ARCHAEOLOGY

a reference handbook

'The other thing that hampers us, in my belief, is the sprawling and gaping disorderliness of our printed literature.' C F C Hawkes 'British prehistory half-way through the century', *Proceedings of the Prehistoric Society* XVII 1951: 1-15.

'The author begs to have it understood, that he does not herein pretend to inform the veteran antiquary; but has drawn up these accounts solely for the use of such as are desirous of having, without much trouble, a general knowledge of the subjects treated in this publication; which they will find collected into as small a compass as any tolerable degree of perspicuity would permit.' Francis Grose, Introduction to *The antiquities of England and Wales*, second edition, 1783.

ARCHAEOLOGY

a reference handbook

Alan Edwin Day
BA, MPhil, Dip Lib, FLA

CLIVE BINGLEY
LONDON

&

LINNET BOOKS
HAMDEN · CONN

To Y D M D
—a companion on many an archaeological tramp
(and much else besides)

FIRST PUBLISHED 1978 BY CLIVE BINGLEY LTD
16 PEMBRIDGE ROAD LONDON W11 UK
SIMULTANEOUSLY PUBLISHED IN THE USA BY LINNET BOOKS
AN IMPRINT OF THE SHOE STRING PRESS INC
995 SHERMAN AVENUE HAMDEN CONNECTICUT 06514
SET IN 10 ON 12 POINT PRESS ROMAN BY ALLSET
AND PRINTED IN THE UK BY REDWOOD BURN LTD
TROWBRIDGE AND ESHER
COPYRIGHT © ALAN DAY 1978
ALL RIGHTS RESERVED
BINGLEY ISBN: 0 85157 242 1
LINNET ISBN: 0 208 01672 4

Library of Congress Cataloging in Publication Data

Day, Alan Edwin.
Archaeology.

Bibliography: p.
Includes index.
1. Archaeology—Dictionaries. 2. Archaeology—
Great Britain—Dictionaries. 3. Archaeology—
Bibliography. I. Title.
CC70.D39 1977   930'.02'02   77-21938
ISBN 0-208-01672-4

PREFACE

My purpose here is threefold: first, to present a descriptive guide to
British archaeology in all its aspects, its antiquarian background, the
history and work of the local and national societies, government departments and agencies, and the museum world insofar as it is relevant;
secondly, to indicate the various forms of literature which now encom-
pass archaeology, publishers' series, textbooks, standard works, learned
and popular journals and magazines, guides and gazetteers, and the
bibliographies, indexes and abstracts which control them; and, lastly,
to recall the life and work of eminent antiquarians and archaeologists.
The first task that confronted me when I rashly embarked on this
venture was obviously one of limitation. In the face of harsh economic
realities which even the most indulgent of publishers could not afford
to ignore, ambition had to be tempered with discretion. In other
words, the pressure of space would not allow me to extend my examination far beyond the confines of mainstream archaeology; however,
I persuaded myself that industrial and nautical archaeology undoubtedly
qualified to be included within this umbrella term. On the other hand
such disciplines, ancillary sciences, and literary material as anthropology,
numismatics, the archaeology and architecture of churches, or tourist
guides to castles, must of necessity be rigorously excluded.

But happily I was not forced to be entirely parochial or insular.
The organization and publications of the British schools overseas could
not justifiably be omitted. A parallel outline of American archaeology
also seemed desirable although the anthropological and ethnographical
nature of the study of archaeology in the United States negated a
complete coverage. In addition, Biblical archaeology, a field in which
both American and British scholars have contributed much, also finds
a mention.

It is impossible to prepare a handbook of this nature entirely in the
study or in any one library. I am indebted in particular to the

5

librarians and their staffs of the Institute of Archaeology and the Yorkshire Archaeological Society not only for allowing me access to their collections but also for answering my importunate requests for help and elucidation with unfailing courtesy and patience.

Leeds, April 1977   A E DAY

1 'Abstracts of New World archaeology' an annual publication of the Society for American Archaeology since 1960, presents abstracts on the archaeology of North, South and Mesoamerica, and is arranged on a geographical basis. An initial general section includes bibliographical sources; the history, theory, scope and role of archaeology; and methods and techniques. There is an author index.

2 'Abstracts of technical studies in art and archaeology 1943-1952' compiled by R J Gettens and B M Usilton, published in the *Freer gallery of art occasional papers* in 1955, contains 1399 abstracts of papers in the ten year period prior to the appearance of *Abstracts of the technical literature on archaeology and fine arts*. Copies may be ordered from Freer Gallery of Art, Smithsonian Institution, Washington DC 20560, USA.

3 **Academic Press**, a subsidiary of Harcourt Brace Jovanovich, publish a number of archaeological titles in two main series, 'Studies in archaeological science' and 'Studies in archaeology' (*qqv*). Many of these titles first appeared under the imprint of the former Souvenir Press.

4 'Aerial photography' in *Anthropological field research* edited by Evon Z Vogt (Harvard University Press, 1974) discusses the latest technical developments in aerial photography and their multiple applications to archaeological and ethnographical research. Some of the papers printed here were read to the sixty-eighth annual meeting of the American Anthropological Association at New Orleans in November 1969. Of particular interest is Thomas S Schorr's 'A bibliography, with historical sketch' which traces the development of aerial photography and the part it has played in anthropology. British readers will find it strange that there is no mention of the works of J K St J Joseph.

5 'Aerial reconnaissance for archaeology' edited by D R Wilson and published by the Council for British Archaeology as No 12 of their Research Reports in 1975 contains most of the papers delivered to an international symposium organised by the Royal Commission on Historical Monuments (England), the CBA, and the Extramural Studies Department of Birmingham University, held at Fortress House, London, 2-4 April 1974. *Contents: Part 1* 'Techniques of remote sensing and survey: soil and crop marks in the recognition of archaeological sites by air photography' (R J A Jones and R Evans); 'Photographic techniques in the air' (D R Wilson); 'Some technical aspects of film emulsion in relation to the analysis and interpretation of aerial photographs' (Jack N Rinker); 'Infra-red techniques' (W A Baker); and 'Transformation of extreme oblique aerial photographs to maps or plans by conventional means or by computer' (Irwin Scollar). *Part II* 'Archaeological interpretation and results: some pitfalls in the interpretation of air photographs' (D R Wilson); 'Aerial reconnaissance in northern France' (Roger Agache); 'Recent archaeological discoveries in Belgium by low-level aerial photography and geophysical survey' (C Leva, J J Hus and H C Bowen); and 'Air photography and the development of the landscape in central parts of southern England' (H C Bowen). *Part III* 'Availability and use of information from air photographs: the organisation of aerial photography in Britain' (John Hampton); 'Problems of town and country planners' (David Baker), 'The application of aerial photography in the Oxford region' (Don Benson); 'Aerial photography and the field archaeologist' (C C Taylor); 'Air, ground, document' (Harry Thorpe); and 'The distant view' (P J Fowler).

6 'Ago' a monthly magazine first issued by the Archaeological Centre, Bournemouth in May 1970, attempted a wide coverage not limited to any period. 'From fossils to industrial relics, from museums to television programmes, from the use of computers to the techniques of underwater archaeology, you will find it all in AGO', its prospectus urged. 'No previous archaeological magazine has been designed for such a large readership.' Unfortunately it never really succeeded in carving out a recognisable niche for itself, a postal strike dealt it a cruel blow, and after ten months it quietly disappeared into *Current archaeology* when that journal acquired its subscription list for just £1.00, thus underlining the difficulties facing such a venture not aimed at a specific audience or enjoying the backing of an established learned society.

7 Air Photographs Unit of the National Monuments Record of the Royal Commission on Historical Monuments (England) was set up in 1965 to compile a record of archaeological features and sites through the medium of air photographs. Over a quarter of a million prints are now stored by the unit of which half are specialist photographs taken from flights organised by the National Monuments Record or by private fliers who deposit their material at the Record. 'Flights by the NMR are based on the twin requirements of the Royal Commission's research programme and the photography of areas of high archaeological interest, where there

8

exists a risk to survival. Great emphasis is placed on the recording of landscapes, and the use of an automatic 70mm camera makes it practical to record even the smallest ditch' (John Hampton 'Organisation of aerial photography in Britain,' *Aerial reconnaissance for archaeology*, CBA Research Report No 12, 1975). The same writer's 'The air photography unit', *Antiquity* XLVI(1) March 1972: 59-61 should also be consulted.

8 '**American antiquity**' *a quarterly review of American archaeology* was launched in 1935 by the newly-formed Society for American Archaeology in the hope that it would be of immediate practical use in coordinating the research work and cementing the friendly cooperation of all students of American archaeology whether amateur or professional. A typical issue contains articles and reports, comments and book reviews, and a current research section. Vols 1-20 are available from Kraus Reprints as a complete clothbound set or as individual volumes with soft covers. Vols 21-33, some from remaining stocks of the original edition, can also be ordered. Vols 34-39 with the exception of vol 37 which is out of print may be obtained from the Society. An index to volumes 1-30 (1935-1964) compiled by Claudia Harris McCracken was published in 1972.

9 **American Association for the Advancement of Science** devoted its meeting in New York, December 1960, to papers on salvage archaeology. These papers, virtually unaltered, were published in the December 1961 issue of *Archaeology*. Titles: 'Salvage in river basins—a world view' (John O Brew); 'River basin salvage in the United States' (John M Corbett); 'Highway construction and salvage problems' (William A Ritchie); 'Saving prehistoric sites in the Southwest' (Alexander J Lindsay jnr); 'Preservation of English and Colonial American sites' (Ivor Noel-Hume); 'Rescuing the past in Canada' (Richard G Forbis); 'Protecting Mexico's heritage' (Luis Aveleyra Arrogo de Anda); 'The threat to Nubia' (John O Brew); 'Archaeological conservation in China' (Frank Ridley); 'Techniques and tools of salvage' (William W Wasley); and 'Physics and archaeological salvage' (Richard E Linington).

10 **American Association of Museums** was founded in 1906 to serve the interests of museums and the museum profession in the United States and Canada. Its purpose is 'to promote the welfare and advancement of museums as educational institutions, as agencies of scientific and academic research, and as community cultural centers; to encourage interest and

inquiries in the field of museology through meetings, reports, papers, discussions, and publications; and to increase and diffuse knowledge of all matters relating to museums.' Twelve regional conferences and associations are affiliated to the association: Midwest Museums Conference, Mountain Plains Museums Conference, New England Regional Conference, New York State Association of Museums, Northeast Regional Museums Conference, Oklahoma Museums Association, Pacific Northwest Museum Conference, Southeastern Museums Conference, Tennessee Association of Museums, Texas Museums Conference, Western Association of Art Museums, and Western Museums League. Addresses and names of officials may be located in *Museums directory of the United States and Canada* (*qv*) which instituted a joint publishing programme of the association and the Smithsonian Institution.

11 'The American Indians' *their archaeology and prehistory* by Dean Snow (Thames and Hudson, 1976) is an anthropologically slanted study whose main thesis it is that there remains convincing evidence to support the claim that the American Indians made a significant contribution to world culture. The arrangement is geographical, the Indians of the Eastern Woodlands, the Great Plains, the Desert West, Far West, and Arctic and subarctic regions coming under scrutiny in turn. Five similarly arranged chronologies, a wealth of illustrations, a bibliography, and end paper maps complement the scholarly text. Published in the US by Viking Books.

12 American Institute for the Conservation of Historic and Artistic Works was until 1972 the American Group of the International Institute for the Conservation of Historic and Artistic Works (*qv*). Its aim and purpose is 'to coordinate and advance the knowledge and improved methods of conservation needed to protect, preserve and maintain the condition and integrity of objects and structures which because of their history, significance, rarity, or workmanship have a commonly accepted value and importance for the public interest.' It endeavours to encourage study and research and to establish standards of practice. A *Bulletin* is issued every six months.

13 American Institute of Nautical Archaeology became an independent research institute of Texas A & M University in 1976. A MSc degree course with a specialization in nautical archaeology is offered.

14 'American journal of archaeology' appeared quarterly 1885-1896 and was regarded as the official organ of the Archaeological Institute of

America from whom it received an annual subvention. In 1897 the council of the institute, on the recommendations of the management committees of the schools at Athens and Rome, determined that all its regular publications should be issued in a journal whose affairs would be conducted by an editorial board representing the several interests of the institute. And so, a new-styled *American journal of archaeology second series: the journal of the Archaeological Institute of America* emerged. Its subject content would be all branches of archaeology and art, oriental, classical, early Christian, medieval, and American. 'The relation of the Journal to American archaeology' vol IV (3) 1888: 259-262 explains its world-wide coverage in response to a complaint that judging by its contents it should be renamed *Journal of Old World archaeology*. It was announced by the editor-in-chief in 1952 that its long-lived bibliographical features would have to be suspended temporarily as an economy measure. Each April abstracts of papers presented at the institute's annual general meeting are printed. Separate indexes of the first series 1885-1896, volumes 1-10 (1897-1906), and volumes 11-70 (1907-1966) have been published. Back numbers and the later index can be ordered from the institute whilst reprints of volumes 1-33 and the 1897-1906 index volume are available from the Johnson Reprint Corporation at 111 Fifth Avenue, New York 10003 or Berkeley Square House, London W1. A microfilm edition of the *Journal* beginning with vol 53 (1949) is issued after the compilation of the printed edition (but only to subscribers of that edition or to members of the institute) by University Microfilms, 313 North First Street, Ann Arbor, Michigan 48106.

15 American Research Center in Egypt was founded in Boston in 1948 as a non-government institution where Americans could learn the languages, customs and culture of the Muslim past and to do what the Metropolitan Museum, the Oriental Institute, and the Museum of Fine Arts, could no longer undertake separately. The establishment of such a center in Cairo was long overdue and it would perhaps have been organized earlier had it not been for the lavish self-sufficiency customarily displayed by American expeditions in the past. The center enjoys the full support of the American Institute of Archaeology.

16 American School of American Research was established by the Archaeological Institute of America in 1907 'to conduct the researches of the Institute in the American field and afford opportunities for field work and training to students of archaeology. The School will direct the expeditions of the local societies, in their respective fields, maintain archaeological research in the various culture areas of the American continent, direct the work of Fellows and collaborate with universities and other scientific organizations, both home and foreign, in the advancement of archaeological research.' In time the school, whose headquarters are at Sante Fe, New Mexico, expanded its area of interest from the American Southwest to Latin America, and broadened its scope into the related fields of history and ethnology. For many years its work was reported at length in the *American journal of archaeology*, nowadays it publishes its own monthly, *El palacio*. The origins of the school are indicated in 'The works of the institute in American archaeology', *AJA* xi, 1907: 47-48 and 'The school of American archaeology', *ibid* xii, 1908: 61-62.

17 American School of Classical Studies at Athens, formed by the Archaeological Institute of America and organized under the auspices of some of the leading American colleges, opened in October 1892 'to give to qualified students the opportunity of studying the antiquities and art, the topography, the history, the language, and the literature of Greece; to prosecute and aid original research in these subjects; and to conduct exploration and excavation of ancient sites.' Its activities were at first reported at length in the *American journal of archaeology* but in 1932 the school began publication of its own annual journal, *Hesperia*, which includes research papers and excavation reports by members of the School. Papers of monograph length are published as *Supplements*. An *Index* to volumes I-X and supplements I-VI published in 1946 was reprinted by Swets and Zeitlinger NV of Amsterdam in 1969, a further *Index* to volumes XI-XX supplements VII-IX appeared in 1968.

18 American School of Classical Studies at Rome was formed by the Archaeological Institute of America 1894-1895 'to promote the study of such subjects as (1) Latin literature, as bearing upon customs and institutions; (2) inscriptions in Latin and in the Italic dialects; (3) Latin palaeography; (4) the topography and antiquities of Rome itself; (5) the archaeology of ancient Italy (Italic, Etruscan, Roman), and of the early Christian, Medieval and Renaissance periods. It will furnish regular instruction and guidance in several or all of these fields, will encourage original research and exploration, and will cooperate with the Archaeological Institute of America, with which it is affiliated.' The circumstances leading up to the school's formation are fully outlined in 'First report of the managing committee . . . ' *American journal of archaeology*,

12

second series, volume 1, 1897: 5-12. The school is now a constituent part of the American Academy at Rome.

19 American School of Prehistoric Research was founded in 1921 as the American School in France for Prehistoric Studies but its scope very quickly widened to the whole of the Old World. For the first five years of its existence its affairs were in the hands of a managing committee drawn largely from the American Institute of Archæology and the American Anthropological Association but it was fully incorporated as a separate institution in 1926 although these two bodies continue to be represented on its board of trustees. The purpose of the school is to train students, to assist them as well as other investigators in the prosecution of their work in the field of prehistoric research, and to enrich museums, both in America and in the lands where researches are conducted, with the material results of exploration. The trustees are authorized to maintain fellowships, instructorships, research stations, and publications; and to raise funds for the support of the same as well as for the endowment of the school. The full text of the Certificate of Incorporation and the by-laws (which includes the school's activities and objectives) is to be found in the school's *Bulletin*, No 2, February 1927. Since 1948 the office of the school has been located at the Peabody Museum of Harvard University where its collections are housed and exhibited. The school conducts excavations in Europe and the Middle East wherever the remains of prehistoric man are to be discovered. The *Bulletin*, an annual publication since 1926, carried reports of the school's activities in addition to accompanying papers until 1953 when simultaneously with a change of format it became an irregular publication printing only long research papers. No *Bulletin* was issued for the years 1940-1947. Kraus Reprint have reissued volumes 1-16 (1926-1948). The background circumstances of the school's foundation may be read in the obituaries of George Grant MacCurdy (1863-1947) and Charles Peabody (1867-1939) both published in the *Bulletin*, 16, 1948.

20 American Schools of Oriental Research. The credit for the original conception of the schools belongs to Joseph Henry Thayer of Harvard University who first broached the idea in his presidential address of 1895 to the Society of Biblical Literature and Exegesis. Enthusiastic support was forthcoming, the American Oriental Society supported the idea, and in 1898 the American Institute of Archaeology agreed to take the proposed new school under its wing, with the president of the institute serving as an ex-officio member of the school, and the chairman of the managing

13

committee similarly appointed to the council of the new institution which was formally established as the American School for Oriental Study and Research in Palestine in 1900. Its historical links with these three bodies is perpetuated in the school's charter, each of them being appointed as a trustee. In 1910 its name was changed to the American School of Oriental Research in Jerusalem. At first its activities were limited by a lack of facilities but at the end of the first world war an elaborate scheme for very close cooperation with the British School of Archaeology in Jerusalem was drawn up and plans made to share a common library, lecture halls, and museum, although the separate identity of the two institutions was strictly maintained. When the articles of incorporation of the society were taken out in 1921 reference was intentionally made to the American Schools of Oriental Research in the plural to reflect the society's determination to set up a parallel school in Baghdad, a plan first mooted by George A Barton in 1913 and approved by the American Institute of Archaeology who appointed a Committee on Mesopotamian Archaeology to consider ways and means. The second school was officially inaugurated in November 1923 and found its first home in the American consulate in Baghdad where it served as a research institution, training archaeologists, and running courses in topography, history and archaeology. The excavation activities of both schools were financially supported by the Fund for Biblical and Oriental Archaeological Research. In Jerusalem a three-building complex was erected as a permanent home for the school 1925-1931, a centre for practically every aspect of archaeology conducted under American auspices. After the Arab-Israeli War of 1967 the political situation demanded a reorganization of the society, the Jerusalem headquarters was renamed the William F Albright Institute of Archaeological Research in Jerusalem after the school's first long-term director in office 1920-1936. At the same time the American Center of Oriental Research was established in Amman as a sister institute to centralise all American archaeological projects east of the River Jordan.

Publications include a quarterly *Bulletin*, an *Annual*, the *Biblical archaeologist* and the *Journal of cuneiform studies* (both quarterlies), an *Archaeological newsletter* which appears ten times a year, and a series of *Bulletin* supplements, dissertaions, and reports on archaeological work. Back issues of all journals and the *Newsletter* are available from Scholars Press, University of Montana, Missoula, Montana 59801. *Bibliography:* the early struggles of the immediate post-first world war period are described in the 'Report of the president (of the school) to the council of the American Institute of Archaeology', *Bulletin of the American schools of oriental research* 5 January 1922: 3-8. A near-contemporary record of the foundation of both Schools appears in James A Montgomery's 'The story of the school in Jerusalem', *Annual of the American schools of oriental research* VI 1924-1925: 1-9, and George A Barton's 'The Baghdad School,' pages 10-12 in the same issue. Philip J King's 'Archaeology at the Albright Institute,' the *Biblical archaeologist*, 38 (3 and 4) September/December 1975: 78-88 is essential reading, as is the same author's *A history of the American schools of oriental research.*

21 American Society for Conservation Archaeology was founded in Denver at a two day meeting of archaeologists and representatives of federal agencies in April 1974, to discuss the urgent need for agreement on 'cultural resource management' *ie* the study and assessment of archaeological resources. It was hoped that the society would provide a forum for communication among those involved in the federal bureaucracy especially in the sphere of planning, negotiating contracts, and estimating costs. The new society also acts as a pressure group, expressing the growing concern of the Society for American Archaeology that there should be strong leadership in establishing standards of archaeological training and professionalism in conservation archaeology.

22 'Analytical archaeology' a formidably academic study by David L Clarke of the modern techniques and procedures now available to the archaeologist, was published by Methuen in 1968. Information and communication theory, topology, cultural ecology, locational analysis, computer applications, and inductive and analytical statistics, are amongst the topics whose influence upon traditional archaeological methodology are described and evaluated. Each chapter ends with a summary (almost obligatory in view of the recondite nature of the text) and a list of definitions. A bibliography heavily weighted with journal articles completes the scholarly apparatus.

23 'Anatolian studies' *journal of the British Institute of Archaeology at Ankara* was first published in 1951. Each annual issue contains articles, a summary of archaeological work in Turkey during the previous year, and a report on the year's work of the institute's staff and scholars. The 1956 volume was a special number in honour of John Garstang, president of the Institute from its inception to his death just before his eightieth birthday. Two cumulative indexes have appeared, *Index to volumes I-X 1951-60* and also for *volumes XI-XX 1961-1970* which include separate lists for contributors, subjects and personal names, and place names.

24 'The ancient burial-mounds of England' by L V Grinsell (Methuen, 1936), a synthesis of information scattered among the proceedings of country archaeological societies and elsewhere, is divided into two parts. 'Aspects of barrow-study' consists of separate chapters on the type and chronology of barrows, burial customs, folk-lore, local names, maps and distributions, fieldwork and excavation. Part II is a survey of barrows in selected regions. Each chapter in both parts concludes with a list of references. An introduction provides a short historical outline of barrow study from William Camden to O G S Crawford.

25 'The ancient civilization series', in which acknowledged authorities present an account of their researches for the general public, has experienced a varied publishing history since its inception by Nagel Publishers of Geneva under the title of *Archaeologia mundi*. Prepared under the direction of Jean Marcadé, professor of Archaeology in the University of Bordeaux, the series was intended as an up-to-date and world-wide view of the problems, methods, and findings of archaeology. Publication in the United Kingdom was first taken over by Frederick Muller and then, from 1971 onwards, it was reissued under its present title by Barrie and Jenkins. Each volume is sumptuously illustrated with on average seventy colour and eighty black and white photographs. Chapter notes, a select bibliography, and chronological tables, complement the text.

Titles: Anatolia I from the beginnings to the end of the second millennium B C (U Bahadir Alkim); *Anatolia II* to the end of the Roman period (Henri Metzger); *Byzantium* (Antoine Bon); *Celts and Gallo-Romans* (Jean-Jacques Hatt); *Central America* (Claude F Baudez); *Central Asia* (Aleksandr Belenitsky); *China* (Vadime Elisseeff); *Cyprus* (Vassos Karageorghis); *Egypt* (Jean Leclaut); *The Etruscans* (Raymond Bloch); *Great Moravia* (Anton Točik); *Greece I* Mycenean and Geometric periods (Nicholas Platon); *Greece II* Post-geometric periods (François Salviat). *Indonesia* (Bernard P Groslier); *Japan* (Vadime Elisseeff); *Mexico* (Jacques Soustelle); *Prehistory* (Denise de Sonneville-Bordes); *Rome* (Gilbert Picard); *Rumania* (Constantin Daicoviciu); *Southern Caucasus* (Boris B Piotrovsky); *Southern Siberia* (Mikhail Gryaznov); *Syria - Palestine I* Ancient Orient (Jean Perrot); *Syria - Palestine II* classical Orient (Michael Avi Yonah); The Teutons (Rolf Hachmann); *Trans-Himalaya: Tibet* (Guiseppe Tucci); *Urartu* (Boris B Piotrovsky); *Mesopotamia* (Jean-Claude

16

Margueron); *Persia I* from the origins to the Achaemenids (Jean-Louis Huot); *Persia II* from the Seleucids to the Sassanians (Vladimir Lukonin); *Peru* (Rafael Hoyle); and *India* (Maurizio Taddei).

26 '**Ancient Egypt**', edited by W M Flinders-Petrie, was introduced in 1914 as the quarterly journal of the British School of Archaeology in Egypt (*qv*), and was intended to keep readers abreast of the discoveries and advances in knowledge of 'the principal civilisation of the Ancient World.' When Flinders-Petrie was obliged to transfer his excavating activities to southern Palestine its title changed to *Ancient Egypt and the East* (1933) becoming at the same time a semi-annual publication. Shortly afterwards it gently expired.

27 '**Ancient history book club**' belongs to the Book Club Associates group owned jointly by W H Smith and Doubleday. As an inducement to enrol three substantial books are offered at a nominal price. Members are committed to purchase a minimum of four books during their first year, at a discount of at least 25 per cent off normal publication prices, selected from a monthly brochure, *The link*, which reviews 6-8 titles, some a few months old, others standard volumes. Archaeological works are well represented in the books offered. Details from PO Box 19, Swindon, Wilts.

28 Ancient Monuments Advisory Council (of Ulster) was established by the Northern Ireland Government in 1926. Its members were responsible for *A preliminary survey of the ancient monuments of Ireland*, edited by D A Chart (HMSO, 1940). In 1950 the council requested the Ministry of Finance to set up an Archaeological Survey of Northern Ireland (*qv*) along the lines of the Royal Commissions on Ancient and Historic Monuments in other parts of the United Kingdom.

29 '**Ancient monuments and historic buildings**' *Government publications sectional list no 27* lists the publications of the Department of the Environment, the Northern Ireland Department of Finance, the Royal Commissions on Ancient and Historic Monuments and Constructions, and the reports of the Ancient Monuments Boards available for purchase. The addresses of government bookshops and booksellers who act as agents for HMSO at home or overseas are also included. The list was last revised to 1 April 1975.

30 Ancient Monuments Board for England is constituted as an advisory board under section 15 of the Ancient Monuments Consolidation and Amendment Act 1913 as extended by section 16 of the Historic Buildings and Ancient Monuments Act 1953. Membership of the board consists of persons nominated by appropriate archaeological and architectural institutions as specified in the first schedule to the 1913 act together with persons nominated by the Secretary of State for the Environment. Its function is to advise the secretary generally on the work of the Directorate of Ancient Monuments and Historic Buildings (refer to Department of the Environment) and more especially to recommend the scheduling of ancient monuments. In this area the board tends to recommend only monuments of clear archaeological importance where either long-term preservation is contemplated, where control of various activities affecting a site is necessary, or where it is considered that efforts should be made to preserve a sample of particular types of monument. The board is required to submit an annual report giving an account of the discharge of its responsibilities during the previous year. The first *Report* of the board appeared in 1954 and up to and including the fifteenth (1968) was published jointly with those of the boards for Scotland and Wales. From 1969 the three have been issued separately. The reports are used to publicly jog the secretary of state's memory, to urge him to act in specific cases, and to air the views of the board on all manner of relevant topics—damage to monuments, marking them with simple notices, reminding owners and occupiers of their responsibilities, emergency excavations, aerial photography, and even such diverse issues as sonic booms and maritime wrecks found on dry land. The total number of monuments recommended for scheduling under the Ancient Monuments Acts during the year, sometimes accompanied by a classified analysis, is included as an appendix.

31 Ancient Monuments Board for Scotland is constituted as an advisory board under section 15 of the Ancient Monuments Consolidation and Amendment Act 1913 as extended by section 16 of the Historic Buildings and Ancient Monuments Act, 1953. Membership of the board is made up of persons nominated by those bodies appropriate to Scotland specified in the first schedule to the 1913 act, and persons nominated by the Secretary of State for Scotland. The work of the board, and the pattern of its annual report, differ in no way from those of the boards for England and Wales.

32 Ancient Monuments Board for Wales/Bwrdd Henebion Cymru is constituted as an advisory board under section 15 of the Ancient Monuments Consolidation and Amendment Act 1913 as extended by section 16 of the Historic Buildings and Ancient Monuments Act 1953, and the Transfer of Functions (Wales) Order 1969 (statutory instrument 1969 no 388). Membership of the board is made up of persons nominated by those bodies appropriate to Wales specified in the first schedule to the 1913 act, and persons nominated by the Secretary of State for Wales. Its functions are similar to those of the board for England, its report follows the same pattern except that it is printed in both English and Welsh.

33 'Ancient monuments in England' *a list prepared by the Department of the Environment* corrected to 31st December 1971 is the sixth edition (1973) of a work first issued in 1954 and records over 10,000 monuments of all kinds which are either officially 'listed' by the Department *ie* those in private hands whose preservation is of national importance, or those in the care of the Secretary of State for the Environment who is required to prepare and publish such a list from time to time by successive Ancient Monuments Acts 1913-1953. The list is arranged alphabetically by historical counties but the next one to be published will correspond to the post-April 1974 local government boundaries. Monuments are classified according to type, and the information provided includes a description, the civil parish in which they are located (this can be misleading and give rise to irritation), and a one inch map and national grid reference. An introductory note explains the significance of 'listing' a monument. Section 12 of the Ancient Monuments Consolidation and Amendment Act 1913 and Section 6 of the Ancient Monuments Act 1931 which set down in detail the procedure to be followed in compiling the list are reproduced in an appendix to this note. A *Supplement* to the 1971 list corrected to 31 December 1973 was published in 1974.

34 'Ancient Monuments in Wales/Rhestr O Henebion Cymru' *a list prepared by the Department of the Environment on behalf of the Secretary of State for Wales* corrected to 31 December 1974, published in 1975, is the first such list prepared by the department exclusively devoted to Wales. Close to 2300 monuments are listed alphabetically under post-April 1974 county headings sub-divided by the old historical counties. In all other respects it corresponds to the English list except that it is bilingual throughout.

19

35 Ancient Monuments Laboratory provides a scientific service to the Directorate of Ancient Monuments and Historic Buildings mainly in connection with excavations undertaken on behalf of the Department of the Environment. It is organized in four sections: geophysics, environmental studies, technology, and conservation. There is also a photographic unit. Approximately forty geophysical surveys to map buried remains in advance of excavation are carried out each year in the British Isles. The environmental studies staff advise on problems on site and use laboratory techniques for pollen analysis, the separation and identification of other botanical debris, charcoal and wood identification, and for reports on human skeletons and cremated remains. Evidence of early industry is the business of the technology section, and conservation procedures are concerned with the scientific examination, cleaning, stabilization, and reconstruction of buried objects. A full description of the laboratory's functions, equipment, and services is included in section V of the *Nineteenth annual report 1972* of the Ancient Monuments Board for England.

36 Ancient Monuments Society founded in 1924 for the study and conservation of ancient monuments, historic buildings, and fine old craftsmanship was the brainchild of John Swarbrick, a Manchester architect disillusioned by the tardy and often ineffectual negotiations conducted by the Ancient Monuments Board. He was convinced that only a society solely dedicated to the task could effectively check the ever-growing destruction. The Society remained Manchester-based until Swarbrick opened a London business office shortly after the war and founded the National Ancient Monuments Society, an independent organization although retaining close links with the senior society in Manchester. The two societies amalgamated in 1953 with headquarters in London and a Northern office kept open in Manchester. Today it operates in two ways: by contesting plans to demolish buildings of architectural or historic interest and putting the case for conservation, if necessary all the way to a public inquiry. The society also keeps a watchful eye open lest the character of conservation areas should be altered by inappropriate new buildings. At the same time as the 1953 amalgamation a new series of the society's *Transactions* was inaugurated, an annual publication containing articles, reports of the society's activities, and book reviews. L M Angus-Butterworth's 'The early history of the society', *Transactions of the ancient monuments society*, new series 20, 1975: 49-84 is especially useful for some case-histories of the society's notable successes in averting damage or destruction to significant ancient monuments. This paper is among the many which the society has made available as offprints.

37 **'Ancient peoples and places'** published by Thames and Hudson, is a series of concise and well-illustrated surveys written by distinguished archaeologists and historians, examining what has been discovered and what has been deduced about various ancient civilizations. 'They're not gee-whiz books, but are directed at the literate general reader, as well as providing up-to-date material for scholars in other fields' (*Sunday telegraph,* 22nd December 1968). Besides an authoritative and readable text and a generous selection of plates, drawings and maps, all volumes contain a detailed bibliography and, for appropriate titles, lists of sites and principal museums to visit.

Titles: The Abyssinians (David Buxton); *The Anglo-Saxons* (D M Wilson); *Archaeology under water* (George F Bass); *The Armenians* (Sirarpie der Nersessian); *Art of the Romans* (J M C Toynbee); *The Balearic Islands* (L Pericot-Garcia); *The Balts* (Marija Gimbutas); *Bones, bodies and disease* (Calvin Wells); *Britain and the Western seaways* (E G Bowen); *Brittany* (P R Giot); *The Bulgarians* (David Marshall Lang); *The Byzantines* (David Talbot Rice). *The Canaanites* (John Gray); *Celtic Britain* (Nora Chadwick); *The Celts* (T G E Powell); *Central and southern Italy before Rome* (David Trump); *Central Asia* (V Masson and V I Sarianidi); *China before the Han dynasty* (William Watson); *The city of Constantinople* (Michael Maclagan); *Colombia* (Reichel-Dolmatoff); *The crusaders in Syria and the Holy Land* (R C Smail); *Czechoslovakia* (E and J Neustupny); *Denmark before the Vikings* (Ole Klindt-Jensen); *The Druids* (Stuart Piggott); *Early Buddhist Japan* (J Edward Kidder); *Early Christian Ireland* (Maire and Liam De Paor); *The early Christians* (Michael Gough); *Early India and Pakistan to Ashoka* (Mortimer Wheeler); *East Anglia* (R Rainbird Clarke); *Ecuador* (Betty J Meggers); *The Egyptians* (Cyril Aldred); *The Eskimos and Aleuts* (Don E Dumond); *The Etruscans* (Raymond Bloch). *Finland* (Ella Kivi-koski); *Food in antiquity* (Don and Patricia Brothwell); *The Georgians* (David Marshall Lang); *The Greeks in Ionia and the East* (J M Cook); *The Greeks in the West* (A G Woodhead); *The Greeks till Alexander* (R M Cook); *The Hittities* (J G Macqueen); *The Iberians* (Antonio Arribas); *Japan before Buddhism* (J Edward Kidder); *Jugoslavia before the Roman conquest* (John Alexander); *The Lapps* (Roberto Bosi); *The Low Countries* (S J De Laet); *Malta* (John Evans); *The Maya* (Michael D Coe); *The Medes and Persians* (W Culican); *Medieval civilization in Germany 800-1273* (Franz H Bauml); *Meroe: a civilization of the Sudan* (P L Shinnie); *Mexico*

21

(Michael D Coe); *The Minoans: Crete in the bronze age* (Sinclair Hood);
The Mongols (E D Phillips); *The Myceneans* (Lord William Taylour); *New
grange and the bend of the Boyne* (S P O'Riordain, Glyn Daniel); *Northern
Italy before Rome* (Lawrence Barfield); *Norway* (Anders Hagen); *Nubia
under the Pharoahs* (Bruce Trigger); *Origins of Rome* (Raymond Bloch);
Pagan Scandinavia (H R Ellis Davidson); *The Parthians* (Malcolm Colledge);
The peoples of the sea (Nancy Sandars); *Peru* (G H S Bushnell); *The
Phoenicians* (Donald Harden); *The Picts* (Isobel Henderson); *Poland* (K˙
Jazdzewski); *The prehistory of Africa* (J Desmond Clark); *The prehistory
of Australia* (D J Mulvaney); *Romania* (D Berciu); *Republican Rome*
(A H McDonald); *Sardinia* (Margaret Guido); *The Sarmatians* (Tadeusz
Sulimirski); *The Seljuks* (Tamara Talbot Rice); *Sicily before the Greeks*
(L Bernabo Brea); *The Slavs* Marija Gimbutas); *South east England* (Ronald
Jessup); *South west England* (Aileen Fox); *Southern Africa during the
Iron Age* (Brian M Fagan); *Spain and Portugal* (H N Sacory); *Sweden*
(Marten Stenberger); *Switzerland* (Marc R Sauter); *Tarquinia and Etruscan
origins* (Hugh Hencken); *Troy and the Trojans* (Carl W Blegen); *The upper
Amazon* (Donald W Lathrap); *The Vikings* (H Arbman); *Wessex before
the Celts* (J F S Stone); and *Writing* (David Diringer). The general editor
is Glyn Daniel. Westview Press of Boulder, Colorado, publish and distribute the series in the United States.

38 'Ancient Scilly' *from the first farmers to the early Christians: an
introduction and survey* by Paul Ashbee (David and Charles, 1974) offers
a comprehensive and profusely illustrated account of the early archaeology of the Isles of Scilly within an economic and social context. A
preliminary chapter, 'Antiquaries, archaeologists and the Isles of Scilly',
provides a pleasant and intriguing background to the more systematic
and scientific studies and investigations of today. A series of appendices
listing the various types of artefact and field monuments, a definitive
bibliography and indexes of personal and place names, complete the
scholarly apparatus.

39 'Ancient Scotland' *a guide to the remains* by Lloyd Laing (David
and Charles 1956) describes archaeological sites from the prehistoric
period to the industrial age. The gazetteer lists those sites judged likely
to be of most interest to the general visitor: access, state of preservation,
and scenic value, take precedence over archaeological significance.

40 'An Anglo-Saxon and Celtic bibliography' (450-1087) by Wilfred
Bonser (Blackwell, 1957) is a comprehensive uncritical bibliography of

textbooks, monographs, general works, and learned journal articles relating to this particular period of English history from the Anglo-Saxon invasions to the compilation of the Domesday Book. Almost 12,000 entries are arranged according to a specially contrived enumerative classification under twelve major sub-headings. Archaeology forms one of these divisions and includes dykes and ditches; Anglo-Saxon, Irish, Scottish and Welsh earthworks; East Anglian, Kentish, Mercian, Northumbrian, Sussex, Wessex, Viking and Celtic cemeteries and finds; implements and utensils, weapons and armour; and physical anthropology. Each item records author and title, an indication of its scope, and a citation if it is a periodical article. There is a list of periodicals and collective works including festschrift volumes abstracted. A separate *Indices* volume provides an author and a subject and topographical index.

41 '**Anglo-Saxon England**', founded in 1972, is an annual publication from the Cambridge University Press. It reflects the contemporary sense of identity and common purpose now pervading, the various academic disciplines with an interest in this period and is intended to encourage their further cooperation, to stimulate a closer investigation of less familiar forms of evidence, and thus to promote fresh areas of knowledge. Each issue contains up to sixteen articles and a classified bibliography of all books, articles, and significant reviews published in any branch of Anglo-Saxon studies during the previous year. Appropriate Council for British Archaeology publications and relevant papers from county society *Transactions* are included in the archaeological section of the bibliography.

42 '**Anglo-Saxon England** by F M Stenton, the second volume of the Oxford History of England, is the standard definitive history of the period. Archaeological sources are listed in the formidable bibliography as the second sub-section to section five: sources of incidental information. The third edition of 1971 is the latest to be published.

43 '**The Anglo-Saxons**' by D M Wilson, volume sixteen in Thames and Hudson's 'Ancient peoples and places' series (*qv*) when published in 1960, 'is intended to give a general view of Anglo-Saxon culture as seen through the eyes of the archaeologist'. An introductory chapter, 'The study of Anglo-Saxon archaeology', describes the progress of the discipline since the end of the nineteenth century and in particular discusses the problem of relative or absolute dating vis a vis the availability of historical and numismatic evidence. The select bibliography is restricted to the principal books used as sources.

44 'An annotated list of motion pictures' *concerning techniques, conservation, display and analysis of works of art and archaeology* edited by Joyce Hill Stoner, Steven H Murden and Ann S Wilson was printed as a supplement to *Art and archaeology technical abstracts* 12 (1) Summer 1975: 181-295. Selected slide and cassette programmes are also included. Each entry by title notes the producer, the running time, whether in colour or black and white, the distributor, and ends with an abstract.

45 'Annual bibliography of British and Irish history' compiled by a team of experts under the editorial direction of G R Elton, the Cambridge historian, is a new venture of the Royal Historical Society, and covers books and articles published in Great Britain, the United States, and Canada. 'The aim is to be as comprehensive as possible without attempting the impossible ambition of exhaustiveness.' It is divided into thirteen main sections: the first is concerned with the auxiliary sciences (*ie* bibliography, archives, reference works and historiography), the second is a general section, and the remainder follow in order of historical period. 'Archaeology' is a sub-section under Roman Britain and 'Society and archaeology' is another under England 450-1066. The entries consist of a bare bibliographical citation and there are author and subject indexes. Published for the society by The Harvester Press in the United Kingdom and by The Humanities Press Inc in the USA, the first volume appeared in the autumn of 1976.

46 'Annual of the American schools of oriental research' was founded in 1920. Before that date the results of the research of the school's staff and students had been published in the *Journal of the American Oriental society*, the *Journal of Biblical literature*, or the *Archaeological journal of America.* Two collections of offprints from the *Journal of Biblical literature* were published separately in 1903 and 1906. Only when the school was enjoying an increased level of support at home at the end of the first world war was it possible for an independent journal to be launched. The first issue contained a selection of papers which had long awaited publication. There was a five year break in publication between 1964 when volumes XXXVI-XXXVII (1957-1958) appeared and volume XXXVIII which eventually arrived in 1969.

47 Anthropological papers of the American Museum of Natural History print the results of research and field work conducted by the staff of the New York museum. Fifty-three volumes appeared in the period 1907-1976.

48 'The antiquarian magazine and bibliographer', a monthly publication founded by Edward Walford after he had severed his connection with *The antiquary* (*qv*), was in his words an 'honest attempt to present the past to English readers in a popular and attractive form'. It carried papers of respectable scholarship, conscientiously chronicled the meetings of learned societies, and like *The gentleman's magazine* which Walford had edited for a brief spell (January 1866-May 1868) markedly featured a correspondence section. Archaeology, in the modern sense of the term, was not conspicuously present in its columns but the magazine, nevertheless possesses an undoubted importance: John Batty's 'On the scope and charm of antiquarian study' which spread over the first three issues January-March 1882 described the science of archaeology as a valid handmaiden to the study of antiquity. The student of archaeology, he declared, was interested 'chiefly in examples showing art perception and development in the construction of monumental erections, old buildings, articles of *vertu*, pottery, jewellery, antique gems, and in treasure-trove generally', an emphasis that would not meet with general agreement today. A change of title to *Walford's antiquarian magazine and bibliographical review* in 1886 did not prevent it from folding with the November 1887 issue. A valedictory note remembered that 'we have endeavoured not only to set before our readers the remains and memorials of the past, but also to note down the changes, whether of true restoration or of wanton destruction, that our own age is working. In our papers are the records of forgotten lives and neglected books brought once more to light, old customs and usages that had faded almost out of recognition, and of those vestiges and shadows of the former time that still linger in the by-ways of the nineteenth century.'

49 'Antiquarian thought in the sixteenth and seventeenth centuries', a paper by Stuart Piggott included in *English historical scholarship in the sixteenth and seventeenth centuries* edited by Levi Fox (OUP, 1956), begins with the early manifestations of unwitting archaeological discoveries recorded by the medieval chroniclers, continues with a brief glance at the more or less conscious antiquarianism of the later middle ages, and then surveys the work and influence of the notable antiquarians of the Tudor and Stuart period when a true field archaeology was almost established before the relapse into myths and speculation after 1730.

50 'The antiquaries journal' *being the journal of the Society of Antiquaries of London* replaced the society's *Proceedings* (*qv*) in 1921 in an effort 'to enlist the support of a wider public'. Apart from a slight enlargement in size in 1946 to allow the inclusion of adequate illustrations of excavations, the journal has altered remarkably little over the last fifty years. In addition to the usual features, papers, notes (*ie* news item) book-reviews, and obituaries, there are also two extremely valuable bibliographical sections, 'Lists of accessions' to the library arranged by alphabetical subject headings, and 'Periodical literature,' a listing of the contents of British and foreign journals. In many ways these are more useful than the excellent Council for British Archaeology bibliographical publications. Very short notes of the society's proceedings are also included, whilst the president's annual state of the society address is reprinted in full thus providing an authoritative and comprehensive year by year record of archaeological affairs. First published as a quarterly the *Journal* now appears twice a year. A *General index volumes I-X* for the years 1921-1930 compiled on a topographical basis was published in 1934. This includes papers read before the society but not printed in the *Journal*. Other cumulative indexes down to and including volume 30 (1950) have also been published.

51 '**The antiquary**' *a magazine devoted to the study of the past* was founded by Edward Walford in 1880 and appeared monthly until December 1914. Walford's intentions were explicitly stated in his prospectus which was reprinted at the front of the first issue: 'Our pages will furnish original papers on such subjects as . . . old abbeys, alchemy and witchcraft, ancient ballads and dramas, ancient castles and seats, local antiquities, archaeology, architecture, arms and armour, ancient and modern art, articles of vertu, autographs, bells, books and bookbinding, bibliography, eccentric and forgotten biography, British and Anglo-Saxon literature, the calendar, cathedrals, ceramic art, church furniture, church restoration, curiosa, dress and vestments, early voyages and discoveries, early printing and block books, epitaphs and inscriptions, engravings, excavations, and exploration at home and abroad, exhibitions of painting and sculpture, family pedigrees, genealogy, heraldry, illuminated manuscripts inns and hostelries, letters and extracts from family archives, local traditions and folklore, manorial customs and tenures, meetings of learned societies, monumental brasses, numismatics, obituary notices of antiquaries, old English poets, travellers, parish registers, picture and art sales, provincial dialect, archaeological and historical books, seals, and English and foreign topography . . . we invite correspondence from those who have a right to speak on their special subjects because they have studied them deeply and lovingly.' Despite the apparent danger of the magazine declining into a vehicle for cranks endowed with highly developed talents for writing specious nonsense on subjects traditionally renowned for attracting this breed of scholar, the contents of *The antiquary* on the whole maintained a high standard of interest and learning. Its articles usually attained a respectable academic level, although there was a noticeable preponderance in subject matter towards ecclesiology, and a typical issue normally included notes on events, accounts of meetings of local and national learned societies, book reviews, and correspondence. An index and list of illustrations was issued annually.

52 'The antiquary's books' were a series of volumes dealing with various branches of English antiquities published by Methuen at the beginning of the century. They were intended to be comprehensive and popular, accurate and scholarly, in order to be 'of service to the general reader, and at the same time helpful and trustworthy books of reference to the antiquary or student'. They are now comparatively rare and stiff prices are paid for secondhand copies. The general editor was J Charles Cox. Titles of especial interest include *Remains of the prehistoric age in England* (B C A Windle); *Celtic art in pagan and Christian times* (J Romilly Allen); and *Archaeology and false antiquities* (Robert Munro).

53 The Antiquities Act 1906 (US), an act for the preservation of American antiquities, remains the fundamental legislation in its field. The full text is conveniently accessible in Charles R McGimsey's *Public archaeology* (*qv*).

54 'Antiquities of the Irish countryside' by Sean O'Riordain, first published by Cork University Press in 1942, largely rewritten for a third edition by Methuen in 1953, and now available in a fourth edition 1965 either in hard covers or as a University Paperback, is not intended for the expert. Its purpose is rather to provide information in a convenient form on the present state of knowledge about the antiquities most frequently encountered. Because the study of monuments belonging to the early Christian period requires architectural knowledge these are excluded. A series of chapters describe and discuss each type of monument in turn and there are extensive suggestions for further reading. A map locates the position of all important sites.

55 'Antiquity' *a quarterly review of archaeology* was founded by O G S Crawford as a 'journal which would raise the general status of archaeology and would popularize its achievements without vulgarizing them—in a word, which would take a place equivalent (both in form and content) to that already occupied by the monthlies and quarterlies in regard to public affairs generally'. The first issue appeared in March 1927 and in his first editorial Crawford nailed his colours firmly to the mast: 'We shall keep our readers informed about discoveries made and books published; and we shall warn them of mares nests. Many so-called discoveries are nothing but newspaper 'stunts'; many best-sellers are written by quacks. The public is humbugged, but it is nobody's business to expose the fraud. Such books are ignored by the learned world. Reviewers in literary papers are therefore tolerant; there is a demand for stuff like this, and the case goes by default. Every page may contain gross errors and wild guesses which pass unchallenged. The antidote is to create a sound and informed body of opinion, and to make it articulate.'

Five years later, on the occasion of the International Congress of Prehistoric Archaeology in London, 1st-6th August 1932, Crawford seized the opportunity of 'setting down in plain words what *Antiquity* stands for'. It was, he remarked, 'primarily an archaeological journal, though we have always reserved the right to publish articles of an historical nature, if we think fit. We are, however, more closely concerned with prehistoric man and his environment; within these wide limits we admit of no restrictions of time or space. We stand for the broadest conception of our subject; we have attempted, often we know with success, to bridge the gulf between the specialist and the reader who is not a specialist in archaeological matters. (It is often forgotten that the specialist in one branch of science is usually a 'general reader' in all such others as he may be interested in) . . . we believe most firmly in the need of studying man not in isolation but in relation to his environment . . . we believe in studying him on the sites where he dwelt . . . not merely in museums and libraries with notebooks . . . In particular *Antiquity* believes in publishing provocative criticism of contemporary affairs: in a free-lance journal like *Antiquity* such matters can be ventilated without malice and with much more freedom than elsewhere . . .'

Crawford continued to edit the journal until his death early in 1958 at which point Dr Glyn Daniel took over as editor with a panel of advisory editors consisting of in the first instance Gerhard Bersu, G H S Bushnell, M E L Mallowan, Stuart Piggott and Sir Mortimer Wheeler, to assist him. Considerable doubt was expressed in the next two years whether the journal, 'a brilliant and essential personal conception in the 1920s' could survive Crawford's death in the 'days of glossy magazines, easy archaeological listening and viewing and of new specialist journals'.

Towards the end of 1960 an opportunity arose of securing the journal's future: the editor and his colleagues determined that it should be owned by an independent archaeological body and not by any one individual or publisher. To this end subscriptions were invited from archaeologists, archaeological publishers, journals, and trusts interested in archaeology, to constitute a fund which would acquire the share capital of Antiquity Publications Limited and thereafter to publish the journal as a non-profit making concern. The response was sufficient for The Antiquity Trust to see these plans fulfilled, the original trustees being R J C Atkinson, Mrs M Aylwin Cotton, M E L Mallowan, I D Margary, Stuart Piggott, and Sir Mortimer Wheeler. A list of individuals, institutions, and trusts who contributed was printed in the June 1961 issue.

The journal has changed remarkably little over the years, and it is still enthusiastic in denouncing quackery and humbuggery. Each issue includes trenchant editorial notes, articles, notes and news, reviews, and a book chronicle feature. A *General index vols I-XXV* (1927-1951) comprising an author-subject-title index of articles and a list of book reviews arranged alphabetically by author was published in 1956. 'A quarter century of antiquity' a felicitous birthday tribute by Jacquetta Hawkes which appeared in the 100th issue, December 1951, includes an analysis of the subject matter of original articles published in the journal. 'Publication', notes on the practical details of writing an excavation report or article, contributed by Crawford, appeared in the March 1953 issue reminding would-be contributors that a good presentation will often turn the scales in a decision whether to publish or not: 'And remember also that (the editor) invariably judges articles by merit only, and is not at all impressed by a case-history of the author.'

'Crawford and *Antiquity*' by Sir Mortimer Wheeler was printed in the March 1958 issue but the most informative and detailed account of how *Antiquity* came into existence is to be found in *Said and done*, Crawford's own reminiscences published in 1955. The completion of fifty years of publication was marked in a most inauspicious manner: financial reasons dictated not only a sizeable increase in subscriptions but also necessitated a reduction in size and a switch to three issues a year instead of four, starting with a combined September/December issue numbered 199/200. It is to be hoped that the journal weathers this latest storm as successfully as it has on previous unsettling occasions in the past.

56 'Approach to archaeology' by Stuart Piggott (A and C Black, 1959) is a brief survey of contemporary archaeological practice and problems which developed out of a series of lectures at an Edinburgh teacher training college and which is primarily addressed to 'the beginner who wishes to know something about the foundations of a subject in which he has become vaguely interested'. Topics discussed include the discipline of archaeology, its sources and techniques, interpretation of the materials revealed, the establishing of the archaeologist's chronological framework, and archaeology's relationship with history and prehistory. There are annotated suggestions for further reading which include a number of articles in learned journals. Photographs and line drawings illustrate the text. A Penguin edition was published in 1966.

57 '**Archaeologia**' *or miscellaneous tracts relating to antiquity published by the Society of Antiquaries*: after twenty years of debate and some opposition the first volume was published in 1770 and consisted largely of a retrospective collection of papers read to the society. Richard Gough, who had been instrumental in persuading the society to embark on this new venture, contributed 'An historical account of the origin and establishment of the Society of Antiquaries' by way of introduction to the first volume. Full details of the circumstances surrounding the decision to issue *Archaeologia* may be found in chapter nine of Joan Evans' *A history of the Society of Antiquaries* (1956). The early volumes continued to include papers read some years previously but this practice was eventually dropped. In all 105 volumes have appeared, the first series ending with the fiftieth volume in 1887, and the second series extends to Volume 55 for 1975. Each volume contains six or seven well illustrated and carefully documented authoritative articles by eminent scholars and distinguished archaeologists. A massive *Index to the Archaeologia . . . from volume I to volume L inclusive* , which included a list of plates and illustrations, volume by volume, was published in 1889 and an *Index to volumes 51-100 (second series, volumes 1-50)*, compiled by V M Dallas, appeared in 1970. This is a classified guide to the papers and authors, not a detailed index to the contents of the volumes. A list of publication dates of the volumes in the second series is to be found facing the title-page.

58 '**The archaeological album**' or *Museum of national antiquities* edited by Thomas Wright (1845) contains a narrative account of the British Archaeological Association's meeting at Canterbury in 1843 together
30

with other papers on British antiquities illustrated by some fine engravings originally issued in parts at two monthly intervals. In view of the imminent deep and lasting schism of the association considerably irony hangs over the editor's concluding remarks on the Canterbury meeting: 'It is impossible to calculate all the benefits to which the exertions of the Archaeological Association may eventually lead. It has been raised to the degree of power and usefulness which it has now obtained by the mutual good feeling and the undisturbed unanimity of purpose which has guided the counsels of the individuals who have founded and hitherto conducted it; and it is most sincerely to be hoped that this unanimity may long continue, undisturbed by the jealousies and dissensions which have too often paralysed the efforts of similar institutions.'

59 '**Archaeological atlas of the world**' by David and Ruth Whitehouse was published by Thames and Hudson in 'The world of archaeology' series in 1975 and contains 103 maps drawn by John Woodcock and Shalom Schotten. The maps (all of which have a grid superimposed on them enabling some 5000 pre- and proto-historic sites to be exactly pin-pointed) are arranged in seven sections: palaeolithic sites in the Old World; Africa; western Asia; the Mediterranean basin; Europe with Russia; south and east Asia; Australasia and the Pacific; and the Americas. Each one is accompanied by a page of explanatory text and a short list of suggested readings. There is an introduction which surveys the origins and growth of archaeological research and an index of sites with grid references. The maps attain a commendable clarity and are well sign-posted by a series of specially selected symbols. A paperback edition is available.

60 '**Archaeological bibliography for Great Britain and Ireland**' replaced the Council for British Archaeology's *Archaeological bulletin* in 1950; Coverage is limited to purely archaeological material relating to the British Isles from the earliest times down to 1600 and a selection of seventeenth century items, and to industrial archaeology. It is arranged in similar fashion to its predecessor *ie* a topographical section under county, period, and subject headings followed by a bibliography providing a complete list of titles arranged alphabetically by author. The list of journals consulted stresses how widely its net is cast. After the first two biennial issues, 1950-1951 and 1952-1953, the *Bibliography* has appeared annually; the present time-lag in publication would seem to be two-three years. As the only comprehensive bibliography of British archaeology published, its value as a research tool is obvious. At the time of writing, however, its future vis à vis *British archaeological abstracts* is under discussion; a publication combining the best features of each might eventually transpire although opinion on this, when expressed, is divided.

61 'Archaeological bulletin for the British Isles', published by the Council for British Archaeology, succeeded the *Report of the earthworks committee* of the now defunct Congress of Archaeological Societies. There are two sections: a topographical selection listing items under county and period, and subject headings, which acts as a chronological and subject index to a bibliography of articles, limited in subject content to the archaeology of Great Britain and Ireland from the earliest times to AD 1600, and published in archaeological periodicals, county journals, regional and county reports, and general periodicals. Three issues only, 1940-1046, 1947, and 1948-1949 appeared under this title, subsequent issues being designated *Archaeological bibliography for Great Britain and Ireland* (*qv*).

62 'Archaeological decipherment' by E J W Barker (Prentice-Hall, 1974) is a comprehensive treatise on the theory and method for working with ancient undeciphered texts. Past achievements are surveyed, sound methods are distinguished from unreliable ones, and there is a discussion on how to set about tackling an undeciphered script, using examples taken in the main from bronze age Aegean material.

63 'Archaeological discoveries in the Holy Land' compiled by the Archaeological Institute of America and published by Thomas Y Crowell in 1967 is an illustrated record of archaeological exploration and excavation in Israel and Jordan since the discovery of the Dead Sea scrolls in 1948. Much of the material first appeared in the pages of *Archaeology*.

64 'Archaeological encyclopaedia of the Holy Land' edited by Avraham Negev (Weidenfeld, 1972) lists in alphabetical sequence almost all of the geographical names mentioned in the Bible. Each one is identified, excavations in its immediate vicinity are described, and an analysis is made of the discoveries made. Historical references to each locality up to the Arab conquest are also included. Several very useful background articles complementing the geographical entries are inserted and three of these, 'archaeology in the Holy Land', 'methods of research', and 'prehistory', are cited as being of especial value. A glossary, chronological tables, brief notes on the ancient sources consulted in compilation, and a profuse number of illustrations, complete a scholarly and serviceable work of reference.

65 'Archaeological excavations' *a brief summary of prehistoric, Roman and medieval sites throughout the country excavated in advance of destruction*, published annually by HMSO for the Department of the Environment, replaced the former *Ministry of Works excavation reports* (*qv*) in 1968. A progress report of rescue archaeology is followed by detailed descriptions of the excavations undertaken directly by the department, the finds yielded and conclusions arrived at, arranged by period of site, are listed alphabetically under county. Then comes a list of grants in aid of excavation allocated to societies, museums, and excavation committees with a similar arrangement of reports on these sponsored digs. Finally there is a list of published papers relating to the excavations. A recent report notes that requests for grants for surveys and excavations of threatened sites was double the money available and that a careful selection of projects was therefore necessary, it being essential to continue a research policy which would add to present knowledge.

66 'Archaeological fakes' by Adolf Rieth was first published in England by Barrie and Jenkins in 1970. It first presents a brief history of faking and then continues with a detailed look at some notorious case-histories. Each stage of how these fakes were planted, how the 'experts' were fooled, and how after much controversy they were exposed, is carefully described and documented. At the end of the day we can only wonder at the misplaced ingenuity of the crooks and rogues and marvel at the ease with which these celebrated fakes were passed off as genuine.

67 'Archaeological fieldwork' by R Rainbird Clarke (1958) forms part C— archaeology, ethnography & folk-life, sections 1 & 2— of the *Handbook for museum curators* published by the Museums' Association in separate fascicles. It is intended as practical advice for junior members of staff of archaeological departments of provincial museums and for archaeologists or those trained in other disciplines who work in smaller museums who may be pressed into archaeological fieldwork in the absence of more expert or experienced staff. Topics discussed include casual discoveries, emergency excavations, the recording of monuments and compilation of museum records, and the publication of results. There is also a short bibliography and a list of useful addresses.

68 'Archaeological guide and glossary' by James Stewart first appeared under the imprint of Titus Wilson of Kendal, Westmorland in 1958, and in a second edition published by Phoenix House in 1960. It is an elementary handbook, suitable for school libraries, and is arranged in four sections—prehistoric, Roman, abbeys and castles—each section consisting of a number of explanatory chapters followed by an illustrated glossary. It has a pronounced British slant.

69 'Archaeological guides' to a number of countries and regions rich in archaeological remains are published by Faber. They are all fully documented, mapped and illustrated. *Titles: Southern England* (James Dyer); *Wales* (Christopher Houlder); *Scotland* (Euan W Mackie); *Denmark* (Elisabeth Munksgaard); *Central Italy* (R F Paget); *Southern Italy* and *Sicily* (both by Margaret Guido); *Malta* (D H Trump); *Southern Greece* (Robert and Kathleen Cook); and *Persia* (Sylvia A Matheson). The general editor is Glyn Daniel.

70 'An archaeological index to remains of antiquities of the Celtic, Romano-British, and Anglo-Saxon periods' by John Yonge Akerman (1847) classifies the sepulchral remains of Britain in descriptive chapters arranged in three chronological period sections. The *Antonini iter Britanniarum*; Ptolemy: the position of the British Island Albion; the *Notitia dignitatum*; the Itinerary of Richard of Cirencester; and a classified index to papers in the (Society of Antiquaries') *Archaeologia* volumes I-XXXI are included as appendixes.

71 'Archaeological indexes' a review article by Sterling Dow, prompted by the publication of an index to volumes I-X of the journal *Hesperia*, appeared in *American journal of archaeology* 54, 1950: 41-57, and is arranged in five sections. The first considers the *Hesperia* index as a whole and serves to introduce the reader to some of the problems associated with the compiling of indexes whilst the second critically examines its general section. These are followed by a descriptive section on the indexes of various European archaeological journals and then comes an attempt to formulate some general principles of indexing. Lastly the writer reverts to the *Hesperia* index once more, this time to appraise its epigraphical section. It is hard to avoid the conclusion that a neater, more logical order of presentation could have been devised.

72 **Archaeological Institute of America** was founded in Boston in 1879 largely at the instigation of Charles Eliot Norton, President of the

Institute 1879-1893, who was anxious to secure for the United States a due share in the field work being undertaken in the classical lands of antiquity and to see a fair proportion of artistic trophies finding a home in America. The purpose of the institute was defined as the promoting and directing of 'archaeological investigation and research by the sending out of expeditions for special investigations, by aiding the efforts of independent explorers, by the publication of archaeological papers and of reports of the results of the expeditions which the Institute may undertake'. There is evidence of initial disagreement as to whether the institute should concentrate its activities on archaeology in America or whether it should cover all kinds of archaeology throughout the world. Eventually the wider view prevailed. To this end the institute has played a prominent role in furthering American archaeological studies abroad by sponsoring affiliated schools to which it entrusted responsibility for research and work in the field. These include the American School of Classical Studies at Athens established in 1881, a similar School at Rome (1895) which was later incorporated into the American Academy there, and other Schools at Jerusalem (1900), Sante Fe (1907) and Baghdad (1923), as well as the American School of Prehistoric Research (1921) (*qqv*). The American Research Center in Egypt (1948) was also fully supported by the institute But it would be erroneous to suppose that its attention was only engaged upon archaeology overseas: in 1884 it was decreed that any local archaeological society in the United States which could boast of at least ten members could by vote of council be affiliated to the institute, and today close on sixty such societies are linked to the institute in this way. From very early in its history the institute has consciously sought to look after the interests of both the scholar and the amateur archaeologist and its present-day activities include the sponsoring of archaeological tours abroad, the arranging of lecture programmes and symposia, and the organizing of field trips. From 1964 onwards it has awarded an annual gold medal for distinguished archaeological achievement. *Publications*: Until 1897 there was no well-defined publishing policy but in that year the *American journal of archaeology* (*qv*) was taken over by the institute as its official organ and largely superseded the heterogeneous series of annual and other reports of the council previously issued as separate pamphlets. In 1948 another quarterly, *Archaeology* was founded in a determined effort to halt the slide in membership and to satisfy the needs and tastes of the non-professional members whilst at the same time acting as a medium to transmit the results of scholarship to a wider public. There is also a mimeographed *Newsletter* which appears midway between issues of

Archaeology and an annual bulletin. A series of learned monographs completes the publishing programme. An *Index to publications 1879-1889* compiled by William Stetson Merrill (1891) is an invaluable aid in the bibliographical control of the institute's early publications. Anne V Dort's 'The Archaeological Institute of America: early days', *Archaeology* 7 (4) December 1954: 195-201 offers a readable historical outline and on page 194 of the same issue, which commemorates the seventy-fifth anniversary of the institute, Henry T Rowell attempts to predict in a short essay what the future might bring.

73 **'The archaeological journal'** began life in 1844 as a quarterly publication of the British Archaeological Association but when internal dissension split the association in two the *Journal* remained in the hands of that faction which in time became the Royal Archaeological Institute. It is now an annual publication with reports on the institute's meetings, papers, book reviews, and since 1974 a section known as 'British antiquity' which revived and extended a bibliographical feature of the early 1930s when Christopher and Jacquetta Hawkes contributed an annual survey of the periodical literature dealing with prehistoric Britain. Now different reviewers survey all literature—books, periodicals and foreign publications—related to six different periods: palaeolithic-mesolithic; neolithic-bronze age; iron age; Romano-Britain; post-Roman and pagan Anglo-Saxon; western Britain, Irish and later Anglo-Saxon; with a consolidated list at the end of each section. An index covering vols 1-25 (1844-1868), the work of a band of volunteers, was published in 1878; a more professional approach is evident in *General index to the archaeological journal volumes 26 to 50 for the years 1869-1893* (1955) which attempted to classify information contained in the *Journal* in accordance with contemporary knowledge. This was followed in 1973 by a similar volume compiled by Ann Morley for volumes 51 to 75 for the years 1894-1918.

74 **'Archaeological museums in Great Britain and Northern Ireland'** a pamphlet issued by the Council for British Archaeology in 1951, is a completely unannotated list of museums arranged alphabetically by counties.

75 **'The archaeological newsletter'** began publication as a monthly in April 1948 and quickly established a niche for itself in archaeological circles, its general articles, reports and notices of meetings, reviews of

books and journals, all tidily presented, earning it a good reputation. It assumed a more glossy, pictorial appearance when taken over by Phoenix House in December 1956. Nine years later it somewhat unaccountably ceased publication.

76 'An archaeological perspective', included in the Academic Press series 'Studies in archaeology' (1972), is a collection of conceptual papers by Lewis R Binford reflecting his search for a valid scientific approach to archaeology, most of which were contributed to various American archaeological and anthropological journals. Professor Binford is firmly entrenched in the school which regards archaeology as an anthropological discipline and not merely the history of artefacts. The papers are arranged in four sections —archaeological method and reasoning; data collection; theory and assumption; and analysis—each introduced by a short essay. The author also includes a personal introduction which traces his academic progress as the leading proponent of 'the new archaeology' in American universities.

77 'Archaeological photography' by Harold C Simmons (New York University Press and University of London Press, 1969), is intended for the professional archaeologist wishing to acquire a modicum of photographic expertise, the amateur photographer wanting an outline of the archaeological aspects of photography, the amateur archaeologist who needs specific photographic instruction, the student uncertain of which career to follow, archaeology or photography, and for the advanced history of art student who may more fully comprehend archaeology and archaeological photography after being introduced to its complex problems and possibilities. For all these people the author has provided a practical work on the selection of photographic equipment and materials, with chapters on photography in the field and in the studio, and with particular notes on special aspects of the subject such as aerial photography, photogrammetry, underwater, infra-red, ultra-violet, x-ray photography, photomicrography, motion pictures, and museum photography. A bibliography is included.

78 Archaeological Placement Service, established in 1974, is a specialized employment agency. Prospective excavation workers, skilled or inexperienced, can seek help in finding temporary or permanent work. Directors of excavations can consult the service either to fill individual vacancies or to recruit an entire site team. Details from 4 Larkfield Road, Sunderland.

79 'Archaeological recording systems' is the title of an article by Stephen A Le Blanc which considers the labelling of artifacts and other collections in the light of contemporary archaeological needs. Four criteria are suggested: information content, accuracy, efficiency and complete compatibility. A flow chart and drawings complement the text of the article which appeared in *Journal of field archaeology* 3 (2) 1976: 159-168.

80 'The archaeological review' *a journal of historic and prehistoric antiquities*, edited by G L Gomme and published by David Nutt, appeared monthly for two years from March 1888 before it was merged into the journal *Folklore*. It was an ambitious project even during a period when ambitious publishing schemes abounded in that it attempted to weld archaeology in Britain into a coherent, concentrated, and well-directed discipline and profession. In modern terms it was an early manifestation of campaigning journalism, it was in its columns that J Charles Cox adumbrated the formation of what eventuated as the Congress of Archaeological Societies although this shadowy organization was not to his pleasing (*Arch rev* 1 (2) April 1888: 158-160). Gomme introduced a number of novel features in the journal's make-up—although admitting that archaeology as a science should be treated as a whole—he divided the *Review* into four self-contained sections:'anthropological archaeology' (*ie* ethnology and the history of man); 'archaeology' (the record of geology as it revealed the doings of man, the remains of prehistoric man, legends and traditions of the past, dialects, and monumental relics of historic times); 'history' (antiquarian subjects); and 'literature' especially the literature of archaeology. After the articles in each of these four sections he placed what he called 'index notes', forming an ongoing subject index and bibliography, a sort of piecemeal contribution to a cumulative index. As was subsequently evident in the *Index of archaeological papers* he compiled for the Congress of Archaeological Societies, Gomme was very conscious of the part previous research could play provided it was adequately recorded and he introduced in the *Review* a list of the papers appearing in the *Transactions* etc of the various local archaeological societies. He then attempted a retrospective coverage by printing in an appendix to each issue a list of papers published prior to 1886, paginated separately so that they might be easily bound up together in volume form. In many respects it was a pity that such a journal so much aware of the need for archaeological and bibliographical research did not last longer but Gomme was ahead of his time and the *Review* was unable to establish itself on a firm basis.

81 'The archaeological site index to radio carbon dates for Great Britain and Ireland' was issued as a supplement to *British archaeological abstracts*

38

in 1971 in loose-leaf form to allow for revision and updating. Arrangement is by archaeological period, then by categories and sub-categories, and then chronologically. In cases where sites extend over more than one archaeological period they are listed under each one involved—all information on these sites may be retrieved by using the alphabetical site index. Entries give site name and category, a national grid map reference, the name of the collector of the sample, a description of this with details of stratification if known, a laboratory number, the carbon-14 date expressed in standard form, and bibliographical references to the site or to its radiocarbon date. Most entries are abstracted from *Radiocarbon*, an American journal although a few are from elsewhere; a list of British and Irish libraries where this journal can be consulted is included. *Addenda* were published in 1972 and 1973.

82 '**Archaeological site science**' by Frank Goodyear (Heinemann Educational Books, 1971) first offers the practising archaeologist a sound guide to the possibly unfamiliar scientific aspects of the archaeological environment (the atmosphere, soil and water); the organic and inorganic materials of antiquity; and the interaction of those materials with their surroundings. Then follow sections on the work of archaeological laboratories, on scientific aids to excavation, and archaeological prospecting. In this way both the principles of scientific applications on site and laboratory investigation methods are appraised and elucidated. A glossary of scientific terms and definitions is appended.

83 '**Archaeological sites of Britain**' by Peter Clayton (Weidenfeld, 1976), part gazetteer, part guide book, part topographical exposition, describes over 250 of the most notable archaeological sites and monuments in Britain, and is arranged in seven broad geographical divisions. Within each area only selected monuments receive detailed treatment 'ones which it is hoped will prove to be of general interest as places to visit, enough to make a detour to see on a car journey'. All sites mentioned are located by National Grid references and over 170 illustrations, a glossary, and a valuable regional guide to the more important museum collections, add to the usefulness of this most engaging and informative guide, which should find a welcome place on college and public reference and lending library shelves.

84 Archaeological Survey of Northern Ireland was established by the Ministry of Finance in 1950 after the Ancient Monuments Advisory

Council had urged the setting up of a body analogous to the Royal Commissions on Ancient Monuments in England, Scotland, and Wales. The task of compiling an archaeological record of the province is based on the Department of Archaeology, Queen's University, Belfast, within the framework of the Ministry of Finance (*qv*). Work commenced in Co Down and the *Archaeological survey of Co Down* is the first result of the survey's operations to appear. Progress of the survey is regularly reported in the *Ulster journal of archaeology*. A preliminary note by E M Jope, volume 13, 1950: 4-5, describes the circumstances of the survey's origins.

85 'The archaeologist in fiction', an erudite and entertaining digression by Charles Thomas, printed in *To illustrate the monuments* (*qv*), wanders lightly over a wide variety of novels of the last seventy or eighty years in search of the portrayal of the antiquarian and archaeologist in English fiction.

86 'The archaeologists' year book' *the international directory of archaeology and anthropology*, first published in 1973, is issued biennially by the Dolphin Press, now incorporated in Blandford Press. It provides directory type information on university archaeology departments, museums, archaeological societies, councils, committees, trusts, research groups, and other useful addresses including those of government departments and agencies. In each instance there are separate sections for British and overseas institutions.

87 'Archaeology' *a magazine dealing with the antiquity of the world* was introduced by the Archaeological Institute of America in 1948 in an attempt to halt a disastrous slump in membership and was part of a bold strategic plan of expansion put in motion by Sterling Dow when he became president of the society in December 1945. A quarterly until 1976 it now appears as a bi-monthly, publishing authoritative but not exhaustive, profusely illustrated articles, written by experts for readers not technically equipped in the discipline of archaeology but who relish and enjoy 'the good and amusing things of the past'. It claims in fact that no other technical magazine exists which similarly draws upon all the world's archaeology and using the whole range of modern photography. Jothan Johnson in his nostalgic essay 'Anniversary', *Archaeology* 10 (4) December 1957: 230-231, remarked that 'it has introduced some notion of what archaeology is really about to thousands of people who otherwise depended on Sunday supplements and picture weeklies, and it has made itself a landmark in the area of public relations, a model of what a learned society can do when it sets out to explain to the public what it does with funds which, in the final accounting, are derived from the public'. An index to volumes 1-10 (1948-1957) compiled by Gloria Saltz was published in 1959 followed fifteen years later by *Index to Archaeology volumes 11-26 (1958-1973)* compiled by Bea Riemschneider.

88 '**Archaeology**', *an illustrated introduction* by Liam de Paor first published by Penguin Books in 1967 and still in print discusses the beginnings, methods, and achievements of archaeology. A wealth of illustrations closely incorporated with the text make the book an attractive proposition for school and college libraries.

89 '**Archaeology A-Z**' *a simplified guide and dictionary* by Geoffrey Palmer and Noel Lloyd (Warne, 1968) contains over 700 profusely illustrated entries relating to sites and artifacts, cultures and the great names in archaeology, plus some technical terms. In addition to the dictionary proper other features include an outline of the principles of field archaeology, a list of particularly important sites in Britain to visit arranged by archaeological period, an alphabetical list of museums and notes on the national societies. Although it cannot be compared with Warwick Bray's and David Trump's *Dictionary of archaeology* it should, nevertheless, find a place on the school library shelves.

90 **Archaeology Abroad Service**: the idea of a register of job opportunities abroad for archaeologists originated in the summer of 1970 when the British schools abroad reported an increasing number of enquiries concerning employment on excavations. After some informal discussions the Society of Antiquaries set up a small committee to consider what action should be taken; it soon became clear that many organizations would welcome such a service which accordingly came into existence on a formal basis the following year with an address at the Institute of Archaeology in London. The service is not an international organization, nor is it an employment agency, and it will provide the names of suitable persons from its register of those who wish to take posts in excavations or field work abroad only if approached by expedition leaders or by the established British schools and other official bodies. The work of the service is mainly with students but where openeings exist for beginners and untrained people it will assist. After five years it was evident that the service had established itself, a central secretariat was in being, and although its status has not yet been acknowledged by any public or private body in the form of financial assistance, it enjoys sufficient support by way of the general subscriptions of institution and corporate members to justify optimism as to its future. *Publications*: *Archaeology abroad*, first issued February 1972 and now published annually contains an account of the current activities of the Schools, and lists not only vacancies in excavation work abroad with details of fares, board, salary etc, but also study tours and courses, scholarships and awards, and insurances. *Bulletins* and *Newsheets* are published at more frequent intervals.

91 **'Archaeology and agriculture'** *a survey of modern cultivation methods and the problems of assessing plough damage to archaeological sites* by George Lambrick was published jointly by the Council for British Archaeology and the Oxfordshire Archaeological Unit in 1977. It offers amateur and professional fieldworkers basic information on modern cultivation techniques and equipment and considers how archaeologists can best cope with the problems these present. There is a valuable bibliography of articles drawn largely from non-archaeological journals. The pamphlet is the first of a series of such publications on aspects of agriculture and archaeology to be issued by the council.

92 **'Archaeology and government'** *a plan for archaeology in Britain* originated in a draft policy document, *In search of history*, on the possible future structure of archaeology in Britain, forwarded by RESCUE early in 1974 to the Council for British Archaeology for their consideration and comment. A final version prepared by a specially convened joint working party was published under the imprint of the two organisations later in the year and copies sent to all MPs, chief executives of the counties and regions, and to the national and specialist press. In January 1975 a copy was formally presented to a Minister of State at the Department of the Environment who accorded it a guarded welcome. Following an introduction outlining various proposals and discussions at national and local level, attention is concentrated on the suggested composition and functions of national and local archaeological advisory committees and the parts to be played by the department, the universities, museums, and Royal Commissions, in the structure of the national archaeological service. The recruitment and training of archaeologists is also touched upon. There are three appendixes: the text of a DoE statement 20 September 1973 on the new arrangements proposed for rescue archaeology, for more money for the Historic Buildings Council and for excavation; the text of a ministerial statement of 23 May 1974 on archaeological rescue excavations and the new regional arrangements; and thirdly a diagram of the proposed administrative structure. Although it encountered a mixed reception from the CBA's membership (there was some opposition to hiving off excavation and surveys from the work of the Inspectorate and the creation of a new national archaeological service) it would be difficult to over estimate the importance of this modest little booklet of some two dozen pages and the influence it exerts on professional archaeological thinking in the United Kingdom. For the first time in years the CBA had completed a fundamental review of the state of archaeology in Britain and initiated a general debate which must surely result in a viable structure for British archaeology for years to come.

93 'Archaeology and the landscape' *essays for L V Grinsell* edited by Peter Fowler and published by John Baker in 1972 is an excellent festschrift volume. Whilst all the essays are demonstrably cohesive in character and genuinely merit publication in their own right, one essay is particularly felicitous and that is Nicholas Thomas' 'Leslie Valentine Grinsell, field archaeologist', an appreciative outline of Mr Grinsell's career and achievements. Other contents include Part I Fieldwork reviewed: 'Field archaeology: its origins and development' (Paul Ashbee); 'The present significance of fieldwork in the light of the Cornish parochial check-list survey' (Charles Thomas); and 'Field archaeology in future: the crisis and the challenge' (Peter Fowler). Part II Fieldwork in practice: 'Barrows in Gloucestershire: patterns of destruction' (John Drinkwater); 'Ring-ditches in eastern and central Gloucestershire' (Isobel Smith); 'Early boundaries in Wessex' (Desmond Bonney); 'Somerset AD 400-700' (Philip Rahtz and Peter Fowler); 'Earthworks of the Danelaw frontier' (James Dyer); 'Medieval notes in Cambridgeshire' (Christopher Taylor); and 'Bibliography of L V Grinsell's publications 1929-1971' (Nicholas Thomas and Peter Fowler). All the essays conclude with an extensive bibliography.

94 'Archaeology and the microscope' *the scientific examination of archaeological evidence* by Leo Biek (Lutterworth press, 1963) provides a detailed discussion of the ways in which science increasingly confirms and interprets the archaeological record. The value of pollen analysis, geophysical surveys, aerial photography, carbon-14 dating and X-ray fluorescence spectrometry is examined and the author draws upon his experience as head of the ancient monuments laboratory of the former Ministry of Public Buildings and Works to provide specific examples of science

aiding the archaeologist. Some eye-catching photographs, a number of analytical tables, an unusual combined bibliography and author index, and a subject index, complete the scholarly apparatus. Sir Mortimer Wheeler contributes a foreword.

95 'Archaeology and the state' by Grahame Clark, published in *Antiquity* VIII (32) December 1934: 414-428, considers 'the growth of state interest, the limits of state control . . . and the main lacunae which appear to exist in the mechanism for the preservation of our national antiquities'. Government measures including the formation and function of the Inspectorate of Ancient Monuments, the Royal Commission on Historical Monuments, and the Ordnance Survey are examined under four headings: the preservation of monuments; the mapping of antiquities; the preservation of loose antiquities; and museums. Sir Henry Miers' report on the public museums of the British Isles to the Carnegie United Kingdom Trust is also considered.

96 'Archaeology as a career', an article by John Howland Rowe based on a circular prepared at the University of California, Berkeley, to answer students' enquiries, first appeared in *Archaeology* 7 (4) December 1954: 229-236. It attempted to give a precise definition of archaeology, explained its connection with art-history and anthropology, outlined career prospects, noted federal and state government research programmes, discussed local and national archaeological societies, provided succinct information on research grants, courses and training, and the techniques of excavation, and ended with a booklist. So successful did the article become that the journal issued 20,000 offprints in three years. It was rewritten in the light of experience and the revised text appeared in *Archaeology* 14 (1) March 1961: 45-55.

97 'Archaeology by experiment' by John Coles, published in Hutchinson's University Library in 1973, presents experimental archaeology (the collection of facts, theories and fictions in the reconstruction of ancient remains) in all its stages from straightforward copies and simulations to continued series-experiments designed to produce a number of varied results. There are three main sections on food production, and heavy and light industry with a summary assessing the contribution of experimental archaeology to the study of the past. An impressive, wide-ranging bibliography supports the text. A paperback edition is also available.

98 'Archaeology: discoveries in the 1960s' by Edward Bacon, for many years archaeological editor of the *Illustrated London news*, was published by Cassell in 1971. It is a continuation of the same author's *Digging for history* (*qv*) and records in detail the most interesting excavations and discoveries made on the major sites of the world during this time. Three underlying trends in archaeology are perceived: 'the discovery and successful exploitation of a number of scientific techniques such as carbon-14 and fluorine dating; the identification by Michael Ventris of the Linear-B language with primitive Greek; and the discovery of the importance of Anatolia as a cradle of urban civilization'. Obviously intended for the intelligent general reader or undergraduate the text is accompanied by eleven maps and almost eighty photographs but there are no indications of further readings, a strange and inexplicable omission.

99 'Archaeology for the historian' by D P Dymond was published in 1967 by the Historical Association in their pamphlet series 'Helps for students of history'. It discusses 'the special nature of archaeology, in the hope of removing some of the historian's doubts and misunderstandings, and thereby fostering further cooperation'. Topics discussed include 'Historians and archaeologists', 'Can archaeology be trusted?' and the impact of archaeology on history and historians. Other features are a practical note on how historians should seek archaeological opinions, a select list of archaeological societies and publications, and a classified bibliography.

100 'Archaeology in Britain' is the cover title adopted for the Council for British Archaeology's annual *Report* since the 22nd report for the year ending 30th June 1972. News of the past year is outlined and discussed in an introduction and the regular features include notes on the work of the CBA, its publications during the year, grants, information on insurance policies and superannuation for the self-employed archaeologist, the activities of regional groups, the work of state agencies in archaeology and on excavation trusts and units. Appendices include a complete list of CBA publications in print and also a list of the constituent organisations of the council. From time to time important documents or memoranda issued by the council like *Archaeology and government* (*qv*) are printed in the *Report*. The presidential addresses delivered by each incumbent at the end of his three-year term of office also find a place. An overall view of the complex and varied activities of the council, especially of its changing relationship with the state, is nowhere better gained than from a perusal of its successive issues.

101 'Archaeology in 1851' a farewell presidential address to the Royal Archaeological Institute by Dr Joan Evans reviews the organization of archaeology at that time with especial reference to the activities of the national societies. Brief reference is also made to the scientific attainments of British archaeologists at home and abroad. The address is printed in *The archaeological journal* CVII 1950: 1-8.

102 'Archaeology in England and Wales 1914-1931' by T D Kendrick and C F C Hawkes (Methuen, 1932) is a comprehensively documented and well-illustrated period by period survey of archaeological scholarship and discovery for these years with a select bibliography of works published in and after 1914 arranged topographically and chronologically. From 1932-1935 an attempt was made to continue the bibliographical coverage of periodical literature in a feature, 'Prehistoric Britain', written first by Hawkes alone and then in conjunction with his wife Jacquetta in the *Archaeological journal* which took the form of a connected review classified according to period and subject.

103 'Archaeology in schools', an article by David Revill, discusses the practicalities of teaching archaeology in junior forms and includes useful hints on planning the syllabus and on possible extramural activities designed to catch and hold the interest and attention of pupils. The GCE A-level option offered by the Cambridge Local Examination Syndicate is noticed and two specimen examination papers reproduced. A list of frequently used books divided into those suitable for adults and senior pupils and those for junior reading, together with details of slides, postcards and models, is also provided. The article appeared in *Current archaeology* III (10) No 33 July 1972: 268-272.

104 'Archaeology in the field' a series published by Dent 'aims to give students, practising archaeologists and historians and all those interested in the environment . . . an overall understanding of various aspects of the landscape'. Titles published or announced include *Fields in the English landscape* (Christopher Taylor), *Trees and woodland in the British landscape* (Oliver Rackhaus), *The landscape of towns* (Michael Aston and James Bond) and *Villages in the British landscape* (Trevor Rowley).

105 'Archaeology in the field' by O G S Crawford, published by J M Dent in 1953 and kept in print in various impressions and revisions, is primarily intended for 'the intelligent layman interested in a pursuit which has now developed its own techniques and come to maturity'. It first surveys the history of field archaeology, then investigates its close connections with maps (as befits a distinguished scholar who was archaeology officer of the Ordnance Survey for twenty five years), describes the various types of structures and remains, and concludes with some comparative studies. There are a number of appendices including some characteristically trenchant remarks on 'crankeries'—always a bee in the author's illustrious bonnet. Over twenty quite excellent photographs and twice that number of text figures admirably complement the enthusiastically written text. A carefully compiled bibliography contains much material gleaned from the *Proceedings* of learned societies.

106 '**Archaeology in the Holy Land**' by Kathleen Kenyon (Benn, 3ed 1970) relates how archaeologists have pieced together the history of the Holy Land from the earliest times down to the end of the Hellenistic period. The author naturally concentrates on those sites at Jericho and in Samaria where she herself played such a distinguished part in uncovering the remains of the early civilizations. A list of excavated sites together with bibliographical references is appended.

107 '**Archaeology in Wales**', the newsletter of Group II of the Council for British Archaeology started publication in 1961. It covers excavations and discoveries in Wales over the whole period of archaeological interest down to and including industrial archaeology. There is also a bibliographical section.

108 '**The archaeology of Anglo-Saxon England**' edited by David M Wilson (Methuen, 1976) does not attempt to sum up the entire archaeological knowledge relating to the period but is content to point out certain major features and to provide 'a true and documented estimate of the present state of certain aspects of Anglo-Saxon archaeological studies'. *Contents*: 'Agriculture and rural settlement' (P J Fowler); 'Buildings and rural settlement' (P A Rahtz); 'Towns' (Martin Biddle); 'Ecclesiastical architecture' (Bridget Cherry); 'Monastic sites' (Rosemary Cramp); 'Craft and industry' (David M Wilson); 'The pottery' (J G Hurst); 'The coins' (Michael Dolley); 'The animal resources' (Juliet Clutton-Brock); and 'The Scandinavians in England' (David M Wilson). 'A gazetteer of Anglo-Saxon domestic sites' (P A Rahtz) is included as an appendix and there is a list of sources.

109 '**The archaeology of Berkshire**' by Harold Peake was issued as one of Methuen's 'County archaeologies' in 1931. The main part of the book consists of a general impression of the county's archaeological background down to the Norman invasion, whilst the gazetteer includes (by parish) every monument, every antiquity found within the county, and a complete bibliography of each. Public collections in museums and private collections of Berkshire antiquities are also listed. A select bibliography appears at the end of each chapter.

110 'The archaeology of Britain' a new series announced by Routledge and Kegan Paul in 1974 will cover the archaeology of Britain up to and including the medieval period. Each volume will be contributed by a distinguished scholar and will incorporate the results and thinking of the latest research. The first volume issued was *Iron age communities in Britain* by Barry Cunliffe who also acts as general editor for the series. Other volumes planned will deal with neolithic Britain, bronze age Britain, the military archaeology of Roman Britain, the archaeology of the Saxon countryside, and Saxon towns.

111 'The archaeology of Cornwall and Scilly' by H O'Neill Hencken (1932) is a little more academic than other books in Methuen's 'County archaeologies' series, a number of chapters originally formed part of a doctoral thesis for Cambridge University. Besides the archaeological survey of the county and the gazetteer listing sites and antiquities by parish, there is an indication of collections containing Cornish antiquities. Chambered barrows in the Scilly Isles, burial chambers on the Cornish mainland, stone circles, and large cists, are also enumerated. There is a general bibliography.

112 'The archaeology of early man' by J M Coles and E S Higgs (Faber, 1969) describes and evaluates aspects of human behaviour in the stone ages and surveys for students 'some of the most important methods by which the material remains of early man may be dated and placed in their proper environmental and economic situations'. The arrangement is on a geographical basis with brief descriptions of many of the more significant sites. Author, site and general indexes, and a wide-ranging bibliography, further add to the usefulness of this work. A Penguin paperback edition became available in 1976.

113 'The archaeology of Exmoor' *Bideford Bay to Bridgwater'* by L V Grinsell (David and Charles, 1970) is a comprehensively documented 'account of places and things from inspection, as well as a digest of what
48

has previously been written on the subject', arranged in a chronological sequence of sites. A series of appendixes includes guides to archaeological touring of the area either by road or on foot in addition to a collection of period inventories, based on distribution maps, which supply the National Grid references of each site and indicate those museums where objects recovered from the sites may be inspected.

114 'The archaeology of Ireland' by Peter Harbison (Bodley Head, 1976) is a beautifully illustrated account of the country's archaeology ranging in time from the last ice-age to the medieval period with a final chapter on the underwater discovery of the wrecks of several ships of the Spanish Armada which foundered in Irish waters. The author is archaeologist to the Irish Tourist Board.

115 'The archaeology of Ireland' by R A S Macalister, originally published by Methuen in their 'County archaeologies' series in 1928, was extensively revised for a second edition in 1949 to take notice of the enormous increase in knowledge during the intervening period. The later edition was shorn of the pre-war series characteristics, the archaological gazetteer and list of museums have both vanished, but an up-to-date, authoritative, systematic account of Irish archaeology remains. For an authoritative critique see E E Evans' 'R A S Macalister and the archaeology of Ireland', *Ulster journal of archaeology*, 14, 1951: 1-6.

116 'The archaeology of Kent' by R F Jessup, published in Methuen's 'County archaeologies' series in 1930, is a descriptive survey of the archaeology and antiquities of the county down to the Norman Conquest. An archaeological gazetteer lists finds and their printed references by parish and a list of museums exhibiting Kentish antiquities is appended.

117 'The archaeology of late Celtic Britain and Ireland c400-1200 AD' by Lloyd Laing was published by Methuen in hard covers and as a paperback in 1975 and has strong claims to be regarded as the standard textbook for the period. Based on a course of lectures for first year undergraduates at Liverpool University it is arranged in two sections. The first consists of a series of surveys of field monuments region by region, whilst the second discusses in some detail the material culture of the early Christian Celts. Both are fully documented in the bibliography and although this includes a brief list of general non-specialist works on the history and archaeology of the period in addition to a catalogue of site excavation reports, it is clear that this particular work is not intended for the general reader. The scholarly apparatus also encompasses extensive notes to each chapter and two appendices, one on Celtic manuscript art, the other a chronology of historical personages mentioned in the text. The book is distributed in the United States by Barnes and Noble.

118 'The archaeology of Middlesex and London' by C E Vulliamy was published in Methuen's 'County archaeologies' series in 1930. In addition to the text, a period by period survey down to the Norman Conquest, an archaeological gazetteer provides a list of principal sites arranged by parishes and an inventory of their most noteworthy objects. Each chapter ends with a select list of further readings and a bibliographical note at the beginning of the book reviews the standard works and journals.

119 'The archaeology of Roman Britain' by R G Collingwood, one of the earliest of Methuen's handbooks of archaeology when it was first published in 1930, was immediately acknowledged as a unique single-volume handbook to the field monuments and antiquities of Roman Britain. A new edition revised by Ian Richmond appeared in 1969 which, expanded and brought up-to-date, retains all the authority of the original. There is a meticulously detailed list of references in every chapter and the text is illustrated with over a hundred line drawings besides twenty-six half-tone plates (including air photographs) of the principal sites, coins, inscriptions and other artefacts of the period. B R Hartley contributes a chapter on Samian Ware.

120 'The archaology of Somerset' by D P Dobson, included in Methuen's 'County archaeologies' series in 1931, summarizes archaeological discoveries in the county down to 1930. An archaeological gazetteer records all the chief sites and objects of archaeological interest. A list of Somerset museums follows and there is also an appendix providing dimensions of Romano-British and Saxon skeletons.

121 'An archaeology of south-east England' *a study in continuity* by Gordon J Copley (Phoenix House, 1958) is in two parts. Part I consists of period surveys forming an illustrated outline of the prehistory of the region intended for the enthusiastic and active amateur archaeologist. Part II is a gazetteer of important sites and finds arranged alphabetically by parish and county with approximate national grid references. Each chapter concludes with its own bibliography and the general bibliography

is especially useful for its list of local periodical publications. Ten distribution and twelve regional maps are also conveniently included.

122 'The archaeology of Surrey' by D C Whimster was published in Methuen's 'County archaeologies' series in 1931. It provides a firm outline of the county's archaeological record and a gazetteer arranges lists of sites and antiquities by parish. Scheduled ancient monuments in the county are also listed as are those museums which include Surrey antiquities among their collections.

123 'The archaeology of Sussex' by E Cecil Curwen, first published in 1937 as one of Methuen's 'County archaeologies' series, was issued in a revised edition in 1954. Unlike other volumes in the series it stops short of the Saxon conquests and the gazetteer is omitted altogether because it would, in the author's opinion, appeal only to a small number of specialists whereas the book is intended to cater more for the interests of the general reader. Museums containing Sussex antiquities are listed as are the various local archaeological societies within the county.

124 'The archaeology of the Anglo-Saxon settlements' by E Thurlow Leeds was, when first published by the Oxford University Press in 1913, one of the earliest attempts to consider the problems of early Anglo-Saxon archaeology as a distinct entity. It reflected the author's chagrin at the cavalier disregard of Anglo-Saxon archaeology scarcely concealed by research workers in other disciplines. Chapter two 'Methods of study and history of Anglo-Saxon archaeological research' is of especial importance in the development of methodology in this particular area of studies.

125 'The archaeology of the Channel Islands' was published in two volumes by different authors, by different publishers, nine years apart: vol 1 *The Bailiwick of Guernsey* by T G Kendrick (Methuen, 1928); vol 2 *The Bailiwick of Jersey* by Jacquetta Hawkes (Société Jersiaise, 1937). Their pattern is similar, a description of prehistoric remains by type, and an archaeological investigation island by island, parish by parish.

126 'The archaeology of the Industrial Revolution' edited by Brian Bracegirdle (Heinemann Educational Books, 1973) is a lavish full-colour pictorial survey of the remains of Britain's industrial revolution which affords an instructive and readable guide to some of the key sites of industrial history. Sad to relate some of the sites illustrated have already been destroyed. *Contents*: 'An introduction to industrial archaeology' (Brian Bracegirdle); 'Inland waterways' (L T C Rolt); 'Railways' (Charles Lee); 'Other means of communication' (A Ridley); 'Natural sources of power' (Rex Wailes); 'Power from steam' (Neil Cossons); 'Electric power' (Brian Bowers); 'Coal and other fuels' (Will Slatcher and Brian Bracegirdle); 'Iron and steel' (W K V Gale); and 'Building for industry' (Jennifer Tann).

127 '**Archaeology of the Mammoth Cave area**', edited by Patty Jo Watson, was published in the Academic Press series 'Studies in archaeology' in 1974 and is a detailed account of excavations in Mammoth Cave, National Park, Kentucky since 1969. The work is more wide-ranging than its title would suggest: not only is the surface work in the National Park described, other caves here and elsewhere, notably at Wyandotte Cave in south Indiana, are also discussed, and there are chapters on the aboriginal use of caves and the identification of botanical material recovered. Full bibliographies are included.

128 '**The archaeology of Wessex**' *an account of Wessex antiquities from the earliest times to the end of the pagan Saxon period, with special reference to existing field monuments* by L V Grinsell (Methuen, 1958) is a chronologically arranged thematic account of field monuments based on personal inspection over a thirty year period, each chapter beginning with a short sketch of the archaological background of the period in question. The work is very carefully documented, there are references at the end of every chapter (usually to journal articles) in addition to a full-scale thematically grouped bibliography modestly described as 'suggestions for further reading'. A map section consisting of six period distribution maps, an appendix listing archaeological museums containing Wessex material, a gazetteer of sites, and a generous selection of photographs and drawings, all ensure that the work is exploited to the full.

129 '**The archaeology of Yorkshire**' by Frank and Harriet Wragg Elgie was included in Methuen's 'County archaeologies' series in 1933 and was the first attempt to outline Yorkshire's prehistoric, Roman and Anglo-Viking archaeology as a whole. The arrangement is by chronological chapters followed by four geographical 'archaeological gazetteers'—East, North and West Riding, and York, which list the most important discoveries, sites and field antiquities. Each chapter concludes with a brief bibliography. Although research over the last forty years has rendered some of its terminology and conclusions obsolete it still retains much interest and value and in 1971 it was republished by S R Publishers of East Ardsley, Wakefield, with a new Foreword by T G Manby, as one of their 'County history reprints' series.

130 'Archaeology under water' by George F Bass was published in Thames and Hudson's 'Ancient peoples and places' series in 1966 and is described by the author as 'a long essay on underwater archaology to show what it is and how and why it has reached its present stage of development'. Although not strictly a technical manual the book is divided into chapters which discuss such matters as working under water, search and survey, draining and raising operations, the salvaging of artefacts, mapping and recording, tools, excavation and an indication of possible future developments. The bibliography, arranged on a chapter basis, is not restricted to purely archaeological entries but includes many references to items of general underwater interest. There are over sixty photographs and numerous drawings. A Penguin paperback edition appeared in 1970.

131 'Archaeometric clearinghouse' is a register consisting of the names of American archaeometrists, their particular individual abilities and expertise, work and interests and their institutional addresses, compiled by Curt W Beck which first appeared in the *Journal of field archaeology* 2 (2) 1975: 169-178.

132 'Archaeometry', a research journal dealing with the involvement of the physical sciences in archaeology and art history, began life in 1958 in cyclostyled typescript form as the 'Bulletin of the research laboratory for archaeology and the history of art', Oxford University. At that time it was almost solely concerned with the publication of interim reports on work undertaken in the laboratory but since its fourth issue it has included accounts of similar work in hand at other institutions on an international basis. Because of the interdisciplinary nature of its interest, authors are encouraged to write with the non-specialist in mind and to include an explanatory introduction if their subject matter is highly technical. Review articles are also printed on occasion providing up-to-date summaries in this rapidly developing field. Since 1970 the journal has appeared twice a year, in February and July, and each issue normally contains articles (including a short abstract), research notes, and application reports.

133 Architectural and Archaeological Society for the County of Buckinghamshire was formed in November 1847 'to promote the study of architecture and antiquities, by the collection of books, drawings, models, casts, brass-rubbings, notes and local information, and by mutual instruction at meetings of the Society in the way of conversation and by reading original papers on subjects connected with its designs'. Seven years later there appeared the first issue of a quarterly journal, *Records of Buckinghamshire, papers and notes on the history, antiquities, and architecture of the county together with the society's proceedings.* A special issue to commemorate the society's centenary in 1947 contained G Eland's 'One hundred years of the records'. Other items of general interest include M W Beresford's 'Glebe terriers and open fields in Buckinghamshire', XV(6) 1952: 283-298 and XVI(1), 1953:1-28 which contains a summary list of deserted villages within the county; J F Head's 'Buckinghamshire AD 450-700', XIV 1946: 301-340, a comparison of documentary and archaeological evidence with a schedule of sites and a bibliography; 'Moated sites in Buckinghamshire', a list prepared by the county museum archaeological group, XIX(3) 1973: 336-339; and C N Gowing's 'A hundred years of the museum', XVII(1) 1961: 82-87.

134 Architectural and Archaeological Society of Durham and Northumberland was founded following a meeting of the Yorkshire Architectural Society in Durham in the autumn of 1861 when it was suggested that a former architectural society in the city should be revived. The steering committee decided, however, that the society should cover the whole diocese. Its objects were: 'To bring under the notice of its members whatever of Architectural and Antiquarian interest may be embraced within its district' and 'to preserve from destruction (as far as possible in an age so destructive to ancient works) all remains illustrative of the genius, taste and skill in manufacture of the Architects, artists and manufacturers of by-gone ages'. The society was careful to point out that 'in pursuing its legitimate objects it will not interfere with any of the existing societies ... inasmuch as these societies are principally concerned with the literary section of antiquarian subjects, and deal more with documentary than with material evidences'. Although on its own admission not chiefly a publishing society, looking more to excursions to places of interest 'to beget a spirit of scientific research amongst its members', a series of *Transactions* was very quickly set in motion, the first issue being dated 1862. The first series of eleven volumes came to an end in 1965 being replaced three years later by a new series in a larger crown quarto format with the text printed offset from typescript to make it possible to publish a big and well illustrated volume every other year, each issue being complete in itself and numbered independently. Papers of note include C E Whiting's 'Some northern antiquaries', IX(1) 1939: 87-111; Stuart Piggott's 'Innovation and tradition in British prehistory', ns III, 1974: 1-12; D W Harding's 'County Durham in the prehistoric period', ns II, 1970: 27-30 and B Dobson's 'Roman Durham', pages 31-43 in the same issue. Back numbers of the old series can be obtained from Periodicals Department, University Library, Palace Green, Durham.

135 '**Art and archaeology technical abstracts**' is now published for the International Institute for the Conservation of Historic and Artistic Works from the Institute of Fine Arts at New York University. The first five volumes (each volume contained four issues over two years) were published under the title of *Abstracts of the technical literature on archaeology and fine arts*, usually known as the *IIC abstracts*, which commenced publication in 1955. For coverage before that reference should be made to *Abstracts of technical studies in art and archaeology*. All items listed were at this stage included under one of five headings: 'Museology' (*ie* those dealing with display, lighting, atmosphere, humidity and pollution, preventive care against fungi and insects, or fire prevention); 'Materials and techniques' of objects of art, archaeology, buildings and paintings; 'Conservation and restoration treatment, materials and methods'; 'Analysis of material and technical examination'(the physical and chemical methods used in analysis, the study of techniques and dating, microchemical analysis etc). and 'Authentification and forgery' especially those discussing examples which have either been confirmed as genuine or condemned as forgeries as a result of scientific examination.

A system of volunteer abstractors working under the direction of regional editors in all parts of the world was gradually built up, a tradition that remained unaltered by a change of title, of editor and of publishing arrangements which took effect with volume six in 1966. There was no change either in the philosophy that motivated *IIC abstracts* namely that it would continue to serve all concerned with the study and preservation of historic and artistic works through the dissemination of information on technical advances, workshop techniques and discoveries.

The editor took space in the first of the new-style issues to lay down the principles to be used in the selection of items for abstracting: all articles dealing with the examination, investigation, restoration, preservation, or documentation of historic or artistic objects; all publications containing information on or describing techniques potentially applicable to their study and treatment; all reports relating to the physical or chemical properties of substances in their structure or treatment *eg* drying oils, pigments, or adhesives, detergents, coating agents; and articles of general interest like progress reports of excavations, accounts of discoveries, or notes on objects authenticated or proved false. A change was made in the method of arrangement: items would in future be listed under general methods and techniques, paper, wood, textiles, paintings, glass and ceramics, stone and masonry, metals, or animal and vegetable products.

Some measure of retrospective coverage was also put in train insofar as abstracts of articles in older literature that contained particularly valuable information which had not been abstracted previously were to be included. At the same time it was announced that a number of critical annotated bibliographies integrating all literature, past and present, on selected topics would be published from time to time. Beginning with volume nine (1972) each volume covers one year (two issues). A subject index to vols 1-5 *IIC abstracts* and vols 6-10 (1955-1973) appeared as a supplement to the first issue of volume eleven (1974) and an author and abbreviated title index volumes 1-10 compiled by N L Kunz and J H Stoner in the second issue of volume twelve (1975). An obituary of Rutherford John Gettens who played a key part in the *IIC abstracts* and its successor from its inception was published in the first issue of volume eleven, summer 1974.

136 'Art index' is one of the wide range of periodical indexes published by the H W Wilson Company of New York. It is a single author subject index to the contents of almost two hundred periodicals, each entry contains the author and title of the article together with full bibliographical details. Among the journals indexed are *American journal of archaeology, Antiquity, Archaeologia, Archaeological journal, Archaeology, The Biblical archaeologist, Expedition, Hesperia, Journal of Egyptian archaeology, Journal of Hellenic studies, The museums journal,* and *Studies in conservation.* The *Index* is issued quarterly with permanent bound annual cumulations reaching back to 1929.

137 Ashmolean Museum, Oxford was founded when Elias Ashmole (1617-1692) offered the university his collection of coins, antiquities, and other items on condition that a museum was built to house them. The university agreed and the museum first opened its doors to the public in 1683. In the nineteenth century the natural history, medical and ethnographical specimens were dispersed to the university and Pitt-Rivers museums and the Ashmolean is now administred in three department: antiquities, classical archaeology, and fine arts. The antiquities collections which are world-wide in scope, were heavily augmented by the excavations of Flinders Petrie in Egypt and Arthur Evans in Crete; the department also holds collections of manuscripts and antiquities originally in the possession of illustrious antiquarians like John Aubrey and James Douglas. G W G Allen's collection of air photographs of sites in the Oxford and adjoining districts also finds a home there. A summary guide to the collections has been published which 'makes no attempt to mention every object or even group of objects in the galleries, but tries to point to those exhibits which seem likely to be most interesting and instructive for the non-specialist visitor, and to provide just enough archaeological and historical background to enable him to thread his way through exhibits of the great diversity and scope and origin which the Department is fortunate enough to possess'. A pocket-size, stiff-paper folder guide and plan to the floors and galleries is also available. Various other cataogues and pamphlets are published: in 1950 the Museum assumed responsibility for *Notes on archaeological technique*, a pamphlet intended to serve as an elementary guide for the beginner in excavation from the initial arrangements to the final report, originally prepared by the Oxford University Archaeological Society. *Elias Ashmole (1617-1692) his autobiographical and historical notes, his correspondence, and other contemporary sources relating to his life and work*, edited with a biographical introduction by C H Josten was published in five volumes by Oxford University Press in 1966.

138 'Aslib index to theses' *accepted for higher degrees by the universities of Great Britain and Ireland and the Council for National Academic Awards* (1950-) is currently issued twice a year. Information provided includes author, university, title, for which degree accepted, and where known the British Library Lending Division accession number. It is arranged under subject headings, 'archaeology' being a sub-heading under 'history'. There are also notes on the availability of theses.

139 Associated Architectural Societies was a cooperative publishing venture on the part of a number of societies all springing up in the 1840s and 1850s for the study of Gothic architecture and ecclesiastical antiquities. Their aim was to obtain a larger circulation for their papers and transactions and to minimise the cost of publication. The *Reports and papers* *read at the meetings of the architectural societies of* . . . were first published for 1850 and continued until 1937. Each society was allotted a specified number of pages although if one society wished to take up more than its agreed share this could be mutually arranged with one of the others subject to a redistribution of costs. The individual society's reports etc were printed separately so that they might at some future time bind up their own papers. A general secretary was appointed to superintend the publication but enjoyed no greater authority than was necessary to see the volume through the press, each society being responsible for its own report and each writer for his own paper. *An index to the first eight volumes . . . during the years 1850-1866*, containing an analysis of each paper, compiled by George Rowe, was published in 1867. Indexes to vols IX-XIV (1867-1878), XV-XIX (1879-1888), XX-XXV (1889-1900) followed. Societies participating included at one time or another the architectural societies of the Archdeaconry of Northampton, the Diocese of Worcester, and the County of Yorkshire; the architectural and archaeological societies of Bedford, Lincolnshire, Leicestershire, Sheffield, and St Albans. In many ways the joint enterprise proved advantageous but one by one the reformed archaeological societies began to publish their own *Transactions* etc, and the combined *Reports and papers* were eventually discontinued. A total of forty-two volumes had been published.

140 Association for Field Archaeology is an American organization devoted to the promotion of field archaeology and the interests of field archaeologists. Its purpose is 'to serve as an instrument for the discussion of and action concerning the recovery, restoration, and primary interpretation of excavation material and the protection of antiquities'. Its organ is the *Journal of field archaeology* (*qv*).

141 The Association for Industrial Archaeology was established in September 1973 to promote the study of industrial archaeology and to act as a pressure group at national and local levels. It sees its functions as threefold: one, to pursue a higher degree of coordination between industrial archaeologists than had hitherto been achieved, and to supervise the arrangements for an annual conference; secondly, to secure a truly professional standard in the recording of industrial monuments especially those in imminent danger of destruction; and, thirdly, to achieve a rational and effective conservation policy. In the long term the association is striving for the creation of a national fund for industrial conservation drawn either from private or public funds, and even the possible outright purchase of selected industrial monuments, or at least putting them in the care of responsible museums, trusts or local authorities. More immediately the association plays an important role with regard to 'unprotected' monuments *ie* those already assessed by the Department of the Environment and not given protection or those not yet assessed. To this end it is seeking to establish a network of watchdogs to report on structures threatened by demolition, alteration, or simply by neglect, and a complementary network of recorders to assume responsibility for ensuring that an adequate record for a monument so threatened either already exists or that one is made as a matter of urgency. The association publishes a bulletin six times a year which includes news of events and activities of local societies and groups, discoveries and educational courses, etc. At one time the association acknowledged a connection with the quarterly *Industrial archaeology* but when that journal was experiencing internal difficulties the connection was discontinued. Now the association is linked with Oxford University Press in the publication of *Industrial archaeology review (qv)*.

142 Association of County Archaeological Officers, formed in June 1973, is intended to provide a forum for the discussion of common problems. It is also concerned with appropriate levels and grading of appointments in local government. A guide to the compilation of sites and monuments records is in preparation and will be the association's first publishing venture.

143 'Atlas of ancient archaeology' edited by Jacquetta Hawkes (Heinemann, 1974) examines on a comparative basis the cultures and civilizations of the world down to the classical period. The pattern of arrangement is by region: an introduction and a regional map depicting cultural areas precedes a description of a number of important sites (170 all told) many of which have been discovered or systematically investigated comparatively recently. Although compiled primarily for students of archaeology and ancient history the *Atlas* is also intended for travellers and tourists and accordingly every site is vividly illustrated with detailed maps, plans and drawings. A short list of appropriate books and journal articles also accompanies each site description. Over a score of leading archaeologists, each responsible for a particular region, contribute towards this well-planned, beautifully produced, and tightly edited work of reference which succeeds as few others do in reconciling the vastly different needs of students and laymen. A chronological chart of palaeolithic and other hunting cultures indicates the approximate relative age of the sites described in the atlas and there are other useful adjuncts, a glossary, a note on American period terminology, and information on dating systems and the rough mean dates of glacial and interglacial periods. There is a comprehensive topographical and subject general index. It is intended that this work shall be followed by an *Atlas of classical archaeology*.

144 '**Atlas of the Bible**' by L H Grollenburg was first published in English by Nelson in 1956. W F Albright and H H Rowley contribute a joint foreword and there is a preface by Roland De Vaux. The maps are arranged in historical order so that they are not burdened with extraneous detail although they do bear descriptive comments which themselves serve as historical summaries. But the bulk of the atlas consists of a quite remarkable selection of black and white photographs of ancient monuments, sites, and landscapes. The third element is the text, linking maps and illustrations, and providing a brief outline of Bible history; sections on the technique of Biblical geography and excavations in Palestine are included in an introductory chapter. An exhaustive gazetteer and index complete an impressive piece of book production. *The shorter atlas of the Bible* (Nelson, 1959), with a rewritten text, fewer illustrations, and with maps confined to key periods, is not strictly an abridged version of the main *Atlas* although it clearly descends from it.

145 '**Atlas of the Biblical world**' by Denis Baly and A D Tushingham (The World Publishing Company, New York, 1971) synthesizes material of archaeological, geographical, and Biblical interest, in a composite volume in which text, maps, and photographs are closely coordinated to present a study of the Middle East as a whole and of the Biblical lands in particular. The principal sources consulted in the preparation of the maps are outlined and there is a full general bibliography. Father Roland De Vaux contributes a foreword.

146 '**Atoms of time past**' by David Wilson (Allen Lane, 1975) reviews the swing back to science evident in archaeology over recent years caused largely by the recognition that the techniques of laboratory science could be profitably applied to archaeological material. The impact of these new techniques, especially that of radio-carbon dating and tree ring calibration, and the emergence of 'The New Archaeology' with its more rigid scientific discipline, is particularly well told and documented as is the relatively new concept of archaeology confirming the historical record in addition to uncovering the prehistoric past.

147 Aubrey, John (1626-1697) was granted letters patent by Charles II in 1671 authorizing him to make antiquarian surveys under the Crown and he devoted much time in collecting material for a detailed account of the field monuments of Britain from the prehistoric period down to the Middle Ages. This was never published although his *Monumenta Britannica: a miscellanie of British antiquities* remains in manuscript in the Bodleian Library. He is regarded as the founder of British field archaeology, his name perpetuated in the Aubrey Holes at Stonehenge. Michael Hunter's *John Aubrey and the realm of learning* (Duckworth, 1975), a study of his writings and their background, includes notes on the manuscripts and printed texts of Aubrey's works and on the works now lost.

148 'Authenticity in art' *the scientific detection of forgery* by Stuart Fleming published in London by the Institute of Physics and in New York by Crane Russak in 1976 presents the background of forensic science behind the major art scandals of recent times. For the archaeologist it outlines the reassuring potential of modern scientific techniques such as thermo-luminescence, radio-carbon dating, radiography and infra-red, ultra-violet, and x-rays.

149 'Azania' *the journal of the British Institute of History and Archaeology in East Africa* began publication as an annual volume in 1966. Its papers, notes and book reviews incorporate not only material relating to the former British colonies and protectorates in East Africa but also the wide central areas of Africa not covered by an English language publication. The main channel for the work of the staff and research students of the institute it also welcomes other contributions, preferably in English, although papers in French, German or Italian are also considered. Research work in progress or recently completed is another feature of the journal which takes its title from the Graeco-Roman name of the East African coastal region.

150 'Barrow, pyramid and tomb' *ancient burial centres in Egypt, the Mediterranean and the British Isles* by L V Grinsell (Thames and Hudson, 1975) is divided into two sections: the first discusses the reasons for the different forms of burial in various parts of the ancient world whilst the second describes the funerary monuments themselves. The British Isles are covered in two chapters, one covering Wessex and the South-West, the other Ireland, Wales and Scotland. The American publishers are Westview Press.

151 Bedfordshire Archaeological Council was formed in 1959 by representatives of the leading archaeological societies in the county in order to coordinate their resources for fieldwork and excavation and to produce a permanent annual journal. In fact the first issue of the *Bedfordshire archaeological journal* appeared in August 1962 after considerable efforts had raised a sufficient sum of money to support it. Already a number of important articles have been printed including John Morris' 'The Anglo-Saxons in Bedfordshire with a gazetteer of pagan Anglo-Saxon discoveries', vol 1 1962: 58-76; Nicholas Thomas' 'A gazetteer of neolithic and bronze age sites and antiquities in Bedfordshire', 2, 1964: 16-33; Geoffrey Fisher's 'Archaeology in the *Bedford times* 1845-1850', 6, 1971: 1-8; and D N Hall and J B Hutching's 'The distribution of archaeological sites between the Nene and the Ouse valleys', 7, 1972: 1-16. 'Bedfordshire archaeology', a guide to current fieldwork and excavation in the county arranged alphabetically by site has appeared since volume four (1969).

152 Bedfordshire County Planning Department Conservation Section: Those who doubt the desirability of rescue or field archaeology becoming enmeshed in local government bureaucracy should read David Baker's 'The past reviv'd through publick endeavour OR An archaeological view from Bedfordshire', *Current archaeology*, IV (12) No 47, November 1974; 367-372, a concise account of the work of the section and why it was formed.

153 'Before civilization' *the radiocarbon revolution and prehistoric Europe* by Colin Renfrew (Cape, 1973) traces the reappraisal of fundamental assumptions regarding prehistoric Europe brought about by the collapse of conventionally accepted chronology caused by the latest advances in radio-carbon dating and tree-ring calibration. If, as now seems necessary, we must accept the hypothesis that the megaliths of Western Europe should be dated earlier than the pyramids—and all that implies— then Professor Renfrew's use of the work 'revolution' in his title is clearly justified. And there could be no more startling manifestation of 'the New Archaeology'. The story of the rise and apparent fall of the diffusionist view of European prehistory is recorded in the first part of this extremely well-documented work, whilst the second part attempts to find answers to the formidable problems now confronting archaeologists and prehistorians.

154 'Beginnings in archaeology' by Kathleen Kenyon, published in a second revised edition by Phoenix House in 1961, is now available in Dent's Aldine paperbacks. The author's purpose was to answer those questions she knew from experience beginners ask and at the same time to provide the sort of information as a Director of Excavations that she would like beginners to have. Topics covered include the diverse nature of archaeology, the geographical areas of archaeological research, how to become an archaeologist, and the techniques of fieldwork. There is also a bibliography and notes on archaeological training in universities, the British schools abroad, archaeological posts, and archaeological societies. American details are supplied by Saul and Gladys Weinberg.

155 Berkshire Archaeological Society began life in August 1871 as The Reading Architectural Association with a membership limited to twenty practising architects. A year later it became the Reading Architectural and Archaeological Society and after a further year the society adopted the county designation. A full history of the society has yet to be written although P H Ditchfield's 'History of the society', *Berkshire, Buckinghamshire and Oxfordshire archaeological journal*, XXVII, 1921: 76-87; H T Morley's 'The Berkshire Archaeological Society 1922-1947', 66, 1971-72: 1-5 offer a few desultory pointers. The society's aims as outlined today are 'to collect and diffuse information respecting the History, Archaeology and Architecture of the County and neighbourhood by Lectures, the reading of Papers and by Excursions, arranging of objects of Antiquarian interest, by the publication of the Society's Journal, and by such other means as the Council may determine; to encourage individuals or public bodies in making researches and excavations and afford them suggestions and cooperation, and to encourage the preservation of historical monuments'. Prior to 1890 the society published a few volumes of *Transactions* but possessed no means of preserving a permanent record of papers presented until *The Berkshire Archaeological journal* enjoyed a brief period of publication 1890-1895 during which time three volumes of eight parts each were issued. But the resources of the society were insufficient to support this venture and it was discontinued. However, a proposal that societies in the counties of Berkshire, Buckinghamshire, and Oxfordshire should pool their efforts to produce a joint journal proved successful in part and *The Berkshire, Buckinghamshire and Oxfordshire archaeological journal* flourished 1895-1929 when it abruptly reverted to the title of *The Berkshire archaeological journal.* This assumed a larger and more modern format with volume 58 (1960). Items of general interest appearing in its pages have been G W B Huntingford's 'The ancient earthworks of North Berkshire', 40(2) Autumn 1936: 157-175; F M Underhill's 'Notes on recent antiquarian discoveries in Berkshire', 41(1) Spring 1937: 33-41 and 42(1) Spring 1938: 20-28; L V Grinsell's 'An analysis and list of Berkshire barrows', 39(2) Autumn 1935: 171-191, 40(1) Spring 1936: 20-62, 'Pt III Evidence from Saxon charters', 42(2) Autumn 1938: 102-116, and 'Pt IV Addenda and corrigenda', 43(1) Spring 1939: 9-21; 'List of scheduled ancient monuments in Berkshire' (corrected to 31 December 1952), 54, 1954-55: 125-126; Mrs M Aylwin Cotton's 'Berkshire hill-forts', 60, 1962: 30-52; M W Beresford's first list of deserted medieval village sites in Berkshire, 60, 1962: 92-97; and H W Copsey's 'A list of barrows around the Berkshire-Surrey-Hampshire boundary', 61, 1963-64: 20-27; Archaeological notes from Reading Museum, objects or sites brought to the museum's notice and unless stated otherwise added to its collections, have been a regular feature of recent issues. *An index of the Berkshire, Buckinghamshire and Oxfordshire archaeological journal and of the quarterly journal of the Berkshire Archaeological Society 1890-1919* compiled by F M Bunce was published in 1924, and a further index to volumes 26-50, 1930-1947, was compiled by Mrs K A Sincock.

156 'The Biblical archaeologist' (1938-) is an illustrated quarterly journal published by The American Schools of Oriental Research whose purpose it is to provide a readable, non-technical, yet reliable, account of archaeological discoveries relating to the Bible. There is a regular exchange of articles with the Hebrew journal *Qadmoniot*. It is indexed every five volumes.

157 'A bibliographical list descriptive of Romano-British architectural remains in Great Britain' by Arthur Lyell was published by Cambridge University Press in 1912. It was intended to provide students with all published information regarding excavated sites, and perhaps prevent the needless excavation of sites already explored. Conversely, it might encourage the exploration of sites which had been previously investigated in a cursory manner only. Obscure evidence and burial sites are excluded. The entries (site name plus bibliographical references) are listed alphabetically by English, Scottish, and Welsh counties.

158 'Bibliography of Holy Land sites' compiled by Eleanor K Vogel first appeared as part of the 1971 Hebrew Union College *Annual*. Listing publications on the archaeology of over two hundred sites it is now available as a booklet from the American Schools of Oriental Research who intend to revise it from time to time.

159 'Birmingham and Warwickshire Archaeological Society was formed as the Archaeological Section of the Birmingham and Midland Institute in 1870. At the end of the century it altered its name to the Birmingham Archaeological Society in order to conform to standard practice although it still remained under the parent institution. A change to its present title came in the 1960s. Its fortunes were low, literally and figuratively, at the time of its jubilee: Howard Pearson in his 'Birmingham Archaeological Society 1870-1920', *Transactions* XLVII, 1921: 2-6, had this to say, 'Meanwhile the prospects of our Society call for very serious consideration. We are in arrears for two volumes of the Transactions. Our funds are utterly exhausted, and we are even in debt.' But thanks to a special jubilee appeal the worst was staved off and the society's position slowly improved. The *Transactions, excursions, and reports* were first published in 1870, changing to *Transactions and proceedings* in 1916, and emerging as the *Transactions* plainly and simply in 1967. Other papers of interest are Samuel Timmins' 'Inaugural Address' vol I 1870: 1-6; J T Burgess' 'Early earthworks in Warwickshire' vol III, 1872: 79-89; Matthew Holbeache Bloxham's 'The ancient British, Roman, and Anglo-Saxon antiquities of Warwickshire', vol 6, 1875: 25-38; J O Bevan's 'A plea for the production of an archaeological map and index for the county of Warwickshire', XXIV, 1898: 6-17, based on the writer's similar compilation for Herefordshire; and Philip Chatwin's list 'Scheduled ancient monuments in Warwickshire and Staffordshire', 68, 1950: 121-124. A special volume of the *Transactions* consisting of a selection of papers from the 1970-1971 lecture programme on the archaeology and history of Warwickshire which marked the society's centenary was published for 1974. This included 'An archaeological gazetteer for Warwickshire: neolithic to iron age' by Nicholas Thomas, and Graham Webster's 'The West Midlands in the Roman period: a brief survey' both of which are available as offprints.

160 'The Bodley Head archaeologies' are a little difficult to categorize in that they are produced by the Bodley Head Children's Department although designed for the general public. Each book deals with either a particular civilization or with the civilizations of a particular area and is fully illustrated with line drawings, maps and photographs. Annotated lists of books for further reading are also included. The general editor is Magnus Magnusson who contributes *Introducing archaeology* (1972) and *Viking expansion* *westwards.* Other titles: *Digging up the Bible lands* (Ronald Harker); *The Archaeology of Ancient Egypt* (T G H James); *The Archaeology of Minoan Crete* (Reynold Higgins); *Ancient China* (John Hay); *The Archaeology of ships* (Paul Johnstone); *Rome and the barbarians* (Barry Cunliffe); *The Archaeology of Ireland* (Peter Harbison); *The Archaeology of industry* (Kenneth Hudson); *Ancient Turkey* (James Mellaart); and *Anglo-Saxon England* (David Brown). Further titles are in preparation.

161 Bristol and Gloucestershire Archaeological Society: At about the time of the British Archaeological Association's visit to Bristol in 1874 John Taylor, Librarian of the Bristol Museum and Library, wrote a paper calling attention to the archaeological riches of the area. This paper, placed in the library, undoubtedly supported a growing local feeling that the county should have its own archaeological society comparable to those of its neighbouring counties of Somerset and Wiltshire. A private meeting in September 1875 resulted in the formation of a provisional committee which in December issued a circular for a proposed society, pointing out the favourable geographical location of the county and its consequent host of antiquities, and announcing a public inaugural meeting to be held the following April. There were three signatures to the circular, the first being that of the Earl of Ducie, Lord-Lieutenant of the County, who took the chair at the meeting, remarking that 'Among the landed proprietors, among the local clergy, and among the residents of such towns as Clifton and Cheltenham there must be many people who were fit to be members.'

By this time in fact four hundred respectable and influential citizens of this sort had already become members. The objects of the society were declared as 'whilst not excluding the consideration of matters of general antiquarian interest, shall specially be the cultivation of the archaeology of Bristol and Gloucestershire. With this view it will seek (1) to collect and classify original and existing information on the antiquities of the district and to accumulate materials for an improved country history. (2) To establish a library and museum for the preservation and study of these and other objects of antiquarian value. (3) To promote, by meetings, publication, etc such an interest throughout the district in the monuments of its past history as shall tend to counteract their present liability to inconsiderate and needless destruction.'

These objectives have been faithfully followed: in more recent years the society's customary activities have included field meetings at places of archaeological and architectural interest in the spring and autumn, a

66

summer meeting lasting 2-3 days, and evening meetings at Bristol during the winter months. The society's *Transactions* have been published annually since 1876. From 1900 to 1919 (vols XXIII-XLII) a series of 'Bristol archaeological notes' by John Pritchard were included. A list of the ancient monuments of Gloucestershire scheduled under the 1913 Act appeared in vol XLV, 1923: 295-297 and vol XLVIII, 1926: 391-392. Informative papers on the society's history and activities include 'The inaugural meeting' (vol I, 1876: 7-30); John Pritchard's 'The work of the society' (vol XLI, 1918-19: 11-25), of especial value for its references to the early meetings; and Roland Austin's 'The Society 1876-1926' (vol XLVIII, 1926: 49-56) which considers how far the society had achieved its objectives by its fiftieth year. Contemporary issues contain papers presented to the society notes (including additions to the library), reviews, and official reports and accounts etc. A full range of indexes have been published, the most recent being a *General index to vols 51-60 (1930-1939) with separate indexes to illustrations, lists of officers of the society, and places visted by the society 1876-1939* compiled by Roland Austin who was also responsible for earlier volumes; *General index to volumes 61-70 (1939-1951)* and *volumes 71-78 (1952-1959)* both compiled by Eileen Richardson. *Essays in Bristol and Gloucestershire history* edited by Patrick McGrath and John Cannon, presents a wide range of archaeological, historical, and architectural subjects. Elizabeth Ralph's 'The Society 1876-1976' reviews all aspects of the society's activities in much fuller detail than had previously been available. Another essay included is Glyn Daniel's 'The archaeology of megaliths: an historical note'.

162 'Britain and the western seaways' by E G Bowen published as the eightieth volume in Thames & Hudson's 'Ancient peoples and places' series in 1972 differs from most other volumes in that it does not concern itself with the civilization of a specific ancient people or place. Here the author is dealing with a variety of places in Western Europe and numerous ancient peoples. An introductory chapter sketches archaeologists' successive trends of thought regarding how far the sea facilitated or impeded the spread of early Mediterranean culture to North-West Europe. In order to reduce the vast area of enquiry to manageable proportions attention is focused on the British Isles.

163 'Britain before the Norman Conquest', an Ordnance Survey map published in 1973 in two sheets drawn on the scale 1:625,000 (about ten miles to one inch), attempts to illustrate the history of the two centuries preceding the arrival of the Normans, and completes the survey's coverage of the first thousand years of British history of the Christian era. Symbols indicating political, ecclesiastical, and topographical features are printed in three colours, black for Anglo-Saxon, red for Scandinavian, and blue for Celtic. The explanatory text contains sections on the Scandinavian settlement; the Norse in Scotland, Wales and Man; towns and fortifications in late Anglo-Saxon England; the church in Britain AD 871-1066; Pit-prefix place names in Scotland; and a bibliography.

164 'Britain in the Dark Ages' an Ordnance Survey archaeological and historical map drawn to a 1:1,000,000 scale (*ie* sixteen miles to the inch) was originally published in two sheets, North (1939) and South (1935). It is now available either as a single sheet or else folded within a laminated cover together with an explanatory text and covers the whole of Britain for the period AD 410-871. Different coloured symbols indicate Celtic, pagan and Christian Anglo-Saxon surface features. Because of its lasting influence on the development of the Anglo-Saxon settlements the entire Roman road system is also traced in outline. The explanatory text contains a general historical introduction, a section on recent progress in the archaeology of the period, notes on the various types of remains, some ecclesiastical notes, and a useful bibliography.

165 'Britannia' *a journal of Romano-British and kindred studies* published by the Society for the Promotion of Roman Studies first appeared in 1970. It includes papers of general interest, excavation reports 'of wider than local significance', and aims to review as many books with a bearing on Romano-British studies as possible. Its scope is not limited to Britain during the Roman period, it includes articles on the archaeology of the western provinces of the Roman Empire and also deals with matters relating to the Celtic period before and after the Roman occupation. 'Roman Britain', a long-standing feature of *The journal of Roman studies*, was transferred to *Britannia* on its inception. Correspondents are asked to forward information on sites and discoveries listing their location (parish and national grid reference), the name of the excavation's director, the society or other sponsoring body involved, the name of its draughtsman or photographer, any previous excavation, and recent or forthcoming publication. Year by year a valuable record of current research is thus maintained which is further enhanced by the publication of offprints. The journal suffers a precarious financial position although many of its articles are subsidized.

166 'Britannica Romana' *or The Roman antiquities of Britain* by John Horsley was first published as a folio volume in 1732. It is arranged in three books: Book I *contains the history of all the Roman transactions in Britain, with an account of their legionary and auxiliary forces employed here . . . also a large description of the Roman walls, with maps of the same laid down from a geometrical survey*; Book II *contains a compleat collection of the Roman inscriptions and sculptures which have hitherto been discovered in Britain . . .*; and Book III *contains the Roman geography of Britain, in which are given the originals of Ptolemy, Antonini Itinerarium, the Notitia, the anonymous Ravennas, and Peutinger's table, so far as they relate to this island, with particular essays on each of these ancient authors, and the several places in Britain mentioned by them.* The third of these was not intended for inclusion in the first instance but Horsley was persuaded that it would be worthwhile to complete his evidence with a chronological survey of the geographical sources. He claimed to have travelled several thousand miles 'to visit antient monuments, and re-examine them, where there was any doubt or difficulty' and his work is widely acknowledged as setting a standard for methodical and scientific investigation; his collection of inscriptions must be regarded as the foundation of all later work. It was described by Haverfield in his *Roman occupation of Britain* (1924) as 'till quite lately the best and most scholarly account of any Roman province that had been written anywhere in Europe' (p75). Although Book I has largely been superseded as the definitive source on the history of the period by Professor Frere's *Britannia: a history of Roman Britain* (1967) and Book III by R G Collingwood and R P Wright's *The Roman inscriptions of Britain vol 1* (1965), the work still retains its value and interest, especially for its treatment of the Roman Wall. A second edition reprinted in facsimile by The Scolar Press and published by Frank Graham, 6 Queen Terrace, Newcastle-upon-Tyne, which appeared in 1974, includes historical and critical notes by Professor Eric Birley.

167 The British Academy came into being as a consequence of the first meeting of the International Association of Academies held in Paris in 1900. Whereas the Royal Society was preeminent in the scientific field no comparable institution could claim to represent United Kingdom historical or philosophical societies. The Royal Society invited a number of eminent academics and scholars to discuss the formation of a new umbrella institution for the humanities. At first it was thought that the Royal Society might enlarge its scope but that view failed to find favour by the fellows. Certain of those persons who had received the society's invitation decided to go ahead independently and a meeting was held at the British Museum late in June 1901. A provisional general committee was constituted and in December the new body, with the support of the Royal Society, petitioned the King for the grant of a Royal charter. The British Academy for the Promotion of Historical, Philosophical, and Philological Studies was duly incorporated in August 1902.

When the International Association of Academies met for the second time in 1904 the British Academy took its place along with the Royal Society. A factual summary of its progress may be read in Sir Frederic Kenyon's *The British Academy: the first fifty years* (1952) and a more lively account of its rejuvenation in Sir Mortimer Wheeler's *The British Academy 1949-1968* (OUP, 1970). The general body of the academy is organized in four sections of which History and Archaeology is one. The Academy has often taken the lead in establishing overseas schools of archaeology and their London based sponsoring societies, awarding grants for initial running costs from their own funds. Many learned society journals and excavation teams have also benefited from the academy's generosity. In 1949 it became the normal channel for all Treasury subsidies to societies and schools involved in archaeological research when at last, after years of argument, the Treasury was persuaded that the subsidies would be better controlled if they were made over to the academy in an annual block grant for it to allocate at its discretion.

'Much the heaviest call on the British Academy's resources lies in the group of schools, institutes, and societies which it sponsors. These together represent some two-thirds of its income. These bodies collectively provide an element in British academic life, for which there is no substitute. At the same time they are a valuable national asset in the countries abroad where they operate, creating a British academic presence, alongside the diplomatic and cultural, as represented by the embassies and the British Council. It is incumbent on the academy, backed with the Government grant, to ensure that they are not inhibited by lack of funds from operating effectively alongside the similar missions from France, Germany, America, and other countries' (*Proceedings* LVIII, 1972: 3-4). The academy also administers the Albert Reckitt Archaeological Fund which provides for 'the exploration and excavation of ancient sites in any part of the world with a view to increasing knowledge of early civilizations and the history of mankind; and for the preservation and exhibition of evidence and for the publication of results. Its current activities, research, lectures, publications, are outlined in the annual report printed in the annual *Proceedings* which commented publication in 1903. Most of the papers presented there are issued in pamphlet form. Informative if eulogistic obituaries of deceased Fellows are also to be found in the *Proceedings*. An *Index to volumes I-XX (1901-1934)* consisting of author-title plus a few subject headings, with lists of lectures and publications, was published in 1937. *A cumulative index to the proceedings of the British Academy vol 1 (1903) to vol 54 (1968)* compiled by K Balasundara Gupta was issued by The Scarecrow Press in 1971.

168 'British archaeological abstracts' records and abstracts important articles of wide interest published in more than two hundred periodicals entirely or partially devoted to archaeology in the British Isles. Books of general interest are not abstracted but monographs, corpora, gazetteers, festschriften and reference works, all fall within its coverage. Each issue contains at least 220 concise summaries of articles arranged in order of archaeological period with a large general section, world-wide in scope, on the principles and history of archaeology and on new techniques in field-work, recording and analysis. The citation of each entry includes full bibliographical details, title of article, author, title of periodical, volume and part number, date and page references. In addition, extensive pre-liminary matter—lists of the British and foreign journals and other sources scanned, related bibliographic compilations (government publications, index volumes and the like), an abstract section finder, a cross-reference guide and a section on archaeology in Parliament—add even more value to this extremely useful publication launched by the Council for British Archaeology in 1968 after some intensive market research which included the circulation of a sample number labelled Vol 0 No 0 Autumn 1967. Two issues a year are published in April and October, enabling scholars to keep up-to-date with the vast amount of literature published in journal form, and allowing experts to keep abreast of the latest work outside their own specialisms. A cumulated index to volumes I-V 1968-1972, is in active preparation. An authoritative account of the reasons for the decision to publish the *Abstracts* is contained in Cherry Lavell's 'The CBA and information retrieval', *Museums journal*, 67(2) September 1967: 111-113.

169 British Archaeological Association *for the encouragement and pros-ecution of researches into the arts and monuments of the early and middle ages* was born in December 1843 out of a sense of disappointment that the Society of Antiquaries was not concerning itself as directly or as en-thusiastically as it might in the prevention of the gradual destruction of

ancient monuments; prospective members of the association were reminded
that the society's charter made no mention of the preservation of monuments threatened with decay or injury. And so the association was formed
as an institution 'where persons of different attainments, and knowledge
in different departments of science and art, combine together to elucidate
the events and memorials of past ages'. It was decided to establish a central
committee 'for the purpose of collecting from correspondents in all parts
of the country information tending to the discovery, illustration, and conservation of our ancient national monuments'.

The archaeological journal, initially intended as a quarterly publication,
was instituted to further the association's aims and purposes but, unfortunately, the high hopes entertained during a highly successful first year, culminating in a most successful congress at Canterbury, were shattered in
December 1844 by an unseemly dispute centring around the publication of
a work called *The archaeological album* written by Thomas Wright, one of
the association's founder members. At this remove it would appear to be
a classic case of faulty communications within the organization but the
dispute got out of hand, tempers flared, and the association divided into
two factions each claiming the title of the British Archaeological Association. Eventually the majority of the original central committee party
reformed as the (Royal) Archaeological Institute of Great Britain and
Ireland (*qv*).

In the words of Sir Thomas Kendrick it was 'the largest and angriest
row in the history of antiquarian societies in this country, a row still
commemorated by the grouping of their descendents into the two bodies
into which in 1845 they exploded themselves'. There were indecisive
moves for a reconciliation but these proved abortive. In the meanwhile,
putting the past behind them, members continue to hold their winter
meetings and to attend their summer congresses to this day. The aims
and purposes of the association remain essentially the same—to encourage and assist original work, to popularize archaeological studies 'by
making known to those less well informed the work of specialists in particular branches of study'. The work is still aided by county correspondents whose task it is to bring the association's notice to undesirable
activities which might threaten the preservation of antiquities and also
to report the latest local information for incorporation in a monthly
Bulletin circulated to members who have traditionally included both
interested amateurs and professional archaeologists and historians.

Publications: the first four issues of *The archaeological journal* are
to be regarded as much the organ of the association as of the Royal

Archaeological Institute—the editor aligned himself with the faction that became the Archaeological Institute of Great Britain and so that body retained the *Journal* although it conceded the title of the association. In reply the *Journal of the British Archaeological Association (qv)* was launched . The association also published *Collectanea archaeologica* designed to include those papers delivered at the summer congresses which were too long for the *Journal* or which required extensive illustrations. Two volumes only were published, the first in 1862 which included all papers read at the congresses held in Shropshire and Devon, and the second in 1872 (papers from the meetings at Exeter, Leicester and Leeds 1861-1863).

Bibliography: the introduction to the first issue of *The archaeological journal* March 1844 outlines the objects of the Association whilst T J Pettigrew's 'On the study of archaeology and the objects of the British Archaeological Association', *Journal Brit Arch Assoc* VI October 1850: 164-177 is useful for the personalities who were responsible for its formation. The views and opinions of the surviving association on the causes of the dissension and on the subsequent events are delineated at length in the first issue of *Journal of Brit Arch Assoc* pages I-XIII and in the third issue pages I-VIII. Joan Evans' 'The Royal Archaeological Institute a retrospect', *The archaeological journal* CVI, 1949: 1-11 should also be consulted.

170 'British Archaeological Institution' was the name given to a proposed professional institution for archaeologists which the Council for British Archaeology hoped would cater for the professional archaeologist in providing a series of qualifications and at the same time enhance the status of the part-time worker. The proposal first saw the light of day in the general euphoria released after the Department of the Environment had announced the increased funds that were to be made available to archaeology in its statement of 23 May 1974 when it seemed likely that archaeology was on the brink of becoming a full-time profession. The executive board of the CBA acted swiftly (too swiftly it transpired) and set up a broadly-based steering group which issued its first progress report in July 1974. Unfortunately this report was very critically received in some quarters and opposition to the apparent haste with which the proposals were steaming ahead hardened, a demand for more consultation very quickly made itself heard.

At the moment the CBA is currently engaging its attention to a Diploma in Archaeological Practice (*qv*) but it is interesting to look back to the suggested criteria for Founder Associateship of the Institution and for full membership contained in the steering group's second report: *Associateship* (a) several months field experience (excavation and survey) under competent direction; (b) a sound outline knowledge of British archaeology; (c) a theoretical and practical knowledge and understanding of the processes of *either* excavation *or* field survey; (d) an ability to prepare and present original illustrative material, including drawing; (e) an ability to apply scientific techniques and principles to archaeology; and (f) an ability to write a paper based on personal work.

Membership: (a) a minimum of five years' full-time employment in archaeology or in a recognized related field; (b) an ability to complete and present a substantial piece of original work; (c) a knowledge of the history and organization of archaeology and its role in modern society; (d) a theoretical knowledge and practical experience of (i) management, administration and public relations (ii) the whole process of excavation up to and including publication (iii) the whole process of field survey up to and including publication (iv) scientific methods and techniques, including field conservation (v) the scope and application of documentary sources to archaeology (vi) historic buildings—analysis and survey; (e) a particular expertise/authority on one of (d)(ii)-(vi); and (f) a scholarly appreciation of British archaeology in its European setting. It is perhaps not surprising that the proposals were not universally applauded or that for the moment they seem to be in abeyance. The text of the steering group's first report 'A professional institution for archaeologists', giving background to the proposal, the role of the CBA, the administrative arrangements, and its suggested implementation, may be found in *Current archaeology* 43, vol IV(8) March 1974: 235-236. Editorials in the March and July 1974 issues should also be consulted.

171 '**British Archaeological Reports**' is a publishing enterprise established in 1974 designed to alleviate the costs of conventional printing and publishing by utilizing the offset litho process which eliminates the necessity for conventional typesetting. The text of the reports is typed on an electric typewriter and is then reproduced photographically. Another advantage of this method is the speed with which they can be published as compared to the normal book. Most of the reports are either academic theses or excavation reports. *Titles*:

1 *Cuddesdon and Dorchester-on-Thames* (Tania Dickinson)

2 *The deserted medieval village of Broadfield, Herts* (Eric Klingelhofer)

3 *A corpus of early Bronze Age dagger pommels from Great Britain and Ireland* (Ron Hardaker)

30 *Studies in the archaeology and history of Cirencester* (Alan McWhirr)

31 *The production and distribution of metalwork in the middle Bronze Age in Southern Britain*, 2 vols (M J Rowlands)

32 *Roman military stone-built granaries in Britain* (Anne Gentry)

33 *Settlement and economy in the third and second millennia BC* (C Burgess and R Miket)

34 *Bronze Age spearheads from Berkshire, Buckinghamshire and Oxfordshire* (Margaret R Ehrenberg)

35 *Medieval moated sites of South East Ireland* (Terence B Barry)

36 *Edwardian monetary affairs 1279-1344* (N J Mayhew)

37 *Studies in Celtic survival* (Lloyd Laing)

A supplementary series is also published. Full details from 122 Banbury Road, Oxford.

172 'A British archaeologists's bookshelf' by Jacquetta Hawkes is a pleasant ramble through the early classics of British antiquarian literature with a glance at a few modern works. It appeared in *Books,* the journal of the National Book league, No 283, January-February 1954: 27-30.

173 'British archaeology', a booklet published in the Library Association's Public Library Group Readers Guide series in 1975 was compiled by David M Browne. Its intention is 'to help those who are interested in studying the past of the British Isles by archaeology to gain access to the basic modern literature on most aspects of the subject'. The two-line author-title-publisher-price (if in print) entries are grouped under General archaeology (history, theory, excavation and fieldwork techniques, and scientific methods and conservation); general studies (regional studies); archaeology by period (coverage extends down to the end of the medieval period); and a final list of periodicals. This title replaced the *Reader's guide to books on British prehistory and Roman Britain* (1957) and *Readers' guide to books on archaeology* (2ed, 1967), both published by the former County Libraries Group of the Library Association.

174 'British archaeology' *an introductory booklist*, compiled by Joyce Kewley and published by the Council for British Archaeology in 1976 in booklet form, 'is intended to provide guidance for teachers, young people, and others keenly interested in archaeology who wish to become better informed on the subject'. It is clearly arranged under form and period headings with a regional section covering the British Isles and with two final sections for young persons aged nine to twelve and thirteen to sixteen. Entries are arranged alphabetically by author within each section and provide all essential bibliographical detail. Most of the works cited were in print at the time of going to press. It follows two other similar CBA lists, *British archaeology: a book list for teachers* (1949) compiled for those 'who wish to acquaint themselves with archaeological material and discoveries, and with their current interpretation by British archaeologists' and *British archaeology: a book list* (1960) for those 'who come new to a subject embraced by a large body of books, journals and pamphlets of varying standards and wide range.

175 'British archaeology abroad' was the name given to an annual feature published in *Antiquity* 1963-1970 in which the directors of the various overseas schools of archaeology reported on their current activities. Their reports were presented in order of the schools' establishment. Much shorter accounts of the schools' work now appear in *Archaeology abroad.*

176 British Association for the Advancement of Science, founded in 1831, exists to 'promote general interest in science and its applications'. Its main activity is the organization of annual conferences in different towns and cities in the late summer. A substantial volume about the locality where the conference is held is prepared for those attending; these were formerly described as handbooks but nowadays they are more usually entitled *A scientific survey of . . .* or in the style *Norwich and its region.* They often contain useful summaries of the archaeology and geology of the places concerned. H C Bowen's *Ancient fields: a tentative analysis of vanishing earthworks and landscapes* was published by the Research Committee on Ancient Fields in 1962 and P A Jewell's *The experimental earthwork on Overton Down, Wiltshire 1960* by the Research Committee on Archaeological Field Experiments in 1963.

177 'British barrows' *a record of the examination of sepulchral mounds in various parts of England* by William Greenwell (1877) takes its place in the ranks of the acknowledged 'classics' of archaeological literature. Following a long introduction on barrow types and their contents the bulk of the work consists of descriptions of barrow excavations in Yorkshire and Westmorland.

178 British Broadcasting Corporation (BBC) has produced many radio and television programmes concerned with archaeology and antiquities—

The archaeologist (radio), *Animal vegetable mineral, Buried treasure, Chronicle* and, more recently *BC The archaeology of the Bible lands.* These and other programmes have spawned a number of books intended for the intelligent armchair archaeologist: Paul Johnstone's *Buried treasure* (Phoenix House, 1969); Glyn Daniel's *Man discovers his past* (Duckworth, 1966); Barry Cunliffe's *Cradle of England* (BBC, 1972) and *The making of the English* (BBC, 1973); and Magnus Magnusson's *BC The archaeology of the Bible lands* (BBC and The Bodley Head, 1977). Glyn Daniel's 'Archaeology and broadcasting' (*The archaeological news letter* 2, May 1948: 1-2) and his 'Archaeology and television', (*Antiquity*, XXVII(12) December 1954: 201-203) provide details of early pre-war and immediate post-war days at the BBC and express one man's faith in the future of archaeology as a subject of popular appeal on television.

179 'British Egyptology 1549-1906' by John David Wortham, first published by the University of Oklahoma Press in 1971, presents an erudite and comprehensive chronological account of the origins and early development of Egyptology in Britain. It provides a salutary corrective to those who imagine that Egyptology in general began with the French savants of Napoleon's expedition 1798-1800 and that British participation was slight before Flinders Petrie's arrival in Egypt in 1880. Notes on the text and a substantial bibliography of primary and secondary sources emphasise the scholarly nature of Professor Wortham's study. The English publishers are David and Charles.

180 British Institute in East Africa, now situated in Nairobi, owes its origins to the initiative of the British Academy which submitted proposals to the government in October 1955 for the establishment and financial support of a school or institute of history and archaeology in East Africa. Its purpose is to provide a base for British Commonwealth students and encourage and undertake research relating primarily but not exclusivly to the former British colonies and protectorates of Kenya, Uganda, Tanganyika and Zanzibar. *Azania*, the journal of the Institute, began publication in 1966.

181 British Institute of Afghan Studies, Kabul opened its doors in July 1972 providing accommodation, a library, study facilities, and a base for field archaeology, for British scholars working in archaeology, history, languages and topography. Its sponsoring society in London is the Society for Afghan Studies.

78

182 British Institute of Archaeology at Ankara was established in 1948 as a research centre providing facilities for British students of the archaeology of the Near and Middle East after the pattern of the School in Baghdad. Its journal *Anatolian studies* began publication in 1951.

183 British Institute of Persian Studies in Teheran was established in 1961 to provide accommodation for senior British scholars and teachers in universities where they could reside from time to time and meet their Iranian colleagues. Although the institute is concerned generally with Persian culture, special emphasis is placed on the development of archaeological techniques and the resolving of archaeological and historical problems. One of its primary tasks is to undertake a fresh appraisal of previous discoveries in an effort to find new material and new sites. The institute's annual publication, *Iran*, first appeared in 1963.

184 The British Museum is 'the National Museum of Archaeology, recording and illustrating the ancient cultures of the world, and it is a collection of works of arts in all media (except paintings) dating from primitive times to the present day'. In addition it houses the British Library Reference Division. Its foundation may be traced to an Act of Parliament 1753 authorising the purchase of the museum and collection of Sir Hans Sloane and the Harleian Library assembled by the first and second Earls of Oxford and for the housing of these and the collection formed by the Elizabethan antiquary, Sir Robert Cotton, in a general repository 'for the better Reception and more convenient Use of the said collections'. Its growth since then, for the most part by private benevolence, has bequeathed the museum with a serious congestion problem although plans to move the library to a new site have been in existence for some years. At the moment, however, the museum is forced to discharge its day-to-day work, 'the conservation, arrangement and display of the collections, their augmentation and recording, service to students and the answering of inquiries from the public' under conditions which reflect no credit on the nation.

Under the terms of the British Museum Act of 1963 the museum is controlled by a Board of Trustees consisting of fifteen nominees of the Prime Minister, one of the Crown, one appointee each by the Royal Society, the Royal Academy, the British Academy, and the Society of Antiquaries, and five members elected by the board itself which also elects its own chairman. The collections are administered on a departmental basis: coins and medals; ethnography; Egyptian; Western Asiatic; Greek and Roman; medieval and later; Oriental; prehistoric and Romano-British antiquities; and a research laboratory (*qv*).

79

From time to time in its history the museum has actively engaged in archaeological fieldwork, a notable example being Leonard Woolley's excavations at Ur in the 1920s. Full details of a large-scale publishing programme, administered for the trustees by British Museum Publications Ltd, and designed to fulfil the museum's obligations both to scholars and the general public, ranging from multi-volume catalogues and inventories of the collections and learned monographs to more 'popular' guidebooks and postcards, are listed in an annual catalogue of books in print. At various times guidebooks to the collections have been published: in the 1920s a series of departmental guides, case by case, gallery by gallery, were available, but in the 1950s a new type guidebook was prepared. These were not intended to imply an itinerary of the galleries or to indicate the contents of each case but aimed at providing an introductory text with notes on the museum's collections. Titles of interest: *Flint implements*, 3ed 1968, an account of Stone Age techniques and cultures; *Guide to the antiquities of Roman Britain* 3ed 1951; and *Later prehistoric antiquities of the British Isles*, 1953.

Bibliography: Treasures of the British Museum (Thames and Hudson, 1971) edited and introduced by Sir Frank Francis, Director and Principal Librarian 1959-1968, presents a general historical introduction followed by a more detailed examination of the work and chief treasures of each department written by a senior member of staff. J Mordaunt Crook's *The British Museum* (Allen Lane The Penguin Press, 1972) is restricted to architectural politics and investigates the museum's functions and failings against a background of changing economic circumstances. Perhaps the most authoritative and satisfying account of the museum's history and activities is *That noble cabinet* by Edward Miller (Deutsch, 1973) which traces the museum from its confused beginnings to its present pre-eminence in comprehensive fashion. The author, a senior librarian of the British Library Reference Division, enjoyed access to much previously unpublished material which is listed in his extensive bibliography. The successive issues of *The British Museum Report of the Trustees* are important especially that of 1966 which is in effect an account of the work of the museum from 1939 onwards. Vera Watson's *The British Museum: its antiquities and civilizations from perhistory to the fall of the Roman empire* is rather different in conception—each chapter consists of an historical summary of the civilization which provides a background to the exhibits of the departments of prehistoric and Romano-British, Western Asiatic, Egyptian, and Greek and Roman Antiquities—and is specifically designed as an illustrated reference book for the visitor, describing the galleries room by room in a series of suggested itineraries. There are lists of books 'generally to be found in public libraries or in paperback editions' for further reading, each section is adequately illustrated and mapped, and it is itself available in hardback or paperback form.

Undoubtedly the most authoritative handbook to the collections is the *British Museum guide*, first published by the trustees in 1976, a superbly illustrated exposition of the museum's treasures, department by department and including the Museum of Mankind (Ethnography) housed since 1970 in new galleries in Burlington Gardens. Coloured outline plans of the ground floor and upper levels are printed on the end papers whilst a detailed plan of each department appears in the appropriate section of the text. Sir John Pope-Hennessy contributes an introduction and he concludes by remarking that 'In 1975 attendance figures rose to a total of over three million. Despite this the trustees and staff are very conscious that the educational potential of the British Museum has yet to be exploited to the full and it is their hope that this *Guide* will enable visitors, whether their interests are archaeological, artistic, or historical, to derive greater benefit from its incomparably rich collections'.

Three articles in *Antiquity* throw much light on the museum's functions. Sir Thomas Kendrick's 'The British Museum and British antiquities, XXVIII(111) September 1954: 132-142, describes how the museum came to change its mind on the question of British antiquities, suggests that it was largely due to this that there came about a general revaluation of the status of British prehistoric studies, and asks whether it would have been better to have entrusted the serious care of British antiquities not to the British Museum but to a separate museum specially formed. Christopher Hawkes' 'The British Museum and British archaeology', XXXVI(144) December 1962: 248-251 discusses the pros and cons of a national museum apropos local pride in local institutions and argues that in order to re-establish its pre-eminence the museum should draw upon its whole range of material for a permanent exhibition, that a perpetual run of temporary special exhibitions showing new material on loan should be arranged so that it becomes necessary to go to the museum in order to keep abreast with current developments, and that a substantial and continuous publishing programme should be set in motion. Such a policy would stifle calls for a new museum of British antiquities. Sir Frank Francis' 'The British Museum and British antiquities' XXXVII(145) March 1963: 50-53 is largely a response to, and in some instances a rebuttal of, these criticisms. The comparative functions of the British Museum and provincial museums is discussed by R L S Bruce-Mitford in his 'Archaeology: a national museum viewpoint' and by D T-D Clarke in 'Archaeology: the provincial point of view', both printed in 'The relationship of national and provincial museums', *Museums journal* 66(2) September 1966: 99-110. The museum's attempts to grasp the public relations aspect of its functions are outlined in Sir Frank Francis' 'Blowing one's own trumpet', *Museums journal* 64(3) December 1964: 233-242.

185 'The British Museum quarterly' was established by the Trustees in 1927 principally as a journal describing and illustrating the museum's most recent acquisitions but it also served to report the results of the museum's excavations abroad, to publicise the temporary exhibitions, and to call attention to the museum's latest publications. Very soon its scope widened to include research papers based on the museum's collections. But in the late sixties and early seventies the *Quarterly* sadly declined, it appeared more and more infrequently, and in 1973 a decision was taken to cease publication altogether when the manuscript and printed books departments, traditionally heavy contributors, were incorporated into the British Library. Almost immediately, however, plans were prepared to launch a successor and in 1976 the *British Museum yearbook* (*qv*), in many ways a direct descendant of the *Quarterly*, made its debut.

186 The British Museum Society was formed in the 1968-1969 winter with the initial purpose of making the unique nature, functions and needs of the museum better known and as the first move in a campaign by the trustees to extract desperately needed funds from private and public sources. A low subscription was sought in order to enlist the moral support of a wide cross-section of people who had the interests of the museum at heart and who would strengthen the efforts of the trustees and staff to provide the best possible service to scholars and to the general public. In return for their subscriptions members receive a regular *Bulletin* three times a year intended to serve as a means of communication with the trustees. The programme for members also includes special lectures, receptions, and visits to exhibitions and private collections at home and abroad. The society was viewed with a certain suspicion in some quarters notably by the ever vigilant editors of *Current archaeology* who pointed out in their editorial to the May 1969 issue that the prospectus issued 'gives no hint of the constitution of the society, no name of the proposed president, no idea of how the subscriptions are to be spent, and most important of all, no indication of how any criticism of the trustees can be effected'. They concluded that 'in the absence of such information the presumption must remain that the society is to be simply the creature of the trustees of the museum, to act as a milch-cow, and to protect them from criticism'. In their view the society needed a ginger group to act as a focus for current discontent and to press for a full scale investigation by outside management consultants into the running of the museum. One can only venture to assume that this was not exactly what the trustees had in mind. 'Lord Eccles outlines the objects of the newly-formed British Museum society and raises questions concerning the museum's future' appeared as an article in *TLS* of the 16th January 1969.

187 'The British Museum yearbook' (1976-) designed as much for the museum visitor interested in art and archaeology as for the scholar, will present each year a number of major articles written around a central theme not only by the museum's staff but also by outside contributors. In addition each volume will contain short departmental notes on recent acquisitions much along the same lines as the old *British Museum quarterly* (*qv*). Volume 1 *The classical tradition* includes 'Magenta ware' (Reynold Higgins), 'Parthian gold from Nineveh' (J E Curtis), and 'Gold and silver coin hoards and the end of Roman Britain' (R A G Carson), each article being fully documented with bibliographical notes.

188 'British prehistory' *a new outline* edited by Colin Renfrew and published by Duckworth in 1974 consists of papers delivered to a conference organised by the Department of Extra-Mural Studies of the University of Sheffield in May 1972 which cumulatively assess the results of the new chronology in British prehistory made possible by the refinements in precise dating brought about by the general acceptance of the calibration of radiocarbon dating method and technique. In the knowledge that the days when one man could hope to cover the whole field are long since over each division of prehistory was assigned to a recognized authority who was required to review the archaeological material for his period and to 'set that material in a new order, in the light of developments in chronology and of recent discoveries'. *Contents:* 'British prehistory: changing configurations' (Colin Renfrew); 'The palaeolithic and mesolithic' (Paul Mellars); 'The neolithic' (I F Smith); 'Scottish chambered tombs and long mounds' (Andrey Henshall); 'The bronze age' (Colin Burgess); and 'The iron age' (Barry Cunliffe). A short bibliography listing the main works on the period together with notes containing more detailed references is provided for each chapter.

189 'British prehistory half-way through the century' a presidential address by C F C Hawkes to the Prehistoric Society discusses the differences between everyday and scholarly terminology and puts forward a case for a 'cognitional system of nomenclature for prehistory'. The terms he proposed and the periods he suggested they should cover were as follows: 'Antehistoric' *ie* before all history (palaeolithic, mesolithic, and primary neolithic); 'Telehistoric', far-off history (secondary and diffusive neolithic and early metal ages); 'Parahistoric', alongside history (1500 BC in Britain); 'Penehistoric', almost history (300 BC in Britain); 'Protohistoric', beginning to be history (50 BC in Britain); and Historic (opening dates in Britain varying according to Region. Roman, Celtic, Saxon and Viking). The address was printed in *The proceedings of the Prehistoric Society* XVII, 1951: 1-15.

190 British School at Athens: a scheme for a British academic centre in Greece was first proposed by Sir Richard Jebb in the *Contemporary review* for November 1878 but his arguments were at first not heeded by the Council of the Society for the Promotion of Hellenic Studies who were expected to take the lead in forming a British school. Jebb was not to be denied however and a later article, 'A plea for a British institute in Athens', in *The fortnightly review*, May 1883, attracted widespread and distinguished support including that of the Prince of Wales. A circular was issued defining the lines on which the proposed school should operate, the society had second thoughts on the matter and was represented on an executive committee charged with drawing up a scheme in detail. At length the school opened its doors in Athens in 1886 to welcome four students under the direction of Francis Penrose. The purpose of the School was outlined as follows: 'to promote the study of Greek archaeology in all its departments . . . the study of Greek art and architecture in their remains of every period; the study of inscriptions; the exploration of ancient sites; the tracing of ancient roads and routes of traffic. Besides being a School of Archaeology, it shall be also, in the most comprehensive sense, a School of Classical Studies . . . The school shall also be a centre at which information can be obtained and books consulted by British travellers in Greece. For these purposes a library shall be formed, and maintained, of archaeological and other suitable books, including maps, plans and photographs.'

Bona fide students are admitted to the school on condition that they stay for a minimum period of three months to pursue a course of study of some aspect of Greek history or archaeology. At the end of their stay they are expected to present a report to the director who may decide to publish it. Students are allowed to attend lectures and use the library facilities at the other foreign schools in the city. In 1974 a fully equipped research laboratory was opened. At first the results of work completed were published in the *Journal of Hellenic studies* but it was soon recognized that the school should have its own journal although there were some misgivings by the society that material for their *Journal* would dry up, these fears were proved premature and unfounded. *The annual of the British school at Athens* made its first appearance following the 1894 session, its main purpose being to make more accessible the contents of the reports of the excavations undertaken by the society. Supplementary papers are also published containing material considered to be too extensive for *The annual*; these are now published by Thames and Hudson. Vols I-XXXII of *The annual* and their two accompanying index volumes have been reprinted by Kraus Reprints. A third index covers vols XXXIII-XLVIII.

191 British School at Rome, modelled in many respects on the school at Athens, was opened in 1901 as the result of the efforts of many scholars and academics notably Henry Pelham, president of Trinity College, Oxford, principally as a training school for students fresh from the universities, as a centre for mature students, and as a source of information for visitors. The province of the school was not restricted to purely archaeological matters, for one thing excavation was not possible in Italy, but included all periods of Italian and Roman history, art, antiquities, and literature. In 1911 the school was reconstituted when the Royal Commissioners for the Exhibition of 1851 negotiated a royal charter for the school conferring upon it the power to institute a national academy for the study and practice of the fine arts in addition to archaeology, the original committee emerging as the Faculty of Archaeology, History, and Letters. An illustrated booklet, *British school at Rome: a note on the school and its scholarships*, first published in 1921 and reissued since at intervals, should be consulted for further details of its history and activities. Patricia Clough's 'Digging in on a starvation diet', *Times higher education supplement*, 19th July 1974, quotes the school's director as saying 'Our job is to help and advise scholars, to put them in touch with people who can be useful to them and show them where they can find material they need. The school is not an educational sausage machine, it is an instrument to enable people to study here. Everyone who comes here is an individual, and usually already a specialist in his own subject, and gets on with his own work in his own time'. *The papers of the British school at Rome* (1902-) were intended to publish in the first instance research articles by the staff of the school and by students and past students on the archaeology, history and literature of Italy and other parts of the Mediterranean area up to modern times. A series of supplementary volumes is also published to accommodate work on a larger scale than is suitable for the *Papers*. Volumes I-XXIV have been reprinted by the Johnson Reprint Corporation, Department SL, Fifth Avenue, New York NY 10003. Selected offprints taken from vol XI (new series vol XXVII) 1972 onwards are available.

192 British School of Archaeology in Egypt emerged in 1905 from the Egyptian Research Account, a fund-raising organization set up in 1894 by William Flinders-Petrie when Edwards Professor of Egyptology at University College London to finance his expeditions to Egypt. Its declared objectives were the excavation of sites for Egyptian history, the full publication of the results, the training of students, the issue of standard reference volumes, and the publication of a quarterly journal, *Ancient Egypt*, to give an account of foreign journals and books and to supply articles on new discoveries. In addition lectures and a summer exhibition were arranged annually at the college. All these objectives were achieved largely through the superhuman efforts of Petrie himself. After he was forced to turn his attention to southern Palestine the school established its field base in Jerusalem (its constitution allowed it to work in any country ever subject to Egypt). Only a person of Petrie's stature was capable of seeing nothing anomalous or incongruous in this arrangement! The school was dissolved in 1954, twelve years after Petrie's death.

193 British School of Archaeology in Iraq was brought into being in January 1932 specifically to 'encourage, support and undertake archaeological research, including excavations', and has consistently followed a policy aimed at tracing the development of man in Mesopotamia from neolithic times until the end of the Assyrian empire. The idea of a British school to provide British students in Iraq with badly needed facilities originated with Gertrude Bell who bequeathed £6,000 on trust for the purpose. In recent years the school has experienced many vicissitudes, its hostel and library being forced to close their doors on the orders of the Iraqi government in August 1973. However, since then archaeological work has continued under the aegis of the British Archaeological Expedition in Iraq which apparently suffers no hindrances. *Publications*:

it is the proud boast of the school that none of its work has remained unpublished, most of it appearing in the school's own journal *Iraq* (*qv*). To commemorate its silver jubilee the school published *Twenty-five years of Mesopotamian discovery 1932-1956* by M E L Mallowan (1956) which also served as a handbook of an exhibition of finds from the Tigris and Euphrates valleys held in the Assyrian basement of the British Museum.

194 British School of Archaeology in Jerusalem, modelled on the older schools in Athens and Rome, was formed in 1919 on the initiative of the British Academy and the Palestine Exploration Fund to provide training in the field for young archaeologists, to maintain a library in Jerusalem, and to assist senior scholars in their work. In its early years the school performed many of the functions of a government department of antiquities especially in the conservation of sites and buildings of historic or architectural importance and when the Palestine Department was founded the school's first Director, John Garstang, became its head, and relations between the two institutions always remained very close. It was not until 1956 that the school moved into its own headquarters; until then it relied much on the goodwill of the French and American schools to give the necessary facilities to scholars and students. By and large the school assumed responsibility for the field work previously undertaken by the Palestine Exploration Fund. Its best-known excavations are those in Samaria (pre-war), at Jericho when work recommenced in 1952, and its excavations in Jerusalem lasting for seven seasons from 1961 onwards, in collaboration with the Royal Ontario Museum and the Dominican École Biblique et Archéologique (for three years), with substantial financial support from the British Academy. Kathleen Kenyon's *Jerusalem: excavating 3000 years of history*, published in Thames and Hudson's 'New aspects of antiquity' series in 1967, is a full report. The school's activities were at first recorded in its *Bulletin* but this was halted when the fund's *Quarterly statement* was transformed into the *Palestine exploration quarterly*. In 1968 the School began publication of its own annual journal *Levant* (*qv*). Miss Kenyon's 'The British school of archaeology in Jerusalem', *Archaeological news letter*, 4(1) August 1951: 1-2 tells the school's story in brisk fashion. The same writer's 'The British school of archaeology in Jerusalem: the new school building', *Palestine exploration quarterly*, 1957: 97-100 should also be consulted.

195 'The bronze age round barrow in Britain' *an introduction to the study of the funerary practice and culture of the British and Irish single-grave* *people of the second millennium BC* by Paul Ashbee (Phoenix House, 1960) is a comprehensive and fully documented study of British bronze age technology based on the archaeological investigation of round barrows and their contents. A preliminary chapter presents a historical survey of barrow exploration from the early days of John Leland to the recent work of O G S Crawford and L V Grinsell. There are five appendixes listing ancient and modern literature in addition to an extensive general bibliography. A generous provision of photographs and text figures adds further distinction to this definitive and scholarly work.

196 'Bulletin of the American Schools of Oriental research' appeared irregularly December 1919 to September 1921 and thereafter has been published quarterly. It appeared in a larger format as from October 1974 and now includes minutes of the Board of Trustees and various papers. An index to volumes 1-184 compiled by John R McRay has been published.

197 'Bulletin of the Institute of Archaeology' replaced the *Annual report* as the institute's principal publication in 1958. The *Report* itself (1937-1957) had been designed to contain a resume of the developments and work done by the institute during the previous year and summaries of lectures of outstanding general interest. Special papers or monographs were also published. From 1958 until the eleventh *Bulletin* which appeared in 1973 a full scale report on the administration of the institute, its teaching and research, and a survey of the activities of each department were included, but the next two issues carried only papers by the institute's staff or students, book reviews, and summaries of undergraduate and postgraduate project reports. Whether or not this pattern continues remains to be seen.

198 'By South Cadbury is that Camelot . . .' *The excavation of Cadbury Castle 1966-1970* by Leslie Alcock, published in Thames & Hudson's 'New aspects of antiquity' series in 1972, takes its title from John Seldon's description in the early seventeenth century. It was written 'for the enthusiasts who came, in tens of thousands, to see the excavation of Cadbury Castle, and for everyone like them, with no special knowledge but a lively interest in Arthur, in archaeology, or in history. It attempts to answer the kind of questions which they asked then, or have since asked my colleagues and myself when we have talked about Cadbury to non-specialist audiences'. Part I 'Exploration' outlines the historical background of the
88

identification of the site with Arthurian Camelot and describes how and why the excavation was planned, how policy was decided, and how the discoveries emerged; Part II analyses the results yielded. Over a hundred photographs, fifteen of them in magnificent colour, support the text.

199 'CBA calendar of excavations' issued for many years in stencilled form achieved the dignity of print in 1966 and now appears monthly March-September, in November, and concludes with a January issue summarising the previous season's activities. It consists of announcements concerning conferences, residential and week-end courses, training and other excavations, listed by county in alphabetical order, appointments and scholarships and overseas tours. It is undoubtedly one of the Council for British Archaeology's most popular publications.

200 Cadbury Research Committee was formed in June 1965 with the express purpose of promoting a large-scale excavation of Cadbury Castle and was composed of representatives of the Society of Antiquaries, the Society for Medieval Archaeology, the Somerset Archaeological Society, the Honourable Society of Knights of the Round Table and the Pendragon Society. At a later stage the Prehistoric Society, the Society for the Promotion of Roman Studies, The University of Bristol, the Board of Celtic Studies of the University of Wales, and Somerset County Council also nominated representatives. Dr Ralegh Radford was appointed chairman, Geoffrey Ashe acted as secretary and Sir Mortimer Wheeler accepted the position of president. The committee invited Leslie Alcock to serve as its director of excavations and it was he who supervised the 1966 reconnaissance investigations and the excation carried out over the next three summers. The full story is recounted in Alcock's *By South Cadbury is that Camelot (qv)* published in 1972.

201 Cambrian Archaeological Association: it is not often that a journal begats a national archaeological society but so it was in this case. *Archaeologia Cambrensis* was ushered into the world in January 1846 under the pastoral care of two Welsh clergymen, John Williams and Henry Longueville Jones, as a quarterly record of the antiquities of Wales and its Marches. That the formation of a Welsh antiquarian society was in the forefront of their minds is indicated in this extract from their first editorial: 'We hope that we have struck a chord in the hearts of Welsh antiquaries that will resound not harshly in the ears of the Welsh public; and that, by describing and illustrating the antiquities of our dear native land, we shall meet with the lasting support and sympathy of all who love those venerable and delightful associations connected with the very name of Wales.'

Evidence that these soul-stirring words had not fallen on barren soil is to be detected in a long communication, over the signature of 'A Welsh antiquary' which appeared in the third issue of the journal in July. This proposed 'that an Antiquarian Association be formed, to be called "The Cambrian Archaeological Association for the study and preservation of the National Antiquities of Wales": that it be a perfectly gratuitous Society, consisting of all persons whose taste and knowledge may induce them to unite for this purpose; that the most eminent Welsh antiquaries and other personages, the natural friends and protectors of the antiquities of the country, be requested to put themselves at the head of this Society . . . and, lastly, that the *Archaeologia Cambrensis* be adopted as the official organ of the Society'. The editors were quick to respond: 'Our sole object in publishing this Work, at a very considerable sacrifice of time and money, has been to awake a love of antiquities among our fellow countrymen; and we are quite ready to do anything within the compass of our limited abilities for the furtherance of the common good.' Those interested in forming a society along these lines should 'take the trouble to communicate their opinions upon it to us through the medium of the publisher'.

A list of antiquaries approving the formation of an association appeared in the following issue in October and the editors suggested that these gentlemen should be considered members unless they indicated to the contrary by the new year. They further recommended that in the meantime a code of laws and regulations similar to those of the Archaeological Institute of Great Britain should be adopted. The columns of *Archaeologia Cambrensis* were offered to 'the gentlemen who are desirous of constituting this Association, for the purpose of regularly publishing their reports, proceedings, and papers; and we would request of them, in case they accept our proposal, to add to our title that of "Journal of the Cambrian Archaeological Association". The association duly came into being at Aberystwyth in 1847 to 'examine, preserve, and illustrate, all Ancient Monuments and Remains of the History, Manners, Customs and Arts of Wales and its Marches.'

Despite the enthusiastic support of the Welsh ecclesiastical authorities the early days of the association were not entirely harmonious: even before it had been formed Longueville Jones had expressed concern lest internal dissensions should threaten its future. And so it proved. A special preface to the 1854 volume of *Archaeologia Cambrensis* speaks of 'opposition which has been manifested in some quarters towards the Association and its periodical . . . It would appear that the Proceedings of the Association are in some degree offensive to two classes of persons. Some dislike its objects, and others its mode of pursuing them'. Three years later fears were still being voiced: 'Our Association has now lasted long enough, and its labours have been sufficiently important, to entitle it to rank with the higher European Archaeological Societies; and as long as it can ward off the influences of local prejudice, narrow party views, and morbid national vanity, it may hold its place.'

The Association managed to avoid the threatened disruption and takes its place today as one of the most respected archaeological societies in the United Kingdom. Among the papers in *Archaeologia Cambrensis* which should be mentioned are O G S Crawford's 'Archaeological surveys in Wales: some suggested subjects', vol XVII(3) sixth series July 1917: 274-287; Mortimer Wheeler's 'Some problems of prehistoric chronology in Wales', LXXVI, 7th series vol 1(1) June 1921: 1-18 and his presidential address, 'The administration of archaeology in Wales', LXXXVI(2), December 1931: 340-352, a historical survey which includes a plea for a Welsh equivalent to the *Victoria history of the counties of England*; H J Fleure's 'Problems of Welsh archaeology' LXXVIII 7th series III(2) December 1923: 225-242; D Morgan Rees' 'Industrial archaeology in Wales: an introduction', CXIII, 1964: 129-149; and A H A Hogg's presidential address 'Field archaeology in Wales', CXXII, 1973: 1-17, a summary of the present position with indications of the progress of the Royal Commission on Ancient and Historic Monuments in Wales and Monmouthshire.

A list of the *Transactions* etc of corresponding societies held in the association's library housed at the National Museum of Wales is printed in vol CXXI, 1972: 142-143. A report of the work of the Ancient Monuments Advisory Board for Wales 1945-1948 was included in vol C 1949: 56-60; at the time it was hoped that annual reports would be published but these failed to materialise after 1951. However, a further summary for the years 1951-1957 appeared in vol CVI, 1957. 'Periodical literature in Wales', a résumé of the contents of the journals of other Welsh local and national historical and archaeological societies has been an annual feature since 1959: 'Other periodical literature on Welsh archaeology' was added in 1970. A bewildering succession of different series afflicted *Archaeologia Cambrensis* in early years although this has improved since the seventh series faded out into consecutive numbering of the annual volumes. *An alphabetical index to the first four series 1846-1884* with an introduction (a brief sketch of the association's history) and lists of articles and illustrations was published in 1892. A similar index to the fifth series followed in 1902. Two other indexes, more professional in appearance, have been published in recent years: *Index to Archaeologia Cambrensis 1846-1900* compiled by Lily F Chilty (1964), and a similar volume for the 1901-1960 period compiled by T Rowland Powel arrived in 1976,

202 Cambridge Antiquarian Society was formed in 1839 'to encourage the study of History, Architecture, and Antiquities, especially in connection with the University, Town, and County of Cambridge; to meet for the discussion of these subjects; to print information relating to them; and to collect antiquities or promote their preservation *in situ*'. A lasting monument to the society's work in the exploration and recording of local archaeology is the University Museum of Archaeology and Ethnography which came into existence when the society donated its collections to the university. In its early days members ranged far and wide in the realm of antiquarian scholarship, contributions to their meetings were by no means limited to local or even national topics. Latterly, however, the society has directed its energies into excavation on a scale which places it in the forefront of active county archaeological societies. In 1952 it incorporated the Cambridgeshire and Huntingdonshire Archaeological Society, and it plays a full part in the deliberations of the Cambridgeshire Archaeological Committee.

The *Reports* of the society were published annually 1841-1850 but thereafter their numbering becomes confused: *Cambridge antiquarian communications: being papers presented at the meetings* include both *Reports* (retaining their serial number) and *Communications* which begin a sequence of their own. This pattern continued until volume VII (1888) when there was a title change to *Proceedings of the Cambridge antiquarian society with communications made to the society* with an additional 'new series' number. Some sort of rationalization came in vol XXV (1922-23) which dropped the new series number altogether; further modernization came with vol XXXV (1935) which shortened its title to *Proceedings*. In 1942 the society was one of the first to adopt the (by now) familiar larger quarto format but in 1973 it reverted to an octavo size.

Papers of especial interest include P V Addyman and Martin Biddle's 'Medieval Cambridge: recent finds and excavations', vol LVIII, 1965: 74-137, which describes the rescue excavation and recording of archaeological material discovered on building sites in Cambridge 1958-1961, and C C Taylor's 'Cambridgeshire earthwork surveys', LXIV, 1973: 35-43. Volume LXV part 1 is *An archaeological gazetteer of the city of*

Cambridge 1973 by David M Browne, commissioned by the Cambridgeshire Archaeological Committee. The purpose of this brief survey is to warn of the wealth of historical material beneath the streets and buildings of Cambridge threatened with destruction. It is the result of the county archaeological committee's realisation that such a survey was urgently needed in their efforts to prevent this wealth of material from being destroyed without record. The *Gazetteer* is based on a series of maps with the written text being kept to a minimum; it shows the areas of maximum interest where rescue excavation is required, and indicates the measures needed to ensure that archaeological evidence is adequately recorded. An extensive bibliography is included. The two most recent cumulative indexes are *Index to proceedings vols IX-XXIV 1895-1922* (1927) and *General index vols XXVI-LXII 1923-1969* (1971).

203 Camden, William (1551-1623) published his *Britannia sive florentissimorum regnorum Angliae, Scotiae, Hiberniae, et insularum adjacentium ex intima antiquate chorographica descriptio*, the first comprehensive topographical and antiquarian survey of the three kingdoms, in 1586. His intention is made clear in his introductory remarks to the section on Cornwall and Devon: 'in each county I mean to describe its antient inhabitants, estymology of its name, its limits, soil, remarkable places both ancient and modern, and its dukes or earls from the Norman Conquest'. The framework of the book was the Celtic tribal areas of Britain as recorded in the pages of the classical geographers with the English shires superimposed. It was a well researched work. Camden himself reported 'I have diligently perus'd our own Writers; as well as the Greek and Latin ones, that mention the least tittle of Britain. I have examin'd the publick records of this Kingdom, Ecclesiastical Registers, and Libraries, Acts, Monuments, and Memorials of Churches and Cities; I have search'd the ancient Rolls, and cited them upon occasion in their own stile'.

But the *Britannia* is by no means a library based work entirely, Camden had travelled the length and breadth of Britain and had himself inspected much of what he described. Its popularity may be gauged by the number of editions it went through in Camden's lifetime, the fifth edition appeared in 1600 although the first English translation was not published until 1610. The respect it continued to command is witnessed by the publication of an enlarged edition, still based on the original Celtic tribal framework, at the end of the seventeenth century. A team of scholars including Thomas Tanner, John Aubrey, John Evelyn, Samuel Pepys and White Kennet, under the editorship of Edmund Gibson, contributed extra material to bring the work into line with contemporary antiquarianism. The new edition was published in 1695, again in folio, and although there was a later revision under the supervision of Richard Gough it is this 1695 edition that is regarded as definitive. It includes a life of Camden, 'a catalogue of some books and treatises relating to the antiquities of England', and Antoninus's Itinerary through Britain. The arrangement is by county sections each of which is accompanied by a map.

A facsimile edition with an introduction by Stuart Piggott, reprinted from the *Proceedings of the British Academy* 37, 1951: 199-217, was published by David and Charles in 1971. T D Kendrick's *British Antiquity* (1950) offers a brief exposition of Camden's aims and intentions, his methods and arrangement, and also follows his dispute with Ralph Brooke, the York Herald, who challenged some of Camden's detail in order to discredit him. But Camden's achievement and his influence on antiquarian studies in this country are today unquestioned; it has truly been said of him that he represents the fulfillment of embryonic archaeology in terms of Tudor antiquarian activity.

204 '**Camera techniques in archaeology**' by V M Conlon (John Baker, 1973) is a practical guide for those who are not professional photographers but who frequently have occasion to use the camera, and covers all aspects of the planning, preparation, and execution of archaeological photography on site and in the studio. W F Grimes contributes a foreword.

205 '**The care of ancient monuments**' *an account of the legislative and other measures adopted in European countries for protecting ancient monuments and objects and scenes of natural beauty, and for preserving the aspect of historical cities* by G Baldwin Brown was published by the Cambridge University Press in 1905 and retains an historical interest for the part it played in the appointment of the Royal Commissions on Ancient and Historical Monuments. A copy came into the hands of Lord Pentland, Secretary of State for Scotland, who was disturbed to read 'When we compare the ample machinery for the official and semi-official care of monuments on the Continent, with what has actually been done on similar lines in our own country, we are inclined to describe our own measures as only shy and tentative efforts at arrangements which across the Channel and the North Sea are well-equipped and in full working order', (p 154). Lord Pentland resolved that in Scotland at least this backwardness should be remedied and largely on account of his efforts the first Royal Commission was appointed in 1908.

206 'Careers in museums' a Museums Association information sheet, is prepared principally for those seeking employment in museums. It provides brief notes on qualifications; prospects; requirements for individual subjects; conservation, design and technical work; qualifications offered by the association; postgraduate certificates in museum studies; trainee posts in teaching museums; Museums Association studentships; and where posts are advertised. A third edition was issued in 1973.

207 **Carter, Howard** (1874-1939) crowned his career with the discovery of Tutankhamen's tomb in November 1922 after long years of searching in the Valley of the Kings. His *The tomb of Tut Ankh Amen* (three volumes 1923-1933) was condensed into a single volume published to coincide with the Tutenkhamen exhibition at the British Museum in 1972. P E Newberry's obituary, *Journal of Egyptian archaeology*, 25, 1939: 67-69 is a concise summary of his life and work.

208 **Cassell's 'Introducing archaeology'** series consists of beautifully illustrated books of less than one hundred pages catering for the increasing popular interest in archaeology stimulated by press coverage and television programmes. The complete series is intended to be world wide in scope, ranging from the prehistoric to the Byzantine period. Although also designed as introductory primers for students the strange lack of bibliographies would appear to effectively thwart this intention. *Titles: Introducing archaeology* (Michael Avi-Yonah); *Ancient pottery* (Rivka Gonen); *Jewellery in ancient times* (Renate Rosenthal); *Ancient scrolls* and *Ancient mosaics* (both by Michael Avi-Yonah); *Origins of the alphabet* (Joseph Naveh); *Marine archaeology* (Elisha Linder and Avner Raban); *Weapons of the ancient world* (Rivka Gonen); and *Introducing prehistory* (Avraham Ronen). Further titles are reported to be in preparation but as heavy stocks of the first volumes were 'remaindered' it may well be that no more will be issued.

209 **'The cataloguing of archaeological collections in museums'** by Adrian Rance, *The London archaeologist*, 2(4) Autumn 1973: 90-93, discusses the successful application of site-orientated catalogues which may result from a close cooperation between excavators and museum curators. The best methods of cataloguing material recovered from sites are discussed with special reference to individual objects, grave groups, small finds, pottery, collected materials (*ie* that for which no trench layer sequence is available), excavation material already sorted, and coins.

95

210 '**Celtic Britain**' by Nora K Chadwick was published in Thames and Hudsons's 'Ancient peoples and places' series in 1963. The author remarked 'I have sought to introduce the reader to some of the pleasant places of ancient Celtic Britain at the time when the Romans had left and the Anglo-Saxons had not yet penetrated in force, or established a Teutonic order widely in these islands. It is the brief period when the Celtic languages and the Celtic customs and institutions were universal here'. The evidence of Celtic monuments and discovered hoards is well to the fore.

211 **Ceram, C W** published a remarkable series of popular archaeological works in the 1950s which professional archaeologists readily admitted to have read and enjoyed. The best known of them, *Gods, graves, and scholars* deliberately written to appeal to the widest general public, was so successful that it was translated out of its native German into twenty-six other languages. It unrepentantly set out to portray the dramatic qualities inherent in archaeology, recounting the most exciting episodes in Near Eastern, classical and American archaeology, Ceram himself heralding it as 'a hymn of praise to the archaeologist's brilliant accomplishments, his penetration and indefatigability'. *A picture history of archaeology* followed the same pattern of tracing the historical cultural continuity extending Sumeria-Babylon-Assyria-Crete-Greece and Rome—to our own times. These two volumes together with *The secret of the Hittites* and *Hands on the past* constituted, so their author claimed, the most comprehensive history of archaeology ever published for the general reader. Ceram also edited *The world of archaeology: the pioneers tell their story* (1966) an anthology of extracts from the writings of nineteenth and twentieth century archaeologists.

212 '**The chambered tombs of Scotland**' by Audrey Shore Henshall (Edinburgh University Press, 2 vols, 1963-1972) is a systematic account of the known tombs county by county. Each volume is divided into three sections: a survey of each of the main types of tomb on a geographical basis; a catalogue of sites and associated finds, giving locality, a description, map references, and an indication of printed sources of information; and, lastly, a catalogue of plans. Stuart Piggott contributes a foreword. 'A guide to chambered tombs in Scotland' compiled by the same writer was printed on the inside back cover of *Current archaeology* III (12) No 35 November 1972. The brief one-line entries refer to articles in the previous (September 1972) issue of the magazine devoted entirely to Scottish archaeology.

213 Chester Archaeological Society formed in 1849 for the collection and publication of archaeological and historical information relating to the city and county of Chester and its neighbourhood and the preservation in a permanent museum of the remains of antiquity, has experienced many changes of name in its history, but the traditional sphere of its activities has remained the County Palatine and North Wales. Its *Journal* was first published in 1849, the three volumes of the original series in twelve parts down to the year 1885. The new series commencing in 1887 achieved a more regular and frequent publication, usually annually or at least biennially. A larger format was adopted in 1951 (vol 38) when there was a simultaneous switch to consecutively numbered annual volumes. A further change came in 1976 (vol 59) which was printed by the offset litho process in a slightly larger format still in order to cope with the inflated costs of printing and paper. Items of general interest in the *Journal* include J Romilly Allen's two papers 'The early Christian monuments of North Wales', ns IV, 1890-91: 34-51 and a similar survey of Cheshire, ns V, 1893' 133-174; Robert Newstead's 'Records of archaeological finds at Chester', ns XXVII(2), 1927:59-162, a consolidated report of Roman archaeological finds from casual excavations in Chester, arranged by site, and ending with a list of references and authorities; and the same writer's 'Records of archaeological finds', ns XXXIII, 1939: 5-117 and ns XXXVI (1) 1948: 50-177. P H Lawson's 'Schedule of the Roman remains of Chester with maps and plans' ns XXVII(2) 1927: 163-189 was a useful adjunct to the first Newstead paper. A *Subject index to the old series volumes 1-3 1849-1885 and new series volumes I-XVIII 1887-1911* was published in 1912 and a *Subject index and index of authors to volumes XVIII-XXVIII (1911-1929) of the new series* in 1929.

214 Childe, V G (1897-1957) was the author of a number of works postulating theories of social evolution stemming from a close examination of archaeological evidence: *Man makes himself* (1936); *What happened in history* (1942); and *Progress and archaeology* (1945). Other published work includes *Prehistory of Scotland* published in 1935 but still of value; *Prehistoric communities of the British Isles* (1940); and *Skara Brae* (1931). *A Short introduction to archaeology* (1956) is a good summary of archaeological techniques. Stuart Piggott's obituary notice in *Proceedings of the British Academy* XLIV, 1958: 305-312 is a sympathetic outline of Childe's life and work.

215 'A chronological table of prehistory' by Miles Burkitt and V Gordon Childe (*Antiquity* VI (22) June 1932: 185-205) was described in the editorial as 'intended to enable the reader to visualize the cultures or civilizations . . . in organic relationship with those which preceded and followed them'. A general introduction discussing the difficulties involved in defining and dating specific periods is followed by numbered notes headed: Ice ages; 'Eolithic' period; Lower palaeolithic period; Earliest flake industries; Middle palaeolithic period; Upper palaeolithic periód; Mesolithic period; Fossil man; Neolithic period; Copper and bronze ages; Iron age Halstatt period; La Tene period; Mesopotamia; Egypt, Aegean cultures; Beakers and Megalithic tombs. An index completes a summary which in the opinion of the editor was 'a definite advance on anything of the kind yet published'. It was subsequently issued as a pamphlet and incorporated in later editions of Childe's *The dawn of European civilization*. Colin Renfrew's *Before civilization* (*qv*) demonstrates how 'this agreeably logical picture has been completely disrupted, first by the introduction of radio carbon dating and more especially by its calibration through tree-ring studies'.

216 '**Chronicles in Old World archaeology**' edited by Robert.W Ehrlich (University of Chicago Press, 1965) replaces *Relative chronologies in Old World archaeology* (1954). The significance of the revised title derives from the introduction of the radio-carbon dating technique which provides 'more secure patterns of relative dates, and presumably a closer approximation to absolute ones'. Each region is treated separately so that revisions that may become necessary are easily assimilated, the time span involved ranges from the earliest known appearance of neolithic culture to the most convenient breaking point in the early part of the second millenium BC. Areas and regions covered include Egypt and its foreign correlations before the late bronze age (Helen J Kantor); Palestine before about 1500 BC (William F Albright); North Syria and North Mesopotamia from 10,000 BC to 2000 BC (Patty Jo Watson); Anatolia (Machteld J Mellink); Mesopotamia: seals and trade 6000-1600 BC (Edith Porada); Mesopotamia: pottery sequence at Nippur from the Middle Uruk to the end of the Old Babylonian period 3400-1600 BC (Donald P Hansen); Iran 6000-2000 BC (Robert H Dyson); Afghanistan, Baluchistan and the Indus Valley (George F Dales); the Aegean in the stone and early bronze ages (Saul S Weinberg); the northwestern Mediterranean (Donald F Brown); Northwestern Europe and Northern Europe (both by Homer L Thomas); East Central Europe (Robert W Ehrich); neolithic and chalcolithic cultures in Eastern Europe north of the Balkan Peninsula and the Black Sea (Marija Gimbutas); and China to the end of Chou (Kwang-chih Chang). Each of these consists of an explanatory text supplemented by maps, chronological tables, figures, and extensive bibliographies.

217 'Circles and standing stones' by Evan Hadingham (Heinemann, 1975) discusses and explains in simple terms the startling new theories concerning the purpose of the 900 or so prehistoric monuments of Britain either standing alone or in circles which have gained currency in recent years as a result of extensive ground surveys. The author follows his descriptive chapters with an enquiry into the image of ancient Britian as depicted by antiquarian writers over the last three centuries. There are three appendices: a list of conventional radiocarbon datings of various sites; a reading list by chapter; and 'Exploring early Britain', a county by county list of monuments with a brief description and finding instructions.

218 'Classical county histories' is a photographic reprint series, complete and unabridged, of recognized classics of English county history mostly published between 1650 and 1850 which are now virtually unobtainable in their original editions. They have been prepared with the assistance of the county libraries concerned and each work contains a new introduction describing the author's life and assessing the importance of his history in relation to other works. The general editor is Professor Jack Simmons of Leicester University who contributes a number of the introductions.

Titles published so far: *The history and antiquities of the County of Leicester* (John Nichols); *The antiquities of Nottinghamshire* (Robert Thoroton); *The history and topographical survey of the County of Kent* (Edward Hasted); *History of Hertfordshire* (John Edwin Cussans); *The history and antiquities of the County Palatine of Durham* (Robert Surtees); *The history and antiquities of the County of Rutland* (James Wright); *Antiquities historical and monumental of the County of Cornwall* (William Borlase); *The history and antiquities of the County of Dorset* (John Hutchins); *Lake's parochial history of the County of Cornwall* (Joseph Polsue); *The ancient and present state of Glostershire* (Robert Atkyns); *The history of the County of Cumberland* (William Hutchinson); *South Yorkshire* (Joseph Hunter); *The history of the Isle of Wight* (Sir Richard Worsley); *The history and antiquities of Staffordshire* (Stebbing Shaw); *The history and antiquities of the County of Surrey* (Owen Manning and William Bray); and *The ancient history of Wiltshire* (Sir Richard Colt-Hoare). Illustrated brochures describing each of these titles are available on request from E P Publishing Ltd, East Ardsley, Wakefield, Yorkshire. A L Rowse in his review article 'Classics of county history', *Books and bookmen* 19 (2)

No 218 November 1973: 18-20 commented: 'An enterprising Yorkshire publishing concern . . . has come to the rescue . . . I can only say how grateful we have reason to be for their initiative, imagination and public spirit—they should all be made earls for their good work: earls have been made for less . . . Here we are with already a small library produced, folios, big quartos, all with their original complement of plates, in their latest and best editions, printed on good substantial paper, firmly and well bound, at reasonable prices.'

219 '**Collingwood, John Bruce**' (1805-1892) is chiefly remembered as a field archaeologist on the Roman Wall and for his studies of Roman inscriptions. His best known book is the definitive *The Roman Wall* (1851). *The handbook* (in early editions *The wallet*) *to the Roman Wall* was first published in 1863 and is now available from Harold Hill & Son Ltd, Newcastle-upon-Tyne, in an extensively revised form edited by Sir Ian Richmond. This provides a general account of the various constructions of the wall followed by local descriptions from Wallsend to Bowness-on-Solway. There is a bibliography giving references to original first-hand accounts of excavations and discoveries on the line of the wall and an historical summary of early literature is included in the introductory chapter. Twelve maps, photographs and many drawings (some retained from earlier editions) add to the handbook's practical value. An abbreviated version, *A short guide to the Roman Wall* revised by Sir Ian Richmond is also available.

220 '**Collins field guide to archaeology**' by Eric S Wood, published in a fourth edition in 1975, is divided into four parts: Part I 'General background' includes the structure of Britain and the patterns of settlement, climate and the cultures of Britain from the beginnings to the modern age; Part II 'Field antiquities' identifies earthworks and outlines the types of field antiquities and surface finds; Part III considers the technical and legal aspects of archaeology; whilst Part IV indicates how to seek out further information (libraries, museums, societies, training etc), lists sites to visit, and suggests worthwhile books and articles to read. All this, together with eighteen maps and numerous illustrations, is compressed into a remarkably readable and compact volume which must be regarded as indispensable for every general, school or specialized archaeological library. Sir Mortimer Wheeler adds an introduction.

221 '**Collins' pocket guide to the undersea world**' by Ley Kenyon (1956) includes less than twenty pages on archaeology off the shores of Britain and Europe but it does offer a survey of the principal diving clubs of the world.

222 Committee for Aerial Photography was formed in the University of Cambridge in 1949 in recognition of the part aerial photography played in the university's teaching and research programme in many diverse disciplines. An annual programme of aerial reconnaissance was put into operation at first in coordination with Royal Air Force training flights and from 1960 onwards in their own aircraft. *The uses of air photography* edited by J K S St Joseph (1966) is composed of papers written largely by staff of the department and includes many of archaeological interest viz 'The scope of air photography' (J K S St Joseph); 'Air photography and the scientific study of soils' (R M S Perrin); 'Air photography and archaeology' (J K S St Joseph); and 'Air photography and history' (M D Knowles). Each paper concludes with a bibliography. The Cambridge University Press have also published a number of studies under the general title of Cambridge Air Surveys: *Monastic sités from the air* (David Knowles and J K S St Joseph); *Medieval England: an aerial survey* (M W Beresford and J K S St Joseph); and *The early development of Irish society: the evidence of aerial photography* (E L Norman and J K S St Joseph).

223 Committee for Rescue Archaeology in Avon, Gloucestershire, and Somerset (CRAAGS) was established as a permanent sub-committee of Council for British Archaeology Group 13 in the autumn of 1973 and is composed of representatives of all major archaeological interests in the area. It acts as a coordinating committee for assessing threats to archaeology and for the allocation of Department of the Environment grants. It also conducts excavations and surveys on its own behalf and is engaged upon a site and monument record for the county of Avon. Informed comment on the committee's activities appears in 'Notes and news', *Current archaeology*, IV(8) No 43, March 1974: 228-229.

224 Committee for the Recovery of Archaeological Remains is a very small group of leading American archaeologists who seek 'to insure sufficient salvage of archaeological, historical, and palaeontological information from sites destroyed by the expansion of modern technology'.

225 'The concise encyclopaedia of archaeology' edited by Leonard Cottrel, first published by Hutchinson in 1960, was reissued in a revised and more convenient format in 1970. It was compiled to help the intelligent amateur who 'wants to know more and more, and is sometimes prepared to wrestle with serious professional works which may occasionally take him out of his depth'. In a single alphabetical sequence there are entries on the great discoveries, essential technical terms, biographies of eminent archaeologists, historical surveys of regional archaeology, scientific processes, cities and civilizations, and the decipherment of ancient scripts and languages, written by acknowledged experts. However, the editor admits to limitations: there are few references to the archaeology of classical Greece and Rome but many to Far Eastern and American antiquities even though some are dated as recently as the sixteenth century AD. This is justified on the grounds that there are a great many books on classical archaeology but far fewer on sites in Asia or America. Selection of entries depended upon many diverse considerations and criteria: the interests of both general readers and specialists, the desirability (and necessity) of including items from all parts of the world, and the need to achieve a balance between famous sites and discoveries of universal interest and recondite terms, sometimes encountered in the more academic books and articles. Entries are initialled (almost fifty archaeologists contributed to the writing of the encyclopaedia) and there is a classified list of entries for those wishing to study a particular topic in detail. Ten maps, a comparative chart of the cultural traditions of early man, a list of further readings arranged by subject and notes on the contributors, are also included. Hawthorn Books published the American edition.

226 **'Concise encyclopaedia of archaeology'** *from the Bronze Age* by Georges Ville was first published by Librairie Larousse in 1968 and in English translation by Collins in 1971. Entries arranged in dictionary form are world wide in coverage, describing briefly and to the point significant peoples and cultures, towns and sites, and explaining why these are important. Archaeological terms, techniques and methods also find a place. The *Encyclopaedia* is intelligently and profusely illustrated, there is a comprehensible map section pinpointing sites mentioned in the text, and a chronological table shows selected sites representing cultural periods which illustrate how culture developed at different times in different places. The list of books for further reading is divided into a general and six geographical sections.

227 **Conference of young archaeologists** was conceived by Richard Reece, Rosalind Dunnett and Barry Cunliffe as an annual forum for young archaeologists, university students reading for higher degrees mostly, where they could exchange views and ideas by means of papers and discussion on recent excavations and the techniques of excavation and discovery. The conference got off to a good start in December 1962 when the theme was 'Recent discoveries in prehistoric, Roman, and Medieval Britain' but in the years following the high level of the initial meeting was not maintained. A marked improvement came in 1975 when for the first time a list of invited speakers was drawn up, the previous system of speakers 'emerging' had not always worked to good effect. A J Lawson writing in *Antiquity*, XLIX (196), December 1975: 300 concluded that the conference 'offers to the student and the professional, topics that are not to be heard elsewhere, with an opportunity for both formal and informal discussion of these, and so provide a valid contribution to archaeology and the ever-growing number of other subjects'.

228 **'Conference on the future of archaeology'** *held at the University of London, Institute of Archaeology August 6th to 8th, 1943* (Occasional Paper No 5, Institute of Archaeology, 1944) prints abridged versions of the papers presented to the conference which was convened to discuss the problems archaeology would face in the post-war period. Although now obviously long overtaken by events it remains a cardinal document in the history of British archaeology.

Contents:

1 The contribution of archaeology to the post-war world (J D G Clark)
2 The future of discovery: archaeology at home
    Prehistoric archaeology (C F C Hawkes)
    Romano-British archaeology (I A Richmond)
    Medieval archaeology (T D Kendrick)
3 The unity of archaeology (V Gordon Childe)
4 The future of discovery: archaeology overseas
    Greek and Roman archaeology (J L Myres)
    Syrian, Palestinian and Turkish archaeology (C F A Schaeffer)
    The archaeology of Iraq, Baluchistan and India (Ernest Mackay)
    Islamic archaeology (H A R Gibb)
5 The training of archaeologists
    Training for fieldwork (Miss K M Kenyon)
    University training (J D Beazley)
    Training in interpretation and presentation (D B Harden)
    Training in the subsidiary sciences (F E Zeuner)
6 Records and discovery—local and national (Cyril Fox)

7 Planning and independence of societies
>The need for planning (J N L Myres)
>Societies working at home (H St George Gray)
>Societies working overseas (Han Gardiner)

8 Archaeology and the state at home (W F Grimes)

9 Archaeology and the state overseas (Leonard Woolley)

10 Museums and the public
>National Museums (C F C Hawkes)
>Other Museums (F S Wallis)

11 Archaeology and education
>Elementary schools (Mrs D P Dobson)
>Secondary and public schools (Philip Corder)
>Universities (a) Oxford (H R Wade Gery)
>(b) Cambridge (D S Robertson)
>(c) Other universities (W J Varley)
>Adult education (Mrs D J Chitty)

12 Summing up (Cyril Fox)

At the end of the conference a resolution 'That the problems raised by the conference be referred to the appropriate organizations' was passed unanimously.

229 The Congress of Archaeological Societies came into existence as the result of a memorandum signed by a number of fellows of the Society of Antiquaries submitted to the president and council in the autumn of 1888. A conference of delegates from the leading local archaeological societies was convened to discuss the more effective organization of archae-oligical research. Just what the society had in mind is clearly outlined in the invitations which were couched in the following terms:

'Each Society will be requested to send not more than two Delegates to the Congress, the object of which will be to consider in what manner to promote

1 The better organization of antiquarian research; and

2 The preservation of ancient monuments and records.

It is thought that the most effective means of obtaining these results will be

A To establish a group of local societies which shall be in correspondence with the Society of Antiquaries of London;

B To request these societies to report from time to time to the Society . . . on all important discoveries within their districts, in doing which the Local Secretaries of the Society . . . will be ready and willing to afford assistance;

C   To encourage the formation of lists of ancient objects of different
    kinds in each local Society's district, and to assist in devising the
    best system on which such lists can be drawn up;
D   To consider in what manner a general archaeological survey of
    England and Wales by counties, on the plan approved of by the
    Society . . . and begun in Kent, may be completed;
E   To define the limits within which each local Society should work;
F   To promote the foundation of new local Societies where none
    exist, and the improvement and consolidation of existing Societies
    where advisable.'

A large number of societies accepted the invitation and attended a
conference 15th November. This was adjourned to the following May
with a view to forming a register of 'Societies in Union' and the first congress proper was held 17th July 1889. A measure of useful bibliographical
work was set in hand: an annual *Index of archaeological papers* appeared
1891-1910 when it was abandoned owing to lack of support from affiliated societies, and a retrospective volume, *Index of archaeological papers
1665-1890* (*qv*) edited by G L Gomme was published in 1907. The index
was not revived but the congress's Earthworks Committee presented a
select bibliography in its annual report. These reports included an increasing amount of information concerning the discovery and excavation of
sites which came under firm control with the publication of *Index of reports
of the Earthworks Committee for the years 1905-1926*. In 1931 the
Earthworks Committee was replaced by the Research Committee whose
reports continued to list work on sites in Britain and an annual bibliography
until 1939. The congress was dissolved 30th November 1945 and was replaced by The Council for British Archaeology. The beginnings of the
congress are etched in *Proceedings of the Society of Antiquaries*, second
series, XII, pages 233-235, and B H St J O'Neil contributed a valedictory
article 'The Congress of Archaeological Societies', *Antiquaries journal*
XXVI 1946: 61-66.

230 **'Conquistadores without swords'** *archaeologists in the Americas*, an
account with original narratives, by Leo Deuel, published in 1967 in
London by Macmillan and in New York by St Martins Press, is an outline
history of American archaeology along regional, historical and chronological lines. Each regional section (Andean South America; Central
America; Central and Southern Mexico; Maya lands; United States; Earliest
Americans; and Northernmost America; *ie* Eskimos and Vikings) consists
of an introductory essay and a number of excerpts from the printed

accounts of pioneer archaeologists many of which have been long out of
print. An extensive bibliography is composed of monographs, articles
and popular books 'capable of directing the beginner in his further readings
of the archaeological literature'.

231 '**The conservation of antiquities and works of art**' *treatment, repair
and restoration* by H J Plenderleith, Keeper of the Research Laboratory
British Museum, was first published by the Oxford University Press in
1956. It was intended as a handbook for the collector, the archaeologist,
and the museum curator, and as a workshop guide for the technician, and
as such was accepted by the Museums Association as their official textbook on the conservation of museum objects. For the archaeologist it is
of most use in tracing the scientific methods available for the restoration
of antiquities recovered from excavations and in revealing unsuspected
facts during laboratory investigations and treatment. The book was brought
up-to-date in a second edition in 1971 with the help of A E A Werner who
was Plenderleith's successor at the British Museum Research Laboratory.

232 '**Contemporary archaeology**' *a guide to theory and contributions*
edited by Mark P Leone (Southern Illinois University Press, 1972) is a
compendium of papers presenting the theory and results of recent developments in anthropological archaeology and is intended as a handbook for
the professional archaeologist interested in assessing what is new in archaeological thinking. The editor introduces each section and a major bibliography is also included.
 *Contents: Part 1 'The scope of the changes in contemporary archae-
ology'* includes 'The revolution in archaeology' (Paul S Martin); 'Issues
in anthropoligical archaeology' (Mark P Leone); 'Old wine and new skins,
a contemporary parable' (Walter W Taylor); 'Interpretive trends and linear
models in American archaeology' (Raymond H Thompson). *Part 2 The
origins of contemporary change:* 'The urban revolution' (V Gordon Childe);
'Conjectures concerning the social organization of the Mogollon Indians'
(Paul S Martin); 'The economic approach to prehistory' (Grahame Clark);
'The conceptual structure in Middle American studies' (Clyde Kluckhohn);
and 'Review of James A Ford's measurements of some prehistoric design
developments in the south-eastern states' (Albert C Spaulding). *Part 3
The theoretical base of contemporary archaeology:* 'Archaeology as anthropology' (Lewis R Binford); 'Culture history *v* cultural process: a debate
in American archaeology' (Kent V Flannery); 'Archaeology as a social
science' (James F Deetz); 'Historical and historic sites archaeology as
106

anthropology: basic definitions and relationships' (Robert L Schuyler); 'Archaeological systematics and the study of culture process' (Lewis R Binford). *Part 4 The methodological base of contemporary archaeology:* 'Archaeological systems for indirect observation of the past' (John M Fritz); 'A consideration of archaeological research design' (Lewis R Binford); and 'A review of techniques for archaeological sampling' (Sonia Ragir). *Part 5 Archaeological strategy for the study of hunter-gatherers:* 'Lithic analysis in palaeoanthropology' (Edwin N Wilmsen); 'The Clovis hunters: an alternate view of their environment and ecology' (Frederick Gorman); 'Archaeological systems theory and early Mesoamerica' (Kent V Flannery). *Part 6 Archaeological strategy for the study of horticulturalists:* 'Postpleistocene adaptations' (Lewis R Binford); 'The ecology of early food production in Mesopotamia' (Kent V Flannery); 'Carrying capacity and dynamic equilibrium in the prehistoric southwest' (Ezra Zubrow); 'Explaining variability in prehistoric southwestern water control systems' (Fred T Plog and Cheryl K Garrett); 'Changes in the adaptations of southwestern basketmakers' (Michael A Glassow); 'The Hopewell interaction sphere in riverine—western Great Lakes culture history' (Stuart Struever); 'Archaeology as anthropology: a case study (William A Longacre); 'A prehistoric community in eastern Arizona' (James N Hill); 'The Olmec Were—Jaguar motif in the light of ethnographic reality' (Peter T Furst). *Part 7 Archaeological strategy for the study of complex agriculturalists:* 'Some hypotheses of the development of early civilizations' (Robert M Adams); 'Praise the gods and pass the Metates: a hypothesis of the development of lowland rainforest civilizations in Mesoamerica' (William R Rathje); 'State settlements in Tawantinsuyu: a strategy of compulsory urbanism' (Craig Morris); and 'Death's head, cherub, urn and willow' (James F Deetz and Edwin S Dethlefsen).

233 'Contributions to American anthropology and history', a series of occasional research papers published by the Carnegie Institution of Washington collected four or five in a volume, were reprinted by The Johnson Reprint Company of New York in 1970. Volumes I to IV (1931-1937) were originally published under the title of *Contributions to American archaeology*.

234 Cornwall Archaeological Society was founded as the West Cornwall Field Club which in turn traces its origins to the Cornwall Excavation Committee formed in 1933 and sponsored by the Royal Institution of Cornwall and the Federation of Old Cornwall Societies. It was three years later that the director of the committee decided that archaeology in West Cornwall should be placed on a more sound footing and in 1936 the field club was inaugurated 'to establish, as closely as may be possible, the detailed chronology of West Cornwall for the approximate period 500 BC-400 AD. It is considered that, apart from its direct advantages, a firmly fixed chronology for that period is essential for those whose interests lie mainly in the earlier bronze age and in the succeeding dark ages, for which information and remains are far more fragmentary than for the nine centuries in question. Thus the main purpose of the club is twofold in that it aims at fixing the chronology of a period which has not yet been worked out in detail, and at the same time providing a pied-a-terre from which investigations can be made backwards from 500 BC and forwards from 400 AD.'

A two part volume of *Proceedings* was published 1937-1938 and a new series began in 1952. Papers of interest include C B Croft's 'History and policy of the West Cornwall Field Club' ns 1 July 1953: 3-6; 'The Club's publications 1935-1956' ns 1(4) 1955-56: 153-156 which lists the early reports of the excavation committee. A special twenty-fifth anniversary number, 'Archaeology in Cornwall', 1933-1958, volume 2(2) 1957-58 coincided with the Prehistoric Society's spring conference at Penzance. This contained several important survey articles: 'The palaeolithic and mesolithic periods in Cornwall' (Charles Thomas); 'Neolithic Cornwall' (J V S Megaw); 'The bronze age in Cornwall' (Bernard Wailes); 'Cornish bronze age pottery' (A R Apsimon); 'The early iron age in Cornwall' (Dorothy Dudley); 'Roman Cornwall' (C A Ralegh Radford); 'Cornwall in the dark ages' (Charles Thomas); and 'The medieval period in Cornwall' (A Guthrie). In 1961 the club transformed itself into a county-wide archaeological society at the instance of a group of members who were of the opinion that the club's name no longer truly reflected the scope of its activities. The society's annual journal, *Cornish archaeology/Hendhyscans Kernow*, first appeared in 1962 and continued three research features which had appeared in the *Proceedings* namely 'Digest of Cornish periodicals' which lists notes and articles bearing on the archaeology, history, and material culture of the county; a 'Parochial check list of antiquities, hundred by hundred, with notes on extant remains, location details, and bibliographic references (a guide to those published to date appeared in vol 8, 1969: 113-114); and lastly, the 'Cumulative index of Cornish archaeology', a bibliography of publications arranged in order of archaeological period, which from 1973 onwards appears every second year. Other noteworthy items are C A Ralegh Radford's 'The neolithic in the southwest of England', vol 1, 1962: 4-9; H L Douch's 'Archaeological discoveries recorded in Cornish newspapers before 1855', 1, 1962: 92-98; 'List of Cornish museums' 1, 1962: 99-101, compiled from information gleaned from curators, which includes all those open to the public; J V S Megaw's 'The neolithic in the southwest of England', a reply to Radford's article, 2, 1963: 4-8; and Paul Ashbee's 'The chambered tombs of St Mary's, Isles of Scilly,' 2, 1963: 9-18. From the outset the society has taken a keen interest in industrial archaeology: Kenneth Hudson's 'Industrial archaeology in the southwest' 3, 1964: 80-83 and S W Beard's 'The industrial monuments survey of Cornwall, 6, 1967: 74-77, both being valuable contributions in this sphere.

235 Cornwall Committee for Rescue Archaeology, founded February 1975 and funded by the Department of the Environment, is currently engaged upon compiling a sites and monuments record for the county.

236 'Council for British Archaeology' was called into existence in 1944 following a suggestion mooted at the 1943 Oxford conference of the Society for the Promotion of Roman Studies that the Society of Antiquaries should invite delegates from archaeological societies to discuss the requirements of post-war archaeology in the United Kingdom. A number of serious problems to be faced during the immediate post-war period were looming up: the considerable rebuilding necessary, especially in London, and the inevitable spread of urban and rural development, would clearly pose formidable problems which the limited and isolated resources of local societies could claim no prospect of solving. Some sort of central organization to speak authoritatively for British archaeology as a whole would be urgently required. The Congress of Archaeological Societies, founded in 1888, was deemed too cumbersome a body to act effectively in this role and in fact it readily agreed to suspend its activities for two years in order that the new body could establish itself on a firm footing.

The new council met for the first time 8th March 1944 and consisted of one representative from each national society approved by the conference of the previous August—Society of Antiquaries of London, Society of Antiquaries of Scotland, Society for the Promotion of Roman Studies, Prehistoric Society, Royal Archaeological Institute, British Archaeological Association, Cambrian Archaeological Association, Royal Anthropological Institute, British Records Association, Royal Historical Society, Royal Numismatic Society, British Association for the Advancement of Science, and the British Academy; one representative from each of the national museums similarly approved *viz* British Museum, Victoria and Albert

Museum, National Museum of Wales, National Museum of Antiquities of Scotland, Guildhall Museum, and Tower Armouries; two representatives from each of those universities which included the teaching of archaeology in their curriculum, Oxford, Cambridge, Edinburgh, Liverpool, London, Durham, Leeds, Wales, and Manchester; Nine representatives and six from Scottish and Welsh societies respectively, and three from each of ten English regional groups; one representative from each Regional Federation of Museums; and ten further members to be co-opted annually.

The council declared its intention to take appropriate action in all matters concerning British archaeology and specifically that it would be its function (a) to urge the necessity for large state grants to deal with problems too vast or too urgent for the resources of any one learned society or regional committee; (b) to urge the strengthening of existing measures for the care and preservation of historic monuments and antiquities; (c) to further and formulate measures to enlighten public opinion concerning the records and monuments of the past; (d) to work for the adequate recognition of archaeology, not only in the universities and schools, but in the wider field of adult education; and (e) to cooperate with any parallel organization that might seek to foster the progress of museum activities.

An executive committee was constituted to act on matters requiring immediate decision; the president of the Society of Antiquaries, Sir Cyril Fox, was elected president and Miss Kathleen Kenyon of the Institute of Archaeology became secretary. The regional groups were recommended to be composed of representatives of county and local archaeological societies, kindred societies, museums, colleges and universities, and perhaps of local education authorities. It was to be their function to act in their own regions on matters of archaeological importance, to consult the council on their more difficult problems, and to report on action taken. A further suggestion was that each regional group might encourage societies to form junior branches.

By 1949, its two year probation period long forgotten, the council could reasonably hope to proceed to a more active role but its ambitions, especially in the publishing field, were frustrated by a serious lack of money. In that year, however, an important and significant step forward was achieved when it was awarded an annual grant from public funds to be divided between administrative and publishing but not towards excavation costs. The government had no wish to duplicate the activities of the Ministry of Works. Clearly the status of the council had been

110

acknowledged and its position as the central coordinating body for British archaeology had been confirmed for all to see.

At the end of its first ten years the council could legitimately take a sanguine view of its achievements: 'The protection of all kinds of archaeological material, the strengthening of existing resources for the care of ancient and historic buildings and the stimulation of an interest in them as records of the past, are all objects which this council has pursued most actively as its reports show . . . The council was also pledged to promote archaeological research and to organize the provision of financial assistance to supplement the resources of learned societies. With the acquisition of a grant-in-aid from the state in 1949, it became possible to implement this resolution and £6000 has been allocated to date in grants to societies for archaeological publications . . . Through its publications and in the support which it has given to training schemes in field archaeology, the council has promoted the recognition of archaeology in education.' (*Report No 4*, 30 June 1954).

The subsequent history of the council's activities is best recorded in the annual *Report* and especially in the presidential addresses delivered according to custom at the end of each three-year term of office. The most significant developments in the 1970s have been the emergence of RESCUE (*qv*) and the council's internal reorganization of its committee structure in an effort to streamline and rationalise its own activities. When RESCUE was formed there were many who questioned the need for another body, arguing that the council could very well undertake its proposed functions but the council itself was quick to point out that RESCUE was seeking the support of individuals in its attempt to raise funds for emergency excavations whereas the council worked through a completely institutional membership and through regional groups and was in fact precluded from spending its treasury grant on excavations. The council therefore welcomed the formation of RESCUE which it regarded as a potentially powerful ally especially in bringing pressure to bear on the government to improve the state archaeological agencies. As it happened the two bodies cooperated very closely to produce *Archaeology and government* (*qv*), a policy document on the possible future structure of archaeology in Britain.

In 1974-75 a completely new committee structure was put into operation. An Executive Board was established to which three other boards would report, each responsible for coordinating the activities of a number of committees. The Finance and General Purposes Board looks after the Publication, Legislation and Government, Consultancy, and Grants

Committees; the Education Board supervises the University, Further Education, and Schools Committees; whilst the Research Board holds a watching brief on the Scientific Research, Implement Petrology, Countryside, Industrial Archaeology, Urban Research, Churches, and Aerial Reconnaissance Committees. Despite this reorganization however, there have been instances when the executive board has attracted criticism for its alleged high-handedness and for its apparent predilection for excessive centralization. The council's plenary meetings have been described as unrepresentative and heavily biased in favour of London and the South East. For its part the board declares that it endeavours to consult members as widely as possible but that its present structure is sorely tried by the loads put upon it in the current swift-moving situation. And so a thorough reappraisal of the council's constitution is promised, hopefully proposals will be formed in time for the council's 1977 summer meeting.

Regional group structure. From their inception the groups were regarded as being in close touch with the requirements of regional archaeology. They were envisaged as forums where bodies of all kinds could meet and discuss problems, and where representatives of the senior county archaeological societies could encounter the younger archaeologists in the active field groups to their mutual advantage. The groups as originally established were as follows (1) Scotland; (2) Wales and Monmouthshire; (3) Northumberland, Durham, Cumberland, Westmorland and Lancashire North of the Sands; (4) Yorkshire; (5) Lancashire, Cheshire, North Staffordshire; (6) Leicestershire, Derbyshire, Rutland and the Soke of Peterborough; (7) Cambridgeshire and the Isle of Ely, Huntingdonshire, Norfolk and Suffolk; (8) Worcestershire, Warwickshire, South Staffordshire, Shropshire and Herefordshire; (9) Oxfordshire, Berkshire, Buckinghamshire, Bedfordshire and Northamptonshire; (10) London, Middlesex, Essex and Hertfordshire; (11) Kent, Surrey and Sussex; (12) Dorset, Hampshire and Wiltshire; (13) Gloucestershire, Somerset, Devon and Cornwall; and (14) Lincolnshire and Nottinghamshire. Group 11 was split into 11A Kent and Surrey and 11B Sussex in 1965. In the last few years concern has been expressed that the groups should coincide as nearly as possible to the Department of the Environment's regional units, it being acknowledged that the existence of an organized CBA regional organization to act as a counterpart to the Area Advisory Committees would be beneficial to both, ensuring proper representation of all archaeological interests. In consequence some boundary changes in the regional group structure have either been effected or are being discussed *eg* groups 6 and 14 have been amalgamated, Norfolk and Suffolk will constitute a new group 6, and
112

the splinter group 11s are to merge again. A proposal that London should form a separate group is aired from time to time, Nicholas Farrant's 'A CBA group for London?' *The London archaeologist*, 3(1) Winter 1976: 24 outlines the pros and cons (and incidentally summarises a group's regular and occasional functions and activities). Most of the groups now issue a newsletter or a bulletin of some description, one or two in permanent form. An annual account of their activities is published in *Archaeology in Britain*.

Publications: from the outset the council has striven to improve the bibliographical control of archaeological literature. *Archaeological bibliography for Great Britain and Ireland* started in 1950, *British archaeological abstracts* was introduced in 1968, the *Calendar of excavations* has proved one of the council's most popular publications since its inception in 1952, *Current archaeological offprints and reports* enables individuals and institutions to secure papers of interest they might otherwise miss, and three booklists with the title of *British archaeology* have been published for use in schools in 1949, 1960 and 1976. All these titles are described elsewhere in this present handbook as are numerous other separate publications.

At the same time as the committee structure was revitalised the council reviewed its publishing programme. Of especial interest was the agreement with the Department of the Environment that the council should publish reports of department sponsored excavations with the department also agreeing that the council should be regarded as a non-profit making body and was therefore eligible for further grants. Fascicles of *Archaeology of York* and *Archaeology of Lincoln* have already made their appearance. The council's annual *Report* has been published since 1950, in 1972 this was given a face-lift and a new cover title *Archaeology in Britain* (*qv*).

Bibliography Kathleen Kenyon's 'The Council for British Archaeology', *Museums journal* 44(6) September 1944: 91-93 is valuable as an early indication of its organization, the problems it faced, and how it perceived its own role in solving these problems. W F Grimes' 'The CBA—the first decade', *Archaeological newsletter*, 5(8) January 1955: 139-145, later issued as an offprint, outlines the council's precursors, constitution, objectives, activities and publications, and its relations with the public over its first ten years. M W Barley's presidential address 'The prospects for British archaeology', *Report No 17*, 1967: 51-56 reviews the council's organization and administration for the period from 1954 onwards, the significance of the financial support it received from the government,

the prospects for a state archaeological service, the scale of the government's expenditure on archaeological research, the prose and cons of
compulsory formal training for excavation, and the relationship between
the council and the state. Charles Thomas' 'Presidential address', *Archaeology in Britain*, 1972-1973: 93-103 explains the council's relationship
with RESCUE, outlines its research and propaganda activities, and comments on its growth into a national pressure group.

237 Council for British Archaeology Research Reports usually emanate
from CBA research committees. Their origins and sales records are recorded year by year in *Archaeology in Britain (qv). Titles:*

1 *Romano-British villas: some current problems*
2 *The recording of architecture and its publication*
3 *The investigation of smaller domestic buildings*
4 *Anglo-Saxon pottery*
5 *The structure of Romano-British pottery kilns*
6 *Romano-British coarse pottery: a student's guide*
7 *Rural settlement in Roman Britain*
8 *Gazetteer of British lower and middle palaeolithic sites*
9 *The iron age in the Irish Sea provinces*
10 *Current research in Romano-British coarse pottery*
11 *The effect of man on the landscape: The Highland zone*
12 *Aerial reconnaissance for archaeology*
13 *The archaeological study of churches*
14 *The plans and topography of medieval towns in England and Wales*
15 *Excavations at St Mary's Church, Deerhurst 1971-73*
16 *Iron age sites in central southern England*

238 Council for Kentish Archaeology changed its name from the Kent
Archaeological Research Groups Council, in November 1969, at the end
of its first five years. It consists of a number of constitutent local archaeological, excavation, and research groups, banded together the better to
promote and coordinate archaeological and historical research in the
county by means of arranging conferences and lectures, the holding of
expensive field equipment and tools in common ownership, and the
quarterly publication of *Kent archaeological review* which first appeared
in April 1968 and succeeded a rather more primitive newsletter. This
deals with current archaeological activity in the county, and contains reports of excavations and discoveries, the work of the constituent groups,
other news items, and details of meetings and lectures. Its chief interest
114

lies in the prehistoric, Roman, Saxon, and medieval periods although articles on 'environmental archaeology', *ie* industrial archaeology and other sundry matters of interest, occasionally appear in its pages. An index to the first thirty issues compiled by John Parson was published in 1975. Mr and Mrs M Leonard's 'Select bibliography on Kent archaeology 1970' appeared in volume 24, Summer 1971: 114-115 and this was updated in Peter Couldrey's 'Kent bibliography 1970-74', vol 43, Spring 1976: 74-76.

239 The Council for Nautical Archaeology was formed in 1964 'to ensure that the many underwater archaeological discoveries being made by divers should not go by default through lack of contact with the appropriate learned bodies and to act as a channel of communication with the many interests that were growing up in this new field of research and exploration. The council seeks to establish standard methods of recording and to instil surveying techniques and the proper conservation of archaeological finds. It aims to cover all aspects of nautical archaeological research . . . and to publish the results. A principal aim has been the promotion of legislation for the protection of nautical archaeological sites.' Museums and academic institutions and the British Sub-Aqua Club are represented on the council. *The international journal of nautical archaeology and underwater exploration (qv)* is now published quarterly.

240 'The county archaeologies', published by Methuen in the 1920s and 1930s were well regarded in their time. Each volume was divided into two parts, the text consisted of a period by period survey of the county in question's archaeology, and an archaeological gazetteer listed finds parish by parish. Museums exhibiting antiquities from the county were also listed and their collections briefly described. In view of the upsurge of archaeology in popularity since the second world war it is surprising that the series was discontinued although two volumes were issued in revised editions and at least one other was reprinted with a new foreword. *Titles: Ireland* (R A S Macalister) 1928, 2nd rev ed 1949; *Middlesex and London* (C E Vulliamy) 1930; *Kent* (R F Jessup) 1930; *Berkshire* (Harold Peake) 1931; *Somerset* (D P Dobson) 1931; *Cornwall and Scilly* (H O'Neill Hencken) 1932; *Surrey* (D C Whimster) 1931; and *Sussex* (E Cecil Curwen) 1937, 2nd rev ed 1954. The general editor was T D Kendrick.

241 'COWA surveys and bibliographies'. The Council for Old World Archaeology was founded as a non-profit making corporation by Lauriston

115

Ward, Curator of Asiatic Archaeology at the Peabody Museum of Harvard University to enable professional archaeologists, scholars in allied subjects, and students, to keep abreast of the increasing volume of literature on the prehistoric archaeology of the Old World. The principal activity of the council is the publication of *Surveys and bibliographies*, a triennial series of area reports on Old World archaeology from palaeolithic to recent historical times. Each area report covers two-three years of archaeological activity and consists of a survey of current work and an annotated bibliography of the more important books and articles in the main publishing languages. A complete series contains upwards of 4000 bibliographical entries. *The British Isles* is No 1 of the eight European areas, the Council for British Archaeology being responsible for the descriptive survey arranged by archaeological periods, with separate sections for Northern Ireland and the Republic of Ireland. The bibliography is arranged alphabetically by author. Four series have been completed covering the period 1956-1967.

242 Crawford, O G S (1886-1957) played an important part in British archaeology in the inter-war years. As the first Archaeology Officer of the Ordnance Survey he was responsible for the compilation of OS maps from the point of view of archaeological information, he also started the survey's series of period maps beginning with the *Map of Roman Britain* (1924). His prime interests were twofold: field archaeology as witnessed by his *Field archaeology* (1932) and *Archaeology in the field* (1953); and aerial photography in which he was an enthusiastic pioneer: *Air survey and archaeology* (1924), *Air photography for archaeologists* (1929) and with Alexander Keiller, *Wessex from the air* (1928) in which there is a history and bibliography of archaeology from the air by way of introduction. He was the founder-editor of *Antiquity* (*qv*), at the time said to be the only independent archaeological journal in the world. His typically ebullient autobiography *Said and done* appeared in 1955. *Aspects of archaeology in Britain and beyond: essays presented to O G S Crawford* edited by W F Grimes (1951) includes John L Myres' 'The man and his past', J K St J Joseph's 'A survey in pioneering in air-photography past and future', and a bibliography of Crawford's extensive writings. 'Ghosts of Wessex', the second chapter of Leo Deuel's *Flights into yesterday* (1971) assesses Crawford's influence in the development of aerial archaeology.

243 Cumberland and Westmorland Antiquarian and Archaeological Society was formed at a meeting at the Crown Hotel, Penrith, 11th September

1886 'for the purpose of investigating, describing, and preserving the antiquities of Cumberland, Westmorland and Lancashire north of The Sands'. The founder members were mainly concerned with research into history, biography, pedigrees, unprinted documents and records of the district and also with prehistoric remains, ecclesiastical and secular architexture, inscriptions, and ancient arts, institutions and industries. The society's *Transactions* date from 1866 and have included much interesting material down the years. John Flavel Curwen's 'Notes on the early history of the society', XXXIII new series 1933: 1-6 is based on personal recollections whilst Eric Birley's 'The archaeology of Cumberland and Westmorland' an address to the Carlisle Meeting of the Royal Archaeological Institute July 1958, and printed in volume LVIII ns 1959: 1-13 ranges over the history of antiquarian studies in the area, the foundation of the society, its personalities notably the Collingwoods father and son, the editors of the *Transactions* etc. 'The present state of antiquarian research in Westmorland and Cumberland', a paper read at the society's inaugural meeting appeared in the first issue, 1866-67: 1-18. W G Collingwood's 'An inventory of the ancient monuments of Cumberland', XXIII ns 1923: 206-276 listed all sites and remains alphabetically by parishes arranged in twelve districts according to a scheme approved by the Inspector of Ancient Monuments for the supervision of antiquities by local correspondents and included bibliographical references and an index. A similar list for Westmorland and Lancashire—North-of-the-Sands was subsequently printed in volume XXVI ns 1926: 1-62. The reports of the Cumberland Excavation Committee were a regular feature for many years and R G Collingwood's 'Ten year's work on Hadrian's Wall 1920-30' XXX ns 1931: 87-110 should also be noted. The society was unusually fortunate in finding volunteers to index the *Transactions*: Archibald Sparke compiled a *Catalogue-index . . . vol 1 (1866) to vol XVI (1900)*, Daniel Scott followed with *An index-catalogue to the second series . . . vols 1-XII (1901-1912)*, and W G Collingwood provided an *Index to vols XIII-XX (1913-1925)*. The two latest to appear were both printed in the *Transactions*: C and J E Spence's 'A subject index to the *Transactions* . . . new series volumes 1-45', XLVI ns 1947: 1-66 and J Melville's similar work for volumes 46-72, LXXIII ns 1973: 1-24.

244 Cunnington William (1754-1810) together with his friend and patron, Sir Richard Colt Hoare, 'may very properly be called the fathers of archaeological excavation in England' (Glyn Daniel: *One hundred and fifty years of archaeology*). Colt Hoare's *The ancient history of South Wiltshire*

(1812-1821) was partly based on Cunnington's excavations and collection of antiquities which he generously put at Colt Hoare's disposal. The collection is now housed at the Wiltshire Archaeological and Natural History Society's museum at Devizes.

245 **'Current archaeological offprints and reports'** published by the Council for British Archaeology since 1951, first as a quarterly, then twice a year, has appeared annually since October 1972 when it changed its title from *Current and forthcoming offprints on archaeology in Great Britain and Ireland*. It is compiled with the cooperation of county and local societies and is intended to facilitate the purchase of offprinted articles. Subscribers are notified that offprints will not usually be supplied to residents within the area covered by the society unless they are already members. Very few papers issued by national societies are included. Items are arranged in three sequences—Europe, England and Counties— each sub-divided by period and the information listed includes title, author, pagination etc, provenance, when available and price. The list is now divided in the annual issue into two parts: current and forthcoming offprints, and papers announced previously but still available. Papers of philological, genealogical, local record, or purely historical interest are excluded as are papers on subjects allied to archaeology published in non-archaeological journals.

246 **'Current archaeology'** began publication in March 1967 as an illustrated magazine to cater for the large number of amateur archaeologists in contrast to the academic and specialized journals published at local and national level, and to act as a bridge between the career archaeologists and the general public. From the first its articles, perceptive book reviews, and its diary of people and events, have consistently hit exactly the right note, not too specialized and yet not sacrificing professional integrity in a vain search for over-simplification. Trenchant editorials face up to the pressing issues of the day and comment in a sensible and responsible manner. Primarily concerned with British archaeology there is from time to time a special issue devoted to the archaeology of a foreign country depending upon where the intrepid editors take their summer holiday. Latterly a good deal of editorial attention and space has been directed on the activities of RESCUE and in the summer of 1976 it was announced that the magazine in conjunction with that organization would henceforward award an annual trophy to independent archaeologists working as a group 'for the best and most original contribution to rescue
118

archaeology'. Other regular features include an annual list of digs to visit and the *Current archaeology job finder*, a leaflet carrying advertisements of professional appointments. An American opinion of the magazine came in a letter from Leonard J Kerpelman of Baltimore printed in the March 1971 issue: 'You are very cheeky, outspoken, opinionated, and you always have a point of view in your editorial column . . . your articles are detailed, specific, and I am sure dull for anyone who does not have an interest in either history or archaeology.' The editors' own view of their publication was expressed in the twenty-first (July 1970) issue: 'We report achievement rather than failure. We ignore petty strife rather than encourage it. We deal with the real issues of archaeology rather than surface glossiness. And we aim, above all, to produce a magazine to be read: and we believe that in doing so we have produced The Magazine of the Future.' At the moment six issues a year are published. An introductory brochure with information on its aims, purpose and contents, together with subscription details, is available on application from 9 Nassington Road, London NW3 2TX.

247 'Dating in archaeology' *a guide to scientific techniques* by Stuart Fleming (Dent, 1976) explains the various methods now employed to establish the age of archaeological finds and other objects of artistic or historical value. Dendrochronology; radio-carbon dating; radioactive decay techniques; and the thermoluminesce, fission track, obsidian hyradation, archaeomagnetic, and chemical methods, all come under scrutiny. The principles on which each method is based are described, a number of case histories exemplifying their use are highlighted, and the strength and weakness of each process is also indicated. Chapter notes and a general bibliography ensure that the guide is efficiently documented.

248 'Dating methods in archaeology' by Joseph W Michels (Seminar Press, 1973) examines the new scientific techniques of dating now available to archaeologists. Sequence dating by stratigraphic analysis and by seriation, dendrochronology and the archaeomagnetic, radio-carbon, potassium-argon, fission-track and obsidian hydration processes, are all investigated and elucidated.

249 'The dawn of civilization' *the first world survey of human cultures in early times* edited by Stuart Piggott, the initial volume in Thames and Hudson's costly 'Great civilizations' series, was first published in 1961 and is a massive sumptuously illustrated encyclopaedic work intended to 'bring together not only the visible remains of man's past achievements but the less impressive though no less important minutiae of the scholar, the pot-sherds, plans, and sections which are the archaeologist's basic tools no less than his trowel'. Its purpose is 'to tell the story of those peoples who laid the foundations upon which were built all the civilizations of antiquity'. In all there are fourteen chapters, each the work of an acknowledged subject specialist, but each contributing to the general underlying theme of man's development as a social animal as depicted and reconstructed by archaeological discovery.

Contents: 'Introduction: The man made world' (Stuart Piggott); 'The first half-million years: the hunters and gatherers of the stone age' (Grahame Clark); 'Roots in the soil: the beginning of village and urban life' (James Mellaart); 'The birth of written history: civilized life begins, Mesopotamia and Iran' (M E L Mallowan); 'The rise of the god-kings: the first flowering in ancient Egypt' (Cyril Aldred); 'The first merchant venturers: the sea peoples of the Levant' (William Culican); 'Melting pot of peoples: the early settlement of Anatolia' (Seton Lloyd); 'The home of the heroes: the Aegean before the Greeks' (M S F Hood); 'Ancient India: the civilization of a sub-continent' (Sir Mortimer Wheeler); 'A cycle of Cathay: China, the civilization of a single people' (William Watson); 'The sea-locked lands: the diverse traditions of South-East Asia' (Anthony Christie); 'The Royal hordes: the nomad peoples of the steppes' (E D Phillips); 'Barbarian Europe: from the first farmers to the Celts' (T G E Powell); 'The crimson-tipped flower: the birth and growth of New World civilization' (G H S Bushnell); and 'Epilogue: the heritage of man' (Stuart Piggott). A select bibliography arranged by chapter, is included prefaced by a note which reads: 'In a subject as necessarily technical as archaeology, and in a book as all-embracing as *The dawn of civilization*, it would be impossible to give anything like a complete bibliography. The selection . . . has been made primarily with an eye to availability, and wherever possible general works in the most common European languages have been given preference. However, in certain areas of the world—China, Russia, and South East Asia for example, such summaries are rare or non-existent, and thus specialist references have been noted to fill the gaps.'

250 Dawson, William & Sons of Cannon House, Folkestone, Kent, are specialist publishers of learned journal reprints both in conventional form and on microfiche. Several archaeological societies have handed over back runs of their journals to take advantage of the firm's expertise in marketing this type of material. Their back issues department holds the largest stock of scientific, technical and scholarly journals certainly in England and probably in Europe. A pamphlet, *Available books and journals on theology, archaeology and ecclesiastical history, local records* is available from the above address. There is also a world-wide subscription service for current journals. Dawsons of Pall Mall, the antiquarian booksellers, are an associated company.

251 'Degree course guide: history' is published every two years by Hobsons Press, Bateman Street, Cambridge for Careers Research and Advisory Centre Cambridge (CRAC), providing comparative information about first degree courses in history and archaeology at British universities, polytechnics and colleges. In addition to the list of courses available, information is also given on the different approaches to the subject, teaching methods, seminars and tutorials, examinations, drop out rates, continuous assessment, and dissertations. Other topics discussed are course contents, language requirements, entrance and selection procedures, and grants. For information concerning postgraduate courses reference should be made to the centre's annual publication, *Graduate studies.*

252 The Department of the Environment as the successor of the Ministry of Public Building and Works (July 1962-November 1970), the Ministry of Works (1941-1962), and HM Office of Works (Prior to 1941), derives its archaeological powers and functions from a series of parliamentary acts beginning with the Ancient Monuments Protection Act 1882, by which for the first time the government acknowledged its responsibilities for ancient monuments and the Commissioner of Works was empowered to acquire by purchase, gift or bequest any monument mentioned in the accompanying schedule to the act and also to accept the guardianship of monuments remaining in private hands. Guardianship was defined as responsibility for 'the fencing, repairing, cleansing, covering-in, or doing any other act or thing which may be required for the purpose of repairing any monument or protecting the same from decay or injury'. This act also decreed that one or more inspectors should be appointed to report to the commissioner 'on the condition of ancient monuments and on the best method of preserving the same'.

The Ancient Monuments Consolidation and Amendment Act 1913 strengthened the provisions relating to the purchase and guardianship of monuments and outlined the procedure to be followed in the process of 'scheduling', ruling that landowners must give three months notice if they intended to demolish or alter monuments. If, at the end of the three months statutory period, the owner could not be dissuaded from his intention, then as a last resort the 1913 act enabled a Preservation Order to be issued. The Commissioner was authorized to set up one or more Ancient Monuments Boards to include representatives from appropriate archaeological and architectural institutions whose duty it would be to advise on the scheduling of monuments. Subsequent legislation followed in 1931, 1953, and in 1972 when the Field Monuments Act provided means whereby financial aid could be given to landowners for the care of monuments of no beneficial use which in the opinion of the Secretary of State were in danger of injury in the course of agriculture or forestry. The full story of the early legislation is told in Grahame Clark's 'Archaeology and the state', *Antiquity*, VIII(32) December 1934: 414-428 whilst B H St J O'Neils' 'Ancient monuments and historic buildings: the function of the Ministry of Works', *The archaeological newsletter*, 3(8) February 1951: 121-124 and 3(9) March 1951: 137-141 traces the growth of the powers granted to the ministry and outlines their meaning, scope, and limitations. Chapter IX 'The state as guardian of the past', in Sir Harold Emmerson's *The Ministry of Works*, published in Allen and Unwin's 'The New Whitehall series' in 1956, presents an authoritative account of the ministry's responsibilities and its internal organization at the time of writing.

The reorganization of the former Ministry of Public Building and Works and the Ministry of Housing into a new super-ministry in 1970 offered an opportunity to bring together the Inspectorate of Ancient Monuments concerned with the preservation of monuments under the Ancient Monuments Acts and the Building Investigators concerned with the listing of Historic Buildings under the Planning Acts in a new Directorate of Ancient Monuments and Historic Buildings. The chief inspector and his staff assumed responsibility for scheduling monuments of all periods and types (unless they were churches in ecclesiastical use or inhabited buildings) whose preservation they considered to be of national improtance.

Two inspectors are responsible for the monuments in guardianship, for the preservation of archaeological evidence, the supervision of excavations, establishing on-site museums, the publication of guidebooks and postcards, and advising private landowners, in each of three geographical regions (North, Midlands, South) into which England is divided. Nowadays the Inspectorate rarely conducts excavations itself although the 1931 Act authorized them to do so and during the war the construction of various defence sites encouraged them to take a more active role in this area. An illustrated booklet, *War and archaeology in Britain:*

the excavation of ancient sites and the preservation of historic buildings
(HMSO, 1947) is a brief record of the ministry's wartime activities. An
alternative source is B H St J O'Neils' 'War and archaeology in Britain',
Antiquaries journal, XXVIII, 1948: 20-44. But since the war excavations
under the aegis of the department have increased enormously, so much
so that it has become standard practice for the Inspectorate to contract
out the actual digging on an agency basis. A full review of the work of
the Directorate is to be found in Andrew Saunders' 'The state archaeology
service', *Current archaeology* IV(7) No 42, January 1974: 204-208 which
includes two diagrams, one indicating how the department's overall professional team of archaeologists, architectural historians, and scientists
is related to other sections of the Directorate and to the wider range of
the department's responsibilities, and the other providing a closer analysis
of the division of duties within the Inspectorate itself. Mr Saunders'
conclusion is that 'while the resources . . . may not, in every case, match
those of state archaeological services in other countires, it may be claimed
that Britain possesses a fully integrated and coordinated government archaeological organization'. That is as may be but certainly the department
is the largest single employer of archaeological students and workers in
Britain.

As a response to the apparent crisis in rescue excavation, and no doubt
influenced by the pressure of RESCUE (*qv*) it was announced at a meeting of field archaeologists convened by the Department in February 1973
that a number of regional units were to be set up in different parts of the
country whose functions were to include the maintenance of an archaeological archive; accomplishing a close liaison with local authority planning departments; recommending sites for preservation; supervising rescue
operations and publishing the results of these in accordance with regional
and national policies; the coordination of amateur activities; and the
effective maintenance of high professional standards. The text of the
official statement of 20 September 1973 concerning the new arrangements for rescue archaeology and the allocation of extra funds for excavation is printed as Appendix A in *Archaeology in Britain 1973-1974*.
Appendix B contains the text of the ministerial statement of 23 May
1974 which sketches the new regional basis whilst Appendix C consists
of a diagram of the administrative structure. All three appendices are
also printed in *Archaeology and government* (*qv*).

Thirteen Area Archaeological Advisory Committees for England were
established—North of England, Yorkshire and Humberside, North-West
England, East Midlands, West Midlands, East Anglia, Cambridge/Essex/

Herts, South Midlands, Avon/Gloucester/Somerset, South-East England, Wessex, and Greater London—to assist the department on survey and excavation policy and priorities, on the applications received for grants, and on joint resources to support the early publication of excavation reports. At first these proposals met with a generally warm welcome, it seemed that a truly national archaeological service at least for rescue excavations was about to come into existence but later a measure of disillusionment set in, the Council for British Archaeology for one feared that this comprehensive scheme was in danger of being abandoned in favour of a rather less structured plan than was originally envisaged. Michael Jarrett's 'A revolution in British archaeology', *Antiquity*, XLVII (187) September 1973: 193-196 is especially instructive for its investigation of the budget and manpower required. This network of advisory committees came into operation in 1975.

The department's powers regarding the listing of buildings stem from the Historic Buildings and Ancient Monuments Act 1953, Town and Country Planning Act 1962, Local Authorities (Historic Buildings) Act 1962, Civic Amenities Act 1967, and Town and Country Planning Act 1968. Four criteria are used in compiling the lists of buildings of special historic or architectural interest: the value of a building as an illustration of a type or in social and economic historical terms, its technological importance, its links with famous people or events, and its value in association with other buildings. Its features and those of other structures fixed to it or forming part of the land on which it stands are also allowed to be considered—this includes machinery and equipment and so of distinct significance in the industrial archaeology field. The department's inspectors first compile provisional lists which classify buildings in three grades: Grade 1 includes buildings of outstanding interest: Grade 2 buildings of special interest which warrant every effort to preserve them; and Grade 3 which are considered important enough to be brought to the attention of local authorities so that the case for preserving them may be fully discussed. Under the Civic Amenities Act 1967 local planning authorities may designate areas of special architectural or historic interest as Conservation Areas. Statutory lists are based on the provisional lists but are by no means identical—particular cases may have been redesignated. The practical effects of listing buildings are limited, it does not imply that even Grade 1 buildings *will* be preserved, simply that its demolition will be delayed until its case has been fully examined. Funds are not automatically available although the department may make grants for the repair or maintenance of Grade 1 buildings. Local
124

authorities on the other hand may make grants or loans for any building considered to be of interest, listed or not. In cases where the Secretary of State concludes that reasonable steps are not being taken for the proper preservation of listed buildings he may authorize local authorities to acquire them by a compulsory purchase order. Listing buildings is not by any means a quick process but a building preervation order with an effective delaying period of six months can be served on owners in an emergency. Further details and an actual case history may be found in section two, 'Industrial archaeology and the law' in Kenneth Hudson's *A pocketbook for industrial archaeologists* (1976). R Gilyard-Beer's 'The Ministry of Public Building and Works: museums and monuments', *Museums journal*, 70(2) September 1970: 58-60 outlines the department's responsibilities in this area. The department's library houses the largest single collection of air photographs in the United Kingdom including those taken by the Royal Air Force from 1944 onwards and the Ordnance Survey material to 1966.

Publications: Conserving the past for the future, a profusely illustrated booklet available gratis, is designed for the general public and describes in broad terms the work of the department. Topics discussed include the identification and recording of documents and their scheduling, conservation areas, grants and payments, and there is an interesting final section on the skills employed in research and preservation work. Other publications noticed separately elsewhere in this handbook include *Illustrated regional guides to ancient monuments* (6 vols), *Archaeological excavations, Ancient monuments in England*, and the *List and map of historic monuments in the care of the department . . . open to the public*. A vast number of official guides to buildings and monuments in the care of the department are listed in *Sectional list no 27 ancient monuments and historic buildings*, last revised as from 1 April 1975. Several regional illustrated brochures on historic places in the department's care are also available gratis. Since 1971 the Departmental Library Services has prepared *An annual list of publications*. Mention must be made of the *Season ticket to the history of Britain*, valid for one year from the date of issue, which allows holders free and unlimited entry to all the monuments in the care of the department and open to the public in England, Scotland and Wales. At the time of writing this costs £2.00 for adults and 75p for children under the age of sixteen (United States and Canada $4.00 and $1.50) and can only be described as one of the few copper-bottom bargains still to be found in an uncertain world. Enquiries should be directed to the Department of the Environment (AMHB/P), RM G1, 25 Savile Row, London W1.

253 'Department of the Environment annual list of publications 1975' gives full details of all publications of more than local interest and available to the public issued by the department. There are sections for departmental publications, acts, statutory instruments, department circulars, the publications of the department's research stations, and for maps, all arranged under alphabetical subject headings of which 'Ancient monuments, historic buildings and archaeological remains' is one. Previous lists 1971-1974 are still available from the DoE Sub-library building, 6 Victoria Road, South Ruislip, Middx.

254 'Department of the Environment archaeological reports' were introduced in 1956 as a definitive series of reports of major excavations on outstanding monuments in the care of the department, and of equally important rescue excavations of archaeological sites in advance of their destruction by modern development. Titles published and forthcoming in numerical order include *Excavations at Jarlshof, Shetland* (J R C Hamilton); *Excavations at Clausentum, Southampton 1951-54* (M Aylwin Cotton and P W Gathercole); *Excavations on defence sites 1939-1945 mainly neolithic-Bronze age* (W F Grimes); *The West Kennet long barrow excavations 1955-56* (Stuart Piggott); *The Romano-British cemetery at Trentholme Drive, York* (Leslie P Wenham and others); *Excavations at Clickhimin, Shetland* (J R C Hamilton); *Yeavering: an Anglo-British centre of early Northumbria* (Brian Hope-Taylor); *Excavations at Chew Valley Lake, Somerset* (P A Rahtz); and *Excavations at Winterton Roman villa and other Roman sites, North Lincolnshire 1958-1961* (I M Stead). Descriptive notes and an order form are contained in an illustrated pull-out, semi-stiff brochure available either from the Department or from Her Majesty's Stationery Office. J R C Hamilton is the general editor.

255 The Derbyshire Archaeological Society, formerly the Derbyshire Archaeological and Natural History Society, was instituted 'to examine, preserve, and illustrate the archaeology and natural history of the County of Derbyshire' at a large and influential meeting at the Midland Hotel, Derby in January 1878. It is now organized in four active sections *viz* an archaeological research group, architectural, industrial archaeological, and local history sections, all of which arrange fieldwork visits, and lecture programmes, in addition to those organized by the main society. A short-lived junior section was suspended in 1974. The first issue of the *Journal of the Derbyshire archaeological and natural history society* was dated January 1879, it officially became the *Derbyshire archaeological*
126

journal in 1961 (vol LXXXI) at the same time as changing to a larger, quarto format to facilitate the inclusion of modern excavation reports. Successive editors have been hospitable in accommodating lists of the ancient monuments in the county scheduled under the successive Ancient Monuments Acts. These appeared under various titles annually 1932-1938 (Thomas L Tudor), again in 1950, and a complete 'List of scheduled ancient monuments in Derbyshire to 31st December 1957', arranged by parish and accompanied with notes and bibliographical references, LXXVII, 1957: 30-37, and supplemented in the 1961 volume (J P Heathcote). Tudor also contributed 'Minor monuments and lesser antiquities of Derbyshire on or near the highways, disused roads and ancient boundaries' in LV ns vol VIII, 1934: 64-78 and LVI ns IX, 1935: 80-87. These were in a classified order, according to type of monument, giving location complete with Ordnance Survey one inch map references, with descriptive notes. Other articles of general interest include D V Fowkes' 'The records of the Derbyshire archaeological society', XC 1970: 1-3, an indication of the wide range of archival material deposited in the Derbyshire Record Office, and A N Tunley's 'A progress report on conservation areas in Derbyshire', XC 1970: 72-93, divided into four parts, an exposition on the implications of the Civic Amenities Act 1967, a list of proposed conservation areas submitted in May 1969, the resolution of the County Council on policy in this matter, and some notes on 21 areas designated in January 1971. A *Complete index to the journal vols 1-25 (1879-1903)* was published and in 1954 there appeared *A subject index to the journal of the Derbyshire archaeological and natural history society 1879-1952.* A subject and author index to volumes 73-82 (1953-1962) was printed in the *Journal* LXXXIV 1964: 139-149 and later issued as an offprint. At the time of writing the society is engaged upon the preliminary work towards a history of its early years in preparation for its centenary in 1978.

256 '**Deserted medieval villages'** *studies* edited by Maurice Beresford and John G Hurst (Lutterworth Press, 1971) must be the starting point for all archaeological and historical research into the subject. The editor's introduction affirms that this is one area where it is absolutely necessary for the historian and the archaeologist to work in conjunction 'since written evidences and archaeological evidences (including in this case fieldwork also) may each be available, occasionally overlapping and confirming each other but more commonly proving supplementary'.

Contents Part One: England 'A review of historical research' (M W Beresford), a long, critical survey of the literature down to 1968; 'A review

127

of archaeological research (to 1968)' (J G Hurst) which reports on the origins of medieval archaeology and the formation of the Deserted Medieval Villages Research Group; 'Gazetteer of excavations at medieval house and village sites (to 1968)' (J G Hurst) listing 290 sites where excavation or recording has taken place arranged by county: 'An historian's appraisal of archaeological research' (M W Beresford), a sympathetic treatment of the constraints imposed on the archaeologist's work and an appreciation of the results yielded; 'County gazetteers of deserted medieval villages (known in 1968)' (J Sheail) arranged by historical counties; 'Select bibliography, England' (J G Hurst), a conspectus of published historical and archaeological work in alphabetical order of authors. *Part two: Scotland* 'The study of deserted medieval settlements in Scotland (to 1968)' 1 Rural settlement (H Fairhurst), 2 The peasant-house (J G Dunbar); 'Select bibliography, Scotland' (J G Dunbar and H Fairhurst). *Part three: Wales* 'The study of deserted medieval settlements in Wales (to 1968)' (L A S Butler), a historical introduction; 'Gazetteer of excavated sites in Wales' and 'Select bibliography Wales' (L A S Butler). *Part four: Ireland* 'The study of deserted medieval settlements in Ireland (to 1968)' (R E Glasscock); 'Gazetteer of deserted towns, rural-boroughs, and nucleated settlements in Ireland' and 'Select bibliography, Ireland' (R E Glasscock). Appendix 1, prints the texts of two memoranda submitted on behalf of the Deserted Medieval Villages Research Group to the Inspectorate of Ancient Monuments regarding the preservation of sites in England and Scotland. Appendix 2 is a fieldwork questionnaire offering guidance to those interested in carrying out fieldwork and providing them with an opportunity to make a permanent record of their work in a form which could be filed at the group's offices for general access.

257 Devon Archaeological Exploration Society came into being at a meeting in Exeter Guildhall in November 1928 with the object of promoting active archaeological research in the county. In the following February the society became affiliated to the Devonshire association. Volumes of *Proceedings* were published until 1962 at which point the system of volumes and parts was discontinued in order to simplify bibliographical reference and to avoid confusion between notional dates of issue and actual dates of publication. From 1963 each separate issue bears a serial number and a year of publication only so that volume V, Parts 5 and 6 1957/8 (actually published in 1962) will be known in future as No 20, 1962. A change of title to *Transactions* was effected at the same time but after only three issues it reverted to *Proceedings* because of the similarity to the *Transactions* of the Devonshire association. E H Rogers' 'What the Devon archaeological exploration society has achieved in its first twenty-five years', V(1) 1953:3-7 considers the society's archaeological work. Other papers of interest include Aileen Fox's 'Prehistoric and Roman settlement in Devon and West Somerset', 27, 1969: 37-48; and L V Grinsell's 'The barrows of North Devon', 28, 1970: 95-129.

258 Devon Committee for Rescue Archaeology a sub-committee of the Devon Archaeological Society, has assumed responsibility for all aspects of rescue archaeology in the county excluding Exeter and Plymouth.

259 Devonshire Association for the Advancement of Science, Literature and Art was established in 1862 at the instigation of William Pengelly. The objects of the association were 'to give a stronger impulse and a more systematic direction to scientific inquiry, and to promote the intercourse of those who cultivate science, literature or art in different parts of Devonshire, with one another, and with others'. Because the terms of reference were at times interpreted a little too widely, the subject of papers accepted for the *Report and transactions* were limited from 1876 onwards to those related specifically to Devonshire. Science tended to predominate at first but in later years historical and archaeological papers have become more and more prominent. As a matter of deliberate policy the association's annual meetings are held at a different venue every year thus keeping interest alive all over the county. In 1912 the Ancient Monuments Committee was appointed to prepare a list of monuments in Devon which it was considered desirable should be handed over with the consent of their owners to the guardianship of the Office of Works. A Barrows Committee was also in existence for many years. In 1926 a general feeling that the association had relapsed into a publishing society which met for an annual picnic led to a reassessment of its aims and purposes. As a result local branches were formed as were specialised sections for the benefit of members with particular interests. One of these was the archaeological section formed in 1928-29 with the object of studying the archaeology of the county by fieldwork and excavation and by the publication of material already found but improperly recorded, its principal interest being prehistoric archaeology. Almost at the same time an independent Devon Archaeological Exploration Society was formed and affiliated to the association, the two institutions have always worked very closely one with the other and each is represented on the other's committee. The association's archaeological section was dissolved as 'it was felt that excavation could be more conveniently organized and carried out by the DAES'. An archaeology and early history section came into existence later and prepared an annual report, printed in the *Transactions*, on archaeological remains discovered and acquired by a public museum. In November 1969 an industrial archaeology section was formed 'to promote the discovery, recording and understanding of the physical remains of industry and technology in relation to the county of Devon'. W Harpley's 'A short account of the origins of the association' *Report and transactions* XLIV, 1912: 154-156 is vastly extended in Hilda Walker's 'The Story of the Devonshire Association 1862-1962', XCIV, 1962: 42-106, a year by year summary of events and accomplishments worthy of its theme. Mrs Hester Forbes Julian's 'William Pengelly FRS, FGS, father of the Devonshire Association', XLIV, 1912: 157-191; XLV, 1913: 424-444; and XLVII, 1915: 257-284 is also esssential reading. The *Report and transactions*, published annually since 1862, include papers and reports from branches and sections. *A key to the transactions of the Devonshire Association I-LX* by R Pearse Chope was published in 1928; a *General index* to vols I-LX, LXI-LXX, and LXXI-LXXX has appeared at regular intervals.

260 '**A dictionary of archaeology**' compiled by Warwick Bray and David Trump was published by Allen Lane, The Penguin Press in 1970. It was intended particularly for 'the many people who have been made aware of archaeology . . . but who have found difficulty in taking their interest further. The necessary technical terms are intimidating, and many archaeological books assume that the reader already knows more than he in fact does'. Over 1600 entries, photographs and drawings, cover ancient cultures, important sites, artefacts and monuments, technical terms, pioneer archaeologists and modern research, in an attempt to elucidate puzzling and obscure terminology. Seventeen maps and a regional index are included. A Penguin paperback edition was issued in 1972. It was published in the United States as *The American heritage guide to archaeology*.

261 '**The dictionary of national biography**' is mentioned here as a reminder that authoritative accounts of the life and work of all notable antiquarians and archaeologists, many of them written by former colleagues are to be found in the appropriate volume according to their dates of death. Published by Oxford University Press the full series comprises Vols I-XXI A-Z (1884-1901); Vol XXII, an updating supplement; and *Twentieth century DNB* in decennial supplements.

262 '**Digging for history**' *a survey of recent world archaeological discoveries* by Edward Bacon (A and C Black, 1960), had as its purpose 'to record conveniently all the principal archaeological discoveries made since the war; to arrange them geographically . . . to recount and illustrate especially the most interesting or most successful; but also to give as full a picture of world archaeological effort as possible, indicating . . . the significance and intention of each dig; and since this is basic to all, to include a description of some of the new equipment and techniques which science and engineering have made available to archaeologists'. It is a substantial but readable compendium.

263 Diploma in archaeological practice: proposals to establish a diploma of this sort emerged when the controversial British Archaeological Institution (*qv*) project was shelved; they received approval at the Council for British Archaeology's summer meeting in 1975 when a provisional examination board under the chairmanship of Professor Leo Rivet was appointed to devise a detailed syllabus and administrative procedure. The diploma is envisaged as a qualification for full-time but otherwise unqualified field workers, for the serious spare-time archaeologist, or for the honours graduate intent upon a career in field archaeology. Pass or credit grades would be awarded as the result of a combination of examinations, assessment, and the submission of practical work covering a spread of relevant topics *viz* fieldwork, excavation, artefact studies; archaeological evidence and sources, interpretation and presentation, and the structure and academic background of British archaeology. These could be sat singly or collectively; the academic status of the diploma would be judged as coming somewhere between a General Certificate of Education A level and a first degree in archaeology. A number of university extra-mural departments, polytechnics and colleges have expressed more than a passing interest.

264 '**The directing of archaeological excavations**' by John Alexander was published by John Baker in 1970 and offers experienced advice on the wide variety of periods and types of evidence, each with its own problems, that confront directors of excavations. Topics discussed include the education of a field director and his assistants, assessing the problems and planning the excavation, the organization whilst excavations are in progress, the writing and publication of the report, and the field problems of environmental archaeology. The second half of the book expands on the special expertise needed for different types of sites. The Humanities Press Inc of New York are the American publishers.

265 '**The directory of museums**' edited by Kenneth Hudson and Ann Nicholls (Macmillan Press, 1975), a mammoth publication of 860 A4 size pages, presents the essential details of museums the world over—full name and address, opening hours and a brief guide to contents. Coverage includes all museums with permanent collections but not zoos, botanical gardens or historic houses that do not attempt to make either the building or its contents of interest to visitors. Other features include an essay on the museum world today, a glossary, and a classified index of special collections. The directory entries are strictly descriptive and not evaluative but the inclusion of a museum's contents in the classified index signifies editorial opinion that these are of more than average interest and importance. Arrangement is by country.

266 '**Discovering regional archaeology**' is a series of slim, pocket-sized paperback volumes published by Shire Publications, Princes Risborough, Aylesbury, Bucks. They are designed to help the increasing numbers of the general public who find pleasure and instruction in visiting ancient monuments to choose the sites with most to offer the untrained eye. Although of no small value to the hiker or cyclist they cater primarily for the motorist and so list only those sites reasonably close to adequate parking facilities. They are arranged alphabetically by county and each is provided with finding instructions, including Ordnance Survey sheet numbers and National Grid references, and a brief description. Maps and photographs add further interest. An introductory volume, now in a fourth edition, *Discovering archaeology in England and Wales* by James Dyer, editor of the series, discusses the methods used by archaeologists to discover sites, how they dig and date their finds, and suggests ways in which anyone can take part in organized excavations.

Titles: Central England ie Cheshire, Derbyshire, Herefordshire, Leicestershire, Northamptonshire, Nottinghamshire, Rutland, Shropshire, Warwickshire, and Worcestershire (Barry Marsden); *Cotswolds and upper Thames*, Berkshire, Gloucestershire, Oxfordshire (James Dyer); *Eastern England*, Bedfordshire, Buckinghamshire, Cambridgeshire, Essex, Hertfordshire, Huntingdonshire, Lincolnshire, Norfolk, and Suffolk (James Dyer); *North eastern England*, Durham, Northumberland, Yorkshire—East & North Ridings (Barry Marsden); *North western England*, Cumberland, Lancashire, Westmorland, Yorkshire—West Riding and City of York (Barry Marsden); *South eastern England*, Greater London, Hampshire, Kent, Surrey and Sussex (Edward Sammes); *South western England*, Cornwall, Devon and Somerset (Leslie Grinsell); *Wales* (Ilid
132

Anthony); and *Wessex*, Dorset and Wiltshire (Leslie Grinsell and James Dyer).

267 'Discovery and excavation in Scotland' (1956-) is an annual publication of the Scottish Regional Group of the Council for British Archaeology. Its purpose is to list by counties all discoveries in Scotland over the past twelve months. The work of the Ordnance Survey, the Inspectorate of Ancient Monuments, and the Royal Commission on the Ancient and Historical Monuments of Scotland is noticed separately. A Scottish bibliography, arranged by archaeological periods, completes a most useful publication.

268 'Dolphin archaeologies' is a series of books covering a wide range of topics published by the Blandford Press. They present original research enhanced by a wealth of illustrations, for the general reading public in hardback and paperback editions. Titles: *The prehistoric rock art of Argyll* (Ronald Morris); *The megalithic art of the Maltese islands* (Michael Ridley); *Mesolithic cultures of Britain* (Susann Palmer); *New Grange* (G Coffey); *Megaliths, myths and men* (Peter Lancaster Brown); *Pompeii* (Alfonso de Franciscis); *Treasures of Islam* (Philip Bamborough) and *Treasure of China* (Michael Ridley).

269 The Dorset Natural History and Archaeological Society came into existence as the Dorset Natural History and Antiquarian Field Club in March 1875 at an inaugural dinner held at the Digby Hotel, Sherborne. Two papers were read to the twenty or so founder members who attended, one on the aims and objects of natural history field clubs, and the other on the working of some established field clubs. This convivial meeting was the culmination of the efforts of three men, James Buckman, professor of geology and botany, Cirencester Agricultural College, who became secretary; the Rev H H Wood, rector of Holwell, the first treasurer; and J C Mansel-Pleydell, a local landowner and geologist of national repute, the club's president for twenty-seven years.

The objects of the club were 'to promote and encourage interest in the study of the physical sciences and archaeology generally, especially the natural history of the county of Dorset and its antiquities, prehistoric records, and ethnology. It shall use its influence to prevent, as far as possible, the extirpation of rare plants and animals, and to promote the preservation of the antiquities of the county.' The Dorset County Museum became the home of the club in 1883 and in 1928 the two institutions were formally merged into one society. The museum and library are maintained as a centre where objects, records, and reference books are available for public inspection or private research. Winter meetings are held in the library and places of interest inside the county and out are visited during the summer months. The society also takes an active part in archaeological excavations in the county.

Publications: an annual volume of *Proceedings* commenced in 1877 and a regular pattern of contents which in the main still continues started in 1933. First comes an annual review (membership lists, names of officers, reports of meetings, accounts etc), followed by a reports and papers section for the natural sciences and for archaeology and history. This latter division now includes a feature 'archaeological fieldwork' in Dorset for the year, more detailed excavation and other papers. 'Notes on the present condition of the Dorset County Museum', contributed by the curator appeared in Vol 31, 1910: 24-27 and E R Sykes' 'The Dorset county museum, its history and founders' in Vol 63, 1941: 82-91. 'A list of ancient monuments in Dorset scheduled under the Act of 1913' classified under type of monument or structure, compiled by Vere L Oliver, was printed in Vol 50, 1929: 203-206 whilst R A H Farrar's 'A list of scheduled ancient monuments and historic buildings in Dorset' appeared in Vol 74, 1952: 79-84 similarly arranged. 'The work of the Royal Commission on Historical Monuments' (in Dorset) was outlined in Vol 64, 1942: 110-111. Indexes to the *Proceedings* have been issued from time to time: *A general index of the Dorset Field Club Proceedings comprising volumes I-XLI* compiled by Harry Pouncy in 1921, and an *Index to authors of papers etc published in volumes I-LV* probably being of most use. The Society also publishes L V Grinsell's *Dorset barrows*.

270 Douglas, James (1753-1819) published his *Nenia Britannica or a sepulchral history of Great Britain, from the earliest period to the general conversion to Christianity* in parts 1786 to 1793 when it was bound up as a folio. It contained descriptions of British, Roman, and Saxon sepulchral sites and of the contents of several hundred barrows opened under his personal supervision or inspection and was illustrated with aquatints. Douglas' intention had been 'to draw a line between all speculative fancies in antiquities and on hypotheses founded on reason and practical observations' and in this he undoubtedly succeeded although his success did not earn the recognition it deserved, his book met with an unenthusiastic not to say hostile reception. However it marks an important stage in British archaeological studies, he was among the first to call attention
134

to the significance of colour differences in the soil, and he also realised that inscriptions and coins provided the only sure and reliable guide to definite dating. On his death his widow gave his collection of Saxon antiquities to Sir Richard Colt Hoare who in turn eventually passed it on to the Ashmolean Museum. A lively account of James Douglas' background and work is to be found in Ronald Jessup's *The Story of archaeology in Britain* (1954).

271 '**Drawing archaeological finds for publication**' by Conant Brodribb (John Baker, 1970) is designed 'to help beginners, students, and amateur archaeologists to acquire a basic skill in drawing objects by the several processes of printing now in vogue'. Topics discussed include tools and materials, the techniques of drawing archaeological finds, finishing touches, and drawing from photographs.

272 '**The Druids**' by Stuart Piggott, published as volume 63 in Thames and Hudson's 'Ancient peoples and places' series in 1968, draws upon three types of source material to present a dispassionate survey of contemporary factual knowledge of Druidism: archaeological evidence, literary references from Greek and Roman writers, and the antiquarian speculation of the seventeenth and eighteenth centuries.

273 '**The early barrow diggers**' by Barry M Marsden, published in Shire Publications' 'Folk life library' in 1974, describes the careers and methods of the more distinguished of the eighteenth and nineteenth barrow diggers, ranging in time from William Stukeley to General Pitt-Rivers, who were responsible for opening many thousands of ancient burial mounds in Britain during this period.

274 '**Early Christian Ireland**' by Maire and Liam de Paor was the eighth volume of Thames and Hudson's 'Ancient peoples and places' series when it appeared in 1958. It 'places the emphasis on the material manifestations of early Irish culture' and summarises in lively fashion the evidence recovered from the excavations of the previous twenty-five years in which significant strides forward were made. There is an exceedingly detailed bibliography.

275 '**The early Christian monuments of Wales**' by V E Nash-Williams published by the University of Wales Press in 1950 is a comprehensive study of the inscribed and sculptured stone monuments which elucidate this

135

most obscure period in Welsh history. A typological study is followed by a descriptive list county by county.

276 '**The earthen long barrow in Britain**', *an introduction to the study of the funerary practice and culture of the neolithic people of the third millenium BC* by Paul Ashbee (Dent, 1970), constitutes a thorough review of present-day knowledge of these structures, their form and type, size, furnishings and their origin and affinity. There are no less than fourteen appendixes (betraying the university degree dissertation genesis of the work), the first two of which consist of annotated references to the early and modern literature relating to this type of long barrow. There is also an extensive bibliography arranged alphabetically by author.

277 '**East Anglia**' by R Rainbird Clarke, published by Thames and Hudson in the 'Ancient peoples and places' series in 1960, surveys the archaeology of the area period by period. There is a list of easily accessible and well-defined important visible monuments and another of museums containing significant collections of East Anglian archaeological material. It was reprinted by S R Publishers Ltd of East Ardsley, Wakefield, Yorkshire in 1971 with a new introduction by James Wentworth Day.

278 '**East Anglian archaeology**' is the title of a monograph series of archaeological reports published since 1975 in association with the Scole Committee for Archaeology in East Anglia. The reports emanate from the Norfolk Archaeological Unit, the Norwich Survey, and the Suffolk County Council Planning Department, and are printed with the aid of grants from the Department of the Environment and the local authorities concerned and are usually sold at cost price. The series will be the main vehicle for publication for final reports on archaeological excavations and surveys in the region. Copies and further details are available from the Centre of East Anglian Studies, University of East Anglia, Earlham Hall, Norwich, Norfolk.

279 Egypt Exploration Society was founded as the Egypt Exploration Fund by Amelia Blandford Edwards and Reginald Stuart Poole at a meeting of British Egyptologists at the British Museum in 1882 to promote the study of the history, religion, and culture of ancient Egypt both by excavation and by scientific publication of its monuments. In its early days its support was crucial to William Flinders-Petrie but eventually he left the society to found his own Egyptian Research Account. Since the war the society has concentrated its activities on the completion of an archaeological survey of Egypt and on its excavations at Saqqara. In the 1960s it also played a major part in the response to Unesco's appeal to salvage sites before they were engulfed in the waters of the Aswan Dam. Despite almost continuous financial stringencies the society manages to sustain a heavy publishing programme of excavation memoirs, volumes of the archaeological survey, and a series of Graeco-Roman memoirs, not to mention the annual *Journal of Egyptian archaeology* (*qv*). The society also published Warren R Dawson's *Who was who in Egyptian archaeology* (1951).

280 'Elek archaeology and anthropology', a recently introduced series, intends to stress broad ethnographic and anthropological themes on the premise that archaeology is not simply confined to prehistory or that anthropology is solely concerned with the study of man as an animal. Consequently works on the art and technology of ancient and modern cultures, especially from lesser known regions, are expected to be included. The first volume, John G Evan's *Environment of early man in the British Isles*, appeared in 1975. Other titles in the series include *Medieval Italian pottery* (David Whitehouse); *Roman fortifications of the Saxon shore* (Stephen Johnson); *Aborigine culture of South-East Australia* (R J Lampert and J V S Megaw); *Problems for Greek architects* (J J Coulton); *Parthian art* (Malcolm Colledge). and *The archaeology of ships* (Peter Marsden). Further titles are in preparation. The series editor is J V S Megaw.

281 Emery, W B (1903-1971) devoted his career to Egyptian archaeology and his name will always be associated with the excavations at Saqqara and the search for Imhotep's tomb which he directed for the Egypt Exploration Society in the 1950s and 1960s. H B Smith's 'Walter Bryan Emery' *Journal of Egyptian archaeology*, 57, 1971: 190-201 provides an outline of his life and work and E P Uphill compiled a bibliography of his writings for the same *Journal*, 58, 1972: 296-299.

282 'Encyclopaedia of antiquities and elements of archaeology' *classical and medieval* by Thomas Dudley Fosbroke published in two volumes in 1825' furnishes readers of all kinds with a variety of useful, often curious information, scattered through rare and expensive works'. It was arranged in a series of narrative chapters 'for the advantage of continuous reading' (with an ample index to 'preserve its Encyclopaedic utility') and is designed as an epitome of archaeology. The dedicated antiquarian will find 'Architecture of the Britons, Anglo-Saxons, Normans, and English' (chapter VI) and 'Barrows, camps, earthworks, roads, rude stone-works etc alphabetically arranged' (chapter XI) of some slight historical value as an indication of the state of antiquarian studies in early nineteenth-century England.

283 '**Encyclopaedia of archaeological excavation in the Holy Land**' is published in four volumes to mark the fiftieth anniversary of the Israel Exploration Society and is designed to aid students of Palestinian archaeology 'towards a fuller understanding of the recent discoveries by incorporating evaluations of the archaeological results and achievements and discussing the dilemmas and difficulties they pose.' It covers all excavations over the last hundred years within the historic borders of the Holy Land on both sides of the River Jordan and its chronological limits extend from the prehistoric period down to the times of the Crusaders. Earlier excavations are described from the original records of the people involved whilst much of the recent work is discussed by those who actually directed operations. The arrangement is alphabetical by site: each site being closely identified in its geographical location with analyses of the objects and artefacts discovered and an explanation of their historic and Biblicial significance. A bibliography is included under each entry. There are also a number of composite entries. Published in England by Oxford University Press and in the United States by Prentice-Hall, volume one Abu Ghosh-Dothan appeared in 1975, volume two Eboda—Jerusalem in 1976, the third and fourth volumes in 1977.

284 '**The English archaeologists' handbook**' by Henry Godwin (1867) was designed 'to facilitate the study of archaeology by removing some of the obstacles which obstruct the path of the student, arising from the inaccessibility of the information which he requires'. Annotated lists of sepulchres, tribes, coins, Roman towns, British chiefs and rulers, Danish antiquities etc, etc are arranged in broad chronological divisions: prehistoric, Celtic, British antiquities, Romano-British, Anglo-Saxon, and Norman and medieval periods. It was also intended to act as a manual for the student of history and as a companion to the English tourist. There seems to be no contemporary equivalent publication.

285 '**The erosion of history**' *archaeology and planning in towns* edited by Carolyn M Heighway is a study of historic towns affected by modern
138

development in England, Wales and Scotland published by the Urban Research Committee of the Council for British Archaeology in May 1972. It reflects the alarm of professional archaeologists that if sufficient precautions are not taken immediately our most important historic towns (*ie* those that reached urban status before 1750) will be lost to archaeology within the next twenty years, and is an attempt to convince the government that existing procedures and legislation are inadequate and not sufficiently effective to ensure the preservation of a satisfactory record of urban history. The report is thorough, systematic, well-documented, and determined in its recommendations which include some weighty points requiring legislation. The conclusion that the only effective way to prevent the destruction without record of the archaeology of historic town centres 'is to secure by law that the archaeological potential of any proposed development should be considered when planning permission is granted' is obviously of crucial and fundamental importance. Other very pertinent recommendations are that an archaeologically credited person should be given access to building sites with archaeological deposits and objects; that there should be provision in law to secure time for excavation if required; and that in the case of a site of particular importance a proportion of the contract sum should be devoted to archaeological purposes costed in advance as part of the site's operating expenses. A number of special cases are cited—Abingdon, Cambridge, Gloucester, Hull, Ruthin (Denbighshire) and Stirling.

286 Essex Archaeological Society has striven valiantly over the last two decades to wrench itself into the archaeological world of the twentieth century. Founded in 1852 to promote the study and preservation of the history and antiquities of the county, it found itself in the late 1950s facing the strong possibility of dissolution only a few years after it had celebrated its centenary. Registered paid-up members were down to three hundred at a time when general public interest in archaeology was booming, publication of the society's *Transactions* had sadly declined in frequency, and its outmoded format and appearance spoke volumes for the state the society found itself in. The first sign of the desperately needed renaissance appeared on the publication of the first part of the third series of the *Transactions* in a larger format in 1961. This contained a hard-hitting preface 'The second hundred years', by J S Brinson, taking stock 'in the light of the past, with an eye to the future'. An immediate overhaul of the society.s activities was set in train, more frequent meetings were arranged over a far wider area of the county, a programme of practical archaeology in the field was embarked upon, and the membership promptly doubled. A great leap forward was accomplished and the revised objectives of the society have a modern ring about them: (1) To promote the study of the archaeology and history of the county of Essex; (2) To collect and publish the results of such studies in annual issues of *Transactions* and other publications. (3) To make researches, undertake excavations and field surveys, and assist in the preservation and recording of ancient monuments, earth works, historic buildings, documents, and objects of archaeological interest and importance; (4) To provide library facilities for members and approved students. In 1972 the *Transactions* were renamed *Essex archaeology and history* with the specific purpose of recording the story of the county and making it more widely known. Two index volumes have been published: a *General index to the transactions vols I-V (1858-1873) and vols I-V new series (1878-1895)* in 1900, and *vols VI-XV new series 1896-1920* in 1926.

287 Evans, Sir Arthur John (1851-1941) is remembered for his uncovering of the Minoan civilization at Knossos in Crete 1899-1907. Of especial significance was the discovery of thousands of incised tablets in the Linear B script not deciphered until Michael Ventris succeeded in the early 1950s. Evans's most important publications are *Scripta Minoa* vol 1 (1909), vol 2 edited by J L Myres (1952) and *The palace at Minos: a comparative account of the successive stages of the early Cretan civilization as illustrated by the discoveries at Knossos*, four volumes in six, (1921-1936). Evans was criticised for not releasing many of the tablets for examination, thus seriously impeding their decipherment, and in 1960 doubts were expressed as to the accuracy of his scholarship when it was suggested that his monumental history of the palace had not always accurately reflected the excavation journal maintained by his assistant. Evans was Keeper of the Ashmolean Museum 1884-1908 during which time he was instrumental in reorganising the collections. Joan Evans' *Time and chance: the story of Arthur Evans and his forbears* (1953) is an authoritative account of his life and work.

288 Evans, Sir John (1823-1908), father of Arthur Evans, was the author of two standard works, *The ancient stone implements, weapons and ornaments of Great Britain and Ireland* (1872) and *The ancient bronze implements, weapons and ornaments of Great Britain and Ireland* (1881) which established the sequence of these implement forms.

140

289 'The excavation of Roman and Medieval London' by W F Grimes (Routledge, 1968) summarises the excavations undertaken in the City of London under the auspices of the Roman and Medieval London Excavation Council, established on the initiative of the Society of Antiquaries in 1946 to take advantage of the widespread destruction caused by German bombing in the second world war. The Roman fort of Cripplegate, the London Wall, and the celebrated Temple of Mithras receive special attention but excavations at various minor sites are not overlooked. Traces of the medieval buildings of London are infinitely more difficult to uncover but an impressive number of secular and ecclesiastical sites explored by the Council are described. All inexperienced archaeologists should make a point of reading Professor Grimes' introductory chapter which sets out the problems involved, the methods adopted to overcome them and the interpretation of results, in exemplary fashion. Over a hundred photographs and fifty or so line drawings (many of which were completed on site) elucidate the text which furthers to no small extent our understanding of the remains of early London.

290 'Expedition' *the magazine of archaeology/anthropology* replaced the Bulletin of the University Museum, University of Pennsylvania in 1958. It is a lavishly illustrated quarterly publication designed to appeal to nonspecialist readers, its scope is excavation world-wide, highlighting the work of the university museum especially. Occasionally a special issue appears devoted to a particular theme, for example the Fall 1962 issue focused on Biblical archaeology and that of Fall 1965 on Tikal: ten years study of Maya ruins in the lowlands of Guatemala.

291 Fausset, Brian (1720-1776), the excavator of an incredible number of Roman and Saxon graves in East Kent, kept a journal of his operations in which he meticulously recorded their contents. This remained in manuscript until it was edited by Charles Roach Smith and published under the title *Inventorium Sepulchrale: an account of some antiquities dug up at Gilton, Kingston, Sibertswold, Barfriston, Beakesbourne, Chartham and Crundale in the county of Kent from AD 1757 to AD 1773* (1856). Fausset's collection of antiquities, especially notable for its Anglo-Saxon ornaments, was offered for sale to the British Museum by his descendants in 1853. The trustees declined to purchase the collection which ultimately found a home in Liverpool. Thomas Wright's 'On Anglo-Saxon antiquities, with a particular reference to the Fausset collection', *Transactions of the Historical Society of Lancashire and Cheshire*, VII, 1854-55: 1-39 is a useful source.

292 'Field archaeology' by R J C Atkinson, originally published by Methuen in 1946, is an elementary manual designed to provide 'an outline of the general principles and methods of research work which are universally applicable and with which the amateur student should be familiar in order that his early experience in the field may profit both himself and those men whose guidance he seeks'. It refers throughout to work within the British Isles and emphasizes especially small-scale operations conducted by only a few workers where the amateur archaeologist may best be of use. It is arranged in four sections: Search for evidence (fieldwork and excavation); The record of the evidence (archaeological survey, recording, photography); The interpretation of the evidence; and Publication. A glossary of archaeological terms and a select bibliography complete a compact introduction which must have been the constant companion of successive post-war generations of budding archaeologists.

293 'Field archaeology in Britain' by John Coles (Methuen, 1972) is intended as 'a guide to some of the techniques of observation and recording of the material remains of man's past, to the processes of their recovery and conservation, and to the aims and methods of archaeologists in treating the evidence' for those 'who may wish to understand the techniques of archaeology, and the reasons behind them, who will on occasion assist in small or large-scale excavations and field projects, or who will sometimes undertake their own fieldwork . . .' There are six sections: Prehistoric archaeology (the role of the amateur and the professional); Discovery of the evidence (fieldwork, aerial photography, detection devices); Recording of sites (maps, surveying practices, note-taking); Excavation; Understanding the evidence; and Organization of prehistoric archaeology in Britain. Two book lists are appended: general books on archaeological procedures and guides to types of field monuments and finds; and an annotated list of excavation and field survey reports selected from recent issues of national journals to indicate different approaches to sites and areas. The American distributors are Barnes and Noble.

294 'Field archaeology in future: the crisis and the challenge' is an essay by Peter Fowler included in *Archaeology and the landscape* (1974). Three facts and two assumptions form the keynote of the essay *viz*: the rate, extent and completeness of the destruction of archaeological sites of all periods is increasing so rapidly that few intact sites will remain by AD 2000 unless positive action is taken now; that many more sites exist than all previous estimates have indicated, implying that the scale of
142

current predictable destruction is and will be absolutely greater; and that present archaeological resources are inadequate to cope with this situation (facts); that many people think it worthwhile to do something; and that the nature and scope of archaeology are generally understood (assumptions). In fact the author has grave doubts about the second assumption. 'The crisis in British field archaeology' the memorandum submitted by RESCUE to the Department of the Environment is appended together with 'Archaeology in the seventies: the challenge' originally published in the December 1970 issue of the *Bulletin* of the Bristol Archaeological Research Group.

295 'Field archaeology in Great Britain' (Ordnance Survey, 5ed 1973) outlines for the beginner 'the physical characteristics and the cultural and historical contexts of such antiquities as may be encountered in Britain, with the object of increasing the competence of the private field archaeologist and of helping the public towards a better understanding of the remains of the past which are still to be seen about us'. The work begins with a general chapter on archaeological field work and a short section on time scales and then proceeds to present the various types of field antiquities in chronological order: prehistoric, Roman period, dark ages and the early medieval period, medieval and post-medieval periods and industrial archaeology, ending with a miscellaneous chapter on linear earthworks, trackways, open-air cooking places and mazes and cockpits. Previous editions of this work should not be discarded lightheartedly: the present bibliography, separately arranged in chapter order, omits many references to pioneer works on field archaeology which were previously included but which are now judged to be more suitable for the advanced field archaeologist rather than for the beginner.

296 'Field archaeology: its origins and development', an essay by Paul Ashbee, takes a close look at the foremost figures among British topographers and antiquarians who pioneered field archaeology in these islands over four centuries from John Leland and William Camden down to O G S Crawford and L V Grinsell. The author concludes that 'almost every advance in method and knowledge has been the result of the enterprise of particular persons who have then stimulated others to work along the same line'. The historical background of field archaeology is also noted. An extensive list of references and a chronological plan of the development of field archaeology enhance the essay which is to be found in *Archaeology and the landscape* edited by Peter Fowler (1972).

297 'Field survey in British archaeology' edited by Elizabeth Fowler (C B A 1972) contains the papers given at a three-day conference on 'Field survey and archaeology' held in September 1971 at Southampton University to re-emphasize the importance of non-excavational fieldwork. The papers express current and past attitudes to fieldwork and give examples of results and local applications and interpretations. *Contents*: Section 1 Organisation and methods—'The individual fieldworker' (L V Grinsell); 'A county society: The Cornwall checklists' (Peter Sheppard); 'A museum: Oxfordshire' (Don Benson); 'A university department of archaeology' (Barry Cunliffe); 'A university department of adult education' (George Jobey). Section 2 Analysis and interpretation—'Flint collecting' (J J Wymer); 'Field archaeology on the M5 motorway 1969-71' (P J Fowler); 'Air photography: some implications in the south of England' (H C Bowen); 'Maps, documents and fieldwork' (C C Taylor); 'Demographic implications' (R J C Atkinson). 'The government organization of field archaeology in Britain', an appendix compiled by A H A Hogg, presents a convenient summary of the statutory duties of the government departments responsible for the recording, protection, and preservation of field antiquities *ie* the national museums, the Ancient Monuments Inspectorate, the Ordnance Survey Archaeological Division, and the Royal Commissions on Ancient and Historical Monuments. A bibliography and a topographical index are also included.

298 'Fieldwork in industrial archaeology' by J Kenneth Major (Batsford, 1975) is a guide to the scope and techniques of fieldwork written in the conviction that this must play a large part in industrial archaeology because of the vital necessity for recording industrial monuments before they are lost through demolition and redevelopment. Topics covered include the wide scope of industrial archaeology, the various types of fieldwork possible (a survey of an industry in a particular area, or of a single industrial unit in depth, or an emergency operation), the background research in the library or archive office, photography, how to compile records, and hints on the publication of results. The bibliography classified under fifteen subject headings is designed to give the fieldworker an insight into the subject and to indicate unexpected sources of material like Victorian textbooks of machinery which the author imagines can be picked up cheaply in second-hand bookshops.

299 'Fieldwork in medieval archaeology' by Christopher Taylor (Batsford, 1974) is intended as a handbook for the part-time archaeologist and

144

examines the various ways medieval field archaeology may be conducted. All aspects from planning and preparation to final publication are covered. The work is well illustrated and there is a select bibliography of medieval and later field monuments arranged by type.

300 'Fifty years of the Transactions' by A C Wood refers specifically to the story of the Thoroton Society's journal but it touches upon the fundamental dilemma which confronted most of the county archaeological societies ten or twenty years ago. Should the society continue in its old, comfortable, and accustomed manner, visiting country churches, eating huge teas, or should it turn its energies to the more serious business of planned or emergency excavations? And where should the society's journal stand? Dr Wood presents his own views on the principles of editorship: '(1) To hold the balance fairly between the various interests represented in the society—archaeological, architectural, ecclesiological, genealogical, historical, topographical and all the rest—to see that all get a reasonable hearing . . . (2) To test each contribution by the query—does this add anything new in presentation, arrangement, interpretation, fact or theory to what is already available in print . . . Only so is it possible to build up our historical knowledge and to make the *Transactions* worthy of their claim to be the journal of a learned society . . . (3) To see that articles are so written that they can be read and comprehended by the average member, and that their literary style is reasonably sound and dignified.' *Source: Transactions of the Thoroton Society of Nottinghamshire,* vol L, 1947: 1-12.

301 'First aid for finds' *A practical guide for archaeologists* by David Leigh was published by RESCUE and the University of Southampton in 1972 as a soft-covered booklet intended to offer guidance to rescue archaeologists working in Britain. Advice is given on how objects may be stored so that 'there is something for the conservator to conserve when (they) finally reach him!' There is a list of conservators and laboratories who have agreed to provide advice by post or telephone on particularly difficult and urgent field conservation problems.

302 'Fishbourne' *a Roman palace and its garden* by Barry Cunliffe was published by Thames and Hudson in their 'New aspects of antiquity' series in 1971. It unfolds the exciting story of the accidental rediscovery in 1960 of the great building at Fishbourne in Sussex (which together with its formal garden spreads over ten acres), and relates the progress of eight years of excavation organised by the Chichester Civic Society. Professor, Cunliffe, director of the excavations, places the palace in its Romano-British context, records the alterations to the building which reflect social changes in the second and third centuries, and outlines its history until it was destroyed by fire in the fourth. Plans, drawings and photographs of the excavations and of the magnificent mosaics and other finds admirably support the text.

303 'Flights into yesterday' *the story of aerial archaeology* by Leo Deuel was published by St Martin's Press in New York (1969) and by MacDonald in London (1971). Although the author modestly describes it as a book of a non-specialist written for non-specialists it is in fact a full account of the history and technique of aerial archaeology as a science and of the personalities involved. Its main purpose is to show that aerial archaeology is something more than an ingenious method of discovery and to emphasise that it implies a radical new direction in the study of antiquities. Starting in Wessex the story extends to Western Europe and the Mediterranean before crossing the Atlantic with chapters on 'Lindbergh searches for Maya cities' and 'Wings over ancient America.' A final chapter examines aerial archaeology as a technique with a future, looking at its scientific potential, and considering its post-war growth especially in France, Italy and Germany. Its implications in underwater archaeology and for anthropology are also discussed. An extensive bibliography arranged by chapter includes many items gleaned from non-archaeological journals. A Penguin edition was published in 1973.

304 'Focus on the past' , a series published by the Phaidon Press is designed to share with the general public the startling progress of archaeology over the last two decades with especial regard to the new methods and scientific techniques increasingly employed, and attempts to convey 'the excitement of finding new evidence and then its interpretation'. Titles published so far include *The human revolution: from ape to artist* (Desmond Collins), *Egypt* (Paul Jordan), *The first cities* (Ruth Whitehouse); and *The Vikings* (Michael Kirby). All titles are also available in paperbacks.

305 'The future of archaeological societies', a paper read to the Surrey Archaeological Society by Sir Frederic Kenyon, is concerned particularly with the museums maintained by county archaeological societies and the support these should receive from local authorities. It appeared in *Surrey archaeological collections* XLIX, 1946: 1-5.

306 'The future of the county archaeological societies and of this society' forms the third part of L V Grinsell's presidential address to the Somerset Archaeological and Natural History Society, 'The past and future of archaeology in Somerset', printed in *Somerset archaeology and natural history* 115, 1971: 29-38 and is noticed separately here because its review of the part played by the old established county societies in the development of British archaeology, and their place in the contemporary archaeological scene, deserves a wider audience than the membership of one particular county society. An effective contrast is drawn between the unchallenged supremacy of the county societies up to the outbreak of the second world war and their infinitely less secure position today when it is the smaller archaeological groups that attract the more alert and enthusiastic younger generation of archaeologists.

307 'A gazetteer of British lower and middle palaeolithic sites' compiled by Derek A Roe, the eighth CBA Research Report, published in 1968, is a substantial work covering the whole British palaeolithic sequence to the Mousterian period. It is arranged alphabetically by county and the information listed includes the locality where artefacts have been discovered, a classification by broad artefact class, an indication of where material may be inspected, and reference to published sources. A classified total of artefacts recovered, an alphabetical list of museum collections and documentary sources, summaries in English, French and German, and indexes of place and site names, support the main gazetteer.

308 The gentleman's magazine (1731-1907), originally a miscellany of 'The most remarkable pieces from the various journals', gradually included more and more original material. Items of antiquarian and topographical interest had always been prominent in its contents but when John Mitford was appointed editor in 1824 the amount of antiquarian and archaeological topics covered noticeably increased. Charles Roach Smith's 'Antiquarian notes' are especially remembered. *The gentleman's magazine library: being a classified collection of the chief contents . . . from 1731 to 1868* edited by G L Gomme began publication in 1883 and consisted of a number of volumes, each devoted to one topic, containing the principal articles on that topic extracted from the monthly issues of the *Magazine*, the date and issue they came from being indicated at the head of each article. *Archaeology* Pt 1 (vol 5) included extracts on geological and prehistoric, early historic, and sepulchral remains, and encampments and earthworks. Pt II was given over to stones and stone circles, miscellaneous antiquities of the British period, and early Anglo-Saxon remains, ornaments and antiquities. *Romano-British remains* also extended over two volumes and listed discoveries in Britain arranged alphabetically by county with a separate section for Roman roads and stations. Many of these extracts of course display a lack of scientific method but there can be no doubt that a wealth of raw material was collected together and this deserves to be recorded. Complete sets or individual numbers of the *Magazine* are available from Kraus Reprints.

309 Gerald Duckworth and Co Ltd, one of the few publishing firms remaining wholly in private hands, was established in 1898. In the years following the second world war it has noticeably expanded its academic book list not least in archaeology: 'Peoples of Roman Britain' and 'Perspectives in archaeology' are two eminent series, and Glyn Daniels' *150 Years of archaeology* also comes from this house. Recent catalogues have included '75 years of publishing', a short outline of the firm's history.

310 'Glossary of archaeology' *excluding architecture and ecclesiology* by A Norman was published in two pocket-size volumes as one of Talbot and Company's 'The antiquaries primers' in 1908. It was restricted in scope to the British Isles and was designed to simplify 'certain indiscriminate nomenclature indulged in the middle ages, and the arbitrary transfer of some terms to utterly dissimilar objects at different periods, which sometimes befogs the reconciliation of apparent contradictions'.

311 Gordon, Alexander (1692?-1754?) spent three years visiting different parts of Scotland and Northumberland drawing and measuring ancient remains which otherwise might well have vanished unrecorded. In 1726 he published his *Itinerarium septentrionale: or, a journey thro' most of the counties of Scotland and those in Northern England*. This was arranged in two parts: (1) 'an account of all the monuments of Roman antiquity found and collected on that journey' and (2) 'an account of the Danish invasions of Scotland and of the monuments erected there . . . with other ancient remains of antiquities never before communicated to the publick'. *Additions and corrections by way of supplement to the Itinerarium septentrionale* appeared in 1732.

312 'Gravel, sand and history', a pamphlet published by the Council for British Archaeology in 1951, was prepared and distributed with the agreement and help of the Ballast, Sand and Allied Trades Association. Its purpose was to remind landowners and operatives in the industry of the importance of pottery remains which might be uncovered and to invite their cooperation in reporting such finds.

313 Gregg International Publishers specialise in the publication of learned works and the reprinting of rare books for libraries and scholars. A subject catalogue, *Archaeology* is available from Westmead, Farnborough, Hampshire.

314 Grose, Francis (1731-1791) published *The antiquities of England and Wales, being a collection of views of the most remarkable ruins and antient buildings, accurately drawn on the spot. To each view is added an historical account of its situation, when and by whom built, with every interesting circumstance thereto* in four folio volumes 1773-1787. A quarto edition appeared in seven volumes and a supplement 1783-1797. Many of the drawings were made by himself although a number of other antiquaries contributed to the text. This was followed by *The antiquities of Scotland*, two quarto volumes 1789-1791. Grose died on a visit to Ireland and his two similar volumes *The antiquities of Ireland* (1791-1795) were in large measure seen through the press by Edward Ledwich. Descriptions of druidical monuments, conical towers, vitrified forts, standing stones, Roman works, Norman castles, and ecclesiastical antiquities, all find a place in these volumes which include many full-page engravings. Stuart Piggott describes Grose as 'one of the first journalist-antiquaries who catered for and fostered the growing interest in illustrated serial works on British antiquities'.

315 'A guide to British topographical collections' by M W Barley (Council for British Archaeology, 1974) briefly records alphabetically by county illustration collections—drawings, prints and photographs, housed in public repositories, and is based in almost every instance on a personal visit and examination by either the author or one of his two helpers. Groups of drawings in particular collections are listed under the name of the artist or under the collector responsible for gathering them together. Indications of collections held outside the county to which they refer provide another valuable feature. There is a consolidated list of such collections and also an index of artists represented in more than one collection. A few private collections are also noted.

316 'Guide to periodicals and bibliographies dealing with geography, archaeology and history' compiled by E Jeffries Davis and E G R Taylor, under the direction of a committee representing the Royal Geographical Society, the Historical Association, Society of Antiquaries, the Institute of Historical Research, Royal Archaeological Institute, Royal Historical Society and other institutions, was issued by the Historical Association in their pamphlet series in 1938. Its purpose was to indicate sources of information regarding current work in the three disciplines.

317 '**A guide to prehistoric England**' by Nicholas Thomas (Batsford, 2ed 1977) was compiled 'for people who love the countryside, who are interested in the past and may wish to plan their excursions around visits to prehistoric sites of various types'. The text consists of a gazetteer of sites arranged first by county and then chronologically by prehistoric period: neolithic, bronze age, iron age. Directions include the nearest town and the main A or B roads but it is assumed that the reader will have the appropriate Ordnance Survey one-inch map to hand. Each entry includes a physical description of the site together with notes on any discoveries made and consequent hypotheses. A general introduction, a glossary of archaeological terms, numerous maps, photographs and drawings are also included.

318 '**A guide to prehistoric Scotland**' *a gazetteer* by Richard Feachem (Batsford, 2ed 1977) provides a broad picture of the best preserved and most significant surviving structural remains of the human occupation of Scotland in prehistoric times, and offers a concise description of the monuments themselves. The main gazetteer is arranged in chronological sections (early settlements, chambered tombs, henge monuments, stones and cairns, cup-and-ring markings, homesteads, hill-forts and settlements, brochs, duns, and crannogs) each sub-divided alphabetically by county. They all begin with a general account of the monuments within their section and continue with brief descriptions of individual monuments. There is also a short final section on Pictish symbol stones arranged in the same fashion. Two maps and a general bibliography supplement the text.

319 '**Guide to reference material**' by A J Walford is a three volume work arranged according to the Universal Decimal Classification scheme. 'Archaeology' takes its place in Volume two *Social and historical sciences philosophy and religion* (Library Association, 3ed 1975). Arrangement is first by form (bibliographies, manuals, periodicals, yearbooks); then come 'archaeological discoveries'; this is followed by a geographical/

chronological sequence (China, Egypt, Palestine, India, Mesopotamia, Persia, classical antiquities, ancient Rome, ancient Greece, Britain, Scotland, Ireland, England, Wales, Germany, Russia, Sweden, Islam, Asia, Southern Africa, Americas, Australia); and finally what we might call auxiliary topics (archaeology of religions, epigraphy, and palaeography). This is obviously not an ideal, logical, or consistent sequence but one which is dictated by the idiosyncrasies of the classification scheme used. 'A signpost to reference books and bibliographies published mainly in recent years' the guide is intended 'for librarians in the building up and revision of reference library stock; for use in general and special library enquiry work; as an aid to students taking examinations in librarianship; and for research workers, in the initial stages of research'. All entries receive a brief description, there is a judicious use of statistical evidence, and it is especially useful for its annotations of the great German cooperative works and other foreign language material.

320 'Guide to the antiquities of Roman Britain' first published by the trustees of the British Museum in 1951 is now available in a third edition. It presents a survey of Roman antiquities illustrated by representative pieces from the museum's collections including all the exhibits of outstanding interest either in their own right or because of their archaeological associations. The *Guide* begins with a general introduction to Roman Britain and continues with a number of sections describing various aspects of its art and life with detailed references to specific items. For its size (less than ninety pages) it includes a remarkable selection of maps, photographs and drawings, and there is a short classified bibliography and a glossary of technical terms in addition to an index of find places.

321 'A guide to the historical and archaeological publications of societies in England and Wales, 1901-1933' compiled for the Institute of Historical Research by E L C Mullins (Athlone Press, 1968), lists and indexes authors and titles of books and articles issued by more than four hundred national and local societies. Entries are arranged alphabetically by society and list the contents of their journals, transactions, proceedings and reports in chronological sequence. A general index and an index of authors ensure information is immediately retrievable. In addition brief notes are provided on the objects, date of foundation, subsequent history and any change of name of each society. A short outline of the genesis and history of the work is to be found in the foreword.

322 'Guide to the national monuments in the Republic of Ireland' *including a selection of other monuments not in state care* by Peter Harbison (Gill and Macmillan, 1970) is in effect a second and heavily revised and enlarged edition of *The national monuments of Ireland* formerly published by the Irish Tourist Board. Its main purpose is to provide information about the major monuments in state care in addition to some hundred or so others considered important. The entries are listed alphabetically by county, giving details of location, whether signposted, a general description and history, with references to Ordnance Survey maps and to the map section in the *Guide* itself. Other features include a glossary, a select bibliography, and a list of selected museums and folk parks.

323 'A guide to the prehistoric and Roman monuments in England and Wales' by Jacquetta Hawkes, first published by Chatto and Windus in 1951, was reissued in a revised edition in 1973. Described by the author as a collection of 'itineraries of an informal kind' it provides a detailed account, on a regional basis, of the principal surviving field monuments. These itineraries are supported by notes on the types of monument to be seen, a chronological division of antiquities, five maps, forty full page photographs (sixteen in colour), and a gazetteer of sites which includes the one-inch Ordnance Survey sheet number, the type of monument, and the National Grid reference.

324 'A guide to the Roman remains in Britain' by Roger J A Wilson, published by Constable in 1975, is a comprehensive survey of all visible remains of Roman Britain with the exception of roads and canals, the vast majority of native settlements of the period, mines and quarries, and doubtful Roman antiquities. Designed for those interested in the past but who possess no specialized knowledge it includes an introductory section providing information on the Roman army in Britain, an historical outline, and a glossary of technical terms. Ten chapters arranged on a geographical basis, each with a map preceding the text, group sites according to the type of remains. Full directions as to routes and access are given but only in a very few instances is the reader expected to refer to an Ordnance Survey map. Over 230 sites, almost all of which the author has personally visited, are described in the main body of the text which is profusely illustrated with maps, photographs and drawings. There are three appendixes: (1) a gazetteer of visible remains not mentioned in the text; (2) some museums displaying Romano-British material; and (3) a detailed bibliography intended for the reader who requires more information on specific sites. Two indexes, by site and type of monument, complete a remarkably compact but authoritative guidebook. Professor J M C Toynbee contributes a foreword.

325 H W Wilson Company, founded in Minneapolis in 1898, are specialist publishers of indexes to current literature. *Art index* and *Humanities index* are noticed separately in this present handbook. *Indexes for reference and research*, a booklet describing at length each index in turn and explaining the service basis method of charge, is available from 950 University Avenue, Bronx, New York 10452.

326 Hampshire Field Club and Archaeological Society was established at a meeting on 22 March 1885 attended by five gentlemen. Numbers soon increased however and in less than twenty years a certain glow of satisfaction can be discerned in the words of the society's editor: 'there can be no doubt but that the influence of our society has been of great service in directing attention to . . . antiquities of the county . . . our efforts have also been largely instrumental in protecting, and in several cases averting the threatened destruction of buildings of historic and local interest.' The society's *Papers and proceedings* were first published for the year 1887 and continued under that name until volume XXI (1958) when a change to a larger quarto format provided an opportunity to alter the title to *Proceedings*. It was customary for many years to bind three or four annual issues together as a volume, an idiosyncrasy that was not reformed until volume XXIV (1967) when the more usual practice of numbering each annual volume consecutively was adopted. Articles of note include J P Williams-Freeman's 'List of Hampshire earthworks classified according to the schedule of the earthworks committee', vol VI, 1907-1910:343-349; L V Grinsell's 'Hampshire barrows', XIV 1938: 9-40, a survey undertaken in order to throw light on the distribution and relative chronology of the rarer types of round barrows; 'Archaeology in Hampshire', the text of a presidential address to the society, XIX 1957: 171-176, an outline of archaeological activity in the ten year period after the war; and C F C Hawkes' 'Hampshire and the British iron age' published in the special volume of essays in honour of Frank Warren (a posthumous festschrift), vol XX, 1956: 14-21. Unfortunately J P Williams-Freeman's 'Early days of the Hampshire Field Club', XV 1943: 236-238 is little more than a few random reminiscences. A *General index to volumes I-X (1855-1931)* compiled by F W C Pepper was published in 1932 followed by another for volumes XI-XX (1932-1956) compiled by A J Lee in 1964.

327 'Handbook for expeditions' *a planning guide* was published by the Braythay Exploration Group in association with *The geographical magazine* in 1971. The group, which originated in the Lake District in 1947 as part of the first 'Holidays with a purpose' course run by the Braythay Hall Trust, has organized over the years many expeditions in the British Isles and abroad for sixth-formers and students, and the *Handbook* reflects the wide experience gained. There are six sections all offering expert advice: the initial considerations listed are the idea, the selection of members, and the range and scope of the expedition; fifteen field studies (of which archaeology is one) are considered; the principles of field recording, photography and surveying are outlined; planning details like travel and timetables, equipment, food and medical supplies, finance and insurance, are examined; organization in the field covers the qualities of leadership, camp routine, communications, and safety; whilst a list of useful addresses, explorer films, the addresses of shops selling special equipment, and a scheme for the study of rural communities, are all contained in an appendix. Lord Hunt of Llanvair Waterdine (*ie* Sir John Hunt of Everest fame) contributes a foreword.

328 'Handbook for industrial archaeologists' *a guide to fieldwork and research* by Kenneth Hudson (John Baker, 1967) is a short working manual on the techniques and methods to be followed in research, fieldwork, recording and publication in this comparatively recent branch of archaeology. National and local institutions and organizations active in industrial archaeology are listed and there is a guide to further reading to complete a remarkably compact and thorough practical handbook. It was replaced in 1976 by the same author's *A pocketbook for industrial archaeologists.*

329 'Handbook of scientific aids and evidence for archaeologists' was published by the Reconstruction Scientific Research Committee of the Council for British Archaeology in 1970 to replace an earlier *Notes for the guidance of archaeologists in regard to expert evidence.* A distinct change of approach is evident: whereas previously it was assumed that archaeologists would wish to call in geologists, zoologists, botanists, soil-scientists, metallurgists whenever it was necessary, now it is expected they will be au fait with some of these ancillary disciplines. The *Handbook* is issued in loose-leaf form to facilitate revision and updating and consists of data sheets arranged in two sections, 'Artifacts and other material' and 'Instrumental techniques (analytical, dating and geophysical)' each in

154

alphabetical order. In the first instance information is printed under the headings 'Potential evidence', 'Sampling or collection', 'Treatment and packing' and 'Bibliography'; and in the second under 'Principle', 'Applicability' and 'Bibliography'.

330 '**A handbook of the prehistoric archaeology of Britain**' compiled by M C Burkitt, V Gordon Childe, Cyril Fox, Christopher Hawkes, T D Hendricks, E T Leeds and C A Ralegh Radford was issued in connection with the first International Congress of Prehistoric and Protohistoric Sciences held in London August 1st-6th 1932. It was not intended as a manual, nor did it attempt to deal with controversial matters, the authors limited themselves to the presentation of facts, suppressing opinions they regarded as personal. It thus served as a summary account of the main features of contemporary British archaeology for native archaeologists and overseas visitors alike. *Contents*: Palaeolithic and mesolithic periods; Character of Britain and its influence on invaders; Neolithic period; Megalithic monuments; Bronze age; Early iron age; Roman period; Early Anglo-Saxon period; and Late Saxon and Viking period. Each section except the second is equipped with its own bibliography. A general bibliography is also included.

331 '**Hertfordshire archaeology**', combining the *Transactions* of two independent county archaeological societies, St Albans and Hertfordshire Architectural and Archaeological Society and East Hertfordshire Archaeological Society, with additional articles from local societies, first appeared in 1968.

332 '**Hill-forts of Britain**' by A H A Hogg (Hart-Davis Macgibbon, 1975) is both narrative and guide. An examination of the various types of structure, their historical and social context, and their distribution, is followed by a gazetteer of a representative sample of hill-forts on the British mainland. Each entry gives the county, the National Grid reference, approximate height and a description of the other main physical features, and bibliographical notes. Maps, drawings, and photographs illustrate both sections.

333 '**Hillforts of the iron age in England and Wales**' *a survey of the surface evidence* by J Forde-Johnston (Liverpool University Press, 1976), is an examination of the 1350 hillforts located south of the Lake District and the North Yorkshire Moors. There is a regional survey; chapters on siting, internal features, types of sites, and entrances; a recommended typological classification; a consideration of typological distribution; and a thorough bibliography.

334 'Historic monuments of England and Wales' by David and Fiona Sturdy (Dent, 1977) is a lavishly illustrated descriptive guide to the outstanding ancient sites and historic monuments open to the public.

335 Historic Sites Act 1935 (US), an act to provide for the preservation of historic sites, buildings, objects, and antiquities of national significance, expanded legislative protection in that sites of local, state, or regional importance became eligible for inclusion. It also allowed federal grants equal to state financial support to be allocated and provided grants in aid to the National Trust for Historical Preservation. The text of the act is included in Charles R McGimsey's *Public archaeology* (*qv*).

336 'Historic Society of Lancashire and Cheshire' was formally established at a public meeting called on the initiative of Abraham Hume, Henry Pidgeon and Joseph Mayer, at the Collegiate Institution, Liverpool, 20 June 1848. By the time of the first ordinary meeting in October 180 members had joined. It is evident from Hume's inaugural address that the society did not intend to follow antiquarian pursuits alone: 'Our basis of operations . . . embraces every subject of historic interest in a given locality. We are circumscribed only in *area*, and that partly from choice and partly from necessity; but it is difficult to conceive of a society more comprehensive in its general principles and its details. It is not, for example, a mere documentary society nor is it archaeological alone, nor genealogical, nor topographical. It is not confined to any branch of natural history, nor to the whole subject; it is not a mere depository of 'folklore', or a chronicler of battles, churches, or ships. With every one of these subjects, aye, and with every other, it claims a connexion, in so far . . . as they tend to illustrate the two counties' (*Proceedings* 1 1848-49: 3-11). Practical advice on the methodology he recommended the society should follow came in Henry Pidgeon's 'On the best mode of carrying out the objects of the society', *Proceedings* 1, 1848: 43-53, summarized as 'the collection, arrangement, and so far as our funds will permit, the publication of all that relates to the history, topography, natural history, statistics, and personal history or biography of the district'. By the late 1870s the society's interests had ranged a little too far and the council inserted an advertisement in the *Transactions* for the 1878-79 session suggesting they restricted themselves to the archaeology and history of the two counties. A somewhat rambling and diffuse history of the society's origins and activities is available in a commemorative address, 'Centenary of the Historic Society of Lancashire and Cheshire: a retrospect' printed in a supplement to volume 100 of the *Transactions* for the year 1948. This is in truth a disappointing publication especially if we compare it for example with the special volumes prepared by the three South Eastern counties of Sussex, Surrey, and Kent to mark their centenaries. Other items include thumbnail biographical notes on the founders of the society and an account of the provenance of the society's ceremonial mace. The society's journal which has been published on a regular annual basis possesses nevertheless a slightly confusing history especially in its early years. The first six volumes were published as the *Proceedings and papers of the Historic Society of Lancashire and Cheshire*, a change to *Transactions* etc coming with volume seven. Since 1860 there has been in turn a new series, a third series, and another new series; mercifully, however, a running volume number has been maintained. In recent years the financial problems of the *Transactions* have been acute and the society has recently discussed the publication of occasional volumes, appearing at the most every other year, intended for retail sale to the public, as a measure to alleviate the journal's precarious position. A number of difficulties will have to be surmounted if this proposed remedy is to be a success. No separate index volumes have been published, it has been the society's policy to print cumulative indexes at regular intervals in the *Transactions*, volumes I-LI 1849-1900 (1902); LII-LXI 1901-1909 (1909); LXII-LXXI 1910-1919 (1922); 72-85 1920-1933 (1934); 86-97 1934-1945 (1949); 98-110 1946-1958 (1959); and 111-120 1959-1968 (1968).

337 'Historical, archaeological and kindred societies in the British Isles' *a list* compiled by Sara E Harcup and published by the Institute of Historical Research, University of London, in a second edition in 1968 gives the name of each society, the date of its foundation, and either its permanent address or the name and address of its secretary. There are three lists in fact: the main alphabetical sequence, a topographical arrangement, and a select list of subjects. Natural history societies are only included if they are partly concerned with archaeology or history.

338 'History from the earth' *an introduction to archaeology* by J Forde-Johnston (Phaidon, 1974), a lavishly illustrated volume, outlines the aims, history, methods and techniques of archaeology and the emergence of man in the palaeolithic age. There is little here that cannot be found elsewhere but the book has few rivals as an attractive introduction to archaeology for the layman and prospective student. Further readings are indicated chapter by chapter. It also serves as the first volume in the 'Introductions to archaeology' series of which the author is general editor.

339 'History in the landscape' series, published by Dent, is one in which 'outstanding archaeologists provide valuable and original insights into particular periods or aspects of archaeological history. The basis of the series is the conviction that archaeology is about people as much as about artifacts, society as much as structures.' The first title to be published is David Hinton's *Alfred's kingdom: Wessex and the South 800-1500* (1977). Other titles on bronze age and iron age Britain are in active preparation. The series editor is Dennis Harding.

340 'A history of American archaeology' by Gordon R Willey and Jeremy A Sabloff was published in Thames and Hudson's 'World of archaeology' series in 1974. It is not intended to serve as a summary of excavations and the finds yielded but rather as an intellectual history of the development of the discipline of archaeology as practised in the Americas. Five periods are discerned: the speculative (1492-1840); the classificatory—descriptive (1840-1914); the classificatory—historical concern with chronology (1914-1940); the classificatory—historical concern with context and function (1940-1960); and the explanatory (1960-); Particular attention is paid to research strategies and methods. The influence of European scholarship in the early part of the nineteenth century is assessed and the relationship of American archaeology to ethnology and anthropology is also remarked. Numerous notes and a major bibliography are regarded as an extension of the text providing necessary detail and examples for the student. A lavish selection of illustrations complements the text.

341 'History under the sea' by Alexander McKee (Hutchinson, 1968), an illustrated account of underwater archaeology and its contribution to history, traces the birth of the science to early nineteenth-century England. In area it covers the coasts of Britain, the Mediterranean, North West Europe, the Caribbean, and the English Channel.

342 'History under the sea' *a handbook for underwater exploration* by Mendel Peterson is a concise account of Western hemisphere locations of underwater sites, expeditions, search techniques, conditions, recovery methods, and identification of shipwreck sites. A classified bibliography and a world list of maritime museums are also included. The handbook was published by the Smithsonian Institution in 1965.

343 Hoare, Sir Richard Colt (1758-1838), indefatigable excavator of barrows and voluminous writer, owes his unrivalled importance in the development of archaeological excavation in England to his down-to-earth approach: 'I shall describe to you what we have found; what we have seen; in short I shall tell you a plain unvarnished tale, and draw from it such conclusions as shall appear not only reasonable, but uncontradictable', he told the readers of his *Ancient history of North and South Wiltshire*, published in two volumes 1812-1821. Volume one, restricted to South Wiltshire and to British antiquities, includes several plans and elevations of Stonehenge, and the whole work records the position and contents of hundreds of barrows opened and explored with William Cunnington. Volume two contains an accurate survey of all Roman roads and tesselated pavements in the county. It was their scientific approach, their careful noting of the difference in types of barrow, their grasping that stratification was crucially important in establishing a relative chronology, their attempt to classify camps and earthworks, that distinguish Cunnington and Hoare from their contemporaries and justifies their claim to be regarded as the first of the modern school of archaeologists.

344 'Humanities index' (April 1974-), one of the latest titles in the H W Wilson family of indexes, descends from the *International index to periodicals* (1907-1965) and *Social sciences and humanities index* (1965-March 1975). When this last was split into two separate publications the coverage of archaeology was increased and it now indexes *American antiquity; American journal of archaeology; Antiquity; Archaeology; Journal of Hellenic studies;* and *Journal of Roman studies.* The *Index* is published quarterly with annual cumulations, author and subject entries are arranged in a single alphabet, complete bibliographical details are included.

345 'A hundred and fifty years of archaeology' by Glyn Daniel published in 1975 is the second edition of a work entitled *A hundred years of archaeology* which first appeared in 1950 in Duckworth's 'Hundred years' series. Although the author writes a modest disclaimer in his preface to the effect that the detailed history of prehistoric scholarship remains to be written, and that this book is no more than a discussion of some of the more significant discoveries and developments of the last century and a half, it must nevertheless be considered as essential reading for all those with an interest in archaeology. The main theme of the book is 'the discovery and description of prehistoric man, and the change in our perspective of our own remote past because of these archaeological discoveries'. The narrative moves forward on a broad chronological and geographical basis with special attention to 'the conceptual development of prehistory, from the epochal attitude of the geological archaeologists, through the culture-study of the anthropological archaeologists, to the historical attitude of modern archaeologists'. The text is unusually well documented and the extensive bibliography is therefore confined to secondary sources. The scholarly apparatus is completed by a glossary and a chronological table of main events in the history of archaeology 1820-1970. A paperback edition is available.

346 'Hutchinson university library', a series of textbooks intended for first year undergraduates and published simultaneously in hard covers and as paperbacks, includes archaeology as one of the many academic disciplines it covers. Recent titles include: *Early farmers of west Mediterranean Europe* (Patricia Phillips); *The northern barbarians 100 BC-AD 300* (Malcolm Todd); *Archaeology by experiment* (John Coles); *Town and country in Roman Britain* (A L F Rivet); and *Hunters, fishers and farmers of Eastern Europe 6000-3000 BC* (Ruth Tringham). For many years C F C Hawkes acted as archaeological editor.

347 'The idea of prehistory' by Glyn Daniel is the printed version of the Josiah Mason Lectures given in the University of Birmingham 1956-1957 and was first published in C A Watts' 'New thinker's library' in 1962. In his preface the author remarks: 'I had already written a short history of the development of prehistory between 1840 and 1940 in my *Hundred years of archaeology*. The Mason lectures seemed to provide a good opportunity for isolating the important events in the history of that hundred years and relating them to what went before and what came after.' An annotated list of books for further reading is included. A Penguin Books edition appeared in 1964 and was reissued in 1971.

348 'Illustrated London news' which commenced publication as a weekly in 1842 has continuously recorded the modern world's uncovering of the past in its pages. A regular feature in the nineteenth century, 'Archaeology of the month' reflected its close interest and since the 1920s the magazine has been regarded as one of the few general periodicals

consistently devoting its columns to archaeology as a matter of course
and not simply when a major discovery was announced. If Roman Britain
and excavations in the Biblical lands have loomed large that is not to say
other periods and areas have been neglected. A sumptuous colourful
anthology of its reports of the most significant and richest archaeological
finds which most aroused public interest was published under the title
of *The great archaeologists*, edited by Edwin Bacon in 1976. Arranged
in chronological order the extracts are linked by summaries of events elsewhere in the archaeological world by the editor who also inserts biographical notes of the archaeologists concerned. Thankfully the transition of
the journal to a monthly publication in May 1971 has not lessened its
archaeological curiosity.

**349 'Illustrated regional guides to ancient monuments in the care of the
state'**, published by HMSO for the Department of the Environment provide visitors with brief outlines of the history and principal features of all
types of monuments to be found within a specific region. Each of the six
pocket-sized volumes contains descriptive essays on the visible remains of
the region, period by period, followed by gazetteer type information on
each main site, listed alphabetically by county. A pull-out map and a
short bibliography are also conveniently included. The guides were devised by W Ormsby-Gore, later Lord Harlech, who was himself the author
of volumes 1-3 and 5, when First Commissioner of Works in the 1930s.
*Titles: Northern England; Southern England; East Anglia and the Midlands;
South Wales* (Sir Cyril Fox); *North Wales*; and *Scotland* (V G Childe and
W Douglas Simpson). All have been continuously revised and reprinted,
the latest edition of each title is indicated in *Ancient monuments and historic buildings* (Sectional List No 27) (*qv*). Many libraries will still have
copies bearing the title *Illustrated guides to ancient monuments in the
ownership or guardianship of the Ministry of Public Building and Works.*

350 'The impact of the natural sciences on archaeology' a joint symposium of the Royal Society and the British Academy (OUP, 1970) marks
the twentieth anniversary of the discovery of radiocarbon dating and consists of the papers presented at a two-day meeting of scientists and archaeologists in December 1969 to discuss the problems of reconciling scientific
and historical dating and how these might be resolved. They outline the
scientific techniques on hand to archaeologists dating their finds. *Contents*:
'Radiocarbon dating' (W F Libby); 'Absolute dating from Egyptian records
and comparison with carbon-14 dating' (I E S Edwards); 'Absolute dating

161

from Mesopotamian records' (A Sachs); 'Ancient Egyptian radiocarbon chronology' (R Berger); 'Critical assessment of radiocarbon dating' (H Barker); 'Evidence for changes in the earth's magnetic field intensity' (V Bucha); 'The contribution of radiocarbon dating to archaeology in Britain' (H Godwin); Dating by archaeomagnetic and thermoluminescent methods' (M J Aitken); 'Techniques used in archaeological field surveys' (R E Linington); 'Magnetic methods of archaeological prospecting— advances in instrumentation and evaluation techniques' (I Scollar); 'Survey techniques in underwater archaeology' (E T Hall); 'A mathematical approach to seriation' (D G Kendall); 'Analytical techniques used in archaeometry' (E T Hall); 'Lead and oxygen isotopes in ancient objects' (R H Brill); 'Neutron activitation analysis of archaeological artefacts' (A A Gordus); 'Analysis of pottery from the Mycenaean period' (H W Catling); and 'Analysis of ancient metals' (A E A Wernher).

351 '**Index of archaeological papers 1665-1890**' edited by George Lawrence Gomme, published under the direction of the Congress of Archaeological Societies in union with the Society of Antiquaries eventually appeared in print in 1907 after it had been planned as an appendix to the *Archaeological review* which started in 1888 but which folded after only four volumes. It lists in alphabetical order of author all archaeological papers printed in the *Transactions* of learned societies in Great Britain and Ireland from the first publication of the philosophical transactions of the Royal Society down to the year 1890 at which point the annual indexes published by the congress take over coverage. There is an appendix comprising entries omitted from their place in the main sequence and also of papers published subsequent to its completion. Originally the editor intended to add a classified subject index which undeniably would have added much to its value as a reference work but the sheer labour entailed in such an undertaking defeated him. The annual *Index of archaeological papers* was published by the congress 1891-1910 and these are usually to be found in libraries collected together in two decennial volumes, 1891-1900 and 1901-1910, bound in similar fashion to the main work. This annual index ceased publication owing to the lack of support from local societies affiliated to the congress.

352 '**Industrial archaeologists' guide**' edited by Neil Cossons and Kenneth Hudson, first published by David and Charles in 1969, was designed as a quick reference tool to provide the sort of information experience told the editors and publishers of the journal *Industrial archaeology* was most often required. Contents include a section on the history and work of the National Record of Industrial Monuments by R A Buchanan, descriptive sections on scientific and technological museums, on-site preservation, some sites worth visiting, and photography and industrial archaeology. There are also lists and details of museums in Great Britain with science and technology collections, of local societies, and of local journals and newsletters. It was intended that the *Guide* would be revised at regular intervals.

353 'Industrial archaeology' by Michael Rix, published in 1967 by the Historical Association as No 65 in their general series of booklets, recounts the development of industrial archaeological studies from the time the author first coined the term in an *Amateur historian* article in 1955, and records the work of various museums with sections devoted to this sphere. The urgency of the need for action to preserve buildings and monuments of the industrial past is examined under three headings providing examples of surviving, lost, and threatened monuments. On a more encouraging note there is a review of sporadic efforts in the past to rescue and record the history of engineering and technology and the field work in progress at the time of writing. A select bibliography constitutes in effect a useful early literature guide to the subject which has of course expanded in spectacular fashion since this booklet appeared.

354 'Industrial archaeology' *an historical survey* by Arthur Raistrick (Eyre Methuen, 1972), is a personal attempt to outline a possible scheme of industrial archaeology which concentrates rather more on the archaeological aspects of the subject, 'a more evenly balanced investigation of industry from pre-Roman times to the present', in the conviction that over-emphasis on the industrial revolution 'will reduce the scope and importance of work which could properly be sponsored under a wider definition'. The text is arranged in three parts, the materials and field evidence, a view of industrial archaeology in Britain, and the place of museums. The bibliography is of particular value in drawing attention to professional and technical journals which although not ostensibly devoted to industrial archaeology often carry papers on a wide variety of subjects of interest to the industrial archaeologist and historian.

355 'Industrial archaeology' *an introduction* by Kenneth Hudson was eventually published by John Baker in 1963 after efforts by the Council for British Archaeology to obtain a grant or subsidy had foundered. It

163

was a pioneering work explaining exactly what was implied by the term 'Industrial archaeology' and drawing attention to the surviving monuments of the industrial age in an attempt to create a genuine public interest and concern. It unquestionably played a full part in establishing industrial archaeology as a serious and proper area of study. Of particular value is the final chapter on the documentation and recording of the subject, and the select bibliography, both of which are designed to guide the enthusiast and the student through the tangled thickets of the literature covering the major industries. A Methuen's 'University paperbacks' edition has also been issued. *Industrial archaeology a new introduction* (1976) contains two up-to-date appendixes: the first an alphabetical list of local societies carrying out research, recording, publishing and political action within the field of industrial archaeology; and the second a classified list of films illustrating industrial and transport history. There is also a gazetteer of industrial sites particularly worth visiting.

356 '**Industrial archaeology**' *the journal of the history of industry and technology* was established in 1964 as a medium for industrial archaeologists to publish the results of their work and to keep in touch with the activities of other groups and individuals. Published quarterly the journal covered the history of mechanical innovations, the sources of power, and the archaeology and history of individual industries and businesses during a creative period in industrial archaeology. Methodology, current research, news, and book reviews were all featured regularly and the journal was always unusually well illustrated with photographs, maps and drawings. An 'Annual review of literature on industrial archaeology and industrial history', compiled by Kenneth Hudson, Ian Donnachie, and John Butt in the form of an alphabetical author list of books with a classified list of periodical articles, appeared in the last issue of every volume 1970-1974. No one could claim that the journal enjoyed a settled existence: during the course of its comparatively short history it experienced a variety of titles and publishers. The first two volumes were published by the Lampart Press as *The journal of the history of industry and technology*, in 1968 it assumed its final title and in 1974 it was transferred to Bratton Publishing Ltd of Edinburgh. At the same time John Butt succeeded Kenneth Hudson, doyen of industrial archaeologists, as editor. This arrangement was shortlived however: Butt resigned at the end of January 1975 leaving material for two issues, those for November 1974 and February 1975 ready for the press but in fact no more were published. The Association for Industrial Archaeology (*qv*) announced that it was severing its previous connection with the journal and now it must be regarded as defunct. In many respects this was regrettable, as for ten years the journal had offered hospitality to a wide range of articles and had undoubtedly played a prominent part in establishing the academic respectability of the whole field of industrial archaeology.

357 'Industrial archaeology in Britain' by R A Buchanan, first published by Pelican Books in 1972, is now available in hardback covers from Allen Lane. Its introductory section on the study of industrial archaeology is particularly useful in defining terms, presenting the historical framework and present organization of the subject in Britain. Other sections discuss the various industrial categories and public services and, lastly, there are regional surveys of industrial monuments which although described by the author as a personal selection provides a most acceptable framework for investigations and visits. The regions are broad geographical units, each section has a map showing the most prominent monuments with national grid references and a short bibliography. In addition each chapter is furnished with notes and bibliographical references.

358 'The industrial archaeology of the British Isles', a new series published by Batsford, will cover all the major industrial monuments and sites of Britain. The first volume to be published is John R Hume's *The industrial archaeology of Scotland: 1 The Lowlands and Borders* (1976) which lists systematically in a county and parish arrangement most of the sites where complete or substantial industrial remains are to be seen. Although the intention is to list as many sites as possible in order to encourage their detailed study this is only an outline guide and the inclusion of a particular site does not necessarily imply that it has been adequately recorded. The general editor of the series is Keith Falconer.

359 'The industrial archaeology of the British Isles' is a series of books published by David and Charles of Newton Abbot. The first group covers the British Isles region by region whilst the second group, the associated volumes, examines smaller areas in greater detail. Both groups are produced in the same format and include a gazetteer, notes and references, and a bibliography; all volumes are copiously illustrated with photographs, maps, and drawings. *Titles*: *Cornwall* (A C Todd and Peter Laws); *Derbyshire* (Frank Nixon); *The East Midlands* (David M Smith); *Galloway* (Ian Donnachie); *Hertfordshire* (W Branch Johnson); *The Isle of Man* (T A Bawden, and others); *The Lake Counties* (J D Marshall and Michael Davies-Shiel);

Lancashire (Owen Ashmore); *North East England*, 2 vols (Frank Atkinson); *The Peak District* (Helen Harris); *Scotland* (John Butt); *Southern England* (Kenneth Hudson); *The Tamar Valley* (Frank Booker) and *Wales* (D Morgan Rees). *Associated volumes: The Bristol Region* (Angus Buchanan and Neil Cossons); *Dartmoor* (Helen Harris); *Gloucestershire woollen mills* (Jennifer Tann); *Stone blocks and iron rails* (Bertram Baxter); and *Techniques of industrial archaeology* (J P M Pannell). The series editor is E R R Green.

360 'Industrial archaeology review', an illustrated journal published by the Oxford University Press in association with the Association for Industrial Archaeology first appeared in September 1976. It intends to provide a meeting point for a wide range of specialist interest but will concentrate on the history of industry and technology in the period of the Industrial Revolution, with an emphasis on the surviving material evidence. Although it is envisaged that most of its contents will be based on British material, it is the intention of the editor, John Butt, to present material of relevance and value to comparative studies. Three issues will be published in each academic year. The circumstances surrounding publication of the *Review* and some disparaging words appear in Philip Riden's note, 'Local interests', *TLS* 7th January 1977, inevitably leading to one of those epistolary duels so favoured by that journal.

361 Inner London Archaeology Unit was established in 1974 by the London and Middlesex Archaeological Society to handle all archaeological work in the London Boroughs of Camden, Hackney, Hammersmith, Kensington and Chelsea, Islington, Tower Hamlets, and the City of Westminster. It sees its primary task as the preparation of surveys and the collating of archaeological information into a sites and monuments record.

362 Institute of Archaeology, University of London, first mooted by the Board of Studies in Archaeology in 1928, was formally opened 29 April 1937 in St John's Lodge, Regents Park, as a centre of academic research and for instruction in those branches of archaeology for which no courses were available in the university. The proposal really took shape when the Society of Antiquaries called a conference in 1932 to consider and develop a scheme which the university could support. The conclusion was that the institute should provide materials for study, instruction in the treatment of antiquities and training in archaeological methods, and a grounding in the methodology and recording of research. Now, forty

166

years on, the institute is the major university school for young, academically qualified archaeologists, providing courses at both undergraduate and postgraduate levels. Another important step forward came in March 1958 when the institute moved into its present purpose-built premises in Gordon Square, shared with the Institute of Classical Studies, which enabled it to become a more effective centre for archaeological activities within the university, and provided space for the first time for all its multifarious needs.

Two notable bibliographical aids provided in the institute's extensive and professionally staffed library are the meticulously compiled subject index to books and periodicals in stock and a most impressive index to archaeological sites, both on slips mounted in massive guard-books. The latter devotes seven of these huge volumes to Britain, one to Australasia, eight to Europe, two to America, five to Asia, and two to Africa. The institute's principal publications are the *Bulletin* (*qv*) and a series of occasional papers.

Bibliography: 'The opening of the Institute', *First annual report* 1937: 9-13 includes the speeches of Sir Charles Pears, chairman of the Management Committee, and the Earl of Athlone, Chancellor of the University; V Gordon Childe's 'University of London Institute of Archaeology', *Archaeological newsletter* 3(4) September 1950: 57-60 discusses its aims and purposes, work and methods, and facilities; M B Cookson's 'The photographic department of the Institute', *Bulletin of the Institute of Archaeology*, 4 1964: 25-27 describes the chief functions of the photographic studio; W F Grimes' 'Archaeology and the University', *Annual report 13* 1956-1957: 37-48 examines the contemporary position of archaeological studies within the university and discusses the anomalies of the various arrangements by which the candidates work for their diplomas; whilst J D Evans' 'Archaeology as education and profession', *Bulletin 12* 1975: 1-2 takes stock of the present status of archaeology, muses on possible developments, notably the instruction of archaeology provided in schools, and its place in the university curriculum, and ends with a consideration of the institute's role in education and research. A graphic account of the events leading up to the institute's foundation is to be found in the pages of Mortimer Wheeler's *Still digging* (1956).

363 International Congress of Anthropology and Prehistoric Archaeology (Congrès international d'anthropologie et d'archéologie préhistorique) emerged from the Congrès international paleoethnologique held at Neuchatel in August 1866, the first ever international gathering devoted to

archaeology. The object of the congress as it developed was to bring together archaeologists from every part of the world to discuss all matters
of common interest connected with prehistoric man. Fourteen congresses
met up to the first world war, all their proceedings are available from
Kraus Reprint.

364 International Congress of the Prehistoric and Protohistoric Sciences
(Congrès international des Sciences préhistoriques et protohistoriques)
came into existence at a representative meeting of prehistorians in Berne,
28 May 1932, at which it was agreed that it would be easier and more
desirable to found a new congress than to revive the old International
Congress of Anthropology and Prehistoric Archaeology (*qv*). The meeting accepted the invitation of the Society of Antiquaries and the Royal
Anthropological Institute to hold the first session in London, 1-6 August
1932. This was followed by further sessions at Oslo (1936), Zurich (1950),
Madrid (1954), Hamburg (1958), Rome (1961), Prague (1966), Belgrade
(1971), and Nice (1976). The affairs of the congress are effectively in
the hands of an executive committee and a secretary-general, there is a
permanent council composed of national representatives (which meets
every two to three years), and a committee of honour of distinguished
archaeologists. The sessions usually take the form of eight simultaneous
programmes of papers and discussion in various sections: non-European;
palaeolithic and mesolithic; neolithic; bronze age; iron age; Roman;
medieval; and anthropology, palaeontology and numismatics, although
the designations sometimes vary.

Continuous preoccupations and activities sponsored by the congress
include the publication of a polyglot archaeological glossary (a number
of European countries seem to have reached an advanced stage with a
glossary of their own, a few have in fact been published), the compilation of an archaeological atlas, and the *Inventaria archaeologica* (*qv*).
Although the congress is the only permanent archaeological association
which attempts to take stock of progress in the whole area of prehistory
and protohistory at regular intervals, there has been growing criticism of
the way in which the sessions are organized especially of the apparent
inability of speakers to content themselves with a concise statement of
essential and relevant information within the usual specified time limit
of twenty minutes. Presidents of sessions have also come under attack
for not being rigorous in their enforcement of this time limit. More
fundamental however is an increasing concern that the congress has
ceased to fulfil a useful function, that it habitually concentrates on the
168

archaeology of one region only to the neglect of the general background of European research.

There is disquiet too that although the congress is representative of over eighty countries, the majority of which are non-European, the sessions are always arranged in European cities and are attended almost exclusively by European prehistorians. Besides which the significance and prestige of the congress is in danger of being devalued as other regional congresses and conferences proliferate. John Alexander in his 'The 1971 Belgrade congress', *Antiquity*, XLVI (183) September 1972: 218-221 recommends that a European-centred congress should be separated from the world congress and that the two should assemble alternatively at five year intervals. He would like to see the papers at the world congress achieve a more equitable balance of interest between continents with a greater emphasis on new methods and techniques. The congress programme could then be arranged along lines other than those of simple chronological or regional summaries, perhaps the wider implications of human prehistory might be aired, or the world-wide problems of archaeology, the wholesale and increasing destruction of archaeological evidence, the illicit traffic in antiquities, could be considered. This would at least fit in with the congress' representative position as the only archaeological member of the International Council (Philosophy and History) of Unesco.

The history of the congress, which changed its name to Union Internationale des Sciences Préhistoriques et Protohistoriques (UISPP) in 1956 is outlined in Siegried J de Laet's 'Un siecle de collaboration internationale dans le domaine des sciences préhistoriques et protohistoriques du congrès de Neuchatel (aôut 1866) au congrès de Prague (aôut 1966)', *Actes du 7e congrès . . . vol 2*: 1423-1439 published by the Academia-Institut d'Archéologie et de l'Académie Tchecoslavique des Sciences à Prague, 1970. This relies for the early period on J Comas' *Historia y bibliografia de los congresos internationales de ciencias antropologicas 1865-1954* published in Mexico 1956. The proceedings of each session are normally printed in the host country and became available two or three years after the session was held. In addition to Hohn Alexander's report quoted above Stuart Piggott's 'The Zurich conference', *Antiquity*, XXIV (96) December 1950: 171-174 and T G E Powell's 'The Hamburg conference', *Antiquity* XXXII (128) December 1958: 247-252 are also illuminating summaries of events.

365 International Council of Museums, a non-governmental institution, was formed in 1946 as a professional organization. Its activities include the organization of seminars in cooperation with Unesco on various general, specialised, and regional aspects of museology. The standing national committees are responsible in turn for arranging triennial conferences. The council publishes *ICOM news*, a comprehensive review of the world's museums. W T O.Dea's 'Working with ICOM', Norman Cook's 'ICOM and the Museums Association', and Sir Philip Hendy's 'ICOM and the future', all appeared in *Museums journal* 64(4) March 1965.

366 International Institute for the Conservation of Historic and Artistic Works was founded in 1950 as the International Institute for the Conservation of Museum Objects. Its task is to coordinate and improve the knowledge, methods, and working standards, needed to protect and preserve precious materials of all kinds. Publications include *Art and archaeology technical abstracts* and *Studies in conservation* (*qqv*). In 1974 the United Kingdom Group published *Conservation in museums and art galleries*, a survey of facilities based on questionnaires sent to all museums, containing a full discussion and analysis of the data revealed and the subcommittee's recommendations for the future.

367 'International journal of nautical archaeology and underwater exploration' (1972-) is now published quarterly for the Council for Nautical Archaeology by the Academic Press. 'The themes of this journal are seas, ships, cargoes, sailors of the past: subjects which have excited interest throughout history. The journal keeps readers abreast of the latest exploration, discoveries, and technical innovations. Studies on ancient ships, harbours, artefacts and cargoes, whether from excavation or documentary sources, will furnish new material for the naval architect, the historian and the archaeologist . . . For scientists, papers relating archaeology to geology, ecology and oceanography will indicate the close association of these disciplines' (introductory brochure). Informative papers of interest include Lucien Basch's 'Ancient wrecks and the archaeology of ships' vol 1 March 1972: 1-58, which sums up the achievements of underwater archaeology from the seventeenth century onwards and discusses the ancient literature of naval architecture and compares it with results from recent ship excavations; Arne Emil Christensen's comment on this outline, vol 2(1) March 1973: 137-145; F M Auburn's 'Deep sea archaeology and the law' in the same issue, pages 159-162; and Angela Croome's 'Table of new maritime museums, galleries and exhibitions (primarily Old World)' 2(2) September 1973: 391-396.

368 'International medieval bibliography' (1967-) is a half-yearly list of all articles on medieval topics published in journals and festschrift

170

volumes directed by P H Sawyer of the University of Leeds. The period covered ranges from 500-1500 and includes works on archaeology, art and architecture, literature and history, philosophy and theology, and is European in scope. Entries are arranged by topic and sub-divided by area.

369 '**An introduction to American archaeology**' by Gordon Willey, published in two volumes by Prentice-Hall 1966-1971, is a descriptive account of New World prehistory spanning the period from Man's first appearance in the western hemisphere to the coming of the Europeans, written for the general reader and the student who requires a narrative guide to the broad field of American archaeology. The author describes the two volumes as an interpretation of the findings of New World archaeologists in their natural environmental context and in the light of recent ethnographic and ethnohistorical information. The work is at the same time a guide to excavated sites and discoveries and an examination of languages, geographical and climatic influences, regional differences, cultural traditions, archaeological periods, and the growth of civilizations. Extensive footnotes and a bibliography ensure that the student who wishes to enquire further into the complexities of pre-Columbian culture is not left entirely to his own resources.

370 '**An introduction to prehistoric archaeology**' by Frank Hole and Robert E Heizer (Holt, Rinehart & Winston, 2ed 1969) is described as an introduction to the science of prehistory, not a summary of facts; it deals with the methods of investigation, what the archaeologist does, rather than what he has found. It is arranged in six parts divided into eighteen chapters: Part I 'Introducing the study of prehistory' (archaeology and the archaeologist, prehistoric archaeology); Part II 'Archaeological evidence' (sites, preservation of evidence, archaeological context); Part III 'Acquiring the facts of prehistory' (survey, excavation and recording, classification and description); Part IV 'Dating the events of prehistory' (by physical-chemical methods, geochronology, using plant and animal remains, other methods); Part V 'Reconstructing cultural subsystems' (Subsistence and economic systems, patterns of settlement, social and religious systems); and Part VI 'Theories and methods of archaeological interpretation' (analysis of culture processes, historical reconstructions in archaeology). Each chapter ends with a list of references and there is an exhaustive bibliography, the authors' response to their realistic appreciation that no single volume, no matter how well conceived can possibly represent the totality of archaeology in all its ramifications.

371 'Introductions to archaeology' is the general title given to a series of
volumes published by the Phaidon Press which not only survey the development of archaeology in particular countries and regions but also examine
the various civilizations uncovered. Titles: *History from the earth: an
introduction to archaeology* (J Forde-Johnston); *Heritage of the Pharaohs:
an introduction to Egyptian archaeology* (John Ruffle); and *From village
to empire: an introduction to the archaeology of the Near East* (C A
Burney). Each is described as 'an expert's foundation study for the layman'. They are available as hardbacks and in paperback. Other titles are
in preparation, the series editor is J Forde-Johnston.

372 'Introductory readings in archaeology', edited by Brian M Fagan and
published by Little, Brown & Co of Boston in 1970, consists of a representative series of extracts from scientific reports and general essays designed
to complement the textbook reading of students.

373 'Inventaria archaeologica', a project for an illustrated card inventory
of important associated finds in archaeology, proposed by the Belgian
archaeologist M E Marien, was accepted by the International Congress of
Prehistoric and Protohistoric Sciences at Zurich 1950, and undoubtedly
constitutes one of that body's major enterprises. Each participating
country produces in a uniform format a series of cards of the finds essential to the understanding of each period it covers. The cards, 215mm x
275mm, are numbered serially in order of appearance in each country's
section. In addition to line drawings and sections, a description of each
item together with a summary of available information about it (bibliography, site, comparisons and analyses) appears on the reverse side of
the card. The British series, which is supported by the Council for British
Archaeology, has so far been restricted to the bronze age although eventually it is the intention to extend to other periods. Material is chosen both
for its relevance to the internal chronology and typology and for its importance in cross-dating with other countries. Sets produced so far in
Britain, each set consisting of ten cards, are:

   1 Grave groups and hoards of the British bronze age, 1955
   2 Bronze age hoards in the British Museum, 1955
   3 Grave groups and hoards of the British bronze age, 1956
   4 Bronze age hoards and grave groups for the N E Midlands, 1957
   5 Early and middle bronze age grave groups and hoards from Scotland, 1958
   6 Late bronze age hoards in the British Museum, 1958

7 Middle bronze age hoards from southern England, 1959
8 Bronze age grave groups and hoards in the British Museum, 1960
9 Late bronze age finds in the Heathery Burn Cave, Co Durham, 1968.
The first seven sets were published by Garraway Ltd but they are now
issued by British Museum Publications Ltd.

374 'Iran' *journal of the British Institute of Persian Studies* (1963-) is
an annual English language publication for articles on Persian studies
written by scholars of all nationalities. Its usual contents include a report
by the institute's director, papers and shorter notices, and a survey of excavations in Persia during the previous year. A statement of its aims and
purposes appeared in volume one.

375 'Iraq' the journal of the British school in Iraq was instituted as an
annual publication in 1932-33 for the studies of the history, art, archaeology, religion, economic and social life of Iraq (and to a lesser extent of
its neighbouring countries where they relate to it) from the earliest times
down to 1700. It is now published twice a year to keep the general reader
informed about the discoveries of the ancient civilizations of Mesopotamia
and to discuss topics of current interest. Volume XXV (1963) is devoted
to the results of excavations at Nimrud where the school has made a
major contribution to the discovery of ancient Assyria; volume XXXI
(1969) in honour of C J Gadd includes a bibliography; and volume XXXVI
(1974) published to similarly honour Sir Max Mallowan prints a bibliography of his writings to 1974.

376 'Ireland in prehistory' by Michael Herity and George Eogan (Routledge, 1977) is a scholarly account of Irish prehistory in the light of archaeological discoveries over the last twenty-five years intended not only for
the general reader but also in the first instance for 'the large numbers of
young people who are now studying archaeology in our universities'. A
short history of Irish archaeology from the seventeenth century is included
in an introduction setting the geographical and historical background; in
the following chapters the authors concern themselves with Ireland's prehistoric economy, technology, burial customs, art and society, and its
surviving remains. In the place of the usual bibliography either arranged
alphabetically by author, by chapter, or in a classified sequence, there is
a comprehensive (pp 256-282) bibliographical index closely linked to the
text.

173

377 'Iron age communities in Britain' *an account of England, Scotland and Wales from the seventh century BC until the Roman conquest* by Barry Cunliffe, published in 1974, is the first volume of Routledge's 'Archaeology of Britain' series. After a valuable introductory chapter examining the development of iron age studies and its associated literature from the mid-nineteenth century onwards, the author looks at the various iron age peoples of Britain first from a chronological and regional standpoint and then from the broader aspect of cultural patterns and social change. The scholarly apparatus is complete and the extensive bibliography emphasises the very real scholarship of the book which is surely earmarked for standard definitive work status.

378 'The iron age in lowland Britain' by D W Harding (Routledge, 1974), is primarily intended as a student textbook although it includes some personal controversial interpretations of the evidence as to the relationship of southern Britain in the iron age with contemporary European cultures. The book falls naturally into two halves: a survey of settlement patterns and structural types, and a chronological investigation of the material remains in an effort to determine whether cultural change derived from continental influences or were generated spontaneously. An impressive full-scale bibliography underlines the fact that this work is not designed for the general reader.

379 'The iron age in northern Britain' edited by A L F Rivet (Edinburgh University Press, 1966) consists of revised versions of papers delivered to a Conference on the Problems of the Iron Age in Northern Britain held in Edinburgh in October 1961 organized by the Iron Age and Roman Research Committee of the Council for British Archaeology. *Papers*: 'A scheme for the Scottish iron age' (Stuart Piggott), a brief conspectus of the history of its study and of the current state of knowledge; 'Metal work and some other objects in Scotland' (Robert B K Stevenson); 'The sequence of Hebridean pottery' (Alison Young); 'The hill-forts of northern Britain' (R W Feachem); 'A field survey in Northumberland' (George Jobey); and 'Forts, brochs and wheel-houses in northern Scotland' (J R C Hamilton). There is a comprehensive classified bibliography.

380 'Journal of archaeological science', published quarterly since 1974 by the Academic Press, was conceived by John Cruise whilst researching for their 'Science in archaeology' series. He decided that there was room for a journal to carry the results of the increasing research in the
174

archaeological sciences that would in all probability not reach publication in book form. The *Journal* aims to publish papers, reviews, and short notes, covering material which combines archaeology with other disciplines such as mathematics, the physical, biological, and earth sciences, and it is intended that all papers shall be understandable in principle, if not in detail, by the modern archaeologist with an elementary knowledge of science. Its present editors are G W Dimbleby and D R Brothwell both of the Institute of Archaeology, London, and H Barker of the British Museum Research Laboratory.

381 'Journal of Egyptian archaeology' was instituted by the Egypt Exploration Fund in 1914 to deal systematically with all branches of Egyptological studies including archaeological excavations. At the time it was intended to cater for both Egyptologists and the informed general public with an interest in Egyptology but it soon became indistinguishable in style and scope from other learned society journals and it would be a brave member of the general public who attempted to read through its pages now. Until about twenty five years ago the *Journal* was acutely aware of its bibliographical responsibilities but of late this aspect of its contents has sadly declined. One or two of its early volumes included reports on the work of the now defunct British School of Archaeology in Egypt. The *Journal* is published annually.

382 'Journal of field archaeology', first published in 1974, stresses the interdisiplinary nature of archaeology and includes studies dealing with all aspects of archaeological projects, the occasional larger interpretative paper, and more frequent summaries of archaeological research. 'The antiquities market', news and commentary on the illicit international traffic in antiquities; 'Perspectives', a forum for the discussion of archaeological matters by the *Journal's* readers; and news items are regular features. 'Staffing opportunities' is a two-way feature designed to be of use to directors of excavations and potential staff. Other articles deal with methodology and the technical problems of field work. Volume 1 consisted of two double issues but from then onwards the *Journal* has appeared quarterly. A subscription includes membership of the Association for Field Archaeology.

383 'The journal of Roman studies', first published by the Society for the Promotion of Roman Studies in 1911, 'endeavours to satisfy the membership by maintaining the high standard set in the earliest volumes;

it is meant for the publication of research and tries to keep abreast of research while maintaining a balance of subject and periods in history and archaeology particularly . . .' In 1921 a feature 'Roman Britain' was introduced, an extensive account of the sites explored during the previous year together with an exhaustive bibliography. It continued almost without break until 1970 when it was transferred to the society's newly established journal *Britannia* (*qv*). I A Richmond's 'Roman Britain 1910-1960' a review of the excavations, discoveries and literature of fifty years appeared in the jubilee volume, 1960: 173-191. Other general articles of note include Richmond's 'Recent discoveries in Roman Britain from the air and in the field', volume XXXIII, 1943: 45-54, his 'Hadrian's wall 1939-1949' XL, 1950: 43-56, and K Jackson's 'On some Romano-British place-names', XXXVIII, 1948: 54-58. An index to volumes I-XXI was published in 1931, a *Consolidated index of volumes XXII-XL 1931-1950* was issued under the auspices of the International Federation of Classical Societies with the aid of an Unesco grant in 1955, and a further *Consolidated index of volumes XLI-LX 1951-1970* appeared in 1975. Kraus Reprint offer individual volumes or a complete set 1911-1935 in cloth or paper covers.

384 'Journal of the British Archaeological Association', 1st series: vols 1-50 (1845-1894); new series: vols 1-41 (1885-1936); third series 1937 onwards, is now an annual publication although when it first appeared as a riposte to *The archaeological journal* it was distributed to subscribing members of the association at quarterly intervals. Recent volumes contain original papers, reports of lectures delivered at the winter meetings and at the annual summer meeting, and book reviews. Several cumulative index volumes have been published.

385 Kent Archaeological Society traces its origins to a meeting at Mereworth Castle, 19th September 1857, called by the Viscount Falmouth at the instigation of his chaplain Lambert B Larking who had received a letter the previous month from George Bish Webb, hon secretary of the Surrey society, proposing the formation of a joint archaeological society for the two counties. Webb was actively canvassing support for this proposal much to Larking's indignation and time was pressing if an independent Kent society was to be founded. And so the society dispensed with the usual public circulars and meetings, the rules of the Sussex society were unceremoniously and hastily adopted, and by the time the inaugural meeting was held in Maidstone museum the following April the membership already exceeded five hundred. No particular objects were set down (even today the society contents itself with the bald statement that its object is 'to promote the study of archaeology in all its branches, especially within the county of Kent') but it was proposed to hold regular meetings 'for the purpose of reading papers, the exhibition of antiquities, or the discussion of subjects connected therewith'. Larking was impatient to publish a volume of *Transactions*, the outward sign of a flourishing society, but owing to various delays the first volume of *Archaeologia Cantiana* although dated 1858 did not appear until July 1859. In his anonymous introduction J S Brewer proclaimed the purpose of the *Transactions*: 'From the memory of things decayed and forgotten, we propose to save and recover what we may, for the present generation and for posterity, of the wrecks still floating on the ocean of time, and preserve them with a religious and scrupulous diligence.' It was hoped that *Archaeologia Cantiana* would be an annual publication but this was only achieved on a regular basis after 1925. A detailed account of the foundation, inaugural, and first annual meetings, including copious quotations from the extraordinarily numerous and long-winded proposals and resolutions etc, may be found in 'Kent Archaeological Society', vol 1, 1858: xxxiii-lxxxv. Frank W Jessup's 'The origin and first hundred years of the society' LXX, 1956: 1-42, based for the early years on Larking's Journals, is a fascinating and detailed account of the society's activities, personalities, social background, finances, and publications. 'Ancient monuments in Kent' LXI, 1948: 122-125 appeared in the absence of an official list of scheduled monuments. 'Researches and discoveries in Kent', a current awareness survey printed in many volumes at the turn of the century, was revived in 1950 and has continued without break since then; 'Investigations and excavations during the year' consisting of reports of excavations supported by the society together with reports from local groups have appeared intermittently since 1968; and 'A Kent bibliography' has been included since 1971. A complete catalogue of the society's library was published in the 1966-71 volumes. Index volumes to *Archaeologia Cantiana* have appeared in the regular numbered series—vols XIX (1892), LII (1940), LXVII (1954), and XC (1975) are all general indexes. An *Index of archaeological matters as published in Archaeologia Cantiana from volume 1 (1858) to volume 83 (1968) covering the stone ages, the bronze age, the iron age, the Roman period and the pagan Anglo-Saxon period*, compiled by John H Evans, was published separately in 1970.

386 Kraus-Thomson Organization Limited is composed of three divisions, Kraus Periodicals, Kraus Reprints and KTO Microforms, and between

them they publish a vast number of informative catalogues describing
their ongoing publishing programmes which can be of the utmost value
to librarians in charge of newly-formed collections likely to be lacking
in older material such as extensive runs of learned journals or specialist
books long out of print. Kraus Reprints' (seventh) *General catalogue*
is published in three parts: *Periodicals, series, reference works* (1974-75);
Monographs in series (1975-76) and *Books* (1975). Each one of these
sale catalogues may be regarded as a bibliography in its own right, together they form an unrivalled bibliographic control tool in academic
publishing. Part I is an international, alphabetic by title, generously annotated, list of periodical sets etc indexed under subject headings of which
'Anthropology, ethnology, and archaeology' is one. There is a thirty page
inset printed on a distinctive coloured paper entitled 'New listings' *ie*
titles and continuations of series added to the Kraus Program since the
previous *General catalogue*. Part II is a straightforward alphabetical list
with no annotation of monograph series and international congresses.
Special-subject catalogues issued by Kraus Reprint include *Anthropology
archaeology folklore*, in which journals, books, and monograph series
are listed alphabetically within each section; and *A comprehensive list
of reprints in the field of art history, archaeology, architecture*. Kraus
Reprint claim that their volumes are produced on paper specially selected
for its strength and longevity in which low acidity content ensures a
greater degree of permanence, and suggest that their editions should be
looked upon as an improved technical product which is in many cases
more suitable for library use than the originals. Kraus Periodicals issue a
special list *Art and archaeology books and periodicals* and KTO Microforms publish a *General catalogue* which includes a section on anthropology, ethnology and archaeology. Most listings in these catalogues
are for complete runs but enquiries for shorter runs are welcomed.
Credit terms are sometimes extended to libraries to allow for the acquisition and immediate use of important publications. Catalogues may be
obtained either from FL-9491 Nendeln, Liechtenstein or from Route 100,
Millwood, New York 10546.

387 Lancashire and Cheshire Antiquarian Society was founded 21 March
1883 at a meeting in the rooms of the Manchester Literary and Philosophical Society at which letters of support from the nobility and gentry
were read. Shortly afterwards an inaugural conversazione was held at
Owens College. The aims and objectives of the society were declared to
be to examine, preserve, and illustrate ancient monuments and records,

178

and to foster the study of history, literature, arts, customs and traditions, with particular reference to the antiquities of the two counties. In addition the society has constantly encouraged and assisted excavation and fieldwork. Two papers in the *Transactions* relate the society's history: J Wilfrid Jackson's 'Genesis and progress of the Lancs and Ches Antiquarian Society', vol XLIX, 1933: 104-112, and the same writer's 'The Lancashire and Cheshire Antiquarian Society 1883-1943', LVII, 1943: 1-17, a decade by decade sketch of the society's activities with especial attention given to the papers printed in the *Transactions* which began publication in 1883. An outstanding feature of the volumes 1890-1903 was a 'Bibliography of Lancashire and Cheshire antiquities' started by Ernest Axon who suggested that the society should subscribe to a press cuttings agency, compile scrapbooks, and deposit them in a public library. Every so often a subject index to the bibliography would also be printed. Other papers of note include Arthur J Evan's 'Megalithic monuments in their sepulchral relation', vol III, 1855:1-31; William Harrison's 'Defensive earthworks and fortified enclosures of Cheshire', XXV, 1907: 146-155: J Wilfrid Jackson's 'The prehistoric archaeology of Lancashire and Cheshire', L, 1934-1935: 65-106, and his 'Some early references to prehistoric and Roman antiquities in Lancashire and Cheshire' pages 162-176 in the same volume. W J Varley's 'Recent investigations into the origins of Cheshire hill forts', LI, 1936: 51-59; J D Bu'lock's 'The bronze age in the north-west', 71, 1961: 1-42; and J Forde-Johnston's 'The iron age hill-forts of Lancashire and Cheshire', 72, 1962: 9-46 should also be mentioned. Decennial indexes are published at the end of every tenth volume.

388 'Landscape archaeology' *an introduction to fieldwork techniques on post-Roman landscapes* by Michael Aston and Trevor Rowley (David and Charles, 1974) describes itself as 'a modest manual of fieldwork techniques which can be employed by individuals or groups working on areas and topics of their own choice' and is designed to help stimulate and guide extra-mural and undergraduate studies. Subjects covered include landscape archaeology, fieldwork techniques, maps, aerial photography, fieldwork in towns, villages and countryside, and the organisation and application of fieldwork. Some examples of efficient documentation are provided in the numerous appendices and there are plentiful notes and references in addition to a brief bibliography.

389 'Larousse encyclopaedia of archaeology' was first published in English by the Hamlyn Publishing Group in 1972 and is a translation of *Larousse* *l'archéologie découverte des civilisations disparues*, a title which perhaps better indicates its true contents. It is divided into two sections: the first, 'Archaeology at work', defines what archaeology is, explains how monuments survive, reveals how sites are located, and examines the techniques of excavation. A final chapter in this section on restoration, exhibition, and publication includes a number of interesting topics like reanimating ruins by son et lumière, the requirements of good museum presentation, or the principle of scholarly ownership in publication, which rarely find the light of day. The second section, 'The recovery of the past', is devoted to a world-wide survey of the cultures and civilisations of the ancient world and how these have been located and uncovered. Illustration is on a lavish scale, no page is complete without at least one photograph and there are no fewer than 40 full page colour plates but it would not be correct to regard the *Encyclopaedia* as just another coffee-table book. Its contributors are all French academics and authorities in their areas and each chapter is furnished with a list of further readings which are all in English for this edition. Nevertheless doubts remain whether this admittedly full-scale work may be truly described as an encyclopaedia, it is almost entirely descriptive and not analytical in method although, to be fair, it does contain 'exhaustive information on some one art or branch of knowledge, arranged systematically' (*Shorter Oxford Dictionary*). However, it is undeniably an attractive and colourful volume which would grace any library shelf. Gilbert Charles-Picard is the general editor.

390 Layard, Sir Austen Henry (1817-1894) is renowned for his spectacular successes in uncovering the palaces of Sennacherib and Ashurbanipal in the desert of southern Mesopotamia. His book *Nineveh and its remains* caused a tremendous stir of excitement when it was published in 1848 as did *Discoveries in the ruins of Nineveh and Babylon* (1853). Gordon Waterfield's *Layard of Nineveh* (John Murray, 1963) is a comprehensive study which relies extensively on the 340 volumes of Layard papers in the Manuscript Room of the British Library Reference Division; M E L Mallowan and R D Barnett contribute comments on his archaeological prowess.

391 Leakey, L S B (1903-1972) immeasurably advanced the study of early hominids and their relation to the origins of human evolution by his remarkable discoveries of fossils and artifacts in Olduvai Gorge, Kenya. His theories and evidence are not easily comprehended by the layman, but it is enough to say that his work in this highly specialized field has
180

established Africa as the probably cradle of humanity. *Adam's ancestors, an up-to-date outline of the old stone age (palaeolithic) and what is known about man's origins and evolution*, completely rewritten for a second edition by Methuen in 1954, may be tackled with confidence by the non-specialist; the full report of his discoveries in Olduvai published by Cambridge University Press should perhaps be left to experts: *A preliminary report on the geology and fauna* (1965); *The cranium and mallixary dentition of Australopitheus (Zinjanthropus)* (1967); and *Excavation in beds 1 + 11 1960-1963* by M D Leakey (1971). Leakey's second volume of autobiography, *By the evidence*, (Harcourt Brace Jovanovich, 1974) includes a 'Publisher's prologue', a sketch of the highlights of his career.

392 Leicestershire Archaeological and Historical Society was formed as the Leicestershire Architectural and Archaeological Society at an inaugural meeting in the Town Library, Guild Hall, Leicester, 10 January 1855, 'to promote the study of ecclesiastical architecture, general antiquities, and the restoration of mutilated architectural remains within the county; and to furnish suggestions, so far as may be within its province, for improving the character of ecclesiastical edifices, and for preserving all ancient remains which the committee may consider of value and importance'. The society was at once admitted to the Associated Societies in the Midland region and the first reports of its proceedings appeared in their *Reports and papers*, but in 1866 the society began to issue its own *Transactions* designed initially to offer a permanent record of papers read to the society since its formation. An account of the inaugural meeting is contained in 'Formation of the Leicestershire Architectural and Archaeological Society' *Transactions* vol 1, 1866: 13-16, and the society's early activities are recorded in W G D Fletcher's 'A brief notice of the work the society has accomplished during the fifty years of its existence', vol IX: 1904-5: 252-257. which presents a long list of distinguished antiquaries connected with the society and underlines its interest in ecclesiology and church restoration. A Hamilton Thompson's 'The Leicestershire Archaeological Society in the present century', vol XXI, 1939-41: 122-148 consists largely of reminiscences of the society stalwarts, mainly in obituary form, and of the illustrious guest lecturers who addressed its meetings. But the most useful and certainly the most analytical study of the society's interests and activities is *The Leicestershire Archaeological Society 1855-1955* published by the society in its centenary year. This contains a masterly investigation of the social background and circumstances in which the society was conceived and nurtured. Its meetings, temporary display museums, lectures, excursions, and publications receive proper attention, the period of stagnation in the 1880s and 1890s, the triumphs of the late 1930s culminating in Kathleen Kenyon's excavations of the Roman remains west of the Jewry Wall in Leicester, are all discussed generously and sympathetically. The society's centenary was also noticed by Jack Simmons' 'A valuable local society', *The Listener*, 17 February 1955 and in 'A hundred years of Midland archaeology', printed in the *Manchester guardian*, 10 January 1955. Contemporary issues of the *Transactions* are markedly more professional in form and content than the pre-war volumes, 'Archaeology in Leicestershire' and 'Leicestershire bibliography' have appeared intermittently since 1953 and 1955 respectively. A 'List of scheduled monuments in Leicestershire and Rutland' to 31st March 1956 was printed in the 1956 volume. *A general index to volumes I to XX* (1855-1939) compiled by L H Irvine appeared in 1951.

393 Leland, John (1506-1552) was commissioned by Henry VIII in 1533 to search the country's libraries for surviving ancient chronicles recording English history. And so for the next eight or nine years he toured England at a time when the dissolution of the monasteries was forging a social revolution and bringing medieval civilisation to an end. As his biographical and historiographical studies progressed Leland began to link them to the material remains of the past, the inscriptions and the field monuments, and conceived the notion of a grand topographical work to be called *De antiquitate Britannica*. But Leland was ahead of his time, the resources for such a work did not then exist, and eventually his ambitious plans overtaxed his brain. The *Britannica* was left unwritten and his manuscripts were not printed until long after his death. The most recent edition of the *Itinerary* is L Toulmin Smith's (1906-1910) reissued by the Centaur Press in 1965 with a new foreword by Sir Thomas Kendrick who also assesses Leland's part in antiquarian studies in his *British antiquity* (1950).

394 Levant *Journal of the British School of Archaeology in Jerusalem* primarily devoted to the archaeology of the Holy Land from the earliest times to circa AD 1800 was instituted by the British School of Archaeology in Jerusalem in 1968. Its appearance took some of the pressure off the *Palestine exploration quarterly*; in future archaeological reports of a detailed or technical nature would appear in the *Journal* and the more popular type of account would be printed in the *Quarterly*. Back issues may be obtained from William Dawson, Cannon House, Folkestone, Kent.

395 Lhuyd, Edward (1660-1709), keeper of the Ashmolean Museum from 1690 onwards, was one of the team of scholars who gathered material for the 1695 edition of Camden's *Britannia*. At the turn of the century he was engaged upon the tour of the Celtic world making observations on the antiquities and languages for a multi-volume *Archaeologia Britannica*. In the event this work experienced inordinate delays and only the first volume, a glossography, an elaborate etymology of the Celtic languages, ever appeared. There was to be a second volume comparing the customs and traditions of the Britons with those of other countries; a third was to have described British monuments in Wales; and a fourth was planned relating the history of the Welsh princes at the time of the Roman evacuation. Frank Emery's 'Edward Lhuyd and the 1695 *Britannica*', *Antiquity*, XXXII (127), September 1958: 179-182 is a readable essay. R T Gunther's *Life and letters of Edward Lhuyd* (1945) remains the most convenient general study; and Glyn Daniel's 'Edward Lhuyd: antiquary and archaeologist', *Welsh history review* 4 (3) 1967: 345-349 assesses his place in the history of British antiquarian scholarship.

396 'Libraries, museums and art galleries yearbook 1976' is the current edition of a work now in its ninth decade although a five year gap in publication occurred 1971-1976 caused by upheavals in the library world. A new edition is hoped for in 1978. 'Museums, art galleries and stately homes' form a section of their own, the entries being arranged alphabetically by town. All information has been supplied by the museums themselves in response to a questionnaire and is set out in the following order: official name; postal address; telephone and telex numbers; name of governing body; name, designation and qualifications of officers in charge; whether or not open to the public; hours of opening; admission charges if any; scope; special exhibits or facilities; and number of full-time professionally qualified, other non-manual, and manual staff. Index entries include general subjects, special collections and names of individual institutions subdivided alphabetically by towns.

397 Lincoln Archaeological Trust has carried out extensive rescue excavations in the city. The importance of many of its discoveries has led to an extensive publication programme in concert with the Council for British Archaeology.

398 'List and map of historic monuments' *in the care of the Department of the Environment in England, Wales and Scotland open to the public,* first published in 1961, is now available in a sixth edition (1972). About 750 immensely diverse monuments managed by the Ancient Monuments and Historic Buildings Branch (acting in Wales and Scotland respectively on behalf of the Welsh Office and the Scottish Development Department) are arranged county by county. Information provided includes hours of opening, a map reference, and indications whether or not admission is free and whether there are easily accessible parking and toilet facilities. A folded map is inserted on the inside back cover of this thirty-page book-let.

399 '**List of archaeological theses in preparation in British universities**', published in stencilled form by the Council for British Archaeology, aims to prevent duplication of study. Eventually it is hoped to compile a con-solidated list of theses since 1960.

400 '**The local historian**', journal of the Standing Conference for Local History, is now published thrice yearly. It started in the autumn of 1952 as *Amateur historian*, a periodical endeavouring to reflect the interests of all those whose hobby was the study of the past, especially that part of the past that was closest to them, their own locality. Then the emphasis was on short articles on documentary and archaeological research method-ology in order to help the untrained amateur historian. Its official con-nection with the standing conference came in 1961 (volume five); seven years later, after much agonizing, the journal changed its name. (The arguments for and against the change are set down in 'Amateur Historian or Local Historian', 7(3) 1966: 78-83 and 'Readers' views', 7(4) 1966: 102-108.) Today the journal is of most concern to the industrial archae-ologist, indeed it was in the pages of *Amateur historian* that the term was first used in academic parlance, in Michael Rix's 'Industrial archaeology', 2(8) October-November 1955: 225-228.

401 **London and Middlesex Archaeological Society** was formed in 1855 on the initiative of a small group who appointed a committee 'to consider the propriety of instituting a society for the purpose of investigating the antiquities of the county of Middlesex'. After resolving unanimously 'that the formation of such a society would be highly proper and condu-cive to the extension of archaeological science', advertisements were placed in the *Times, Notes and queries*, and other journals inviting those interested to communicate with the honorary secretary, the ubiquitous George Bish Webb. It was Lord Londesborough, president of the British
184

Archaeological Association, who first suggested widening the proposed society's area of operations to the City of London. An inaugural meeting, held at Crosby Hall, Bishopgate Street Within, 14 December, saw the society established. Its objects were defined as follows: '(1) To collect and publish the best information on the ancient arts and monuments of the cities of London and Westminster, and of the county of Middlesex; including primeval antiquities . . . and all other matters usually comprised under the head of archaeology. (2) To procure the careful observation and preservation of antiquities discovered in the progress of works, such as excavations for railways, foundations of buildings etc. (3) To make and encourage individuals and public bodies in making researches and excavations, and to afford them suggestions and cooperation. (4) To oppose and prevent, so far as may be practicable, any injuries with which monuments and ancient remains of every description may, from time to time, be threatened; and to collect accurate drawings, plans, and descriptions thereof. (5) to found a museum and library for the reception, by way of gift, loan, or purchase, of works and objects of archaeological interest. (6) To arrange periodical meetings for the reading of papers and the delivery of lectures.'

Great pains were taken to assure all and sundry that the new society had no intention of interfering in the traditional pursuits of the national archaeological institutions with headquarters in London; the sole desire was 'to do our own work on our own ground'. A full account of the proceedings at the inaugural meeting is to be found in 'Prologomena', *Transactions* 1(1) July 1856: 1-22. The society's history is well documented: Charles Welch's 'City archaeology: a retrospect and a glance forward', *Transactions* ns 1 1905: 462-468 reviews the progress of archaeology in the City of London since the society was inaugurated fifty years earlier and concludes that the most pressing need in the future is the 'tabulation and arrangement of results already obtained scattered through so many publications and private and public collections'; Sir Edward Brabrook's 'Sixtieth anniversary of the formation . . .' ns III (11) 1915: 105-122 adds details of the society's publications and relationships with other societies; C W F Goss' 'An account of the London and Middlesex Archaeological Society 1855-1955', *Transactions*, centenary volume 18(1) 1955: 1-12 looks back at the society's foundations, surveys its activities over the years, and reflects on its progress and how far it has remained true to its original objects. Although the society rarely undertakes fieldwork its archaeological activities are far from dormant: an archaeological research committee offers help to affiliated societies in the way of loans of equipment and tools, financial assistance, and the provision of excavation insurance schemes. The committee also keeps an alert eye open on development schemes and arranges an annual conference of London archaeologists at the Guildhall. In addition two other committees, for historic buildings and conservation, and for local history, are equally active. The Middlesex Local History Council was incorporated with the society in 1965. S W Howard's 'London and Middlesex Archaeological Society', *The London archaeologist,* 2(2) Spring 1973: 43-44 presents a lively account of the society's activities in recent years.

The first issue of the society's *Transactions* appeared in July 1856 only seven months after the society was formally constituted which in the light of the frustrating delays experienced by most county archaeological societies can only be regarded as a considerable achievement. The first series consists of six volumes 1860-1885, a new series started in 1905, the centenary volume of 1955 reverted to the original numbering, there was a change to a larger quarto format in 1967 (vol 21), and from 1973 (vol 24) the old system of two parts forming one volume has been abandoned in favour of the more modern trend of numbering each annual volume independently. An analysis of the contents of the six original volumes is included in Charles Welch's 'Thirty-six years work of the London and Middlesex Archaeological Society', ns 1 1905: 1-12. Reports of archaeological finds from the City of London and the historical counties of London and Middlesex added to the collections of the Guildhall and London Museums are now a regular feature. A series of special papers was introduced in 1976, the first published being *The archaeology of the London area: current knowledge and problems* edited by J Kent.

402 'The London archaeologist' a lively quarterly magazine sponsored by the leading archaeological societies in the London region began publication in 1968 in order to 'publish interim excavation reports and other suitable papers on the archaeology and allied history of the London region, to promote cooperation between societies, to provide an independent forum for discussion and to attract more of London's population towards having an interest in the past'. Although its reports on recent discoveries and other articles on current topics are intended to satisfy the professional archaeologist much of the magazine's contents are regarded as a public relations exercise; it pays considerable attention to the activities of London societies and forthcoming events, and from the beginning it has included regular features focusing on individual archaeological societies in the London area. How the editor regards the magazine and a

186

summary sketch of its first four years is outlined in 'The end of volume 1', printed in the Autumn 1972 issue.

403 Lysons, Samuel (1763-1819) is remembered chiefly for his *Reliquiae Britannico-Romanae containing figures of Roman antiquities discovered in England* issued in two folio volumes 1801-1817. Lysons had devoted twenty-five years of his life to this project, it seems odd to say the least that only fifty copies were available for sale to the public.

404 'The making of the past' a richly illustrated series published by Elsevier-Phaidon since 1975, is intended to provide the student and general reader with a complete survey of the early history of the world as revealed by archaeology and related disciplines. Each of the volumes is written by a practising archaeologist, is designed to incorporate the discoveries of recent excavations, and includes four 'visual stories', text and illustrations on either ancient monuments or excavations, in addition to a chronology and suggestions for further reading. There is an advisory board consisting of John Boardman, Reader of Classical Archaeology, Oxford; Basil Gray, former Keeper of Oriental Antiquties, British Museum; and Prof David Oates, Institute of Archaeology, University of London. Titles in series order: *Man before history* (John Waechter); *The rise of civilization* (David Oates and Joan Oates); *The Egyptian kingdoms* (Rosalie David); *The first empires* (J N Postgate); *Biblical lands* (P R S Moorey); *The Aegean civilizations* (Peter Warren); *The emergence of Greece* (Alan Johnston); *The Greek world* (Roger Ling); *The Roman world* (Michael Vickers); *Rome and Byzantium* (Clive Foss and Paul Magdalino); *The Iranian revival* (Georgina Herrmann); *India and South-east Asia* (P Rawson); *The spread of Islam* (Michael Rogers); *Ancient China* (C P Fitzgerald); *Ancient Japan* (J E Kidder); *Prehistoric Europe* (D Harding); *Barbarian Europe* (Philip Dixon); *The new world* (Warwick Bray, Ian Farrington and Earl Swanson). *The kingdoms of Africa* (Peter Garlake) and *Archaeology today*. If the present rate of publication is maintained the series should be completed by 1978. A full colour brochure is available from the publishers at Littlegate House, St Ebbe's Street, Oxford.

405 'Man's discovery of his past' *literary landmarks in archaeology* by Robert F Heizer, first published by Prentice-Hall in 1962, a collection of reprinted articles and excerpts from longer works, included a number of unfamiliar extracts from writings which in their time had nevertheless made a significant contribution to the development of archaeology as a recognized academic and scientific discipline. Previous anthologies were listed in the bibliography. A second edition appeared in 1969 under the imprint of Peek Publications of Palo Alto, California.

406 '**Map of ancient Britain**' *a map of the major visible antiquities of Great Britain older than AD 1066*, ten miles to one inch (1:625,000), derives from a special map produced in 1951 for visitors to the Festival of Britain who might wish to inspect British archaeological monuments. It is now published by the Ordnance Survey in a North and South sheet both of which are obtainable flat or folded together with text material in a laminated cover. Sites are classified according to their prehistoric or archaeological period. The text includes a select bibliography of maps, books and excavation reports, and there is a list of important regional museum collections.

407 '**Map of monastic Britain**' was first published by the Ordnance Survey in 1950 at a scale of ten miles to one inch (1:652,000) in two sheets, North and South, both being available either in a flat or in a folded version complete with text. The south sheet shows the distribution and character of all known sites of religious houses in England and Wales 1066-1540. A brief outline of monasticism during this period, together with explanatory notes on the various religious and military orders, collegiate churches, hospitals, the symbols used, the diocesan boundaries, and a bibliography and index, are all included in the text. These notes are not repeated in the text of the north sheet which concentrates on the religious foundations and ecclesiastical boundaries of Scotland although the English dioceses of Carlisle and Durham also fall within its area. The history of the map's production, its pioneer status, the complexity of its symbols, and the style of type and colouring employed, are discussed in David Knowles' 'The map of monastic Britain', *The archaeological news letter*, 3(9) March 1951: 144-145, the final sentence of which reads 'The abiding impression is one of admiration at the finished product, in which the resources of both scholarship and cartography have been so well deployed.' The second edition of 1954-55 was completely revised and redrawn, the north sheet in particular suffered a severe pruning of unauthenticated 'monasteries'.

408 '**Map of Roman Britain**' drawn on the scale of sixteen miles to one inch (1:1,000,000) has been constantly revised and reissued since it was first published by the Ordnance Survey in 1928. It is now available either
188

in a laminated full colour cover with an explanatory text or as a flat sheet map only. All land and water communications, settlements, villas and temples etc dating from the Roman occupation are marked on the map whilst the explanatory text includes a general introduction, notes on different types of site and visible remains, a chronological table, a list of Roman geographical and chronological terms, four additional maps including the entire British section of the Antonine Itinerary, and a topographical index in which sites are arranged in categories according to the symbols used on the map. The basic problems of presentation and other factors in the map's revision are discussed in C W Phillips' 'O S map of Roman Britain', *The archaeological news letter* 2(5) September 1959: 69-71.

409 '**Map of southern Britain in the iron age**', first published by the Ordnance Survey in 1962, is drawn on the scale of approximately ten miles to one inch (1:625,000). It marked a fresh start in the survey's prehistory publishing programme after stocks of previous period maps had been destroyed in the war. Available either folded in a laminated cover along with an explanatory text or as an unattached flat map, it includes all known remains of the period from the beginning of the seventh century BC to the middle of the first century AD depicted by coloured symbols with a special colour to demonstrate the spread of Belgic influence. A general historical introduction, notes on the various types of remains, a section on Celtic coins, eight distribution maps, and a classified index, are all presented in the full version.

410 Margary Trust Fund for Archaeological Research in the British Isles is administered by the Council for British Archaeology and was established by a donation of £3000 from I D Margary. Income from the fund is used to make grants to CBA regional groups, constituent organisations, and individuals, for projects promoting archaeological knowledge, especially field surveys and the compilation of catalogues although excavation work is not ruled out entirely especially if it forms part of a wider programme. The first award was made in 1965.

411 '**Mathematics and computers in archaeology**' by J E Doran and F R Hodson (Edinburgh University Press, 1975) 'is intended for archaeologists or budding archaeologists who may have no specialised mathematical knowledge, but who wish to assess the relevance of mathematics to their subject and the quality of mathematical work carried out by their colleagues'. There are three parts: basic archaeological and mathematical tools; data analysis; and beyond data analysis: problems and prospects. Many archaeologists will be tempted to murmur that they see no prospect of understanding even the basic problems. For the undeterred there is an imposing and extensive list of references to an impressively wide range of sources.

412 '**A matter of time**' *an archaeological survey of the river gravels of England*, prepared by the Royal Commission on Historical Monuments (England), published by HMSO in 1960, is a short guide to the number and distribution of sites of prehistoric settlement on the gravel terraces abutting the larger rivers. Its intention was to alert field archaeologists to the enormous increase in gravel diggings for industrial purposes, especially by mechanical excavators, and to suggest areas where urgent and detailed surveying might be expedient and where excavation might yield valuable results. Profitable use is made of a number of aerial photographs specially taken by Prof J H St Joseph all of which are extensively annotated. There is a bibliography and an appendix on the sites of the Ouse, Trent, and Welland valleys.

413 '**Medieval archaeology**', first issued in 1957, is the annual publication of the Society for Medieval Archaeology. It includes articles on the problems and results of archaeological, historical, numismatic, and linguistic studies of the medieval period in Britain in an attempt to show the interaction of one discipline upon another. Other features include the usual notes and news, and book reviews, and also 'Medieval Britain', an account of the progress of field work, excavations and news of important chance finds of the previous calendar year divided into two sections, pre-Conquest and post-Conquest. Entries contain a description of the excavation or object, the circumstances of its discovery and its present whereabouts, with a comparison or bibliographical reference if appropriate. Two index volumes covering the years 1957-1961 and 1962-1966 have appeared; each contains a general index (including all objects, types of sites, persons, authors, books received, and authorities cited) and a topographical index of all places in the British Isles with museums included under their localities with the exception of the British Museum and the Victoria and Albert which are listed separately. It is the intention to continue these indexes at five yearly intervals.

414 '**Medieval archaeology in England**' *a guide to the historical sources* by Colin Platt, published by Pinhorns of Shalfleet Manor, Isle of Wight, 190 in 1969, is intended for the archaeologist of the period unaware of the wealth of documentary materials available for consultation or who lacks the technical knowledge to exploit them. The holdings and lists, guides and catalogues of the Public Record Office, the British Library Reference Division, and other repositories, are described and examined and there is a final section on the basic reference works of historical research. A select bibliography of source materials and guides, designed particularly to meet the needs of archaeologists, concludes a most useful pamphlet.

415 Medieval Village Research Group, formerly known as the Deserted Medieval Village Research Group, was set up in August 1952 by a small group of academics of various disciplines to encourage the study of deserted villages. The group's struggle for funds, their (necessarily) limited excavation activities especially at Wharram Percy, near Malton in the East Riding of Yorkshire; their efforts to compile county lists of deserted villages comprising map references (an indication of the quality of historical documentation available), the nature and visual quality of remains, and the period when villages became deserted, are all outlined in M W Beresford's 'A review of historical research' in *Deserted medieval villages*, 1971 (*qv*). Beresford's *The lost villages of England* (1954) includes lists of over a thousand such sites. Two booklets, *The deserted villages of Oxfordshire* (1965) and *The deserted villages of Northamptonshire* (1966) both by K J Allison, M W Beresford and J G Hurst, were published as occasional papers by the Department of English Local History, University of Leicester. 'Wharram Percy', *Current archaeology*, V(2) No 49, March 1975: 39-49 is essential reading to comprehend the activities of the group.

416 'Megalithic enquiries in the west of Britain' is a collection of studies edited by T G E Powell examining new possibilities in tomb classification and cultural backgrounds for the ultimate purpose of providing a fuller understanding of the prehistoric culture-groups who built them, published in 1969 by Liverpool University Press in their 'Monographs in archaeology and oriental studies' series. Inventories of chambered tombs in the Cotswold-Severn region, of megalithic tombs in North Wales, Clyde cairns, and of neolithic artifacts other than pottery found in Kintyre, Argyll, are listed in appendices, and there is an extensive bibliography.

417 'Memorandum on the ancient monuments acts', a leaflet issued by the Council for British Archaeology in a second edition in 1954, was published as a result of the destruction of a number of scheduled earthworks in the west of England which only came to light after a long interval. Its purpose was to remind county archaeological society members of the provisions of the acts and to indicate the steps to be taken to avert damage or destruction. Some societies reprinted it verbatim in their *Transactions.*

418 '**Mesoamerican archaeology'** *new approaches* edited by Norman Hammond (Duckworth, 1974) contains the proceedings of a symposium held by the University of Cambridge Centre of Latin American Studies, August 1972. 'The new approaches are in some cases in the realm of theory, applying new models and techniques to elucidate patterns in archaeological data; in others it is the direction of approach from iconography or ethnohistory, that is more novel to Mesoamerican archaeology; and in yet others, traditional models and techniques are taken into little-known areas of Mesoamerica.' Gordon Willey contributes an introduction which comments at length on the papers included, linking them together, almost in consecutive abstract form. Like all symposia this is no book for the amateur enthusiast, a good grounding of scholarship is needed to grasp the well documented papers presented here.

419 '**Metallurgy in archaeology'** *a prehistory of metallurgy in the British Isles* by R F Tylecote (Edward Arnold, 1962) gathers together the wealth of information supplied by metallurgists, chemists, and other specialists, on the metallurgic aspects of archaeology previously printed only in appendices to excavation reports. Each chapter considers a particular metal in turn and proceeds to discuss its use throughout the prehistoric period. There is a glossary of technical terms.

420 Methuen and Co Ltd, the academic division of Associated Book Publishers Ltd have long been active in the publishing of books of archaeological interest. The Methuen 'Handbooks of archaeology' in particular, have gained an enviable reputation. Titles: *English coins* (C G Brooke); *Greek geometric pottery* (J N Coldstream); *The archaeology of Roman Britain* (R G Collingwood and Ian Richmond); *Greek painted pottery* (R M Cook); *West Africa before the Europeans* (Oliver Davies); *Greek and Roman jewellery* (R A Higgins); *Greek terracottas* (R A Higgins); *Roman coins* (Harold Mattingley); *Western Asiatic jewellery* (K R Maxwell-Hyslop); *Egyptian religion* (S Morenz); *The archaeology of Crete* (J D S Pendlebury); *Greek coins* (Charles Seltman) and *Ancient Egyptian jewellery* (Alix Wilkinson). The American agents for books published by Methuen are Barnes and Noble of New York.

421 Ministry of Finance: Northern Ireland is the government department responsible for archaeology in the province and is concerned with both the protection and the recording of sites, thus combining the functions, of the Directorate of Ancient Monuments (Department of the Environment) and of the Royal Commissions in other parts of the United Kingdom. It publishes two illustrated regional guides: *Ancient monuments of Northern Ireland Vol I: in State care* and *Vol II not in State care*, and a number of official guides to various individual monuments and historic buildings. These are all listed in *Ancient monuments and historic buildings* (Government Publications Sectional List No 27).

422 'Ministry of Works excavation annual reports' developed from lists of excavations undertaken on sites threatened by destruction which were circulated privately to archaeological societies and institutions. Following a specific recommendation of the Ancient Monuments Board it was decided to publish this information in the shape of an annual report when rescue archaeology rapidly expanded in the 1950s. Excavations are listed in three categories: prehistoric, Romano-British, and medieval, arranged alphabetically by county. The reports appeared under this title 1961-1967 and were then superseded by a similar publication, *Archaeological excavations (qv)*.

423 Moated Sites Research Group was formed in 1972 after a week-end conference arranged by the Department of Adult Education, Leeds University with a view to study the problems presented by medieval moated sites and coordinating research into the subject by archaeologists, geographers and historians. A standard field record card has been introduced including as many features as possible relating the site to villages and field patterns, and a central index is maintained, arranged alphabetically by parish within counties. Further information is contained in Jean le Patourel's 'The moated sites research group', *Current archaeology*, IV(3) No 38, May 1973: 92-93. The group's activities are recorded in a *Bulletin* and a report on events and developments appears in *Archaeology in Britain*.

424 'Modern trends of display in archaeological museums' was the theme of a number of articles published in *Museum* 6 (1) 1953. Whilst making no pretence of covering all aspects of archaeological collections the several authors emphasized those developments in making collections more attractive, more understandable, and more instructive to the general public. Methods used to overcome the handicaps of bad-layout, inadequate funds

193

and antiquated equipment are discussed and other topics touched upon include the classification of archaeological material, and the different needs of the student and the layman. *Articles*: 'Problems of display for archaeology' (Grace McCann Morley); 'Aesthetic appeal in archaeological and ethnological museums' (Pal Kelemen); 'Exhibitions of Egyptian material in the Brooklyn Museum' (Elizabeth Riefstahl); 'Recent rearrangements in Italian archaeological museums' (Giovani Becatti); 'Display of the Asiatic archaeological collections in the Musee Guimet' (Jeannine Auboyer); 'The section of regional archaeology in the Musee de Mariemont (G Faider-Feytmans); 'New presentations of the collections in the Archaeological Museum of Strasbourg' (J J Hatt); and 'A new exhibition of archaeological collections in the National Museum of Ireland' (Joseph Raftery).

425 '**Monuments threatened or destroyed**' *a select list 1956-1962*, published for the Royal Commission on Historical Monuments England by HMSO in 1963, is an illustrated handlist of 850 such monuments selected from a far larger number notified to the commission. An analysis of the type of structure included and an assessment of the gravity of actual and potential losses is contained in the introductory report. Lists of archaeological sites individually examined by the commission's staff and of buildings under threat of demolition or drastic alteration are included in two appendices. These lists are arranged alphabetically by county with each entry being accompanied by a short descriptive note and, in some instances, illustrated either by a photograph or a line drawing. The purpose of the list was to alert field archaeologists to potential losses and to suggest where detailed surveying and excavation might prove profitable.

426 '**Museum**', a quarterly journal launched by Unesco in Paris in 1948, surveys museum activities and museographical research. It was seen as the successor to *Mouseion* a pre-war journal published by the International Museum Office of the League of Nations. Although intended primarily for the museum profession it was hoped that it would attract a large world audience and to that end each issue printed all articles in French and English. In recent years a separate English only edition has been published. Most issues have a thematic basis, sometimes on a geographical pattern, or more often on specific museographical problems, consisting of wide-ranging descriptive or discussion papers on new specialities and techniques.

427 The Museum Association was established to promote a better and more systematic working of museums, at a meeting arranged by the
194

Yorkshire Philosophical Society held in York in 1888. The topics then of concern now have an antiquated ring about them but they serve to remind us how far museum services have progressed: the means of interchange of duplicate and surplus specimens; the means of securing models, casts and reproductions; a scheme for a general supply of labels, illustrations, and information; a uniform plan of arranging natural history collections; a scheme for securing the services of specialists; the indexing of museum collections; the importance of library and museum legislation; the promotion of museum lectures to working men; the preparation of small educational collections for circulation to schools; the concerted action for securing government publications and specimens on loan or otherwise; and the publishing of a journal by the association. Today it represents museums and art galleries and those who work in them both in the British Isles and overseas. Its objects remain close to those expressed when the association was formed: 'to promote the establishment and better administration of museums and art galleries and to improve the qualifications and status of museum staffs'. To this end the association awards a diploma to those of its members 'who have had at least three years' full-time experience in a museum or art gallery (or two years, if university graduates) have completed the required courses of study, and have passed the prescribed examinations'. This diploma is the recognized qualification in museum curatorship within the profession. In 1965 a Conservation Certificate for those occupied with the conservation and restoration of archaeological and ethnographical material was instituted and, at the time of writing, plans for a revised certificate and a new Diploma in Conservation are well advanced. The association's publishing programme includes the monthly *Museums bulletin*, the quarterly *Museums journal, Museums yearbook*, a series of information sheets, and a number of handbooks for museum curators. Further details of the association may be obtained from 87 Charlotte Street, London W1.

428 '**Museums and art galleries in Great Britain and Ireland**' is published annually by ABC Historic Publications, a division of ABC Travel Guides Ltd. In the main sequence museums are listed A-Z by town or city, each entry in addition to the usual details of opening hours etc briefly indicates the scope of the collections. Pictorial advertisements enliven the pages and add further details to the information on the larger museums. A subject index, a list of museums by name, and a geographical index add to its usefulness.

429 '**Museums and monuments**' is a series of pictorial handbooks published by Unesco on general and specific topics relating to museum administration,

preservation, and archaeological problems. Among the titles published
are *Sites and monuments: problems of today*; *Manual of travelling exhibitions*; *Protection of cultural property in the event of armed conflict*;
The organization of museums: practical advice; *Temporary and travelling
exhibitions*; *The conservation of cultural property with special reference
to tropical conditions*; *Field manual for museums*; and *Underwater archaeology: a nascent discipline*.

430 'The museums calendar' including a directory of museums and art
galleries of the British Isles, published annually by the Museums Association, also includes a report on national and international events in the
museum world for the previous year and instructive and informative notes
on the association's courses and certificates.

431 'Museums directory of the United States and Canada' published by
the American Association of Museums and the Smithsonian Institution
in a second edition (1965) is arranged in four sections: (1) a geographical
list of museums under state or province with information as to the museum's date of foundation, the opening date of the building currently occupied, its address and telephone number, names and titles of principal
officers, the main subject areas covered, and hours of opening; (2) an
alphabetical list; (3) an alphabetical list of personnel; and (4) a classified
list under subject headings of which 'Archaeology museums and archaeological sites' is one. The *Directory* ends with a list of foreign museum
members of the association, a list of museum associations abroad, and a
subject index.

432 'The museums journal' (1901-) is published quarterly by the Museums Association. Recent articles of archaeological interest include
Colin Renfrew's 'The requirements of the research worker in archaeology'
vol 67(2) September 1967: 111-113, which discusses the desirability and
problems of a National Museum Index (to contents); D F Petch's 'Museums and field archaeology', considering how far museums should com-
mit their resources in this direction and P J Fowler's 'Museums and archaeology AD 1970-2000' assessing British archaeology's likely requirements from museums over the next generation, both contained in 'Museums and archaeology', 70(3) December 1970: 119-121; and Neil
Cossons' 'The conservation of industrial monuments', 74(2) September
1974: 62-66.

433 'Museums of the world' *a directory of 17,000 museums in 148 countries including a subject index* compiled by Eleanor Braun was published by Verlag Dokumentation, Pullach bei Munchen in 1973. Because of the international basis of this massive work the text is in English although the preliminaries and the index instructions are also given in a parallel German translation. The geographically arranged entries provide each museum's full name and complete address, its year of foundation, the name of its curator or director, its type, and information on the fields of its specialised collections—in fact all the criteria suggested by the International Council of Museums in Paris which permitted the compiler access to its files. There is a name index to identify memorial and biographical museums and of ethnographical and geographical terms to locate archaeological sites; a subject index based on the systematic organisation of collections determined by the Centre de Documentation Museographique, Unesco; and a geographical index for the location of every museum listed so that the user may easily find all museums with locally limited collections or, alternatively, all museums within a specific area. The comprehensive nature of this vast conspectus, so readily accessible by name, subject or place, truly entitles it to be regarded as essential for the museum curator and reference librarian. R B Bowker are the London and New York agents.

434 'National ancient monuments year book' was an interesting publication edited by John Swarbrick, the prime mover behind the Ancient Monuments Society (*qv*). It was divided into three distinct parts: (1) matters of topical interest related to ancient monuments, works of art, and craftsmanship; (2) particulars of the ancient monuments protected by legislation and notes on the work of the Ancient Monuments Boards and the Royal Commissions, and a list of societies and organisations interested in the study and conservation of monuments and historic buildings; and (3) matters of interest to owners, architects etc relating to the cause of decay and to the methods of reparation together with lists of artists, craftsmen and firms recommended for various kinds of work, and manufacturers of suitable building materials. The intention was to publish every year in the late spring/early summer 'when the world at large begins once again to explore the countryside and to wander in search of the ancient monuments and historic buildings with which the country, fortunately, still abounds'. But only the 1927 issue ever appeared.

435 National Heritage, launched in 1971 to support, encourage, and protect museums in Great Britain, describes itself as the Museum's Action

Movement. It unites individual members, affiliated museums, and friends of museums, in an alert national lobby dedicated to the promotion of museum interests. Among its activities is the finding of industrial sponsors for special exhibitions and 'effective help on a constant basis for museums with urgent financial or other problems'. For an annual subscription of £4.00 individual members receive an eighty page book, *Museums of Great Britain*, containing brief details of the collections, contents, and opening hours of over 900 museums; a semi-annual illustrated magazine, *Museum news*; and invitations to private views of important exhibitions. *Address*: PO Box 689, London SW1.

436 National Maritime Museum was opened in the Queen's House, Greenwich on 27th April 1937, the conclusion to a campaign begun by the Society for Nautical Research over a quarter of a century earlier. Their efforts had culminated in the establishment of the museum administered by a board of trustees and a director in 1934. The museum's declared objectives are 'to promote and maintain due interest in seafaring and shipbuilding, past and present, particularly British, and in nautical astronomy. To collect, preserve, study, exhibit, and make available to all who are interested, any objects which will explain the story or assist the student'. The museum has assumed a leading role in nautical archaeology in the United Kingdom; a Department of Archaeology of the Ship established in 1973 is actively pursuing an organized research programme. Symposia on different aspects of maritime history are arranged: in October 1971 boat archaeologists gathered to listen to and discuss papers on the excavation of boats at North Ferriby, Sutton Hoo and Graveney, these papers were later published as *Three major ancient boat finds in Britain* in the museum's 'Maritime monographs and reports' series (No 6, 1972). *The Cattewater wreck*, an interim report on the wreck discovered in the Cattewater, Plymouth, 1973 appeared as number thirteen in the same series (1974). In September 1976 an international symposium on 'Boat archaeology—sources, techniques and theories' was held. There is an official *Guide* to the museum and two pictorial guides, *Maritime Greenwich* and *National Maritime Museum* are available in Pitkin's 'Pride of Britain' series. The museum was featured in 'Museum report 1 Great Britain', *International journal of nautical archaeology*, 1, March 1972: 218-219.

437 National Monuments Record was formed in 1941 as the National Buildings Record on the initiative of the Royal Institute of British

Architects when it was feared that large numbers of historical buildings would disappear without record as a result of enemy bombing or else be prematurely pulled down by over-zealous demolition gangs unless urgent measures were put in hand. The Architectural Graphic Records Committee immediately handed over its index of architectural records, the Courtauld Institute transferred its Conway Library of photographs, and various other records were presented by the Victoria County History and the Royal Commissions on Historical Monuments. The record's immediate aims were to prepare and classify lists of buildings of merit, to collect information of existing records and transfer them onto a central index, and to make new records of buildings including those which had suffered war damage. Today the intention is to compile a complete record of architecture in England by means of photographs and measured drawings, to maintain a library in which these records are available to the public for consultation and study, to supply copies of photographs, and to maintain an index of architectural records and to assist and encourage the study of buildings of all periods. In the early 1950s the government proposed that the record should become merged in the Ancient Monuments Department of the Ministry of Works but the council was reluctant to surrender its independent status on the grounds that more than half of its records related to churches with which the ministry had no concern and that its principal purpose was to provide facilities for reference and study to students of architecture and others, and that its services to national and local government departments were incidental to this. However in July 1962 a working group of ministers appointed to investigate the possibility of closer coordination of all government departments and treasury-financed institutions recommended that the record should become part of the Royal Commissions on Historical Monuments and this change in status was duly effected. The function, scope and beginnings of the record, together with suggested methods whereby local committees, architects, photographers, archaeological societies, libraries and museums, could assist its work, are all contained in a paper printed in the *Journal* of the Royal Institute of British Architects, May 1941, afterwards issued as an offprint. 'Keeping records of buildings', the *Times*, 8th April 1959, is a useful interim summary of its work. The record now includes an archaeological section. The Air Photographs Unit (*qv*) works in close cooperation with the Archaeology Division of the Ordnance Survey. National Monument Records departments are also attached to the Royal Commissions in Aberystwyth and Edinburgh.

438 National Museum of Antiquities of Scotland: The formation of a museum was among the original aims of the Society of Antiquaries of Scotland founded by the eleventh Earl of Buchan in 1780. A year later it received its first accessions. At first the museum collections included antiquities from all over the world but gradually it has become more and more national in content. The museum's history is a chequered one, frequent ups and down of fortune were experienced and in 1851 following a slump and then a rise in public interest arrangements were put in motion to make over the society's collections to the government on condition that accommodation suitable for public access would be made available and that responsibility for the museum's management would continue to rest with the society. It was during the ensuing period that the museum began to dispose in earnest of its non-Scottish material and to concentrate on its collection of national antiquities. Most of the finds yielded by excavations in Scotland have subsequently found their way to Edinburgh, perhaps because of its continuing links with the society. R B K Stevenson's 'The National Museum of Antiquities of Scotland', *Museum journal* 54(3) June 1954 is a convenient historical account of the museum whilst the same writer's 'Bringing a nineteenth century museum into the 1970s: shaping a new National Museum of Antiquities of Scotland', *Museums journal* 69(2) September 1969: 50-53 tells of the high hopes and expectations aroused by the National Museum Act of 1954 and includes photographs of a model of the new museum so confidently expected to rise near the University of Edinburgh and the National Library. Sadly, however, the 22nd annual report of the board of trustees talks of the first phase of the new building being indefinitely postponed. A research laboratory was established in 1967 to apply modern scientific techniques to archaeology and conservation, its most recent work has been concerned with developing programmes for the study of prehistoric metalworking, in thermoluminescent dating techniques, and in wood conservation.

   Publications: *A short guide to Scottish antiquities* is a useful illustrated handbook for visitors. On a more scholarly level a stapled, duplicated bibliography, *Scottish material culture, Section A Archaeology* compiled by D V Clarke and A C Grieve, intended largely for internal use, was experimentally circulated in 1975 in the belief that it would be of service elsewhere. This includes 'recently published work dealing with Scottish material culture, studies relevant to Scottish material but not specifically mentioning Scotland, and methodological studies, particularly in science, with possible relevance to Scottish material'. Entries are arranged in a general section, by archaeological period, with a special section for nautical archaeology. The second issue published in 1976 includes a bibliography of 'Rescue and salvage excavation in Scotland 1960-1975' compiled by J N Graham Ritchie and based on the appropriate entries in *Discovery and excavation in Scotland*. The successive annual reports of the board of trustees, published by HMSO in Edinburgh, should be consulted for news of the museum's current activities.

439 National Museum of Wales/Amgueddfa Genedhaethol Cymru at Cardiff received its charter of incorporation in 1907 although it was not until 1912 that the foundation stone was laid, the public first being admitted ten years later. The museum's purpose is 'to picture the kind of place Wales is, and man's life and progress therein'. To this end the museum is administered in six departments: archaeology, art, botany, geology, zoology, and industry. The collections of Cardiff Municipal Museum were transferred to the National Museum on its foundation. The Department of Archaeology covers all aspects of Welsh archaeology from the prehistoric period down to the end of the middle ages; its galleries are divided into early and later prehistory, Roman Wales, and dark age and medieval Wales. In addition the Legionary Museum at Caerleon is a branch gallery on the site of the Roman Legionary fortress of Isca presented to the National Museum by the Monmouth and Caerleon Antiquarian Association in 1930. A new Industrial and Maritime Museum was started in the Bute West Dock area Cardiff in January 1975.

Publications: W F Grimes' *The prehistory of Wales* (1951), a general account of man's activities in Wales prior to the arrival of the Romans illustrated from the museum's collections and a full descriptive catalogue of the collections accompanied by bibliographical and topographical references and illustrations of the more important specimens, replaced an earlier *Guide to the collections illustrating the prehistory of Wales*. In turn this went out of print to be partially replaced by H N Savory's *Guide catalogue of the early iron age collections* (1976) which retains the same form and standard of detail in the catalogue and similar subject and topographical indexes to its predecessor. *National Museum of Wales: a short guide* was published in 1975; the annual report (continuous since 1907-1908) reviews developments and the events of the past year and contains full details of the museum's services and complete range of publications. A folded leaflet *Cyhoeddiadau/Publications* is available on request from the museum bookshop; see also entry 619 *Welsh antiquity. Amgueddfa; bulletin of the National Museum of Wales* is published three times a year. John Ward's 'Welsh Museum of Natural History, Arts and Antiquities, Cardiff', *Archaeologia Cambrensis*, 6th series vol XII, 1912: 295-315 provides a history and description of the museum's foundation collection donated by Cardiff Corporation.

440 National Parks Service (US) was established in 1916 as a national conservation system for natural, prehistoric and historic sites. In the 1960s the service was given the task of operating the National Survey of Historic Sites and Buildings which has developed into a register of over ten thousand sites of national, state, and local significance. Because of the shortage of experienced archaeologists on their staff most excavations carried out are undertaken by qualified contracting agencies, usually museums and universities. John L Cotter's 'Archaeological sites, important national resources', *Archaeology* 25(2), April 1972: 152-153 briefly outlines the service's part in archaeology.

441 'The national record of industrial monuments' traces its beginnings to the moment when the Council for British Archaeology persuaded the government to provide funds for an Industrial Monuments Survey under the joint sponsorship of the Ministry of Public Building and Works and the CBA itself in 1962. Work started the following year conducted in the main through the CBA's regional groups whose members filled in cards devised specially to record the most significant information. When the completed cards flooded into the CBA and the Ministry, the consultant on industrial monuments at the ministry recommended that the Centre for the Study of the History of Technology, Bristol College of Science and Technology (now a constituent part of Bath University) should be invited to record and classify the information provided. The centre accepted this task and the *Record* came into being in the summer of 1965. Each card is classified according to county and industrial group and carries a description of the nature of the site or artefact, its dimensions and present condition, its machinery or fittings if any, a note indicating any danger of demolition, and any printed, manuscript or photographic record. Besides the card at Bath University a duplicate is sent to the CBA and another to the National Buildings Record. At the moment the *Record* is still in its preliminary stages but it is hoped eventually that it will provide a unique source of information on industrial monuments which otherwise might be forgotten. R A Buchanan's 'The national record of industrial monuments', *The journal of the history of industry and technology* 4(4) 1967: 358-365 and Norman Smith's *Victorian technology and its preservation in modern Britain* (Leicester University Press, 1970) should be consulted for further details.

442 'The National Trust' *a record of fifty years acheivement* edited by James Lees-Milne (Batsford, 1945) is a bare outline of the trust's progress

over fifty years and of the varied types of property in its care. *Contents*:
'National Trust and national parks' (Ivor Brown); 'Country and coast'
(Harry Batsford); 'Ancient sites' (Grahame Clark); 'Medieval buildings'
(John Harvey); 'The manor house' (G M Young); 'The country house'
(James Lees-Milne); 'Country buildings' (Basil Oliver): 'Town buildings'
(John Summerson); 'Historic shrines' (John Russell); 'Nature reserves'
(Sir William Beach Thomas); and 'The work of the National Trust' (D M
Matheson). There is an introduction by G M Trevelyan and an index of
properties indicating those owned by the trust and those not owned but
protected by means of restrictive covenants.

443 'The National Trust and the National Trust for Scotland' *complete in
text and pictures* by Peter Ryan (Dent, 1969) covers the whole of Britain
and provides information on all matters of interest to visitors: what to
see at each of the trust properties and whatever is considered particularly
worth mention in the property's history or in the history of the people
associated with it.

444 The National Trust *for places of historic interest or natural beauty*
was founded in 1894 and registered under the Companies Act in January
1895 largely as a result of the efforts of Octavia Hill, Canon H R Rawnsley,
and Robert Hunter who had first mooted the formation of an organisation
empowered to acquire land and buildings for the benefit of the nation ten
years earlier. By 1906 the trust owned 24 properties and 1700 acres and
the executive committee determined that it was time for a more formal
recognition of its privileges and responsibilities, the question of public
access especially needed resolving. The first National Trust Act of 1907
conferred powers on the trust to declare its property inalienable, ensuring
that it could not be acquired by government departments or local authorities without express parliamentary approval, thus reassuring potential
benefactors that they might transfer their property to the trust secure
in the knowledge that it would remain in the trust's ownership in per-
petuity. A further step forward came under the clauses of the 1937
National Trust Act, by which the trust was permitted to accept restrictive
covenants on property, from owners who wished to retain some measure
of privacy, there being no automatic right of public access to covenanted
property. Other clauses allowed local authorities to transfer property to
the trust and to assist financially in its maintenance and opened the way
for the trust to own 'furniture, pictures, and chattels of any description
having national or historic or artistic interest'.

In the late 1960s internal dissension prompted the council to appoint an advisory committee to review the trust's management, under the independent chairmanship of Sir Harry Benson. The *Report by the council's advisory committee on the Trust's constitution, organization and responsibilities*, prepared within eighteen months, was published in 1968. Although endorsing the broad lines of the council's policy, the *Report* recommended changes in its financial and administrative arrangements, and in particular eased the path of the newly instituted regional committees. These changes were embodied in further legislation in 1971. Although the trust's duties and procedures are established by Parliament, and although it receives relief from income tax and government grants, the trust is a completely independent institution financed by members' subscriptions, donations, legacies and rents. At the present time it can boast of approximately 350,000 members. It owns 185 sites and buildings in England and Wales scheduled under the Ancient Monument Acts ranging from prehistoric and Roman remains (Avebury and Fort Housesteads among them) to industrial monuments. Acknowledging that the care of ancient sites demands specialized care the trust has placed many of these under the guardianship of the Department of the Environment.

Publications: *An atlas of places to visit in England, Scotland, Wales and Northern Ireland* (1975) is the new title of what was formerly known as *The National Trust atlas showing places of historic, architectural and scenic interest* (1964), and pinpoints over 6000 buildings and constructions of all types. These are not limited to trust properties. Each double-page map section is followed by its own gazetteer which identifies sites and properties numbered and categorised by conventional signs on the maps. *Prehistoric properties of the National Trust*, a slim illustrated booklet by Phyllis Ireland lists the best known sites owned by the trust arranged alphabetically by county. The physical appearance of each site, its excavation history and the discoveries made, are all briefly recorded and there are references to printed excavation accounts. The whereabouts of artefacts recovered are also indicated. *Properties open: essential information for visitors* is an annual booklet describing each property, with information on how to get there, opening hours, charges, refreshments and picnicking amenities etc. Properties are listed according to post-1974 counties. *Properties of the National Trust*, last published in January 1973, with a new edition expected in 1978, is a descriptive list of all trust owned and covenanted properties. There is a subject guide to special categories of properties placed before the text. *The National Trust year book 1975-76* published for the trust by Europa Publications is the first of an intended

204

annual collection of studies in art history and nature conservation relating to properties in the trust's care, and *Treasures of the National Trust* edited by Robin Fedden is described as a natural companion to *The National Trust guide* (*qv*) and considers the aesthetic importance and rarity of the trust's collections of furniture, ceramics, paintings, sculptures etc. *National Trust* (1968-) is a pictorial magazine issued thrice yearly carrying features on the trust at work, personalities, properties, head office and regional news, and book reviews.

Bibliography: Clough Williams-Ellis' *On trust for the nation* (2 vols, Paul Elek, 1947-1949) describes individual properties and is superbly illustrated with photographs and drawings. Robin Fedden's *The continuing purpose: a history of the National Trust, its aims and work* (Longmans, 1968) is a definitive account and the same author's *The National Trust past and present* (Cape, 1974) tells the same story but in briefer compass and broader outline suitable for the general reader. Michael Beaumont's 'The National Trust and conservation', *Museums journal* 74(3) December 1974: 104-107 is a reliable survey of this particular aspect of the trust's work.

445 National Trust for Historic Preservation (US) is a national private society chartered by Congress in 1949 to encourage the preservation of districts, sites, buildings, and objects of significance to American history and culture. It advises communities on how to raise funds and act as a pressure group; it alerts local groups to threats to historical monuments and architecture; and it acts as a source of information on state and federal preservation programmes. Its quarterly journal is *Historic preservation*. In 1954 the trust absorbed the National Committee for Historic Sites and Buildings.

446 'The National Trust guide' compiled by Robin Fedden and Rosemary Joekes (Cape, 1973) is an official and comprehensive guide to all the important properties of the Trust in England, Wales and Northern Ireland open to the public. There are seven sections each preceded by an introductory essay: 'Houses' (Nigel Nicolson). 'Gardens and landscape parks' (Miles Hadfield); 'Follies, monuments, villages, dovecotes, chapels, and buildings of useful intent' (Barbara Jones); 'Medieval buildings' (John Harvey); 'Industrial monuments' (Sir James Richards); 'Archaeological sites' (Jacquetta Hawkes); and 'Coast and country' (C H D Acland). Within each section properties are described and their contents and main features discussed according to type eg 'industrial monuments' are arranged under windmills, watermills, canals and bridges, presses and beam engines subject headings whilst 'archaeological sites' are classified either as prehistoric or Roman and Romano-British sites. The *Guide* is lavishly illustrated and each section is complemented by a corresponding series of distribution maps. A glossary and county lists of trust properties of lesser importance not included in the text are useful additions.

447 National Trust for Scotland *for places of historical interest or natural beauty* came into being in 1931 on the initiative of the Association for the Preservation of Rural Scotland who were becoming increasingly frustrated by their inability to hold land or buildings in ownership. And so the trust was formed along the same lines as the National Trust south of the border as an independent body but constituted so as to be capable of acting in cooperation with statutory authorities and with powers to hold land and buildings and chattels 'for the benefit of the nation'. The trust's position was further established on a legal basis by the National Trust for Scotland Act 1935 which bestowed upon it the right to declare its property inalienable except by specific parliamentary approval. Among the trust's properties are three sections of the Antonine Wall. A short account of the trust's growth written by the Earl of Wemyss and March is published in *The National Trust for Scotland guide* compiled and edited by Robin Prentice (Cape, 1976), a complete gazetteer to properties classified according to type. The trust publishes a *Yearbook* and several guidebooks to individual properties.

448 'Nautical archaeology' *a handbook* by Bill St John Wilkes (David and Charles, 1971) is a guidebook on all aspects of underwater archaeology intended for small groups lacking the lavish resources of the well-publicised expeditions.

449 The Nautical Archaeology Trust was established by the Council for Nautical Archaeology and was incorporated and registered as a charity in 1972. The objects of the trust include 'the furtherance of research into nautical archaeology and the publication of results of such research and the advancement of training and education in the techniques pertaining to the study of nautical archaeology for the benefit of the public'. The trust organizes lectures and conferences, and publishes *NATNEWS*, a quarterly newsletter. Members are also entitled to special subscription rates to *The international journal of nautical archaeology*.

450 'New aspects of antiquity' published by Thames and Hudson, is a series consisting of monographs by eminent archaeologists recording the discoveries which they themselves have recently made in the field. In the case of specific sites the author actually directed the operations. The series is important in that much of the material included in these volumes is new in book form. The original editor was Sir Mortimer Wheeler. *Titles*: *Akhenaten Pharaoh of Egypt* (Cyril Aldred); *By South Cadbury is that Camelot* (Leslie Alcock); *Catal Huyuk* (James Mellaart); *Cities in the sand* (Aubrey Menen); *The end of Atlantis* (J V Luce); *Europe's first monumental sculpture: new discoveries at Lepenski Vir* (Dragan Srejovic); *Fishbourne: a Roman palace and garden* (Barry Cunliffe); *Great Zimbabwe* (Peter S Garlake); *Ife in the history of West African sculpture* (Frank Willett); *Jerusalem* (Kathleen M Kenyon); *Salamis in Cyprus* (Vassos Karageorghis); *Southern Arabia* (D B Doe); *Timna: valley of the Biblical copper mines* (Beno Rothenburg); *View from the bronze age: Mycenean and Phoenician discoveries at Kition* (Vassos Karageorghis); and *Vindolanda* (Robin Birley).

451 'New Grange and the Bend of the Boyne' by Sean P O'Riordain and Glyn Daniel, number forty in Thames and Hudson's 'Ancient peoples and places' series when published in 1964, examines that remarkable collection of megalithic tombs north of Dublin which constitute one of the most significant prehistoric sites in western Europe, and sets the monuments firmly in their context. Dowth and Knowth receive equal treatment and there is also a comparison with other Irish and British passage graves.

452 'The new world' by Warwick Bray, Earl H Swanson and Ian Farrington, published by Elsevier Phaidon in their 'The making of the past' series in 1975, is an authoritative and beautifully illustrated introduction to the archaeology and pre-Columbian culture of North, South, and Mesoamerica. In addition to the full treatment of the Mayan and Aztec civilisations of Central America, the Incas, and the North American Indians, room is found for a discussion of their prehistoric precursors. A comparative chronological table of the three Americas ranging in time from 27000 BC down to AD 1500 sets each culture and civilisation in context. The reading list is sparse and could profitably have been extended.

453 The Newcomen Society for the study of the history of engineering and technology was formed in 1919 by a small group of engineers after a James Watt commemorative meeting at Birmingham, and must be regarded

207

as a pioneer of industrial archaeology in Britain. The society's chief activity is publishing papers relating to the history of invention or industry in its *Transactions* (1920-), and drawing attention to the importance of specific machines or industrial equipment which merit preservation as industrial monuments either in situ or in a museum or factory. If this proves impossible the society ensures that a suitable photographic or documentary record is deposited in a convenient museum or library. The society owns no premises, its headquarters are at the Science Museum, South Kensington, and so works in close cooperation with established museums. A four day summer meeting is held annually when visits to works and sites of interest are arranged. Stanley Hamilton's 'The Newcomen Society and industrial archaeology', *The journal of industrial archaeology* 1(2) August 1974: 74-75 presents a short account of the society's aims and purposes.

454 **'No stone unturned'** *an almanac of North American prehistory* by Louis A Brennan (Gollancz, 1960) traces for the general reader the development of indigenous cultures from the time man first made his appearance on the continent about forty thousand years ago to the old world discovery of these cultures in the sixteenth and seventeenth centuries. The author's principal thesis is that 'most of what is early American is truly American, invented, created or developed by an American race whose integrality of character is deep enough in time for its differentiation from other races to be recognised by its own racial name.'

455 **'The nomenclature of archaeology'**, an article by T A Richard, discusses the implications of the terms stone, bronze and iron ages and their history; refers to the practice of designating cultures after the locality in which significant discoveries were made eg Chellean, Solutrean, etc; and questions some of the characteristics of classification used. The writer concludes that 'in the present state of knowledge it would appear that human existence may be divided into a primordial age, characterized by the use of wood, bone and shell; the stone age; and lastly, the metallurgic age.' The article appeared in a supplement to *American journal of archaeology* XLVIII, 1944: 10-16.

456 **Norfolk and Norwich Archaeology Society** was founded on the initiative of a small group of gentlement in 1846 to 'collect the best information on the arts and monuments of the county, including primeval antiquities; numismatics; architecture, civil and ecclesiastical; sculpture;

paintings on walls, wood, or glass; civil history, and antiquities; comprising manors, manorial rights, privileges and customs; descent; genealogy; ecclesiastical history and endowments; records etc and all other matters usually arranged under the head of archaeology.' *Norfolk archaeology or miscellaneous tracts relating to the antiquities of the county of Norfolk* was first published in 1847 and appeared irregularly for many years, it is now an annual publication although still numbered four issues to a volume. 'Periodical literature relating to Norfolk archaeology' based on materials held in Norwich Public Library, was a regular feature of every issue 1921-1941. B Cozen-Hardy's 'Scheduling of the Norfolk ancient monuments', XXII, 1926: 221-226 is a list of monuments notified to the Office of Works as being worthy of scheduling under the Ancient Monuments Act of 1913. In recent years the journal has assumed a more modern appearance although still within severe and traditional covers and its contents have reflected a more professional and disciplined approach to field archaeology. Thomas Wake's 'Some recent archaeological discoveries in Norfolk, XXVIII, 1945: 23-28 and J E Sainty's 'Mesolithic sites in Norfolk' in the same issue pages 234-237 are useful survey articles. R Rainbird Clarke's 'Roman Norfolk since Haverfield: a survey of discoveries from 1901' XXX, 1952: 140-155 comprehensively summarizes the chief discoveries in the county since Haverfield's descriptions in the first Norfolk volume of the *Victoria County History*. The same writer's 'Notes on recent archaeological discoveries in Norfolk (1943-8)' XXX, 1952: 156-157 and 'Archaeological discoveries in Norfolk 1949-54', XXXI, 1957: 395-416 are equally useful. Peter Wade-Martin's 'The linear earthworks of west Norfolk', XXXVI(1) 1974:23-38, should also be noted. Most recent issues include interim reports on excavations currently being undertaken in Norwich. *A general index to volumes I-XX and a list of the principal places visited July 1890 to December 1927* compiled by J Olerenshaw was published in 1928.

457 Norfolk Archaeological Unit was established in April 1973 with the aid of a grant from the Department of the Environment to carry out excavations and surveys in the county. Peter Wade-Martin's 'The Norfolk Archaeological unit', *Current archaeology*, IV(9) No 44, May 1974: 281-284 explains the background to its activities.

458 North Staffordshire Field Club was formed in April 1865 largely at the instigation of W D Spanton, a former member of the Sheffield Naturalists Club, whose enthusiasm and drive contributed much to the club's early years. From the start the objects of the club were equally divided

between natural history and archaeology, for a time its official title was
the North Staffordshire Naturalists Field Club and Archaeological Society
but, understandably, that was considered too cumbersome and in 1865
it was abbreviated to its present form. The club published its *Transactions*
1865-1960 but when the University College at Keele suggested that they
should share in the publication of a new journal the club agreed and in
1961 the first issue of the *North Staffordshire journal of field studies*
appeared. Both club and college appointed members to the editorial board
and although most of the papers are contributed by university or polytechnic lecturers the proceedings of the various sections of the club are fully
reported. So far it would appear a happy marriage. W D Spanton's presidential address printed in the *Transactions* XLI 1906-1907: 48-64 is valuable for its account of the club's early activities whilst H V Thompson's
'The North Staffordshire Field Club 1865-1965 a retrospect', *Journal*
6 1966: 1-6 presents some assessment of what the club has been able to
accomplish since its formation in 1865, and at the same time, traces the
impact of changing conditions. Other *Journal* articles of more than passing interest are A J H Gunstone's 'An archaeological gazetteer of Staffordshire: the barrows' volume 5, 1965: 20-63, which identifies in the field
all barrows mentioned in the antiquarian literature of the county and makes
recommendations for the scheduling of well-preserved sites as ancient monuments, and R J Sherlock's 'Industrial archaeology in administrative Staffordshire: an interim report', volume 2, 1962: 96-107 which embodies the results of a pilot survey of industrial remains for the Council for British Archaeology.

459 Northamptonshire Archaeological Society was formed in 1974 as
the successor of the Northamptonshire Federation of Archaeological Societies 'to promote the study of archaeology in all its branches in Northamptonshire and the Soke of Peterborough and to ensure the proper publication and dissemination of the results of archaeological work'. Seven
parts of a *Bulletin* of the federation were published until this was superseded in 1973 by *Northamptonshire archaeology*, an annual journal containing reports on archaeological work in the area and a Northamptonshire
archaeological bibliography.

460 Northern Archaeological Survey was established in May 1974 by the
Department of Archaeology in the University of Durham, with the support
of the Department of the Environment, to set up an effective machinery
for tackling the problems of rescue archaeology in Cumbria, Durham,

Northumberland, and Tyne and Wear, and more specifically, to prepare
a report, if possible within a year, evaluating the archaeological potential
of the region and assessing the likely threats to be feared from development. The report, *Archaeology in the North*, by P A G Clack and P F
Gosling, was published by the survey in the spring of 1976. Two principal
lines of research were followed: the compilation of a comprehensive list
of known archaeological sites in the area in the form of a gazetteer and
distribution maps; and the gathering and collation of information concerning possible development. In addition an assessment was also attempted
of the archaeological resources, the distribution of sites and their localized
concentration, and of the number of societies, museums, and universities
with an interest in exploiting these. The contents of the report include a
consideration of the current crisis in rescue archaeology in the region and
the effect of local government reorganisation, unfortunately coming into
effect just as the survey commenced work; a chronological survey of sites;
a study of the possible developments to be expected from local government,
service and extractive industries, and afforestation and agriculture; and the
survey's conclusions and recommendations. Appendix A consists of twelve
detailed surveys whilst appendix B looks at the legal framework, outlines
a histogram of scheduled ancient monuments county by county, examines
local government responsibilities, reports on the archaeological provision
in museums, surveys air photography in the region, discusses information
retrieval, planning and the computer, and indicates the work and resources
of archaeological societies and institutions. There is an extensive bibliography arranged chronologically and the report is well furnished with
maps, plans, and diagrams.

461 'Observer's book of ancient and Roman Britain' by Harold Priestley
(1976) belongs to Warne's 'Observer pocket book' series of which the
Birmingham post once remarked 'Information that is readily available at
the time when it is wanted in just the right quantity and of the right quality'. There is a brief outline of British prehistory down to the end of the
Roman period but the main part of the text is devoted to a gazetteer of
accessible sites and monuments listed and described in alphabetical order.
One novel feature is the inclusion of a number of 'key points', ie locations
from which several listed sites may be visited during the course of one day's
car travel. A glossary, a bibliography, maps, photographs, and drawings,
complement the text.

462 The Olympia Convention was an agreement between the German
and Greek governments signed on 25th April 1874 regulating German

excavations at Olympia. It was significant in that it became the proto-
type of many such agreements. The full text was printed in English Translation in C W Ceram's *The world of archaeology*.

463 'Opportunities for archaeologists' by John Bishop (RESCUE, 1975),
a booklet originally prepared for careers officers is divided into eight
sections—Archaeology in Britain; Field archaeology; Academic archaeology;
Museum archaeology; Government service; Archaeological publishing; Administration and archaeology; and Jobs—which together represent nothing
less than a complete guide to the present state of British archaeology. The
complexities of the present regional groups; rescue archaeology committees,
Department of the Environment advisory committees; rescue units and
trusts are elucidated; the prospective employers of field archaeologists are
clearly defined; college and university courses are indicated; informative
notes on the organization and function of government bodies involved in
archaeology are outlined; and there is realistic advice on career opportunities
Finally a series of appendixes provide useful addresses, a bibliography, the
text of the DoE ministerial statement of 23 May 1974, a diagram of the
Directorate of Ancient Monuments and Historic Buildings structure; and
the addresses of British schools and institutes overseas.

464 Ordnance Survey, founded in 1791, whose prime responsibility it is
to survey and provide maps of Great Britain, has traditionally included
archaeological detail on its maps although, oddly enough, as C W Phillips
has pointed out, it strictly speaking enjoys no authority for doing so.
The closest official sanction for this practice is to be found in the recommendations of a departmental committee set up under the chairmanship
of Sir J C C Davidison. In its report published in 1938 the Committee
merely stated that 'the Ordnance Survey should continue to publish archaeological maps' accepting a fait accompli with no questions asked.
Here we may usefully divide our examination of the survey's investigation,
recording, and survey of field antiquities into three parts: its practice of
noting archaeological features on its general maps, its archaeological records, and its series of special archaeological and historical maps.
    One inch maps published in the early nineteenth century included anti-
quities but coverage very much depended on the interests and idiosyncrasies of individual field surveyors but the completion of the six inch
survey of Ireland in 1845, which was meticulous in recording landscape
antiquities, served as a model for their subsequent systematic surveying
and recording. In 1865 Sir Henry James issued orders in which reference
212

was made to 'the necessity of officers making themselves acquainted with the local history of, and (by personal inspections) with the objects of antiquarian interest in the districts which they are surveying in order that all such objects may be properly represented on the plans, and fully described in the name books'. But despite this quickening awareness there was still a lack of experience, there was no expert archaeologist at the centre of affairs who could take a broad view and secure a proper archaeological balance. Not surprisingly therefore an increasing number of complaints at the unequal coverage began to be voiced. These reached their climax in an address to the Royal Geographical Society in 1905 by F J Haverfield who deplored the absence of trained and expert knowledge within the Ordnance Survey and listed four areas in which the survey was falling down in its work: the visible archaeological remains were not being surveyed by officers with archaeological experience, local information was being inadquately sifted, printed sources were taken too much on trust, and the conventional signs used to distinguish between ditch and mound, and between those used for visible remains and those buried beneath the surface, were far from perfect. He proposed two ways whereby the survey could effect an improvement: its archaeological information should be published either by the Government or if it was unwilling by county societies for their own areas; and, secondly, the survey should set up advisory committees composed of the ablest men in the country and not rely entirely on local advice of variable and dubious quality.

The first real improvement in the survey's archaeological services arrived when O G S Crawford was appointed as the first Archaeological Officer in 1920 and although his appointment coincided with a period of economic retrenchment he gradually succeeded in formulating a policy which remains the foundation of the Archaeology Division to this day. He also instigated the publication of archaeological period maps. The Archaeology Division was founded in 1947 under C W Phillips who was appointed Crawford's successor. It was obvious that the immediate post-war period would be crucial in the survey's history and might well be the last opportunity to undertake a comprehensive field survey of Britain's surviving antiquities and in addition it was plain that before any attempt to preserve or schedule monuments a reliable record was of prime importance and so the Archaeology Division would have as its first task the proper recording of archaeological information. Unfortunately the Object Name books Sir Henry James had introduced in the nineteenth century had been destroyed by bombing in November 1940 and a completely fresh start was therefore necessary.

The task was twofold. On the one hand the survey would need to act as an information gathering body sifting facts from a variety of sources and reducing them to a basic, easily consulted record; and on the other they would need to collect together an experienced band of field officers with a good knowledge of field archaeology and fully trained in ordnance survey methods. It would be their job to check the records against reality in the field, to search for new sites and to provide the survey with accurately plotted new material for use in the current revision of the general series maps.

That is not to say that the survey attempts to publish on its general maps a definitive record of antiquities and monuments; to be included these have to conform to certain rules. They must either be artificial features, natural features or places associated with well-known historical events or characters, or human dwelling places, and must date in origin to before 1715, with the exception of certain industrial monuments.

Besides information published on its maps the survey maintains an important archive of information on cards at its Southampton headquarters for use not only by other official archaeological bodies but also by the public at large. The basic record consists of a card index arranged by historical counties and each antiquity has its own card on which is noted a standard series of items of information—county, precise location by National Grid reference, six inch map sheet number, parish, character and name of antiquity, bibliographical references, treatment on earlier survey maps, observations by the field staff, and if possible a photograph. This unique combination of documentary and field research is available for consultation by bona fide research workers and copies of the cards may be purchased from the National Monuments Record Branch of the Royal Commission on Historical Monuments. The index is of course of tremendous value in the production of the 'period' maps devoted to archaeology, inaugurated by Crawford in the 1920s and 1930s, which have been known since 1966 as the 'Archaeological and historical maps'. Those currently available are *Southern Britain in the iron age*, *Roman Britain*, *Britain in the dark ages*, *Britain before the Norman Conquest*, *Ancient Britain*, *Monastic Britain*, *Hadrian's wall*, and *The Antonine wall*,*(qqv)*. Another important publication is *Field archaeology (qv)*.

Bibliography: F J Haverfield's address was printed in *Geographical journal*, XXVII (2) February 1906: 165-176; O G S Crawford's 'Archaeology and the Ordnance Survey', *Geographical journal*, LIX (4) April 1922: 245-258 is a brief outline of contemporary practice at the survey in dealing with antiquities; C W Phillips' 'Archaeology and the Ordnance Survey',
214

Antiquity XXXIII (131) September 1959: 195-204 is a pleasant account of the survey's origins ending with comments on its organization of its archaeological activities; the same author's 'The Ordnance Survey and archaeology 1791-1960', *Geographical journal*, CXXVII (1) March 1961: 1-9 covers much the same ground, whilst his 'The special archaeological and historical maps published by the Ordnance Survey', *Cartographic journal*, 2(1) June 1965: 27-31 describes the development of the recording of archaeological and historical sites in Britain and treats in detail each of the special maps. J B Harley's substantial volume *Ordnance Survey maps a descriptive manual* (1975) is essential reading especially chapter ten 'Archaeology and the archaeological and historical maps'. Successive sections on the survey's policy, its records and their compilation, the publication of antiquities on the standard maps, the naming and marking of antiquities, the selection of antiquities for publication, are followed by an account of the development of period maps and detailed notes on the archaeological maps now available. There is a tabular guide to the type of antiquities published in the various map series and a list of period maps compiled under Crawford's direction 1923-1938. Concern and dismay at a recent decision to reduce the comprehensive nature of the survey's card index archive of antiquities is apparent in Grahame Webster's 'Archaeology and the Ordnance Survey', *Current archaeology*, IV(7) No 42 January 1974: 201. O G S Crawford's autobiography *Said and done* (1955) affords a rare glimpse of the day-to-day working of the survey from within.

465 **'The origin of the British people'**: *archaeology and the Festival of Britain*, an article by Jacquetta Hawkes which appeared in *Antiquity* XXV (97) March 1951: 4-8, recounts the conception of the archaeological and physical anthropological pavilion on the South Bank in 1951 and describes its lay-out and contents.

466 **'The origins and growth of archaeology'** by Glyn Daniel, published as a Pelican Original in 1967, chronicles by means of a series of extracts from original writings how archaeology evolved in the course of three hundred years from the fanciful speculations of antiquarians and treasure-hunters into the professional and scientific discipline of today. It is fully documented and illustrated.

467 **'The origins of the English county archaeological societies'**, an admirably documented paper by Stuart Piggott, investigates the social and intellectual forces behind the formation of the local archaeological societies

215

in the latter half of the nineteenth century. Attention is focused primarily on the religious movements earlier in the century, although the effect of contemporary geology and other incidental factors such as the literary heritage of Sir Walter Scott and the unremitting boredom of young ladies in rectories and country houses are not overlooked. Professor Piggott's general conclusion is that 'to provide for shared common interests in archaeology and antiquities, the county societies came into being in Anglican, rural England. The societies were an answer to an intellectual and emotional need . . .' The paper is printed in volume 86 of the Birmingham and Warwickshire Archaeological Society's *Transactions* for 1974 which consists of a selection of papers from its lecture programme of 1970-1971 on the archaeology and history of Warwickshire celebrating the society's centenary. It is now available as an offprint.

468 'Orkney and Shetland' *an archaeological guide* by Lloyd Laing (David and Charles, 1974), primarily intended for the visitor and 'armchair' archaeologist, is a complete guide to the archaeology of the two island groups from prehistoric settlements to the seventeenth century. There is a glossary, suggestions for further reading, and a gazetteer listing all sites worth visiting.

469 Owen, Nicholas (1752-1811) published *British antiquities; or a collection of antiquities relating to Britons* (1777) which includes a biography of Edward Lhuyd but little else of significance or value.

470 Oxford Archaeological Excavation Committee was formed in 1967 in order to carry out a programme of excavations in the city in connection with the first stages of redevelopment. Interim excavation reports by T G Hassall appeared in the 1969-1974 volumes of *Oxoniensia*.

471 Oxford Architectural and Historical Society was founded as the Oxford Society for Promoting the Study of Gothic Architecture in 1839 and for the first twenty years of its existence was devoted almost entirely to the ecclesiological studies associated with the Gothic Revival and the Oxford Movement. In 1860, however, it changed its name to the one it still bears today marking a change of direction in its interests and activities along the path trodden by the county archaeological societies. Agreement was reached with the Oxfordshire Archaeological Society (*qv*) in the summer of 1953 for an interchange of privileges for members and for the county society's *Report* to be printed in *Oxoniensia*. The early history
216

of the society is well sketched in W A Pantin's 'The Oxford Architectural and Historical Society 1839-1939' *Oxoniensia*, IV, 1939: 174-194 and S L Ollard's 'The Oxford Architectural Society and the Oxford Movement', V, 1940: 146-160. A series of *Proceedings and excursions* was published 1860-1900 but these included non-local material and much space was taken up with accounts of the society's meetings and visits. In 1936 the society decided to publish a new annual journal, *Oxoniensia*, dealing with the archaeology, history and architecture of Oxford and its neighbourhood. Papers of note include D N Riley's 'Archaeology from the air in the Upper Thames valley', VIII + IX, 1943-44: 64-106; D B Harden's 'Scheduled monuments in Oxfordshire' (up to 31 December 1952), XIX, 1954: 137-145; J E G Sutton's 'Iron age hill-forts and some other earthworks in Oxfordshire', XXXI, 1966: 28-42, a gazetteer and review complete with bibliography, and Alison Dickson and David Hinton's 'A gazetteer of the late Saxon and medieval objects in the Department of Antiquities, Ashmolean Museum', XXXVII, 1972: 192-197. Don Benson's 'A sites and monuments record for the Oxford region', XXXVII, 1972: 226-237 is noticed separately in this handbook because of its wider significance. T G Hassall's interim reports of recent excavations in Oxford are listed under Oxford Archaeological Excavation Committee.

472 'Oxford Bible atlas' edited by Herbert G May with the assistance of Robert W Hamilton and Geoffrey Hunt, published in a second edition in 1974, takes full account of the discoveries in biblical geography, history and archaeology in the intervening period since the first edition of 1962. Twenty six full-colour maps, each accompanied by a descriptive text, include 'The Near East: archaeological sites'; 'Palestine: archaeological sites excavated or partly excavated 1973'; and 'Jerusalem in Old Testament and New Testament times, both revised in the light of recent archaeological discoveries'. Following the maps R W Hamilton contributes a chapter, 'Archaeology and the Bible', outlining how archaeology has advanced our knowledge of the material background of biblical times. There is a gazetteer containing historical and archaeological data in addition to place names, and nearly one hundred photographs further augment the maps and text. G N S Hunt's 'Producing a Bible atlas', *The Periodical*, XXXIV, Autumn 1962: 281-282 affords a brief but interesting glimpse of the production of the first edition.

473 Oxfordshire Archaeological Society was founded as the North Oxfordshire Archaeological Society in 1853 'for the study and preservation of the antiquities, ecclesiastical, civil and military, of North Oxfordshire and portions of adjoining counties'. The society's history is largely unrecorded although G D Parkes' 'The Oxfordshire Archaeological Society 1853-1953', *Oxoniensia* XVII/XVIII 1952 and 1953: 259-260 provides a bare outline down to the time when steeply rising printing costs caused the activities of the society to be coordinated with those of the Oxford Architectural and Historical Society (*qv*). A list of the society's publications is to be found in its *Report* no 87 (1949).

474 Oxfordshire Archaeological Unit is the executive arm of the Oxfordshire Archaeological Committee. It is cooperating with the Oxford City and County Museum and the Department of Extramural Studies Oxford University in a county-wide survey, parish by parish, to supplement Don Benson's Oxfordshire sites and monuments record. Kirsty Rodwell's *Historic towns in Oxfordshire: a survey of the new county* was published in 1975.

475 Palestine Exploration Fund was founded in 1865 as a society 'for the accurate and systematic investigation of the archaeology, topography, geology and physical geography, manners and customs of the Holy Land' at the instance of George Grove who was anxious to consolidate and extend the excellent survey work conducted in Jerusalem by Charles Wilson, a Royal Engineers officer. As the first scientific society to undertake exploration overseas the fund was a pioneer in archaeology. From the outset the society determined that its work should be strictly carried on along scientific lines and in particular that it would refrain from religious controversy. These basic principles have been adhered to with the result that Christians, Jews, and Muslims have all contributed to the high reputation the society so justifiably enjoys. In 1919 the society was instrumental, together with the British Academy, in setting up the British School of Archaeology in Jerusalem (*qv*) and thenceforward most of the fieldwork previously undertaken by the society was delegated to the school although the society continued to participate in excavations. It also continues to serve as the London base, the centre of studies relating to modern Israel, Jordan, Syria and the Lebanon in the United Kingdom. Today the society's role is very much to aid research workers with facilities and grants and to publish the results of their activities both for specialists and for the general public.

Publications: Dawson's of Pall Mall are now the sole agent for the distribution of all the book publications of the fund, excavation reports,
218

and summaries of work like C M Watson's *Fifty years work in the Holy Land 1865-1915* and *Palestine exploration annuals* many of which were first published up to a century ago. In addition they have recently completed a reprinting programme of the *Palestine exploration quarterly* which began publication in 1869 as the *Quarterly statement* and assumed its present title in 1937. A special feature is the inclusion in the 1869-1870 volume of the reports of the surveys and excavations carried out by Charles Warren 1867-1870 which were not available to the editors of the original volume. Cumulative indexes for 1869-1892, 1893-1910, and 1911-1963 have also been reprinted. A special leaflet is available from William Dawson, Cannon House, Folkestone, Kent. A centenary exhibition mounted at the Victoria and Albert Museum in cooperation with the British School of Archaeology in Jerusalem, October-November 1965, was commemorated by a souvenir album titled *World of the Bible*. Besides the descriptive annotations of the exhibits this also contained introductory sections on 'Palestine in the middle ages: AD 638-1516' (C N Johns); 'Pilgrims to archaeologists: AD 1516-1865' (D R Howell); and three listed under 'Palestine Exploration Fund AD 1865-1965'. Short papers on various topics relating to Palestine's natural environment, prehistory, and history, were also included. Among the maps is one showing the principal excavations with notes recording the British and foreign sponsoring agencies. Francis James' 'A milestone in Palestinian archaeology', *Expedition*, 7(4) Summer 1965: 34-38 is a convenient outline of the fund for American readers. The opening chapter of Kathleen Kenyon's *Digging up Jerusalem* (1974) also contains a useful summary of its activities.

476 Peabody Museum of Archaeology and Ethnology, Harvard University, was founded in 1866 as a result of a benefaction from George Peabody. It quickly established itself as a driving force in the development of archaeological studies in the United States and was also instrumental in pioneering modern museological methods and techniques. Instead of passively acquiring its collections by gift or purchase the museum became actively engaged in mounting archaeological expeditions to the American Southwest and to Central America. Its *Papers*, scholarly research reports, began publication in 1888 when the trustees decided that the museum's *Annual report* did not adequately reflect its activities; their scope is world wide although there is obviously a heavy concentration on North and Mesoamerica. The *Memoirs* published in a near folio format to accommodate the large plates thought desirable are almost exclusively devoted to Central America and to the Maya in particular. Volumes 1-45 (1888-1960) of the

Papers and volumes 1-10 (1891-1952) of the *Memoirs* are currently available from Kraus Reprint whose *General catalogue part 2* is a convenient source for authors and titles.

477 Penguin Books have included many celebrated books on archaeology in their lists over the years and for much of the time Glyn Daniel has acted as their advisory editor. A full list of titles in print and those forthcoming may be found in the current issue of *Penguin humanities catalogue* available from the Information Unit, Penguin Books Ltd, Bath Road, Harmondsworth, Middlesex or from Viking Penguin, 625 Madison Avenue, New York 10022.

478 'Peoples of Roman Britain' a series edited by Keith Branigan and published by Duckworth aims to present a comprehensive picture of the archaeology of Roman Britain. Each volume considers a single *civitas*, its settlement patterns and resources, and its reaction to an alien imposed civilization. The series is written by professional archaeologists recently active in fieldwork and research in the regions concerned. Titles published include *The Regni* (Barry Cunliffe); *The Coritani* (Malcolm Todd); *The Cornovii* (Graham Webster); and *The Trinovantes* (Rosalind Dunnett). Others in preparation are *The Cantiaci* (Alec Detsicas); *The Catuvellauni* (Keith Branigan); *The Iceni* (Helen Clarke and Peter Wade-Martins); and *The Parisi* (H Ramm).

479 'Perspectives in archaeology' is a Duckworth series edited by Colin Renfrew which seeks to apply modern archaeological thinking to concrete problems. The emphasis is on the rethinking of basic assumptions combined with an up-to-date methodology. *Titles*: the first to be published is *The spatial organisation of culture* (Ian Hodder); others to follow include *Early postglacial settlements of northern Europe* (Paul Mellars); *Ecology, economy and demography in the neolithic of eastern Europe* (Paul Dolukhanov); *Culture change in the prehistory of south eastern Europe* (Ruth Tringham); *Population concepts in the study of prehistory* (J Ammerman and L L Cavalli-Sforza); *From hunter to citizen: culture change in peninsular Italy* (Ruth Whitehouse); *Settlement and subsistence in the palaeolithic* (Paul Mellars); *The rise of the Maya* (William L Rathje); *The sea traders: the Indian Ocean* and *The Gulf from the Sumerians to the Portuguese* (both by David Whitehouse); *Human ecology in later European prehistory* (Andrew Fleming); and *The coming of coinage* (John Collis).

480 **Petrie, Sir William Matthew Flinders** (1853-1942) began excavating in Egypt in 1881 and from the outset his forceful personality was well to the fore. He spared no words in condemning contemporary methods of excavating: 'Nothing was done with any uniform plan, work is begun and left unfinished, no regard is paid to future requirements of exploration and no civilized or labour-saving appliances are used. It is sickening to see the rate at which everything is being destroyed, and the little regard paid to preservation.' Petrie's contributions to archaeology are large, his insistence on a meticulous record being kept of all artefacts in their context and his ingenious method of sequence dating being not the least among them. And, in Leo Deuel's words, 'By (the) crossdating of different civilizations by means of datable artifacts Petrie devised comparative archaeology.' Petrie's relations with the Egypt Exploration Fund were less than harmonious so, typically, he founded the Egyptian Research Account (later the British School of Archaeology in Egypt) to find the necessary financial backing for his expeditions. He was assiduous in publishing his excavation reports and many of these were republished in the 1970s by Aris and Phillips Ltd, Teddington House, Warminster, Wilts, and by Joel L Malter & Co, P O Box 777, Encino, California 1974. Petrie's total publishing output was vast, his *Ten years' diggings* (1892) records the finding of the Tell el-Amarna correspondence and relics; *Methods and aims in archaeology* (1904) outlines his method of sequence dating; and *Seventy years in archaeology* (1931) chooses from a 'mass of recollections' those 'which influenced my life and work and which helped or hindered the final outcome of each endeavour'. Chapter XI: 'Sir Flinders Petrie and the development of scientific excavation', in John David Wortham's *British Egyptology 1549-1906* (1971) is a well-documented summary; Percy E Newberry's obituary, *Journal of Egyptian archaeology*, 29, 1943: 67-70 is factual, Sidney Smith's in *Proceedings of the British Academy*, XXVIII, 1942: 309-324 is more analytical and more informative on Petrie's personal relationships and the effect these had upon his career.

481 **'Photography in archaeology and art'** by S K Matthews (John Baker, 1968) is a technical manual for the use of amateur and professional photographers interested in finding new ways of presenting their work for record, exhibition, or publicity purposes. An outline of the laws of copyright reproduced in part from *The British Journal photographic almanac* is included in the bibliography.

482 **'Physics and archaeology'** by M J Aitken, first published by Interscience Publishers of New York in 1961, appeared in a second edition published by the Clarendon Press in 1974. It describes ways in which physics has been closely involved in archaeological research in dating, surveying and the location of remains, in the hope it will provide professional archaeologists with a guide to new techniques, and is clearly not intended for the casual reader, each chapter ending with extensive references to papers in learned journals.

483 'The Picts' by Isabel Henderson, number fifty-four in Thames and Hudson's 'Ancient peoples and places' series when published in 1967, stresses the contribution made by recent advances in identifying a genuine Pictish archaeology and the emerging definition of the Scottish iron age.

484 Pitt-Rivers, General (1827-1900) shares the credit with Flinders-Petrie for urging archaeologists to study all artefacts recovered from excavations and not to restrict their interest to those of obvious artistic value. He is remembered especially for his grand-scale excavations on his estate at Rushmore, Wiltshire, which on account of their meticulous planning and recording, have come to be regarded as classics of British archaeology. He was supremely aware of the need for the prompt publication of the results, his *Excavation in Granborne Chase, Near Rushmore, on the borders of Dorset and Wilts*, privately printed in five volumes 1887-1903, were presented to many public and university libraries. A memoir of the general together with a bibliographical list of his writings 1858-1900 is included in the fifth volume. Brief outlines of his career and place in the history of archaeology are available in Ronald Jessup's *The story of archaeology in Britain* (1964) and Glyn Daniel's *A hundred and fifty years of archaeology* (1975).

485 'A pocketbook for industrial archaeologists' by Kenneth Hudson (John Baker, 1976) is regarded by the author as a replacement of his *Handbook for industrial archaeologists* (1967) (*qv*). It begins with a personal view on how industrial archaeologists should redefine their objectives in the 1970s and 1980s (ie to concern themselves with the second industrial revolution of electricity and petroleum), continues with a very informative section on industrial archaeology and the law, worth a very careful reading, discusses the processing and presentation of facts, lists museums libraries and archives alphabetically by county, indicates other organisations and institutions (including local societies) active in industrial archaeology, and ends with a summary of key inventions and technological developments. The book was planned especially to meet the
222

needs of those whose interest in the subject is comparatively recent as a guide and reference work that can be easily slipped into the pocket and be readily consulted whenever the need or occasion arrives.

486 'Post-medieval archaeology' is the annual publication of the Society for Post-Medieval Archaeology. First issued in 1967 its format closely follows its older stable-companion *Medieval archaeology*: the customary papers, notes and news, and book reviews, are accompanied by a feature 'Post-medieval Britain' divided under two headings 'Excavation and field-work' and 'Periodical literature'. The first covers 'every aspect of activity which could leave traces capable of elucidation by the archaeological method in the future'; entries are arranged into nine different categories—ecclesiastical buildings, military and naval earthworks and canals, towns and corporate buildings, villages, manors and country homes, farms and smaller domestic architecture, industries, communications, and sports and amusements, all listed alphabetically by county. 'Periodical literature' is based principally on periodicals published in Britain during the previous calendar year and follows the same arrangement. *Index of volumes I-V 1967-1971* was published in 1973, it too is similar in arrangement to the indexes of *Medieval archaeology* (*qv*).

487 'Practical archaeology' *an introduction to archaeological field-work and excavation* by Graham Webster (A and C Black, 2ed 1974) is designed to help the serious amateur archaeologist towards an understanding of the practical aspects and basic techniques of archaeology from the initial survey and digging of the first sod to the writing and publication of results. The first chapter, 'Archaeological organisation', provides a useful survey of the structure of archaeology in Britain—the functions of the county societies, the Council for British Archaeology, and the regional museums are examined and there are notes on further sources of information. Other topics discussed include investigation by field work and excavation and scientific examination. Some well-chosen photographs and line drawings complement the text. When first published in 1963 it was designed as a companion volume to Stuart Piggott's *Approach to archaeology*.

488 'Prehistoric and early Christian Ireland' *a guide* by Estyn Evans (Batsford, 1966) is arranged in two distinct parts. An introductory section providing the cultural and historical context is followed by a gazetteer which lists sites and monuments alphabetically by counties. Entries include map references (although the author warns that long years of

experience persuade him that local enquiries are often more reliable),
brief physical descriptions, and at times, an indication of the site's wider
significance. A glossary explains archaeological and architectural terms,
there is a full measure of drawings, plans and photographs, and the bibliography offers references to published accounts of each site.

489 'Prehistoric and early Wales', edited by I Ll Foster and Glyn Daniel,
prints in permanent form the papers given at the British Summer School
of Archaeology held at Bangor in August 1959. It was published in Routledge's 'Studies in ancient history and archaeology' series in 1965. *Contents*: 'The old stone age in Wales' (C B M McBurney); 'Neolithic Wales'
(W F Grimes); 'The bronze age' (H N Savory); 'Early iron age Wales'
(A H A Hogg); 'Roman Wales' (I A Richmond); 'Wales in the fifth to
seventh centuries AD: Archaeological evidence' (L Alcock); and 'The
emergence of Wales' (I Ll Foster). Each chapter is completed with a detailed bibliography. Glyn Daniel contributes an introduction reviewing
the literature of Welsh antiquarian and archaeological studies.

490 'Prehistoric and Roman studies' *commemorating the opening of the
Department of prehistoric and Romano-British antiquities* edited by G de
G Sieveking, was published by the trustees of the British Museum in 1971.
It is made up of papers relating to important individual pieces or classes
of antiquity in the possession of the department which was established
as a separate entity in 1969. All the papers were previously printed in
the *British Museum quarterly*. Some personal reminiscences by Sir Thomas
Kendrick throw an intimate light on some of the museum's personalities
in the 1920s.

491 'The prehistoric annals of Scotland' by Daniel Wilson (Macmillan,
2 vols, 1863) was the second edition of a book originally titled *The archaeology and prehistoric annals of Scotland* first published in 1851. Intended
'to rescue archaeological research from that limited range to which a too
exclusive devotion to classical studies had given rise; and, especially in
relation to Scotland, to prove how greatly more comprehensive and important are its native antiquities than all the traces of intruded arts' (Preface), it was divided into four sections—'The primeval or stone period',
'The archaic or bronze period', 'The iron period', and 'The Christian
period'. Undoubtedly an original contribution to Scottish archaeology,
it has a further claim to fame in that it reputedly first used the word
'prehistoric' in English. A fine appreciation of it and Wilson's other works
224

is to be found in W Douglas Simpson's 'Sir Daniel Wilson and the *Prehistoric annals of Scotland*: a centenary study', *Proceedings of the Society of Antiquaries of Scotland*, XCVI, 1962-63: 1-8.

492 'A prehistoric bibliography' by Wilfrid Bonser extended and edited by June Troy (Blackwell, 1976) is a substantial volume arranged under five main headings: Men and methods in archaeology (archaeologists and their work, general theories, and scientific methods of excavation and their interpretation); Field archaeology; Specific sites; Material finds; and Culture. These divisions are sub-divided into a general section and by zones which correspond in area to the regional group structure of the Council for British Archaeology. Entries provide information as to author, title, pagination and source of each item and are numbered consecutively in order to facilitate their endexing. Owing to unfortunate circumstances which included the untimely death of the compiler and a consequent lack of stringent proofreading, there is a monstrous number of *corrigenda* which are themselves not free from error. In other respects however, this is a valuable addition to Bonser's Romano-British and Anglo-Saxon-Celtic bibliographies.

493 'Prehistoric Britain' by Jacquetta and Christopher Hawkes (Chatto and Windus, 1947) declares that 'it wishes to be no more than the briefest chronicle of the course of human history in the British Isles'. It is in fact far more than that, being an enjoyably urbane and literate synthesis of geology, prehistory, and archaeology, spanning half a million years. A series of chronological chapters, each devoted to a specific archaeological period, tells the story of man in Britain from neolithic times down to the Roman invasions. Then comes a long essay on the history and methodology of British archaeology ending with a bibliography of books published 1932-1946. The second half is given over to a regionally arranged guide to the most significant prehistoric and Roman antiquities of Britain.

494 'Prehistoric Britain and Ireland' by James Forde-Johnston (Dent, 1976) focuses attention on the various types of prehistoric monuments still visible in the British Isles and places them in their archaeological context.

495 'Prehistoric chamber tombs of England and Wales', by Glyn Daniel (Cambridge University Press, 1950), based on a field survey 1933-1937 and an examination of excavated material in museums, is in two parts: (1) a descriptive text (distribution, morphology, ritual, archaeological finds, origins and dating) and (2) a series of regional inventories giving locations, map references, description, and bibliographical references to each tomb in turn.

496 'Prehistoric Ireland' by Joseph Raftery (Batsford, 1951) is a profusely illustrated account of Irish archaeology intended for the interested layman rather than the specialist prehistorian.

497 The Prehistoric Society is the only archaeological society in Britain devoted exclusively to the study of prehistory. It was originally founded in 1908 as the Prehistoric Society of East Anglia at an inaugural meeting in the Norfolk and Norwich Library. The declared objects of the society were to study all matters connected with prehistoric man in East Anglia, to facilitate friendly intercourse between prehistorians, to disseminate knowledge of prehistory by means of papers and exhibitions of implements, to preserve records of all prehistoric remains found in the district, and to see as far as possible that the existing remains of the prehistoric period such as barrows, trackways, camps and settlements, are preserved from destruction. In 1935 the local designation was dropped and the society assumed the name it still retains. Its progress since then is best followed by reading the valedictory addresses delivered every four years by the retiring president. J C D Clark's 'Perspectives in prehistory', *Proceedings of the Prehistoric Society*, XXV 1959: 1-14 discusses the consequences of shedding the society's regional origins, and redefines its purpose: 'we are concerned with the advancement of prehistory, that is with reconstructing the history of preliterate or at any rate non-literate societies. We are therefore . . . necessarily concerned with every means by which information can be obtained about prehistoric man, his environment, his activities, and, in the broadest sense, his beliefs and socially conditioned presuppositions.' He also provides an instructive geographical and temporal analysis of the contents of the society's *Proceedings*, coming to the conclusion that they 'no longer mirror the outlook of flint collectors based primarily on Ipswich and Norwich, but to an increasing degree that of professional prehistorians working predominantly . . . in the British Isles, clearly aware that they can only master their own prehistory in a wider context.' Stuart Piggott's 'Archaeology and prehistory', *Proceedings* XXIX 1963: 1-16 reviews thought and practice in British archaeology and prehistory since the 1920s and then asks some questions about the future. John D Cowen's presidential address, Proceedings XXXV 1969: 1-11 first reviews the society's activities (a week-end spring

226

conference in London, a summer conference in the country lasting a week, and six winter lectures), includes a word or two on nomenclature, and speaks of the growing division in prehistory between the palaeolithic and the rest. T G E Powell's presidential address 'A midterm view', *Proceedings* 39 1973: 1-5, includes some personal reminiscences and goes on to ruminate on the society's responsibilities. Stuart Piggott's 'The Prehistoric Society', *Archaeology*, 3(2) June 1950: 119-120 is a short introductory article for American readers.

498 **'Prehistory'** *an introduction* by Derek Roe (Macmillan, 1970) examines the sequence of events of old world prehistory and investigates some of the ways in which these events are studied. The main emphasis is on British prehistory although this is placed firmly in its European context with reference at times to even further afield. The approach is chronological from the earliest times to the iron age with an introduction on the divisions and subdivisions of prehistory and its relation to archaeology and with a final chapter describing the impact of recent scientific techniques. In an effort to avoid the danger of over-simplification notes are appended to each chapter indicating where the text needs amplification by further reading. Although this introductory account is not intended for 'senior scholars of prehistory' it would be a mistake to suppose it to be addressed to the uninformed layman, the author assumes the reader will have access to an archaeological library and both notes and bibliography contain many references to journal literature.

499 **'Prehistory and the Romantic movement'** by Stuart Piggott, an essay published in *Antiquity* XI (41) March 1937: 31-38, indicates the main features of archaeology in England during the period 1720-1820. The beginnings of field archaeology and its literature, the eighteenth century interest in the Druids, and the growing taste for prehistoric archaeology are among the topics discussed.

500 **'The preparation of archaeological reports'** by Leslie Grinsell, Philip Rahtz and David Price Williams, originally issued in duplicated form by the Bristol Archaeological Research Group in 1962, was published in conventional form by John Baker in 1966 and is now available in a second (1974) edition. It is 'intended as a guide which will enable the potential writer of archaeological reports to infuse into them his own idividuality or even originality, within the framework of what is required by editors and publishers'. Eminently useful and sensible hints and advice on the form of publication, the preliminaries and initial stages, the body of an excavation report (text and illustrations), distribution maps and the final stages, are complemented by lists of abbreviations of international, national and general periodicals and two appendixes–'Some archaeological reconstructions' and 'Some publications recommended for study'. There is also a list of references and a bibliography. Every local archaeological society will need at least one copy of this immensely practical work in its library, although all wise young or inexperienced archaeologists will doubtless prefer to acquire a copy for their own personal use.

501 'Pre-Roman Britain' by Stanley Thomas (Studio Vista, 1965) is a pictorial survey of the prehistoric archaeology of Britain. A brief summary of the present state of knowledge of the period precedes the main part of the book consisting of three hundred or so photographs of sites and monuments from the earliest beginnings down to the first century AD. It should find a place on all sixth form or college library shelves.

502 'The preservation of buildings of historic interest' *a note on the Town and Country Planning Act, 1947* published by the Council for British Archaeology in 1953, summarized the provisions made for the protection of buildings of historic or architectural merit. The procedure for listing buildings was explained as was the operation of the act's preservation clauses.

503 'The preservation of technological material' *report and recommendations*, prepared by a working party of the Standing Commission on Museums and Galleries set up 'to consider the problem presented by the preservation of historical technological relics and records, and to recomment how the necessary finance should be provided and administered', was published by HMSO in 1971. Although chiefly concerned with archive material the working party did not omit industrial monuments from their deliberations and it was recommended that these should remain the responsibility of the Department of the Environment but 'should be the subject of considerably increased expenditure'. Documents submitted to the working party and printed here include a note by the Ministry of Public Building and Works dated May 1970, that is shortly before its absorption into the DoE, on the practical help given by the way of grants and advice in industrial archaeology; a descriptive list of museums in which technological material is preserved, and also of some industrial monuments preserved in situ; and an outline of the work of the Council for

British Archaeology and the establishment of the National Record of Industrial Monuments (*qv*); and indications of some prominent monuments allowed to be destroyed, some that had been saved but which needed financial support, and some that were still in danger of destruction. The working party's main recommendation stated that an annual grant-in-aid should be allocated to the Science Museum to be administered with the help of an advisory committee appointed by the Department of Education. This grant would be for the purpose of helping with the purchase of museum objects and the cost of their transport in cases where 50 per cent of the total cost could be matched from other sources.

504 'Principles and practice in modern archaeology' by David M Browne was published in Hodder and Stoughton's 'Teach yourself' series in 1975 and is 'based on the belief that there is a certain body of data that is traditionally the concern of the archaeologist and that this can only be discovered and studied by archaeological means'. To this end it begins by establishing the framework within which archaeologists operate and then proceeds to examine the ideas and methods current in modern archaeology: finding sites, excavation, conservation, and the analysis of organic and inorganic remains. The emphasis throughout is on modern techniques and on the necessity for professionalism. There is an appendix listing museums with collections of archaeological importance and a general bibliography.

505 'Principles of publication in rescue archaeology' *report by a working party of the Ancient Monuments Board for England Committee for Rescue Archaeology*, published by the Department of the Environment in 1975, is a slim, paper-covered, A4 size, spiral bound, document of fifteen pages. It considers how the various fieldwork records, post-excavation studies, interpretative analyses and other related data may most expeditiously be made available to the public. The Secretary of State welcomed it as a basis on which to build a detailed policy for publication in rescue archaeology, approving the suggested balance between excavation and publication of completed work.

506 Proceedings of the Prehistoric Society (1908-) published annually, have altered remarkably little in seventy years apart from a few typographical changes. Contents include excavation reports, summaries and surveys of archaeological theories and discoveries, and reviews of important books. An *Index vol I-XXX 1935-1964* compiled by Bridget Trump (1974) is in three parts, subject, sites and authors. The subject index lists all cultures and classes of objects dealt with in detail; the site index lists sites under British counties and foreign countries; and the author index includes all articles and books reviewed, but not the writers of the reviews, in one sequence. The old series ie pre 1935, was titled *The proceedings of the Prehistoric Society of East Anglia.*

507 '**Proceedings of the Society of Antiquaries of London**' began publication in 1843 and consisted in the main of condensed abstracts of the society's proceedings along with business details, the election of fellows, obituaries etc, for circulation to members. Of special interest are the presidential addresses, useful for indicating what was exerting the attention of the society at any one time. In later years many papers delivered to the society were printed in full. Two series were published: the first in four volumes 1843-1859 and the second series in thirty-two volumes 1859-1919. There is a general index to the first series at the end of volume four and a separate *General index to proceedings second series, vols I-XX with classified list of illustrations* was published in 1908. Thereafter the indexes of the biennial volumes must be consulted. Since 1921 very short notes on the society's proceedings have been included in *The antiquaries journal (qv).*

508 **Protection of Wrecks Act** 1973 provides wrecks of historical, archaeological or artistic importance with the same sort of protection enjoyed by ancient monuments on dry land. Such wrecks may only be disturbed on licence from the Department of Trade and Industry who first have to be satisfied that applicants command the necessary archaeological competence and facilities.

509 '**Public archaeology**' by Charles R McGimsey III, published by the Seminar Press in their 'Studies in archaeology' series in 1972, is based on two surveys of state-supported archaeological research programmes in each of the fifty states of America in 1958 and 1966, the second of which greatly influenced the legislation establishing and funding the Arkansas Archaeological Survey of which the author was named as director. His report is here updated for those in the archaeological profession who may be about to become involved in developing programmes in their own state and for the increasing number of legislators and other interested citizens showing concern over their state's archaeological heritage, and is intended to encourage state-supported archaeological programmes elsewhere. A chapter on designing such programmes and on drawing up a State
230

Antiquities Act is based on the author's experience in Arkansas; there is a summary of prevailing state and federal support for archaeology including a commentary on the principal federal legislation. This is followed by a detailed scrutiny of the public financial support, the administrative arrangements, and the legislative support, enjoyed by archaeology in each of the states in turn. The text of all federal laws affecting archaeological preservation completes an invaluable survey and reference work.

510 'A reading list in American archaeology' compiled by J Alden Mason appeared in *Archaeology* 2(3) September 1949: 134-139 and consists of an annotated representative selection of reliable works on the archaeology of the Americas for the information and guidance of readers with no previous professional interest in archaeology. The aim was to suggest 'not too technical works in English by recognized authorities, the more recent up-to-date books, and those either purchasable or obtainable in most large libraries'. Books which present a controversial view about the origins of the American aboriginals were not considered for inclusion.

511 'Recent archaeological excavations in Britain' *selected excavations 1939-1945 with a chapter on recent air-reconnaissance* edited by R L S Bruce-Mitford (Routledge, 1956) comprises eleven accounts by distinguished archaeologists of representative excavations during the specified period. Contents include 'Star Carr, a mesolithic site in Yorkshire' (J G D Clark); 'The Snettisham treasure' (R Rainbird Clarke); 'The Brigantian fortifications at Stanwick, Yorkshire' (Sir Mortimer Wheeler); 'The cult of Mithras and its temple at Carrawburgh on Hadrian's wall' (I A Richmond); 'The Lullingstone Roman villa' (G W Meates); 'Excavations in the City of London' (W F Grimes); 'The excavation of the Sutton Hoo ship-burial' (C W Phillips); 'A dark-age settlement at Mawgan Porth, Cornwall' (R L S Bruce-Mitford); 'Jarlshof, a prehistoric and Viking settlement site in Shetland' (J R C Hamilton); 'The Norman motte at Abinger, Surrey and its wooden castle' (Brian Hope-Taylor); and 'Deserted medieval villages and the excavations at Wharram Percy, Yorkshire' (J G Hurst). A concluding chapter by J K S St Joseph outlines the startling finds made possible by aerial photography. The editor also contributes a note on the law and practice of treasure trove. Maps, plates and drawings illustrate the text and each chapter ends with a short reading list.

512 'Recent work in rural archaeology', edited by P J Fowler and published by the Moonraker Press of Bradford-on-Avon, Wiltshire in 1975, 'illustrates some of the sorts of archaeological work at present (ie in 1972) taking place in the British countryside'. Each essay attempts to interpret the broad flow of information resulting from field surveys, air photography, deep ploughing and road building and concludes with a bibliography. These bibliographies, deliberately not standardised in presentation, 'represent the contributors' various responses to an invitation to provide leads to the source material on their particular sites and areas and to the background which has informed the work they describe'. *Contents*: 'The Somerset levels' (John Coles and Alan Hibbert); 'Settlement, farming and environment in south-west England' (Roger Mercer); 'Pattern and interpretation: a view of the Wessex landscape' (Collin Bowen); 'Religion and settlement in Wessex, 3000-1700 BC' (Geoffrey Wainwright); 'The brochs of Scotland' (Euan Mackie); 'The north-western interface' (Barri Jones); 'Roman settlements in the Nene valley: the impact of recent archaeology' (Christopher Taylor); 'Continuity in the landscape? Some local archaeology in Wiltshire, Somerset, and Gloucestershire' (Peter Fowler); and 'The origins of rural settlement in East Anglia' (Peter Wade-Martins). Numerous well-integrated photographs, maps and drawings complement the text.

513 'Reconstructing the past' *a basic introduction to archaeology* by Keith Branigan (David and Charles, 1974) explains in simple terms to the uninformed public just what the archaeologist is trying to do and how he sets about his task, in an attempt to enlist general support for the aims and purposes of rescue archaeology. Each chapter sets out to answer a typical question of the sort long experience has taught archaeologists to expect from casual visitors to their sites—Why are you digging it up? How did it get buried? How did you know it was there? Have you found anything interesting? Why keep broken pieces of pottery? How do you know how old it is? What was it? Why do you take so long? As a succinct and informative guide to the basic techniques of archaeology it surely deserves a place on the shelves of every sixth-form library.

514 'The regional archaeologies', originally published by Cory, Adams and Mackay, now appear under the Heinemann Educational Books imprint. Written for the most part by professional archaeologists these slim, carefully illustrated handbooks are intended as authoritative introductions to local archaeology for schools and adult education classes. In all cases special care is taken to avoid insipid generalizations and instead to argue from the evidence of a particular site to its general context and,

232

whenever necessary, to take into account appropriate geographical and geological factors. Those sites easily visited within the area and the objects to be found in local museums are clearly listed with directions and National Grid map references. Titles: *Roman frontiers of Britain* (D R Wilson); *South Wales* (C Houlder and W H Manning); *North Wales* (Katherine Watson); *East Anglia* (Helen Clarke); *Wessex* (Peter Fowler); *The Severn basin* (K S Painter); *South west Scotland* (Jack Scott); *Edinburgh and south-west Scotland* (Graham and Anne Ritchie); *Yorkshire* (Ian Longworth); and *London* (Ralph Merrifield). General editor of the series is D R Wilson.

515 '**The reliquary**' *a depository of precious relics—legendary, biographical, and historical—illustrative of the habits, customs, and pursuits of our forefathers* began publication as a quarterly in 1860. Although intended to be 'of real value and service to the general historian, the archaeologist, the biographer, the genealogist, the artist, and the topographer', its archaeological contents, in the modern sense of the term at least were often restricted to notes on archaeological progress and developments submitted by the secretaries or editors of the principal county archaeological societies. In 1894 it absorbed the short-lived *Illustrated archaeologist* (June 1893-September 1894) to become *The reliquary and illustrated archaeologist: a quarterly journal and review devoted to the study of the early pagan and Christian antiquities of Great Britain; medieval architecture and ecclesiology; the development of the arts and industries of man in the past ages; and the survivals of ancient usages and appliances in the present.* Publication was discontinued in 1910.

516 '**Report of the committee of enquiry into the arrangements for the protection of field monuments 1966-68**' (Cmnd 3904) was presented to Parliament by the Minister of Public Building and Works in February 1969. The committee had been appointed in May 1966 following ministerial concern, reinforced by strong representations from responsible archaeological bodies, at the increasing damage to ancient earthworks. Their terms of reference were 'to consider whether, in the light of present day conditions, changes are needed in the scope and/or use made of the existing powers and arrangements for the protection of field monuments; and to make recommendations'. After first listening to the views of the Chief Inspector of Ancient Monuments, the committee invited various archaeological organisations, associations connected with farming and land-owning interests, local authority associations, and government departments, to submit evidence. In all the committee met twenty-seven times. Their main conclusions were 'that with the pace of modern development of all kinds, the rate of disappearance of antiquities can only accelerate unless resolute steps are taken to stop it' and that 'it would be a grave national loss if these national monuments, many of which have stood unharmed for thousands of years and offer a rich harvest of knowledge to be tapped at the right moment, should be swept away in relatively few years'. The committee recommended that the scheduling policy of the ministry should be re-examined, more monuments should be taken into guardianship, and that a new category of 'starred monuments' should be introduced, the Ancient Monuments Acts should be consolidated and amended, strengthened and enforced. Other recommendations included payments to landowners for the continued preservation of scheduled sites on arable land, a more frequent inspection of monuments, and the augmenting of the staff of the Inspectorate of Ancient Monuments and of the local authorities. The recording of monuments both in the literature and on the ground would in itself effect a considerable improvement. The *Report* was generally welcomed, the Council for British Archaeology urged all members of the archaeological societies to read it as it was imperative that these bodies should recognize and undertake their responsibilities in the preservation of field monuments. The recommendations of the committee were met in part by the passing of the Field Monuments Act 1972 which allowed payments to be made to private landowners to protect sites of no beneficial use which in the opinion of the Secretary of State were in danger of injury in the course of agriculture or forestry.

517 RESCUE a trust for British archaeology was formed in response to a feeling of anger and despair at the inexorable destruction of archaeological evidence in the United Kingdom in the wake of city redevelopments, the building of new towns, the construction of motorways, and the conversion of the countryside to arable farming and the extensive use of deep ploughing. After two preliminary meetings in 1970 RESCUE officially came into existence at a public meeting held in the Senate House, University of London, 23 January 1971, attended by over 700 people. The objects of the society are 'to promote and foster the discovery, excavation, preservation, recording and study of sites and objects of archaeological importance in Great Britain for the public benefit and to promote and foster public knowledge, understanding and appreciation of archaeology generally and of such sites and objects in particular'.

It was intended that the society should be an association of all interested people with individual membership, and a fund raising body
234

obtaining funds from subscriptions, donations, bequests and appeals. These resources would be used 'to make the public aware of the rapidly accelerating destruction of their archaeological heritage; to encourage the revision and extension of existing legislation concerning archaeological remains, and to seek for new legislation where necessary; to obtain greatly increased funds for rescue excavation and its publication; to press for the extension and the improvement of field archaeological training at all levels; to help to record and conserve the physical remains of Britain's archaeological heritage of every age, and with particular reference to the changing character of the natural environment; and specifically to support surveys, to acquire sites or areas of archaeological importance for permanent conservation, to initiate or support rescue excavations and the consequent work on the results and their publication' (from its appeal leaflet of which 100,000 copies were distributed through the national journals, to the membership of archaeological societies, and to volunteers and visitors on excavation sites).

Two thousand people joined RESCUE in its first eighteen months, a cohort of very distinguished and experienced archaeologists agreed to serve on an adivsory council, a number of eminent persons consented to act as patrons, and the society was well and truly launched. A sophisticated public relations operation bombarded MPs, radio and television, local and national newspapers, with the latest in rescue archaeology stories. Coincidentally or not, the government budget for archaeology was multiplied eightfold. Not that the trust was equally successful in extracting funds from the general public as originally intended but its successes in promoting a wider understanding of the urgency of rescue archaeology at local town hall level cannot be questioned. Lectures, seminars, sponsored excavations, led to some spectacular triumphs but the impetus has to be constantly maintained, the scope for RESCUE is forever expanding, not contracting. As Graham Thomas wisely remarked 'RESCUE must and will retain its completely independent watchdog role. With so many decisions crucial to the future of archaeology taken behind closed doors, it is vital that an organisation exists to review progress and results.'

RESCUE scholarships are awarded from time to time and are designed to assist intending full time archaeologists to obtain experience in selected aspects of archaeology over a period of at least six months. Any person may apply provided they have an appropriate background of relevant academic and/or other experience and an ambition to become an experienced full time archaeologist. Sponsorship it is hoped will descend from several sources—industry, educational trusts, etc. The purpose of the scholarships is to bridge the gap between the increasing number of non-university full-time archaeological posts now being created and the availability of people properly qualified to fill them. It is not intended primarily to produce more excavators but more to enhance the quality of archaeological work as a public service.

Peter Fowler's 'The crisis in field archaeology' *Current archaeology*, 23 November 1970: 343-345 reports on the preliminary moves leading up to the formation of RESCUE; that journal's editorial in the January 1972 issued (No 30) looks back on the society's first year and describes it as a sort of archaeological Fabian Society. Graham Thomas' 'RESCUE: the first five years', *London archaeology* 2(12) autumn 1975: 298-299, 320, assesses its impact and the tasks awaiting it. A fuller account of its origins, development, and activities is to be found in *Rescue archaeology* (*qv*). *Publications*: *RESCUE news* and various other books and pamphlets notably *The future of London's past: a survey of the archaeological implications of planning and development in the nation's capital* by Martin Biddle and D Hudson. RESCUE's initiative in the publication of *Archaeology and government* (*qv*) must also be noted.

518 '**Rescue archaeology**' edited by Philip A Rahtz (Penguin Books, 1974) describes the efforts of professional archaeologists, principally through the formation of RESCUE (*qv*), to prevent further large-scale destruction of archaeological sites in Britain. Contents include Part 1 *Background to the crisis*: 'Archaeology in Britain 1973' (Charles Thomas); 'The world situation' (John Alexander); 'The scale of the problem' (Philip Barker); and 'Survival and archaeology' (Cecil Hogarth). Part 2 *Rescue digging*: 'Rescue digging past and present' (Philip Rahtz); 'Kent, Dover and the CIB Corps' (Brian Philp); 'Rescue digging all the time' (Chris Musson). Part 3 *Special threats*: 'The future of the urban past' (Martin Biddle); 'Motorways and archaeology' (Peter Fowler); 'Ancient mining and the environment' (Barri Jones and Peter Lewis). Part 4 *Crisis areas*: 'York: the anatomy of a crisis in urban archaeology' (Peter Addyman); 'The changing historical landscape seen from the air' (J K St Joseph); 'Destruction in the highlands and islands of Scotland' (Iain Crawford); 'Rescuing museums' (Kenneth Barton); and 'Rescuing finds' (David Leigh). Part 5 *How you can get involved*: 'Training the new archaeologist' (Graham Webster); 'Rescue archaeology and the public' (Graham Thomas and Graham Arnold); 'Archaeology as a hobby and how to start' (Robert Kiln); 'Volunteers' (Philip Rahtz); and 'The origins and development of RESCUE' (Philip Barker).

236

519 Rescue Archaeology Group was formed by Graham Guilbert and Chris Musson in 1970 to carry out surveys and excavation work on sites threatened with destruction. It is patterned on an architectural partnership and all members of the group are skilled archaeologists. The effectiveness of small professional teams in terms of economy and productivity and the problems involved are discussed in their article 'Two winters with RAG', *Current archaeology*, 33, July 1972: 259-263 which includes a tabulated list of their work October 1970-April 1973.

520 'Rescue archaeology in Britain' is a memorandum produced by the Department of the Environment for distribution to local authorities. It outlines in brief what is meant by the term 'rescue archaeology', explains why it has developed so swiftly over the last decade or so, and notes the consequent haphazard structural pattern of this type of work. It also indicates the measure of government financial support and reports the appointment of a Committee for Research Archaeology of the Ancient Monuments Board to advise on national priorities, the organization and needs of support facilities, and on the principles to be followed in publication. Finally the local pattern and the role of local authorities is defined. With the approval of the Chief Inspector of Ancient Monuments it was published as appendix 1 in *Archaeology in Britain 1974-75* (report No 25 of the Council for British Archaeology, year ending 30 June 1975).

521 'RESCUE news' launched in October 1972 now appears three times a year. It is a lively but thoroughly professional tabloid reporting on topics of current interest. 'Already it is performing a very valuable purpose in keeping the members of RESCUE in touch, and though its occasional strident tone may jar on some, yet this is an inevitable part of an avowedly propagandist newsheet, and the whole production is admirably professional.' (Notes and news, *Current archaeology*, 36, January 1973).

522 The Research Laboratory, British Museum was originally formed as a short-term measure in May 1920 (following the return to the museum of many antiquities which had deteriorated in underground storage during the first world war) for the scientific study of ancient materials with special reference to their reaction to various environmental conditions and to evolve appropriate restorative methods of treatment. This work achieved such a degree of success that the laboratory was established on a permanent basis under the direction of the Department of Scientific and Industrial Research. In 1931, largely due to the recommendations of the Royal

Commission on Museums, it was incorporated as a separate department of the British Museum.

More recently attention has increasingly been devoted to developing scientific methods of conservation, devising new techniques as and when these are required in order to solve specific problems. One of the more glamorous 'spin-offs' of its work in this area is the authentication of important objects, many alas being detected as spurious. In the past decade the laboratory has pursued a policy of training staff from other museum departments in the techniques of routine conservation, thus allowing its own staff to concentrate on research activities. The new methods developed and introduced by the laboratory include 'the intensive washing technique for bronzes, the use of polyethylene glycol wax for the consolidation of fragile antiquities, the silver oxide method for the treatment of bronze disease, the use of synthetic resins for the impregnation of fragile antiquities and the consolidation and restoration of metal antiquities, the development of special methods of electrolytic reduction for the cleaning of corroded lead objects, the treatment of 'weeping' glass and the development of a new method for the reduction of completely mineralized silver objects'. (*Report of the trustees 1966*, p26) The museum's reputation in the field of examination and restoration of antiquities may be gauged by the growing number of overseas institutions which avail themselves of its facilities and goodwill.

A short essay on the laboratory, describing its methods and successes, written by Dr A E Werner, Keeper of the Research Laboratory, is to be found in *Treasures of the British Museum* (Thames and Hudson, 1971) edited by Sir Frank Francis. The successive issues of the *Report of the trustees* should also be consulted for nouvelles de la dernière heure.

523 Research Laboratory for Archaeology and Art History, Oxford University was founded in 1955 to develop new methods of physical research for application to archaeological or art-historical objectives. Such work is financed by the laboratory through the experimental stages and when first demonstrated. The facilities of the laboratory are described in the second issue of *Archaeometry* (*qv*). Every spring the laboratory organises an Archaeometry Symposium in Oxford.

524 Reservoir Salvage Act 1960 (US), an act to provide for the preservation of historical and archaeological data (including relics and specimens) which might otherwise be lost as the result of the construction of a dam, was an important measure in American salvage (or rescue) archaeology. Charles R McGimsey's *Public archaeology* (*qv*) includes its text.

238

525 'Responsibility and safeguards in archaeological excavation', a pamphlet edited by P J Fowler and published by the Council for British Archaeology in 1972 is intended 'not as a comprehensive safety code but as a guide to the main areas in which common sense, practical experience, the law and insurance dictate that certain minimum precautions should be taken *before*, *during*, and *after* an archaeological excavation'. Topics covered include excavation and the law, third parties and negligence, precautions against soil collapse, working with machinery, and personal safety and medical precautions. It replaced an earlier four-page memorandum, *Safety precautions in archaeological excavations*.

526 'Retrospective index to theses' *of Great Britain and Ireland 1716-1950* is published in five volumes by the American Bibliographical Center-Clio Press and provides coverage down to the year when the Aslib *Index to theses* (*qv*) commences. The theses are listed under subject headings, each entry giving title, author, degree awarded, date, and university. 'Archaeology and antiquities' (with an alphabetical geographical sub-division) is included in *vol 1 Social sciences and humanities* (1975).

527 'Roman Britain and the English settlements' by R G Collingwood and J N L Myres, the first volume of the Oxford History of England, includes in the bibliographical essay which brings it to an end two sections labelled 'Archaeology and topography' and 'County history and period works'. The first of these is a review of antiquarian and archaeological literature from the days of Leland onwards, whilst the second looks at the part played by the publications of the local archaeological societies.

528 'The Roman forts of the Saxon shore' by Stephen Johnson published by Paul Elek in 1976 describes the Roman castles and fortresses built in the third and fourth century BC to defend Britain from attack by the marauding Germanic tribes. It is well mapped and illustrated and fully documented with notes and a bibliography for each chapter.

529 'Roman roads in Britain' by Ivan D Margary was first issued in two volumes in 1955 but is now available in a third edition (1973) as a single volume published by John Baker. Its main purpose is to provide the reader with a descriptive survey of 7400 miles of Roman roads as they exist now. Ten geographical chapters illustrate the lasting influence the Roman road system exerted on Britain's internal communications. An ingenious road numbering method linked with a special index ensures that the reader can instantly locate particular roads in the text and on the maps of the various road networks. An introductory chapter includes a summary of previous literature, and references to further reading are to be found at the end of each section, thus providing a readily accessible bibliography for each route. The author's survey enjoyed the support of the Council for British Archaeology as an urgent and vitally important research project. The fifteen British sections of the *Itinerarium Antonini Augusti* are listed in an appendix.

530 **'Roman roads in Britain, their investigation and literature'** is the title of a bibliographical essay by Ivan D Margary printed in *The archaeoligical journal* CXIX 1962: 92-102. Chronological in approach it traces the development of the study of Roman roads in Britain and reviews the literature in books, journals and society transactions and proceedings. A preliminary section offers hints on how to examine a suspected route both indoors and on the ground.

531 **'Roman roads in the south-east Midlands'** by the Viatores (Gollancz, 1964) traces the Roman network of roads in the present-day counties of Bedfordshire, Buckinghamshire, Hertfordshire (west of Ermine Street), and part of Northamptonshire, and is the result of six years of inter-county cooperation on the part of individual fieldworkers meeting under the chairmanship of I D Margary, long acknowledged as the foremost national authority of Roman roads and himself the author of a number of books on the subject. The three principal through routes of the region, Watling Street, Akeman Street and the Icknield Way, are each treated in a separate chapter with secondary and minor roads being examined in further chapters. Over 850 miles of Roman road are delineated, the greater part of these being discoveries of the writers. There is a systematic and businesslike traverse of each route and wherever applicable reference is made to previous descriptions and discoveries. The second half of this substantial book is given over to strip maps reproduced from the Ordnance Survey 2½ inch sheets with roads numbered according to the method devised by Margary in his *Roman roads in Britain* (*qv*). The 'Viatores' (ie travellers along Roman roads) is a composite nom-de-plume adopted for brevity's sake by eight authors: R W Bagshawe, D B Baker, G R Elvey, C W Green, D E Johnston, C Morris, E V Parrott, and R H Reid, who initial their several contributions.

532 **'Roman ways in the Weald'** by I D Margary, first published by Phoenix House in 1948 and brought up-to-date in a third edition (1965), describes and maps all Roman roads running from London through the Weald of Kent, Surrey and Sussex to the south Coast. Useful chapters on the form and character of Roman roads and on the methods of research and field work add to the book's worth and standing. There is a briefly annotated bibliography and O G S Crawford contributes a foreword.

533 'A Romano-British bibliography' (55 BC-AD 449) by Wilfrid Bonser (Blackwell, 1964) includes material published to the end of 1959. Three types of user are envisaged: librarians who should be able to satisfy all enquiries on the period; the student and general reader; and research workers who may find the work useful for looking up references which have slipped the memory, or to be sure of what has already been published on a particular topic. The bibliography is purely descriptive, the author offers no evaluation which he insists is the function of the user who must 'exercise his judgement, from the date of the work or his knowledge of its writer, as to what is valuable and reliable, also as to what is now obsolete, redundant, or prejudiced'. To arrange the 10,000 entries a whole enumerative classification is outlined in two parts. Part 1 comprises a conspectus of history and culture divided under a number of major sub-headings of which general archaeology is one. This is sub-divided into general topics: museums; air reconnaissance; funeral customs, goods and structures; earthworks, camps, forts; baths; hypocausts; boats and canoes; embankments; and lighthouses. Part 2 (Sites local history, records of excavations and finds) is arranged alphabetically by county. Each entry gives author, title, an indication of scope and content, and an abbreviated citation if it is a periodical article. There is a list of periodicals and collective works abstracted. Four indexes—author, subject, personal names, and place names—were published in a separate volume in order to facilitate reference to the bibliography proper.

534 **Roy, William** (1726-1790) ended his army career as a major-general in the Royal Engineers and Surveyor-General of Coasts and Engineering for Military Surveys. Keenly interested in archaeology Roy spent twenty-five years mapping Roman remains in England and Scotland, his *Military antiquities of the Romans in Britain and particularly their ancient system of castrametation illustrated from vestiges of the camps of Agricola existing there* . . . was published posthumously in a handsome folio edition by the Society of Antiquaries in 1793. Roy was also responsible for the Geodetical Survey made under the auspices of the Royal Society which later formed the basis of the first Ordnance Survey. *The military antiquities* was reprinted by Gregg International Publishers in 1967.

535 Royal Archaeological Institute traces its origins to the founding of the British Archaeological Association in 1843. At first the new society flourished holding fortnightly winter meetings in London and a very successful summer meeting at Canterbury in 1844 where the members divided into primeval, medieval, architectural and historical sections each with its own president and committee structure. However, by a remarkably unfortunate set of circumstances a seemingly innocuous offer by the *Illustrated London news* to issue an illustrated report led step by step to procedural irregularities, a splinter group, rival circulars and meetings, acrimony, charges and counter-charges, and irremediable rift. For a time there was the nonsense of two societies each claiming for itself the title of British Archaeological Association. In a word it was a row of unholy dimensions and proportions and none of the personalities involved emerged with credit untarnished. On one side was the majority of the original central committee including one of the two secretaries and editor of *The archaeological journal*, the official organ of the association, whilst on the other could be seen the president, the treasurer (with the funds), and the second secretary. Strict legality possibly remained with the central committee but even so it was forced to adopt the name of the Archaeological Institute of Great Britain and Ireland. The quarrel was never formally made up, attempts to mend matters in 1850, when the institute made it known that it would be willing to admit members of the breakaway association as members of the institute without an entrance fee, and again in 1892 and 1896 failed, although a measure of mutual tolerance was achieved after 1851 when the two societies agreed to exchange publications.

Despite these unusual events the institute played its part in the organization of antiquarianism in nineteenth-century Britain. Then as now its efforts and attentions were concentrated on medieval antiquities and even more on ecclesiology; in 1845 through the good offices of the society Lord Proudhoe offered his collection of antiquities to the British Museum 'provided there be a room set apart for the reception of these objects and of any other national antiquities contributed by other gentlemen' which formed the beginning of the Department of British and Medieval Antiquities. In 1866 the institute became the Royal Institute of Archaeology. But for most of the century financial difficulties pressed hard and in 1900 part of the library had to be sold. The remaining books were given to the Society of Antiquaries and in return members of the institute were allowed the privilege of using the antiquaries' library, a privilege they hold to this day.

242

The purposes of the RAI have changed little since the early days, in the words of their Royal Charter granted in November 1961 they are 'to examine, preserve and illustrate the ancient monuments, past history, manners, customs, arts and literature of Great Britain and Northern Ireland and other countries'. The members still hold periodical London meetings, they still congregate in some provincial city in the summer; the ancient quarrel is still not officially healed although a quarter of a century ago Joan Evans in her survey of the RAI's history reflected 'We are still not yet amalgamated with the British Archaeological Association, but I hope it is not vain to anticipate that one day we shall be. We have so many members in common that a fusion would hold no shocks for either party . . . The success of the new Prehistoric Society may gradually lessen our duties in that field and may leave us and the British Archaeological Association identical in scope and interest.'

Publications: Although it lost its own name the institute managed to retain the title of *The archaeological journal* (*qv*) which is now an annual publication. Special volumes of *Proceedings* were issued in addition to the *Journal* 1845-1853 which contained reports of the annual summer meetings followed by papers delivered at them or connected with the places at which they were held. *Bibliography*: the introduction to the first issue of *The archaeological journal* March 1844 discusses the objectives of the British Archaeological Association (*qv*); 'Statement of the committee', *Journal of the British Archaeological Association* 1, 1845: i-xiii records contemporary events seen through the eyes of the breakaway group; A Hamilton Thompson's 'Address in commemoration of the centenary of the Royal Archaeological Institute', *The archaeological journal* C, 1943: 1-15, was a nostalgic glance back at the personalities, early meetings and social occasions enjoyed by members. Joan Evans' 'The RAI: a retrospect', *The archaeological journal* CVI 1949: 1-11 is valuable for the early controversy especially.

536 Royal Commission on Historical Monuments in England was appointed 27 October 1908 'to make an inventory of the ancient and historical monuments and constructions connected with or illustrative of the contemporary culture, civilization and conditions of life of the people in England, excluding Monmouthshire, from the earliest times to the year 1700 and to specify those which seem most worthy of preservation'. The commissioners were authorised to enlist the aid and cooperation of owners of ancient monuments, to call 'such persons as you shall judge likely to afford any information on the subject', and were empowered to visit personally any ancient monuments as might be deemed expedient. Four sub-commissions were initially appointed by the chairman of the commission: for Pre-Roman monuments and earthworks other than Roman; Roman monuments and earthworks; English ecclesiastical monuments; and for English secular monuments. It was early decided that the county should be the unit of publication and the civil parish the unit of record.

In 1913 the commission's sphere of interest was extended to buildings and constructions down to the year 1713. Changes in later years in the commission's establishment and terms of reference include the issue of a new warrant in 1946 which stated that Lords-Lieutenant of individual counties should join the commission when their particular county was being surveyed and that the commission should confer with the council of the National Monuments Record which itself was absorbed into the commission in 1962. In 1955, at the request of the Ancient Monuments Board and various learned bodies, the commission undertook to make emergency surveys of monuments of the prehistoric and early historic periods threatened with destruction by modern developments in agricultural, forestry, and mining techniques. *A matter of time* (1960) and *Monuments threatened or destroyed* (1963) (*qqv*), bear witness to the commissions' activity in this area.

Since the war the commission's surveys have been further extended to cover monuments subsequent to the year 1714. The findings of the commission are published in two forms: the interim reports presented to Parliament by Command, and the full scale, quarto size descriptive and pictorial surveys of a county's earthworks and ancient buildings. The descriptions are of course compressed but each important monument is given an historical introduction, a summary of its main features, and a concise architectural report. Monuments of lesser significance are sometimes grouped under a general description but each structure mentioned has been inspected by the commission and the account of every monument of importance has been checked in situ by the commission's secretary and editor. In addition all photographs have been taken by the commission's own photographers in order to emphasise the outstanding features of interest. The normal arrangement for the surveys is first an introduction, then the commissioners' report which includes a list of the monuments they consider to be especially worthy of preservation, the main inventory alphabetically by parish, a glossary, and an index. County by county an impressive record is being compiled although the commission's surveys have undoubtedly changed their character since the earlier volumes; whereas counties were previously compressed into one, or at most
244

two volumes, four now seem to be regarded as necessary. Admiration for the commission's thoroughness is tempered by a concern at the stately pace of its progress.

Inventories published to date: Hertfordshire (1910); Buckinghamshire, 2 vols (1912-1913); Essex, 4 vols (1921-1923); London, 5 vols (1924-1930); Huntingdonshire (1926); Herefordshire, 3 vols (1931-1934); Westmorland (1936); Middlesex (1937); City of Oxford (1939); Dorset, 4 vols (1952-1972); City of Cambridge, 3 vols (1959); City of York, 4 vols (1967-1975); Cambridgeshire, 2 vols (1968-1972); and Northamptonshire (1975).

A typescript *Union subject index to all volumes so far published 1910-1952* compiled by the Royal Institute of British Architects with the consent of the commission may be found in various libraries. A full list of inventories, reports, and other publications in print is included in the current sectional list 27: *Ancient monuments and historic buildings (qv)*. A microfiche edition of all inventories published by the Royal Commissions for England, Scotland, and Wales 1910-1975, on standard 105mm x 148mm 49 double-frame monochrome silver halide microfiche, each volume starting on a new microfiche, is available from Chadwyck-Healey, 21 Bateman Street, Cambridge or Somerset House, 417 Maitland Avenue, Teaneck, NJ 07666, USA. *Historic buildings in Britain*, a descriptive illustrated folder may be obtained on application.

537 Royal Commission on the Ancient and Historical Monuments and Constructions in Wales and Monmouthshire was appointed 10th October 1908 'to make an inventory of the ancient and historical monuments and constructions connected with or illustrative of the contemporary culture and civilisation and condition of life of the people of Wales from the earliest times, and to specify those which seem most worthy of preservation'. It will be noticed that unlike the English and Scottish commissions the Welsh were not restricted to dates but in practice the Welsh inventories have kept in step with the other two series of volumes. A similar pattern in publication, interim reports and county inventories, may also be observed. *Inventories published so far*: Montgomeryshire (1911); Flintshire (1912); Radnorshire (1913); Denbighshire (1914); Carmarthenshire (1917); Merioneth (1921); Pembrokeshire (1925); Anglesey (1937); and Caernarvonshire, 3 vols (1956-1964); Notes on the procedure adopted, important sources for research, definitions of the terms 'ancient monuments' and 'inventory', and the classification of monuments, are delineated in the commission's *First report* (Cd 5285) 1910.

538 Royal Commission on the Ancient and Historical Monuments of Scotland the first of the three national commissions, was brought into being by letters patent dated 2nd July 1908 appointing commissioners 'to make an inventory of the ancient and historical monuments and constructions connected with or illustrative of the contemporary culture, civilization and conditions of life of the people in Scotland from the earliest times to 1707, and to specify those which seem most worthy of preservation'. The commissioners set about their task in a determined manner and prepared lists of monuments drawn up by county and parish (gleaned from the six inch maps of the Ordnance Survey) which were then circulated to 'ministers of the Gospel, schoolmasters and such other individuals as might be able to supplement them from local knowledge'. They also decided that the secretary to the commission should also 'visit each county in turn, with the object of personally inspecting each monument so as to satisfy the commissioners as to its true character and condition'. The commission fulfills its two functions by publishing county inventories of relevant monuments and also periodical reports to which are appended lists of those deemed worthy of presentation. In 1948 fresh Letters Patent were issued allowing the commission to list and record at its discretion buildings of a later date than 1707. A brief outline of the commission's history and description of its work, methods and progress may be found in Angus Graham's 'The Royal Commission on the Ancient and Historical Monuments of Scotland', *The archaeological news letter*, 2(12) May 1950: 193-195 and 3(1) June 1950: 1-3; In 1975 a booklet, *Recording Scotland's heritage: the work of the Royal Commission on the Ancient and Historical Monuments of Scotland*, was published in Edinburgh by HMSO.

Inventories published to date: Berwick (1909, revised 1915); Sutherland (1911); Caithness (1911); Galloway 2 vols (1912-1914); Dumfriesshire (1920); East Lothian (1924); Outer Hebrides, Skye and the Small Isles (1928); Midlothian and West Lothian (1929); Fife, Kinross and Clackmannan (1933); Orkney and Shetland 3 vols (1946); City of Edinburgh (1951); Roxburghshire 2 vols (1956-); Selkirkshire (1957); Stirlingshire (1963); Peeblesshire (1967); and Argyll 2 vols (1967-1975);

539 The Royal Society, the oldest and the preeminent scientific society in the United Kingdom, formally came into existence in 1660 although a number of gatherings had been held for some years past in London and Oxford. A royal charter of incorporation was granted in 1662 and two years later the *Philosophical transactions* first made their appearance

246

although they were not officially issued by the society until the mid-eighteenth century. The society greatly influenced the development of British antiquarian studies into the embryonic science of archaeology; the scientific method of investigation generally coming into prominence manifested itself in archaeological studies by a growing tendency on the part of antiquarians to place more reliance on strictly archaeological evidence in context as opposed to the more literary sources favoured previously. The printing of archaeological papers in the *Philosophical transactions* encouraged a tight and exact method of describing excavations to the point where a modern type excavation report can be discerned. There are many histories of the Royal Society but the most appropriate source on the archaeological activities of its members during its first hundred years and their significance in the unfolding story of British antiquarianism is undoubtedly M C W Hunter's 'The Royal Society and the origins of British archaeology', *Antiquity*, XLV(178) June 1971: 113-121 and XLV(179) September 1971: 187-192.

540 Royal Society of Antiquaries of Ireland was founded as the Kilkenny Archaeological Society in 1849 by James Graves, who served as hon secretary until 1886, 'to preserve, examine, and illustrate all ancient memorials of the history, language, arts, manners, and customs of the past, as connected with Ireland'. The society's activities gradually spread over the south-east and then embraced the whole of Ireland; and it became in turn the Kilkenny Archaeological Association, the Kilkenny and South-east of Ireland Archaeological Society and, at the end of December 1869, its status as a national society was acknowledged when Queen Victoria granted it the title of the Royal Historical and Archaeological Association of Ireland with the privilege of electing its own fellows. It assumed its present title in January 1890. It very early introduced a system of appointing provincial and local secretaries whose duty it was to inform the society of all ancient monuments discovered in their districts, to investigate local history and traditions, and to warn the society of likely impending damage to monuments so that it might exert its influence to prevent this.

In this way the society carried out as a private institution much of the work of preservation now undertaken by the Irish Government. The history of the society and the story of archaeology in Ireland are inseparably linked as several papers and addresses printed in the society's *Journal* testify. Among these are Robert Cochrane's 'Notes on the Ancient Monuments Protection (Ireland) Act 1892 and the previous legislation connected therewith', vol XXII, 5th series II (IV) December 1892: 411-

429, which includes the text, and a list of monuments scheduled in the act, and notices the work and influence of the society; Thomas Johnson Westropp's 'The progress of Irish archaeology', XLVI, 6th series VI(1), June 1916: 2-25, a history of antiquarian studies since 1630; Robert Cochrane's 'Address delivered at the annual general meeting . . . on 26 January 1909', XXXIX 5th series XIX(1), March 1909: 1-22, which includes memoirs of past presidents of the society, the circumstances in which it came into existence, the other societies active in Ireland in the nineteenth century, the Ordnance Survey of Ireland, the legislation on the care and preservation of remains, and a comparison of the responsibilities of the Commissioner of Public Works in Ireland with those of the Royal Commissions on Ancient Monuments in England and Scotland; and H G Leask's 'The archaeological survey', LXXII 7th series XII(1), March 1942: 1-13 reporting progress in making a full survey and inventory of all Irish ancient remains. Sean P O'Riordain's 'Preserve, examine, illustrate' a commentary on the position of Irish archaeology, LXXXV, 1955: 1-21, looks particularly at the progress in the decade 1944-1955. The circumstances of the society's origins are recalled in Arthur Wynne Foot's 'In Piam Memoriam James Graves', 4th series VIII(1), 1887: 8-23, which reminds us that 'Graves was so completely identified with the progress and interests of . . . the Kilkenny Archaeological Society, that any account of his life must be, more or less, a history of the rise and progress of that now influential and Royal Association.'

The *Journal* of the society began publication in 1849 and apart from a brief period of indecision in the early 1890s when its title was changed to *Journal of the proceedings* for a year and then to *Proceedings and papers* for another it has continued on an even (and distinguished) keel ever since. Papers of note not already mentioned include H S Crawford's 'A descriptive list of early cross-slabs and pillars', XLII, 6th series II (III), September 1912: 217-244, vol XLIII, 6th series III (II) June 1913: 151-209, vol XLIII 6th series III(III), September 1913: 261-265, and a 'Supplementary list', XLVI, 6th series VI(I) December 1916: 163-167; E C R Armstrong's 'The La Tene period in Ireland', LIII 6th series XIII(I) June 1923: 1-33; the same writer's 'The early iron age, or Halstatt period in Ireland', LIV 6th series XIV(I): 1-14 and XIV(II): 109-127; D A Chart's 'The care of ancient monuments in Northern Ireland 1921-1948' LXXIX, 1949: 182-185; Joseph Raftery's 'A matter of time', XCIII(II), 1963: 101-114 which considers the problem of chronology in Irish archaeology; and Peter Harbison's 'The earlier bronze age in Ireland: later third millennium—c1200 BC' 103, 1973: 93-152, complete with maps, notes and references.

The archaeological acquisitions of the National Museum of Ireland
have been described at length since 1957. After fluctuating between
quarterly and half-yearly publications the *Journal* has settled down as an
annual since 1964 when a change to a quarto format was also put into
effect. *The index to the first nineteen volumes of the Journal for the
years 1849-1899 inclusive* (in three parts 1898-1901) has been followed
by other indexes vols XXI-XL 1891-1910 (1915), XLI-LX 1911-1930
(1933).

541 **'Ruins in a landscape'** *essays in antiquarianism* by Stuart Piggott
(Edinburgh University Press, 1976) is a reprinted collection of essays
rambling through the history of antiquarianism in Britain from the six-
teenth to the nineteenth century. They may be regarded as a hors
d'oeuvres to a general study of antiquarian thought of this period which
Professor Piggott hopes to publish in the not too distant future. *Contents*:
'Antiquarian thought in the sixteenth and seventeenth centuries'; 'Brazilian
Indians on an Elizabethan monument'; 'William Camden and the *Britannia*';
'Celts, Saxons and the early antiquaries'; 'Background to a broadsheet:
what happened at Colton's field in 1685?'; 'Ruins in a landscape: aspects
of seventeenth and eighteenth century antiquarianism'; 'The ancestors of
Jonathan Oldbuck'; 'The Roman camp and four authors'; and 'The origins
of the English county archaeological societies'. Each essay is liberally furnished with bibliographical notes.

542 **'Sales catalogues of libraries of eminent persons'** (general editor:
A N L Munby) *Volume 10 Antiquaries* edited with introductions by Stuart
Piggott (1974) includes the catalogues of the sales of the libraries of Ralph
Thoresby, Thomas Hearne, George Vertue, William Stukeley, and Francis
Grose reproduced in facsimile.

543 **'Science and archaeology'** (1970-) is a quarterly journal carrying up
to the minute articles of interest to both archaeologist and scientist, over
a wide spread of subjects which offer a clear opportunity for genuine
inter-disciplinary exchanges, written in a style that will not perplex the
arts-trained archaeologist. Its choice of topics is catholic, ranging from
biodeterioration to computers, ceramics to entomology, and by no stretch
of the imagination can it be regarded as a conventional archaeological or
scientific journal. In order to reduce costs the text is prepared on an
electric typewriter and reproduced by offset lithography. Subject bibliographies, abstracts, and a notes and queries section, are regular features.

Edited by Francis Celoria (University of Keele) and J D Wilcock (North Staffordshire Polytechnic) the journal is published by George Street Press, Fancy Walk, Stafford.

544 **'Science in archaeology'** *a comprehensive survey of progress and research* edited by Don Brothwell and Eric Higgs and published by Thames and Hudson in 1963 consists of over fifty essays contributed by recognised experts in their respective fields 'to provide a systematic conspectus of the bearing of the natural sciences on archaeological investigation'.

Contents: Section I Dating–'Archaeology and dating' (C B M McBurney); 'Analytical methods of dating bones' (Kenneth Oakley); 'Radio-carbon dating' (E H Willis); 'Obsidian dating' (Irving Friedman, Robert Smith and Donovan Clark); 'Archaeomagnetism' (R M Cook); 'The potassium-argon dating of upper tertiary and pleistocene deposits' (W Gentner and H J Lippolt); 'Dating basalts' (J A Miller); and 'Dating pottery by thermoluminescence' (E T Hall).

Section II Environment–'Environmental studies and archaeology' (J M Coles); 'The significance of deep-sea cores' (Cesare Emiliani); 'Soil silhouettes' (L Biek); 'Soil, stratification and environment' (I W Cornwall); 'Cave sediments and prehistory' (Elisabeth Schmid); 'Pollen analysis' (G W Dimbleby); 'Wood and charcoal in archaeology' (Cecilia Western); 'The condition of 'wood' from archaeological sites' (J W Levy); 'Dendochronology' (Bryant Bannister); 'Palaeoethnobotany' (Hans Helbaek); 'Diet as revealed by coprolites' (E O Callen); 'Fauna' (Eric Higgs); 'A scrap of bone' (K A Joysey); 'Osteo-archaeology' (Charles A Reed); 'The rate of evolution' and 'The cave hyena, an essay in statistical analysis' (Bjorn Kurten); 'The science and history of domestic animals' (Wolf Herre); 'The ageing of domestic animals' (I A Silver); 'The origins of the dog' (Juliet Clutton-Brock); 'The palaeopathology of pleistocene and more recent animals' (Don Brothwell); 'Bird remains in archaeology' (Elliot W Dawson); 'Remains of fishes and other aquatic animals' (M L Ryder) and 'Non-marine mollusca and archaeology' (B W Sparks);

Section III Man–'The biology of earlier human populations' (Don Brothwell); 'Microscopy and prehistoric bone' (Antonio Ascenzi); 'Sex determination in earlier man' and 'Estimation of age and mortality' (Santiago Genoves); 'Stature in earlier races of mankind' (L H Wells); 'Cremations' (Nils-Gustaf Gejvall); 'The palaeopathology of human skeletal remains' (Marcus S Goldstein); 'The radiological examination of human remains' (Calvin Wells); 'The study of mummified and dried human tissues' (A T Sandison); 'The hair of earlier peoples' (Don Brothwell and

250

Richard Spearman); 'Palaeoserology' (Madeleine Smith Glemser); and 'Blood groups and prehistory' (J D Garlick).

Section IV Artifacts: 'Artifacts' (L Biek); 'A statistical analysis of flint artifacts' (A Bohmers); 'Petrological examination' (F W Shotton); 'Some aspects of ceramic technology' (Frederick R Matson); 'Optical emission spectroscopy and the study of metallurgy in the European bronze age' (Dennis Britton and Eva Richards); 'Microscopic studies of ancient metals' (F C Thompson); 'The analytical study of glass in archaeology' (Ray W Smith); 'Remains derived from skin' (M L Ryder); and 'Fibres of archaeological interest: their examination and identification' (H M Appleyard and A B Wildman).

Section V Prospecting–'Magnetic location' (Martin Aitken); and 'Resistivity surveying' (Anthony Clark). Each essay is accompanied by references and notes which if assembled together would have amounted to a considerable bibliography. Many composite works of this nature and on this particular aspect of archaeology have been issued but few on such an ample scale (nearly 600 pages, 95 photographs, 92 line drawings and 66 tables) or with such a distinguished and international list of contributors.

545 'Scientific American', the celebrated multi-faceted scientific journal, regularly includes articles of archaeological interest. Many of these are issued as offprints and some have been thematically collected in book form. *Early man in America*, edited by Richard S MacNeish (1972) is concerned with the prehistoric migration of man to the New World, the techniques of modern archaeology being used to reconstruct details of early Indian life. An introduction recounts the twenty years of archaeological progress represented by the articles included. *New world archaeology: theoretical and cultural transformations* edited by Ezra Zubrow (1974) reports on the major archaeological finds, presents the various theoretical approaches to their interpretation, and indicates the techniques and methods employed by practising archaeologists. *Old world archaeology: foundations of civilization* edited by C C Laberg-Karlovsky (1972) forms an introduction to the cultural evolution of mankind. An annotated catalogue *Scientific American books and offprints* is available from W H Freeman & Co, 660 Market Street, San Francisco, Ca 94104; or 58 Kings Road, Reading, Berks.

546 'The scientist and archaeology' edited by Edward Pyddoke (Phoenix House, 1963) consists of nine papers, all contributed by experts with special knowledge and experience, designed to illustrate some of the more important areas in which scientific techniques have been applied to the practical solution of archaeological problems. *Contents*: 'Resistivity surveying in archaeology' (R J C Atkinson); 'Soil-science helps the archaeologist' (I W Cornwall); 'Pollen analysis' (G W Dimbleby); 'Petrological examination' (F S Wallis); 'The examination of ceramic materials in thin section' (H W M Hodges); 'Fluorine, uranium and nitrogen dating of bone' (Kenneth P Oakley); 'The applications of radioactivity in archaeology' (Harold Barker); 'Analysis and microscopic study of metals' (R M Organ) and 'Physical methods of chemical analysis' (E T Hall).

547 Scole Committee for Archaeology in East Anglia came into existence in 1971 when those involved in rescue archaeology in Norfolk and Suffolk frustrated by the lack of a single committee to coordinate regional policy, met at Scole, a village symbolically half-way between Norwich and Ipswich. Today the committee is recognized by the Department of the Environment and by the local authorities as the official regional coordinating body; it was instrumental in 1974 in setting up the Norfolk and Suffolk Archaeological Units.

548 'Scotland: an archaeological guide' *from earliest times to the 12th century AD* by Euan W Mackie is intended for the archaeologically-minded tourist and describes the major sites and monuments in eight geographical zones. A chapter is devoted to each zone, sub-divided by county, and then further by route or area so that the sites are outlined in the order they are encountered on the ground. Because of the long span of time involved from the fourth millennium BC, only a representative number of each type of monument or site in each area is described in detail. Location of the sites is defined by the full six-figure references of the National Grid on the Ordnance Survey maps. An introduction containing an outline of Scotland's past and a regional guide to museums precedes the zonal guides. There is a glossary of archaeological terms and a bibliography which first lists general works on the archaeology and early history of Scotland and then lists of books and sources for each zone. Photographs, maps, plans and drawings abound. The guide was published by Faber in 1975.

549 Scottish Archaeological Forum, an annual meeting usually at the National Museum of the Antiquities of Scotland, was the outcome of a suggestion first put forward by Miss Audrey Henshall and Graham Ritchie towards the end of 1968 that there should be an opportunity for everyone concerned with the problems of archaeology in Scotland to discuss and
252

assess the important new discoveries and the reinterpretation of published or unpublished material. The theme of the first meeting in March 1969 was a broad survey of archaeological matters of topical interest, since then more specific aspects of Scottish archaeology have been discussed. Papers read and discussed are issued in soft covers under the title *Scottish archaeological forum*.

550 Scottish Field School of Archaeology, initiated largely at the prompting of the Scottish Regional Group of the Council for British Archaeology, was at first simply a clearing house for placing students on approved excavations. Subsequently it has developed into an integrated training unit not only arranging on-site training but also lectures and guided excursions. Its activities are regularly reported in the survey of regional groups printed every year in *Archaeology in Britain* (*qv*).

551 Scottish Society for Industrial Archaeology was formed in 1966 to conduct research, record industrial buildings, liaise with local societies and groups, arrange excursions, and to publish a *Newsletter*. Representatives are appointed in each region to alert the society should significant industrial monuments be threatened with destruction.

552 Scottish Summer School of Archaeology, an annual weekend conference discussing the history and antiquities of the district it finds itself in, was inaugurated in Dundee in 1952 and is now known as the British Summer School of Archaeology.

553 'The Shell guides': over the last fifteen years four sumptuous general guides to the British Isles, all more or less following the same pattern, have been published. The first to appear was *The Shell guide to Ireland* (Ebury Press, 1962) edited by Lord Killanin and Michael V Duignan, both of whom were at one time members of the Irish National Monuments Advisory Council. It is not surprising, therefore, that of the four this is the one which pays most attention to antiquities. In addition to the gazetteer section there is also a useful historical introduction to Ireland in separate period sections, the first three being 'Prehistoric Ireland', 'Gaelic Ireland', and 'Medieval Ireland'. A short classified bibliography is also included. *The Shell guide to Scotland* (Ebury Press, 1965) edited by Moray McLaren and *The Shell guide to Wales* (Michael Joseph, 1969) edited by Wynford Vaughan Thomas and Alun Llewellyn are very similar to the Irish volume but *The Shell guide to England* (Michael Joseph, 1970) edited by John Hadfield shows a different approach. Not only is England bigger and more densely populated than the other countries, there is also demonstrably a much more clearly discernible pattern of regional characteristics. And so the English guide is more of a symposium volume: a number of introductory chapters, each by a different hand, providing historical, topographical, architectural, and other information, set the scene. Then comes the main gazetteer, arranged by region, the alphabetical entries preceded in each case by a regional essay. It should be fully understood that these guides, with the possible exception of the Irish volume, are not archaeological guides to field monuments or other antiquities. They are rather general guides which include a tremendous amount of information on sites and monuments. Each one contains an effective map section and they are all illustrated in handsome fashion. *The Shell guide to Britain* is an abbreviated guide to the United Kingdom.

554 'Shire archaeology' is the name given to a pocket-size, paperback series of monographs on the various artefacts found during excavations. They are intended for the non-specialist and explain the importance and relevance of exhibits displayed in national and local collections. Titles: *Bronze age metalwork in England and Wales* (Nancy Langmaid); *Pottery in Roman Britain* (Vivien Swan); *Anglo-Saxon jewellery* (Ronald Jessup); and *Flint implements of the old stone age* (Peter Timms). They are published by Shire Publications, Cromwell House, Church Street, Princes Risborough, Aylesbury, Buckinghamshire.

555 Shropshire Archaeological Society: in December 1876 a few members of an existing Shropshire Natural History and Antiquarian Society (founded 1835) began to discuss amongst themselves the formation of a county archaeological society. Eventually a circular was issued proposing such a society 'for the printing of the historical, ecclesiastical, genealogical, topographical, geological, and literary remains of Shropshire'. It only needed, the circular continued, the cooperation of a few influential gentlemen and its progress would be certain, rapid, and satisfactory. Over two hundred such turned up at an inaugural meeting in Shrewsbury, 2nd May 1877 and the society was well and truly launched with the objects of 'the promotion of archaeological and historical investigation in the county and the preservation of its antiquities'. In particular their energies were to be directed to 'the recording of archaeological discoveries, the editing and printing of documents of local historical importance, and the transcription and printing of parish registers'. Within weeks it was

254

discovered that their aims were almost identical with those of the senior society and the two institutions were merged as the Shropshire Archaeological and Natural History Society. At this remove it is difficult to understand this course of events; doubtless they had their reasons. It was not until 1936 that the society reverted to the name it enjoyed for such a brief period sixty years earlier. The society's *Transactions* have appeared since 1878 although latterly more than the usual delay in publication has occurred, the 1971-72 volume did not make its appearance until June 1976. Volume LVII(1) 1961 marked the change to a larger quarto format, in keeping with a number of other county societies there was a general feeling that it was high time that the *Transactions* should contain fully illustrated excavation reports and plans. 'The itinerary of John Leland as far as it relates to Shropshire' was reproduced in volume IV, 1881: 127-155. A 'List of ancient monuments in the county scheduled at present' (ie December 1951) appeared in vol LIV(1) 1951-52: 155-158. An 'Index of papers published in the first and second series . . . 1878-1900' was printed in vol XII(3) 2nd series, 1900: 371-390; of the third series 1901-1910 in vol X(3), 3rd series, 1910: xix-xxv; and of the fourth series 1911-1930 in vol XII(2) ie vol XLX 1930: xxi-xl. Thomas Auden's *Shropshire* first published in the Oxford County Histories in 1911 was issued to members in place of the *Transactions* for the year 1942.

556 'Signposts for archaeological publication' *a guide to good practice in the presentation and printing of archaeological periodicals and monographs*: In 1973 Professor Vincent Megaw was invited by the Council for British Archaeology to set up a working party to look into the problems of archaeological publication. Questionnaires returned by institutions affiliated to the council were computer analysed and much information was gathered on the practical details of publication. The working party's report was first printed as appendix V to *Archaeology in Britain 1973-1974*: 106-110 and is here considerably expanded as a separate booklet. The original questionnaire was concerned only with serials and journals but the information acquired on design, production, estimates, presentation, standardization, sales outlets, copyright law, etc is considered by the CBA as applicable to all forms and classes of printed matter. The booklet, published in 1976, also includes the list of CBA standard abbreviations for titles of periodicals.

557 'A sites and monuments record for the Oxford region', a paper by Don Benson, explains how the Oxford City and County Museum (founded

1965) tackled the problem of the lack of a locally accessible and comprehensive index of sites and finds, discusses the various methods of data processing and information retrieval investigated, and describes the record and index system eventually adopted. At least, the writer remarks, it provides a starting point for research, and it can also supply essential information to determine priorities in rescue work, field surveys, or excavations, and indicate areas where more work is needed. It plays a vital role in answering enquiries from the public, from local societies, and from professional archaeologists and historians. The paper appeared in *Oxoniensia*, XXVII, 1972: 226-237.

558 Smith, Charles Roach (1807-1890) fell victim early in life to the collecting bug, in his case Roman and British remains. When the Thames was dredged he seized the opportunity to build up a collection of antiquities which in 1854 was offered to the British Museum for £3,000. Although on this occasion the trustees declined, his collection found its way there the following year for a slightly lesser sum to form the foundation collection of the museum's Roman-British antiquities. In conjunction with Thomas Wright he formed the British Archaeological Association in 1843. His published work includes *Collecta antiqua* (7 vols, 1848-1880), etchings and notes on ancient remains, ornaments, and monuments in France, Germany, and Italy; *The importance of public museums for historical collections* (1860); and *Retrospections, social and archaeological*, three volumes of very readable autobiographical papers (1883-1891); Obituary notices may be found in *Proceedings, Society of Antiquaries*, second series XIII, 1889-91: 310-312 and *Journal British Archaeological Association* XLVI, 1890: 237-243 and 318-330.

559 The Smithsonian Institution, Washington DC was founded in 1846 when the Congress accepted a bequest from James Smithson, a natural son of the ducal line of Northumberland. It includes an Office of Anthropology which came into existence in 1965 with the amalgamation of the Bureau of American Ethnology (established 1879) and the United States National Museum Department of Anthropology. The Office is administered in two divisions, physical anthropology, and cultural anthropology which is concerned with archaeology, ethnology, and linguistics. Unlike the former bureau the office does not restrict its interests to the American continent; its research activities have expanded in Africa, Asia, and the Pacific area. The extensive publishing programme of the institution has included many monographs and series of archaeological interest: the

256

bureau's *Annual Report* (from 1880) and its *Bulletin* (from 1886) remained a valuable source of archaeological material until 1964. A year later, in consequence of the amalgamation, the *Smithsonian contributions to anthropology*, monographs, and research reports by the staff of the institution or based upon its collections, were first published. At the time of writing twenty-one volumes have appeared and have been distributed to libraries on a world-wide basis. The history of the Smithsonian is well-documented, there is a convenient bibliography in the *Encyclopaedia Britannica*.

560 Society for Afghan Studies was founded in June 1972 under the auspices of the British Academy. Its purpose is to support and maintain the British Institute of Afghan Studies in Kabul.

561 Society for American Archaeology was formed in Pittsburgh in 1934 with the object of stimulating research in New World archaeology which was defined as the accumulation, preservation, and interpretation by recognized archaeological methods of all the pertinent information on the history and lives of the aboriginal inhabitants of the Americas. This was to be achieved by strengthening professional bonds among practising archaeologists, by closer relations with amateurs in the field, and by controlling or eliminating the commercialization of archaeological objects. W C McKern's 'The society for American archaeology', *American antiquity* 1(2) October 1935: 141-151 is an early record of the society's formation and prints its constitution, by-laws, and rules of procedure. Besides this quarterly journal the society also publishes its *Memoirs*, a monograph series examining particular facets of the archaeology of the two Americas; *Archives of archaeology*, microcard records of the primary documentation of archaeological investigations, published in conjunction with the University of Wisconsin Press; and *Abstracts of New World archaeology*. No new items have been published in the *Archives* since 1971, a list of those still available appeared in the July 1969 issue of *American antiquity*. The *Memoirs* vols 1-17 (excluding No 10) 1941-1961 are available from Kraus Reprint in paper or cloth.

562 Society for Historical Archaeology (US) founded in 1967, is composed of archaeologists, historians, and anthropologists whose aim it is to study historic sites and to develop 'generalizations concerning historic periods and cultural dynamics as these may emerge through the techniques of archaeological excavation and analysis, and the study of documents'.

Its main centre of interest is the western hemisphere. A *Newsletter* is published quarterly: the society's journal, *Historical archaeology*, is an annual publication.

563 The Society for Libyan Studies came into existence on 4th June 1969 largely as the result of the expressed desire of the Libyan government that British museums and universities should continue to send expeditions to work in Libya. The British Academy asked a committee organising a fund in memory of Richard Goodchild, Controller of Antiquities in Cyrenaica 1954-1967, to consider the formation of a society which would act as the centre of Anglo-Libyan studies in Britain; sponsor research in all fields of Libyan studies, in the natural sciences, linguistics and history as well as archaeology; and encourage relations between British and Libyan scholars. The academy made a grant of £1500 to cover initial running costs and advanced another £3500 so that the society could embark on field work with the minimum of delay. An account of the background events leading to the society's formation may be read in the *First annual report* issued for 1969-70. This also contains 'British archaeology in Libya 1943-70', an extremely useful résumé of the work of British archaeologists during this period, which ends as follows: 'The foundation of the society gives the opportunity to provide a solid basis for the completion of existing research programmes and for the development of new fields of study. The society is also aware of its responsibility in the field of publication so that important researches which have been undertaken in the past are fully and worthily recorded.'

564 Society for Lincolnshire History and Archaeology has experienced a bewildering number of names. Starting off in 1844 as the Lincolnshire Society for the Encouragement of Ecclesiastical Antiquities; it became the Lincoln Diocesan Architectural Society in 1853, then the Architectural Society for the Counties of Lincoln and Nottingham, before emerging as the Lincoln Architectural and Archaeological Society. In 1966 this society merged with the Lincolnshire Local History Society (founded 1930) which in turn united with the Lincoln Archaeological Research Committee in 1974 to form the present society. The founding fathers enlisted the society as one of the Associated Architectural Societies (*qv*) when they combined in 1850 and so its first reports and transactions appeared in that body's *Reports and papers*. An independent series was published 1938-1964. This was superseded in 1966 by *Lincolnshire history and archaeology*, an annual publication, designed to strike a
258

balance between the specialised articles previously printed in *Reports and papers* and the material of more general interest formerly published in *The Lincolnshire historian*. The feature 'Archaeological notes', an illustrated gazetteer-type record classified by period of archaeological finds reported to the City and County Museum, Lincoln, and of current excavations in the county, which first appeared in *Reports and papers* in the early 1950s was carried over to *Lincolnshire history and archaeology*. When that journal was modernized in 1975 the old format was abandoned and a change of name to 'Archaeology in Lincolnshire' effected. This now concentrates on short notes on the more important excavations, discoveries, fieldwork, and research projects during the year. The society is administered by the Community Council of Lincolnshire and its affairs are managed by an executive committee with sub-committees for archaeology, industrial archaeology, and local history. Sir Francis Hill's 'Early days of a society', *Lincolnshire history and archaeology*, 1, 1966: 59-63 clarifies the society's somewhat tortuous beginnings.

565 The Society for Medieval Archaeology was founded at a public meeting chaired by Sir Mortimer Wheeler at Burlington House, 13th June 1957 after support and approval had been indicated by the Society of Antiquaries, the Royal Archaeological Institute, the British Archaeological Association, and the Society for the Promotion of Roman Studies. It exists 'to further the study of British history since the Roman period by publishing a journal of international standing dealing primarily with the material evidence, and by various other means, for example holding annual week-end conferences outside London'. All archaeological aspects of the Anglo-Saxon period are included within the society's interests and activities but for the post-Conquest period emphasis is laid on fieldwork and excavated articles rather than on art or architecture although the society regards itself as a medium for coordinating the work of archaeologists and historians. *Publications*: *Medieval archaeology* (*qv*) and a series of monographs dealing with particular aspects of the archaeology of the British Isles AD 400-1600. These are listed on the inside back cover of the current issue of *Medieval archaeology*.

566 Society for Museum Archaeologists was formed in 1976 'to promote active museum involvement in all aspects of archaeology and to emphasize the unique role of museums within the essential unity of the archaeological discipline'. In particular it wants museums to participate in field archaeology either in collaboration with archaeological units or (more controversially) by assuming complete responsiblity for this sphere of operations. The society also sees a part for museums to play in the maintenance of sites, monuments, and finds records.

567 The Society for Post-Medieval Archaeology was formed out of the three years old Post Medieval Ceramic Research Group in 1967, 'to promote the study of the archaeological evidences of British and Colonial history of the post-medieval period before the onset of industrialization'. Two annual conferences are held: one in the spring at which general papers are read, the other in the autumn which caters for specialized interests within the society. The beginnings of the society are outlined in K J Barton's 'The origins of the Society for Post-Medieval Archaeology' in their journal *Post-medieval archaeology* I 1967: 102-103.

568 The Society for the History of Technology was formed in 1958 to promote the study of the development of technology and its relationship to science, politics, social change, the arts and the humanities, and to economics, and to make these elements of knowledge available and comprehensible to the educated citizen. To this end *Technology and culture* is published quarterly. The society holds alternate annual meetings with the American Association for the Advancement of Science and the American Historical Association. Melvin Krauzberg's 'At the start', *Technology and culture* 1(1) winter 1959: 1-10 and 'A brief history' in the same issue, pages 106-108, together make useful reading for events leading up to the society's formation and for its philosophy and purpose.

569 The Society for the Promotion of Hellenic Studies was the brainchild of George Macmillan who, after a visit to Greece in 1877 which laid the foundation of a life-long interest in Greek archaeology, determined to form a society in England similar to the French *Association pour l'encouragement des etudes grecques.* He enlisted the support of Professor A H Sayce and in March 1879 letters went out to a number of distinguished figures who had already visited Greece. Support was forthcoming and an inaugural meeting was held at the Freemason's Tavern in June. The first general meeting took place in the Royal Literary Fund's rooms in the Adelphi in January 1880. The objects of the society were defined as follows: 'To advance the study of Greek language, literature and art and to illustrate the history of the Greek race in the ancient, Byzantine and neo-Hellenic periods by the publication of memoirs and unedited documents in a journal to be issued periodically . . . To organise means by which members of the society may have increased facilities for visiting ancient sites and pursuing archaeological researches in countries which, at any time, have been the sites of Hellenic civilization.' Today meetings are held four times a year in London at which papers are read and there are also joint meetings with local branches of the Classical Association in the provinces. The society works very much in conjunction with the British School at Athens (*qv*). *The journal of Hellenic studies* has appeared annually since 1880 and is regarded as one of the most esteemed learned journals within its field. George Macmillan's 'An outline of the history of the Hellenic Society' in vol XLIX 1929: i-li takes a close look at the society's administration, finance, excavations and explorations, library, and other activities. The library is maintained jointly with the Society for the Promotion of Roman Studies at the Institute of Classical Studies, 31-34 Gordon Square, London.

570 The Society for the Promotion of Roman Studies was created in 1910 after a memorandum from the Director of the British School in Rome to the Hellenic Society requesting an annual grant similar to that made to the School in Athens had sparked off a debate amongst the members of the Hellenic Society and the Classical Association as to the proper course of action to follow in order that British studies in Italy should be set on an equal footing with those in Greece. The general conclusion was that an independent society on the lines of the Hellenic Society would be the best solution. Accordingly the society came into being 'to promote the study of the history, archaeology, and art of Italy and the Roman Empire, from the earliest times down to about AD 700; to publish a journal which shall contain original articles, reports of recent research and exploration in Roman lands, and notices of recent literature; to form a library and to collect photographs, lantern slides and other materials for study and to offer facilities for study to those working on the subjects to be promoted by the society'. The society would also work with and make grants to the British School at Rome. The goodwill of the Hellenic Society was manifest from the beginning and, despite some signs of strain from time to time especially when the younger society's funds sank dangerously low, a general harmony was preserved. The two societies maintain a joint library and lantern slide collection covering every aspect of classical antiquity, including the archaeology and history of Roman Britain. Meetings of the society are held four times a year in London at which papers are read, provincial meetings are also arranged in conjunction with other societies, and every three years a joint conference with the Hellenic Society and the Classical Association is held either at Oxford or Cambridge. The society's annual *Journal* was first published in 1911 and *Britannia* started in 1970. M W Taylor's 'The Society for the Promotion of Roman Studies, 1910-60' printed in the jubilee volume of *The journal of Roman studies* 1960: 129-134 records in outline the society's history and activities.

571 The Society of Antiquaries of London is the premier national archaeological society of Great Britain; membership is restricted to those who can point to a distinguished contribution to archaeological scholarship and election to the society is by ballot. Although attempts have been made to trace a direct link between the society and the Elizabethan College of Antiquaries, its true origins are to be discerned in a tavern club formed early in December 1707 by Humphrey Wanley, John Talman, and John Bagford which assembled at the Bear in the Strand every Friday evening to discuss the antiquities and history of Great Britain up to the reign of James I. The little coterie grew in numbers but its organized and recorded meetings lapsed the following February and were not revived until July 1717 when twenty-three gentlemen, including six known to be members of the earlier gatherings, Wanley, Talman, and Peter Le Neve, the new president, among them, founded the Antiquarian Society London. The first secretary of the new society was William Stukeley who was intrumental in drawing up eleven articles of association for the formal constitution of the Society of Antiquaries London in January 1718. Its progress from the comparatively humble beginning to the preeminence it enjoys today is admirably narrated and fully documented in Joan Evans' *A history of the Society of Antiquaries*, a rambling but totally absorbing book put in hand as part of the celebrations of the bicentenary of the Royal Charter granted by George II in November 1751, and published by the society in 1956. The progress of the society, the manner in which it recognized and acknowledged the changing course of the study of antiquity, the development of its library and its publishing programme, are all traced there in detail. The part played in the original ancient monuments legislation, in the formation of the Congress of Archaeological Societies, in the events leading up to the replacement of that body by the Council for British Archaeology, and in the setting up of the Institute of Archaeology, is remembered with affection; and the personalities involved are revived for a brief spell before they once more pass into the shades. Less formidable accounts are *The Society of Antiquaries of London: notes on its history and possessions*: an illustrated booklet by R L S Bruce-Mitford (1951) and *The Society of Antiquaries of London:*
262

a short guide to its history, activities and possessions, a pamphlet produced in 1968. An active publishing programme has traditionally been sustained by the society: besides its regular publications noticed separately in this present handbook (*Archaeologia*, the *Proceedings*, *Antiquaries journal*, *Vetusta monumenta*, and *Reports of the research committee*) occasional papers, exhibition catalogues etc have all appeared from time to time.

572 **'Society of Antiquaries of London: Reports of the research committee'** have been published since 1913. Titles in numerical sequence:

1-2, 4	*Excavations on the site of the Roman town at Wroxeter, Shropshire* (J P Bushe-Fox)
3	*Excavations at Hengistbury Head, Hampshire* (J P Bushe-Fox)
5	*Excavation of the late Celtic urn field at Swarling, Kent* (J P Bushe-Fox)
6-7, 10, 16	*Excavation of the Roman fort at Richborough, Kent* (J P Bushe-Fox)
8	*Report on the excavation of the Roman cemetery at Ospringe, Kent* (W Whiting, W Hawley, and Thomas May)
9	*Report on the excavation of the prehistoric, Roman, and post-Roman site in Lydney Park, Gloucestershire* (R E M Wheeler and T V Wheeler)
11	*Verulamium: a Belgic and two Roman cities* (R E M Wheeler and T V Wheeler)
12	*Maiden Castle, Dorset* (R E M Wheeler)
13	*The tombs and moon temple of Hureidha (Hadramaut)* (G Caton Thompson)
14	*Camulodunum, first report on the excavations at Colchester 1930-39* (C F C Hawkes and M R Hull)
15	*Excavations at the Jewry Wall site, Leicester* (Kathleen M Kenyon)
17	*The Stanwick fortifications* (Sir Mortimer Wheeler)
18	*Alalakh* (Sir Leonard Woolley)
19	*Hill forts of northern France* (Sir Mortimer Wheeler and Katherine M Richardson)
20	*Roman Colchester* (M R Hull)
21	*The Roman potters' kilns of Colchester* (M R Hull)
22	*Skorba* (D H Trump)
23	*Excavation of the Roman fort at Richborough, Kent 5th report* (Barry Cunliffe)

24	*Roman Bath* (Barry Cunliffe)
25	*Excavations at Brough-on-Humber 1958-1961* (J S Wacher)
26-27	*Excavations at Fishbourne 1961-1969* (Barry Cunliffe)
28	*Verulamium excavations* (Sheppard Frere)
29	*Durrington Walls excavations 1966-1968* (G J Wainwright and Ian H Longworth)

573 Society of Antiquaries of Newcastle, one of the oldest of English provincial antiquarian societies, was called into existence at a meeting attended by seventeen gentlemen at the invitation of John Bell, a local bookseller, in the Long Room of Loftus' Inn at Newcastle on 23rd January 1813. This convivial gathering resolved to draw up rules and regulations for an antiquarian society and, incredibly, less than a fortnight later the society was established for 'inquiry into antiquities in general, but especially into those of the North of England, and of the counties of Northumberland, Cumberland, and Durham in particular'. The full history of the society has yet to be written although it can be noted that after a drift into the doldrums in the 1870s the society reinvigorated itself to good purpose. In the last forty years it has concentrated its attention naturally enough on the Roman wall and its stations. However, a remarkable anniversary issue of *Archaeologia Aeliana*, 'Records of the Society of Antiquaries of Newcastle-upon-Tyne, centenary volume 1813-1913' volume X, 3rd series, 1913 provides a wealth of source material. 'History of the society 1813-1913' (John Crawford Hodgson) is concerned mainly with the society's migrations in search of a permanent home but 'The society's museum' (Richard Oliver Heslop) and 'The society's library' (Charles Hunter Blair) help to fill in this rudimentary outline. Chronological and alphabetical lists of members follow and then comes undoubtedly the most impressive section of all, 'Biographies of contributors to the society's literature' compiled by Richard Welford and John Crawford Hodgson. 'A classified catalogue of papers printed in *Archaeologia Aeliana* 1813-1913' and an index to the biographies bring this superb celebration volume to an end. The society's regular publications are its *Proceedings* and *Archaeologia Aeliana or miscellaneous tracts relating to antiquity*, commencing in 1822, which have now reached a fifth series with a change to a larger format in 1973. *A general index to the Archaeologia Aeliana volumes I-IV 4to and I-XVI 8vo and to the Proceedings volume I old series and volumes I-V* was published in 1896. A substantial successor appeared in 1925, and further author and subject indexes have been printed in the *Aeliana* vols XIII-XXIV, 4th series in vol XXIV (1946) and vols XXV-XXXVI in volume XXXVI (1958).

574 Society of Antiquaries of Scotland was founded by the eleventh Earl of Buchan in November 1780 for 'The promotion of archaeology, especially as connected with the antiquities and historical literature of Scotland'. It was incorporated by royal charter in May 1783. Its early history is best told by David Laing's address to the society printed in volume five of *Archaeologica Scotica*. The society's *Proceedings* were first published for the year 1852. Papers of general interest include J Y Simpson's 'Address on archaeology', vol IV(1) 1860: 5-51, a survey of the whole field of Scottish archaeology; George Black's 'Report on the antiquities found in Scotland and preserved in the British Museum etc in London, and in the Museum of Science and Art Edinburgh' vol III 3rd series 1892-93: 347-368; R A S Macalister's 'An inventory of the ancient monuments remaining in the Island of Iona', XLVIII, 1913-1914: 421-430; Abbe Breuil's 'Observations on the pre-neolithic industries of Scotland', LVI, 5th series VIII, 1921-1922: 261-281; J Graham Callander's 'Scottish bronze age hoards', LVII, 5th series IX, 1922-1923: 123-166; Cecil L Curle's 'The chronology of the early Christian monuments of Scotland', LXXIV, 7th series 11, 1939-1940: 60-116. described as an endeavour to establish a classification and a tentative chronology; John Coles' 'Experimental archaeology', XCIX, 1966-67: 1-20; A D S Macdonald and Lloyd R Laing's 'Early ecclesiastical sites in Scotland: a field study', 100, 1967-68: 123-134 and 102, 1969-70: 129-145, the first report of visits by the Inspectors of Ancient Monuments beginning a programme of scheduling early Christian sites throughout Scotland 1967-1969; and J T Lang's 'Hogback monuments in Scotland', 105, 1972-74: 206-235. In the late 1920s reports of the Scara Brae excavations were a regular feature as were reports of the Viking site at Jarlshof throughout the 1930s. Additions to the library and museum are listed in each issue. *A general index to the Proceedings vols I-XXIV 1851-1890* was published in 1892; this was followed by other indexes to vols XXV-XLVII 1890-1914 (1936); and vols XLIX-LXXXI, 1914/15-1946/47.

575 The Society of Biblical Archaeology came into being at a public meeting held in the rooms of the Royal Society of Literature 9th December 1870 when it was resolved 'that a society be initiated, having for its objects the investigation of the archaeology, chronology, geography and history, of ancient and modern Assyria, Arabia, Egypt, Palestine and other Bible lands, the promotion of the study of the antiquities of these countries, and the preservation of a continuous record of discoveries now or here-after to be in progress'. The activities of the society were to be 'not to defend systems or destroy theories, but to elicit facts from which scientific writers may freely deduct their own inferences, for subsequent examin-ation to controvert or confirm'. An account of the events leading up to the formation of the society may be read in the introduction, *Transactions of the Society of Biblical Archaeology* 1(1) December 1872: i-iv. A Memoir of Samuel Birch who was instrumental in these events is to be found in *Transactions* IX Pt 1 1893: 1-41 which includes a list of his pub-lished writings. Besides the *Transactions* (1872-1878) the society also published its *Proceedings* (1879-1918) which contained the official busi-ness plus lengthy abstracts of papers read to the society and the ensuing discussion. Decennial indexes were published. In 1918 the society was absorbed into the Royal Asiatic Society.

576 'Soils for the archaeologist' by I W Cornwall (Phoenix House, 1958) may be regarded as the pioneering work of synthesis in this special sub-ject. It was designed to explain how sedimentary petrology and soil science could help the practising archaeologist to draw the correct conclusions from his excavations. An extensive bibliography is included for those who wish to investigate the techniques of soil interpretation in more detail.

577 Somersetshire Archaeological and Natural History Society was formed in 1849 after a number of gentlemen residing in the neighbourhood of Taunton had addressed a circular to every magistrate and clergyman in the county and had organized a meeting at Taunton on 26th September at which the society's objectives were defined as 'the cultivation of, and collecting information on, archaeology and natural history in their vari-ous branches, but more particularly in connection with the county of Somerset, and the establishment of a museum and library'. The society's first home was a room belonging to the Literary Institution but in 1873 the inner ward of Taunton Castle was purchased to save it from destruc-tion and to house the society's museum, and in 1901 the society took up permanent residence there.

An early venture was a questionnaire to members asking them to fur-nish information on local rocks and stones which had become the objects of tradition and popular superstition; ancient roads and trackways; battle-fields; earthworks and encampments; Roman, Saxon, Danish, and Norman edifices; seals, weapons and ornaments uncovered; ecclesiastical buildings;

ancient bridges; and crosses. Another early ambition was the compilation of a *Bibliotheca Somersetensis*, a complete list of all books, tracts, and manuscript documents relating to or published in the county.

In his presidential address, 'The society's work 1849-1949' *Proceedings* XCIV 1948-49: 26-33, Sir Arthur Hobhouse distinguished four aspects of the society's activities: the annual meeting and summer excursions which in his view had encouraged members and kept the society a live organization; its fieldwork and research notably the excavations of the lake villages at Glastonbury and Meere and at Glastonbury Abbey; the publication of the *Proceedings* which he claimed were regarded as being second only to those of the Society of Antiquaries; and, of course, its library and museum.

Today the Society operates a system whereby other groups in the county can become affiliated to it and every autumn a symposium or special lecture is arranged for their benefit. That the society musters within its ranks some members at least who are conscious of the need to move with the times is evidenced by L V Grinsell's presidential address of 1971 in which he urged the society to review its constitution and suggested ways and means by which it could modernize its activities, namely the active development of a junior membership, a prize essay competition, fund raising evenings, Sunday archaeological walks, archaeological trails, a travelling exhibition illustrating the work of the society, the revival of the practice of holding meetings up and down the country, and the securing of professional advice in designing the society's publicity.

The society's *Proceedings* have been published since 1851 with a change to a shorter and more manageable title, *Somerset archaeology and natural history* with volume 112 1967-68. Papers of special interest include Sir Charles Peer's 'Ancient monuments in Somerset' (vol LXXVII, 1932:1-8) which discusses the seven Somerset monuments in the care of the Commissioners of Works. Lists of all the county monuments scheduled under the Ancient Monuments Act of 1913 compiled by Ethelbert Horne appeared in the 1925-1929 volumes. Articles providing useful background information on the society's history are H St George Gray's 'A review of the society's *Proceedings* during the present century' (vol XCVI 1951: 30-40); obituary notices of Gray by C A Ralegh Radford and S W Rawlins (vol 107, 1962-63: 111-116); and L V Grinsell's 'The past and future of archaeology in Somerset' (vol 115, 1971: 29-38) (*qv*). Also of the utmost value is the same writer's 'Somerset archaeology 1931-1965 with a section on recent, including industrial, archaeology by Neil Cossons' (vol 109, 1964-65: 47-77), an account of the progress of archaeology in the county period by period since the publication of Mrs D P Dobson's *Archaeology of Somerset* (1931). This contains ten period divisions each accompanied by a map and each furnished with a bibliography. Recent issues have usually contained the *Proceedings* of the society including additions to the library and a list of articles of Somerset interest in non-Somerset periodicals; various papers; notes; and book notices. Indexes to the *Proceedings* have been issued at intervals, the most recent being *A short index chiefly topographical to the Proceedings of the Somerset Archaeological and Natural History Society vols 1-80 (1849-1934)* published in 1937 and a *General index to volumes 81-115 (1935-1971)* compiled by L A Haldane.

578 '**South east England**' by Ronald Jessup, published in Thames and Hudson's 'Ancient peoples and places' series in 1970, is concerned with the counties of Kent, Surrey and Sussex. The topographical background of these counties is outlined and a survey of successive periods and their remains ends with a long chapter on the Roman occupation. There are detailed descriptions of the better known megalith monuments and the reader's attention is drawn to modern methods of research. In addition to some well chosen photographs the text is supported by a bibliography, a list of easily accessible field monuments, and the addresses of the principal museums in the region.

579 '**South west England**' by Aileen Fox appeared in Thames and Hudson's 'Ancient peoples and places' series in 1964 and traced the history of man in the south-west peninsula from early neolithic times to the Saxon conquest in the seventh century. Almost one hundred well annotated photographs, numerous maps and drawings, a representative list of not too inaccessible monuments to visit, an indication of the range and scope of local museum collections, and a detailed bibliography arranged by chapters, support the text. A revised edition, published by David and Charles in 1973, takes account of new excavations and discoveries and modern scientific dating techniques such as carbon-14 and dendochronology.

580 '**Southern England: an archaeological guide**' *the prehistoric and Roman remains* by James Dyer, published by Faber in 1973, is a personal selection of more than a thousand sites in England south of Birmingham and the Wash intended for the field archaeologist and 'for those who want to seek out ancient sites and to know something of their history'. Sites are listed and described alphabetically by county in gazetteer form. Each entry includes the number of the appropriate 1-inch Ordnance Survey map, a full six-figure National Grid map reference to locate the site precisely, and an up-to-date bibliographical reference to further information. At the end of each county section there is a list of local museums. An essay. 'Southern England in prehistoric and Roman times', a glossary and ten distribution maps, precede the text, and there is a general and a site index. Over a hundred maps, drawings and photographs are provided.

581 Standing Commission on Museums and Galleries was appointed in February 1931 'to advise generally on questions relevant to the most effective development on the national institutions as a whole and on any specific questions which may be referred to them . . . to promote cooperation between the national institutions themselves and between the national and provincial institutions . . . (and) to stimulate the generosity and direct the efforts of those who aspire to become public benefactors'.

582 'The stone circles of the British Isles' by Aubrey Burl (Yale University Press, 1976) reviews and synthesizes all earlier work on Britain's surviving megalithic stone circles. After a consideration of their origins and the problems they pose there comes a series of regional surveys each paying especial attention to their architectural type and to the finds yielded by excavation. A county gazetteer is appended, arranged alphabetically under old county names, giving exact details of their location, size, customary name, bibliographical references, and associated finds. The book is magnificently illustrated and it is obviously destined to become a major work of reference.

583 'The story of archaeology in Britain' by Ronald Jessup (Michael Joseph, 1964) is chiefly concerned with the discovery of antiquities and archaeological evidence first by accident, then by deliberate investigation and excavation, and then by the modern techniques of aerial photography and scientific methods of dating. Other topics discussed include the discovery of fossil man in Britain, archaeological publication, the forgery of antiquities, and the nature and scope of practical archaeology at the time of writing. A brief study of the lives and work of four pioneers of archaeological discovery, William Stukeley, James Douglas, Charles Roach Smith and General Pitt Rivers, and a short guide to ancient monuments in England and Wales, complete an unpretentious but most useful work which although intended for the interested layman might profitably be scanned by the professional archaeologist. A few years earlier Mr Jessup had compiled *Curiosities of British archaeology* first published by Butterworths in 1961 and reprinted by Phillimore in 1973, a personal selection from a wide variety of writings illustrating the history and progress of archaeology in this country. The extracts are arranged 'into obvious categories: the antiquary-archaeologist himself, his tours abroad in the countryside, his digging expeditions, his regard for churches, his discoveries and his attitude to fakes and forgeries, fable and legend, and above all his attention to the grammar of his subject . . .' These are not exactly companion volumes but the one undoubtedly complements the other.

584 'Studies in ancient history and archaeology' published by Routledge consist of volumes based on lectures given at British Summer Schools of Archaeology. *The prehistoric peoples of Scotland* edited by Stuart Piggott prints the papers of the 1954 Edinburgh meeting and *Prehistoric and early Wales* edited by I Ll Foster and Glyn Daniel those of the 1959 Bangor conference. Nelson's 'Studies in history and archaeology' series (*qv*) is also concerned with the proceedings of the summer schools.

585 'Studies in archaeological science' is a research series published by Academic Press providing in-depth treatment of specialized archaeological techniques. Titles: *Methods of physical examination in archaeology* (M S Tite); *Skins, leathers and parchments in archaeology* (R Reed); *Land snails in archaeology* (John G Evans); *The study of animal bones from archaeological sites* (Raymond E Chaplin); *Soil science in archaeology* (S Limbrey) and *Fish remains in archaeology* (R W Casteel). The consulting editor is G W Dimbleby.

586 'Studies in archaeology' published by Academic Press of New York and London are intended for 'advanced and beginning students, as well as laymen inclined toward archaeology'. Each volume is provded with ample illustrations and an extensive bibliography. Titles: *The study of prehistoric change* (Fred T Plog); *The stone age archaeology of southern Africa* (C Garth Sampson); *Archaeology of the Mammoth Cave area* (edited by Patty Jo Watson); *Public archaeology* (Charles R McGimsey III); *An archaeological perspective* (Lewis R Binford); *Dating methods in archaeology* (Joseph W Michels); *The Aztecs, Maya and their predecessors* (Muriel Porter Weaver); *The Casper site* (edited by George C Frison); *Prehistoric man and his environments* (edited by W Raymond Wood and R Bruce McMillan); *Cultural change and continuity* (Charles

E Cleland); *The early Mesoamerican village* (edited by Kent V Flannery); and *Behavioural archaeology* (Michael B Schiffer); Other titles in preparation include *Prehistory in the Nile Valley* (Fred Wendorf and Romuald Schild); *Hunter-gatherer subsistence and settlement* (Michael A Jochim); and *Method and theory in historical archaeology* (Stanley South). The consulting editor is Stuart Struever.

587 'Studies in conservation' *the journal of the International Institute for the Conservation of Historic and Artistic Works*, now established as a quarterly, carries papers and book reviews concerning the material remains relating to the arts, archaeology and ethnography (including standing monuments, libraries, and archival materials), and industrial art. It also deals with the technology and composition of the different types of object, the nature of deteriorative processes and their prevention, and all aspects of storage and display.

588 'Studies in history and archaeology' edited for Nelson by F T Wainwright, were intended as authoritative, comprehensive, and up-to-date 'summaries and surveys of various aspects of the archaeology and early history of Britain'. The editor was for many years honorary director of the Scottish (later British) Summer School of Archaeology which he inaugurated at Dundee in 1952 and although not linked officially with the summer schools, this series of volumes are all written by eminent archaeologists who participated in the school's lectures, excursions and other activities, all of which were designed to revolve round one central theme. *Titles: The problem of the Picts* (edited F T Wainwright); *Roman and native in north Britain* (edited I A Richmond); *The northern isles* (edited F T Wainwright). Reference should also be made to the Routledge series 'Studies in ancient history and archaeology'.

589 'The study of animal bones from archaeological sites' by Raymond E Chaplin was included in the Seminar Press International series of monographs on science in archaeology in 1971. It discusses the more important theoretical and practical aspects of bone studies and describes how certain basic principles can be applied to sites of any period. The text is supported by an imposing list of references.

590 Stukeley, William (1687-1765) travelled up and down the British Isles during the summer months 1711 to 1725 diligently recording and drawing with meticulous accuracy ancient monuments, and it is upon this

271

fieldwork that his reputation rests. In 1724 his *Itinerarium curiosum or an account of the antiquitys and remarkable curiositys in nature, or art observ'd in travels thro' Great Britain*, a work of the utmost significance in the development of British antiquarianism, was published. His descriptions and his drawings provide a contemporary record of many important buildings and monuments now sadly lost or damaged. As a field archaeologist he was very much in advance of his time, he was the first to recognize the significance of cropmarks, and he firmly established the study of prehistoric and Roman antiquities. Unfortunately, in his later years Stukeley became influenced by romantic notions about the Druids witnessed by his *Stonehenge, a temple restor'd to the British Druids* (1740). He played an active role in the early history of the revived Society of Antiquaries being secretary for nine years. By far the most comprehensive study is Stuart Piggott's *William Stukeley an eighteenth-century antiquary* (OUP, 1950) which deliberately concentrates on his work as an antiquarian and on his claim to the title of father of British archaeology. Professor Piggott comments on Stukeley's library in *Sales catalogue of eminent persons vol 10 Antiquaries* (*qv*). Gregg International Publishers have reprinted the 1776 two-volume quarto edition of *Itinerarium curiosum*.

591 Suffolk Archaeological Unit was formed in April 1974 with the help of a Department of the Environment grant and under the auspices of the Scole Committee for Archaeology in East Anglia (*qv*).

592 Suffolk Institute of Archaeology and Natural History was founded in 1848 as the Bury and West Suffolk Archaeological Institute whose objects were 'To collect and publish information on the archaeology and natural history of the district and to oppose and prevent, as far as may be practicable, any injuries with which ancient monuments of every description, within the district may be from time to time threatened, and to collect accurate drawings, plans, and descriptions thereof.' In 1853 the Institute united with the Bury St Edmund's Athenaeum, its scope was widened to include the whole of the county, and its name was changed to the one it bears today. This union however was comparatively short-lived, the connections was severed in 1867, but the institute's activities continued to flourish in the archaeological area although natural history interests, never prominent, declined even further. The institute's *Proceedings* first appeared in 1848 and after an irregular beginning a regular pattern of three annual issues forming a volume has emerged. Articles and papers of interest published in recent years include R L S Bruce-Mitford's 'The Sutton Hoo ship burial', vol XXV(1) 1950: 1-78 and the same writer's 'Excavations at Sutton Hoo in 1938', XXX(1) 1964: 1-43. G Maynard's 'Recent archaeological fieldwork in Suffolk', XXV(2) 1951: 205-216 records the archaeological character of sites examined by the staff of Ipswich Museum, listed alphabetically by location. A feature. 'Archaeology in Suffolk', interim reports of excavations, has appeared in every issue since 1954. The ancient monuments of the county are listed in vols XXVI(3) 1954: 233 and XXXI(2) 1969: 208-209. Leslie Dow's 'A short history of the Suffolk Institute of Archaeology and Natural History' appeared in the centenary volume XXIV(1) 1949: 129-143 which makes full use of the rather sparse documentation still extant for the early period. This is accompanied by an 'Index to articles, *Proceedings*, vols 1-XXIV (1848-1948)' and a list of excursions for the same period.

593 'Summary of archaeological organisation in Britain' published by the Institute of Archaeology, University of London, in 1943, collected information together on the existing official bodies connected with archaeology, the resources and activities of archaeological societies, the university provision for the teaching of archaeology, and on the resources of British Schools of Archaeology abroad, based on the pre-war position. It was issued to provide the necessary groundwork for planning the post-war future of archaeology and as such must be considered a seminal document.

594 Surrey Archaeological Society was 'established in 1852 for the investigation of subjects connected with the history and antiquities of the county of Surrey'. A leaflet circulated by George Bish Webb invited 'the attention of the nobility, clergy, and gentry resident in or connected with Surrey to the establishment of this society, in the hope that it will meet with their support and encouragement'. A number of meetings were held in 1853 although it was not until May 1854 that the society was officially inaugurated at a meeting held at the Bridge House Hotel in Southwark.

The objects of the society were defined a little more closely than those of many other county societies springing to life at about the same time, and read as follows: '(1) To collect and publish the best information on the ancient arts and monuments of the county; including primeval antiquities; architecture; civil, ecclesiastical, and military; sculpture; paintings on walls, wood or glass; civil history and antiquities, comprising manors, manorial rights, privileges and customs; heraldry and genealogy; costume;

numismatics; ecclesiastical history and endowments, and charitable foundations, records, etc, and all other matters comprised under the head of archaeology. (2) To procure careful observation and preservation of antiquities discovered in the progress of works, such as railways, foundations of buildings, etc. (3) To encourage individuals or public bodies in making researches and excavations, and afford them suggestions and cooperation. (4) To oppose and prevent, as far as may be practicable, any injuries with which monuments of every description may, from time to time, be threatened; and to collect accurate drawings, plans and descriptions thereof.'

'A brief history of the society' by A W G Lowther appears in the centenary volume of *Surrey archaeological collections* LIII 1954 which also contains 'A list of excavations carried out by, or in association with the Surrey Archaeological Society'; 'A list of ancient monuments in Surrey'; 'A history of the society's library' (A Muriel Lucas); 'The society's collection of antiquities and records' (E M Dance); 'Excursions and visits made by members of the Surrey Archaeological Society' (W B Billinghurst); and 'Surrey archaeological collections' (J A Giuseppi).

In 1972 the Surrey County Council voted to pay an annual grant to the society on the understanding that an archaeological officer would be appointed to enlarge and develop the society's inventory of sites and finds, to advise the society and the county council on the archaeological aspects of planning applications and proposed developments, to carry out a programme of observation work in cooperation with the society's officers and members, and to advise the society and the county on all aspects of field archaeology. The formation of a full time unit soon created difficulties for the society's officers, the risk of liability on the part of the society was vastly increased, and so a decision was taken to transform the society into a limited liability company. A survey of the general and specific factors leading up to this decision is sketched in J L Nevinson's 'Archaeological Society or Limited Company?' *The London archaeologist* 2(8) Autumn 1974: 198-199.

Publication of the *Surrey archaeological collections relating to the history and antiquities of the county* (the name was copied from the Sussex society's journal) began in 1858 and it now appears annually. Octavius Freire Owen's 'The archaeology of the county of Surrey' vol 1 1858: 1-13 surveys the antiquarian character of the county. Other valuable lists and compilations include A Ridley Box's 'List of papers and illustrations relating to the county of Surrey contained in *The archaeologia, The archaeological journal,* and the *Journal of the British*

Archaeological Association' XV 1900: 128-136 and D Grenside's 'Surrey museums', XXXVII, 1927: 228-236. John Morris' 'A gazetteer of Anglo-Saxon Surrey', 56 1959: 132-158 is compiled from sites published in the *Collections*, the contents of national and county museums, and the records of the Archaeological Department of the Ordnance Survey. *General indexes* to volumes I-XX (1858-1907), XXI-XXXVIII (1908-1930), and XXXIX-LX (1931-1963) were published in 1914, 1936 and 1972. Back numbers are available either on microfilm or as Xerox copies from University Microfilms, St Johns Road, Tylers Green, High Wycombe, Bucks. A quarto size series of 'Research papers' were published during the 1950s and more recently, in 1974, a further series of 'Research volumes' was introduced. At the time of writing it would appear that this is the society's solution to the problem of publishing adequately illustrated modern excavation reports and that they do not intend to emulate other county societies now publishing their annual journals in the larger quarto format.

595 **'Survey and policy of field research in the archaeology of Great Britain'** *I The prehistoric and early historic ages to the seventh century AD* edited by Christopher Hawkes and Stuart Piggott was published by the Council for British Archaeology in 1948 in order to review the state of British field archaeology in the immediate post-war period and to consider its future direction and emphases. It is arranged in two chapters: 'Survey of the present position in British prehistoric and early historic archaeology', period by period; and 'Outstanding problems in British prehistoric and early historic archaeology: policy and recommendations for field research'. A distinguished team of contributors was assembled and throughout the corresponding sections in the two chapters were written by the same hand, so achieving a natural correlation. Work on the survey was begun at the behest of the Research Committee of the Congress of Archaeological Societies in 1938 and was completed under the auspices of the CBA after the congress had been dissolved in November 1945.

596 **'Survey of the megalithic tombs of Ireland'** by Ruaidhri de Valera and Sean O'Nuallain is an enterprise of the Irish Ordnance Survey Office designed to provide a corpus of descriptions, plans and photographs. It is the result of a completely new survey and publication is by county units; it is expected that a few counties will require a volume to themselves, others will be assembled together. A supplement will be published at the end of the series to cover fresh discoveries. Volumes published to date: (1) *Co Clare* (1961) and (3) *Galway, Roscommon, Leitrim, Longford, Westmeath, Laoighis, Offaly, Kildare, Cavan* (1972);

597 'Surveying for archaeologists', a booklet by D H Fryer first published in 1960 by the Durham University Excavation Committee, is now available in a fourth edition dated 1971. It largely consists of expanded lecture notes for students on a training course in Roman archaeology which deal with horizontal measurements, elevation, and how to relate a survey with national maps. Two chapters on contouring and the surveying of large sites have been added. Although the booklet has no pretensions of being a definitive treatise, being designed simply to impart enough information to allow the amateur archaeologist to make an intelligible survey, its success can be gauged by the number of editions printed.

598 Sussex Archaeological Society came into being at a meeting at the County Hall, Lewes, 18th June 1846 convened at the suggestion of a few gentlemen who, 'observing the interest excited by some recent antiquarian discoveries, were anxious to promote a readier acquaintance among persons attached to the same pursuits, and to combine their exertions in illustrations of the history and antiquities of Sussex'. (Report, *Sussex archaeological collections* 1, 1848: vii-xii). Its objects were to embrace 'whatever relates to the civil or ecclesiastical history, topography, ancient buildings or works of art within the county'. Shortly afterwards the first general meeting assembled in the ruins of Pevensey Castle. As early as January 1847 it was resolved in committee 'to prepare and print occasional papers for distribution among the members of the society, to consist of such communications as have been brought before the society', the first volume of *Sussex archaeological collections relating to the history and antiquities of the county* being dated 1848. A notes and queries feature appeared 1854-1933 and this was eventually replaced by a separate quarterly journal *Sussex notes and queries.*

W H Blaauws's 'On Sussex archaeology', a paper read at the society's second meeting in Brighton, September 1846, which surveyed the opportunities for research, period by period, and suggested by what means the society could best exert its energies, appeared in vol 1, 1848: 1-13. L V Grinsell's 'Sussex barrows', an important analysis and list based on the six-inch Ordnance Survey quarter-sheets was printed in vol LXXV 1934: 217-275 with a 'Supplementary paper', LXXXI, 1940: 210-234 which included three distribution maps and 'Supplement No II' LXXXII, 1941: 115-123. A record of scheduled ancient monuments is kept with meticulous care, the latest consolidated list to 31 December 1961 was published in vol C, 1962: lxvii-lxxii. An annual feature innovated in the 1972 volume is 'Shorter notices' designed to record discoveries found by

276

chance or by small-scale excavations of the type rarely noticed by major archaeological journals.

'A history of the Sussex Archaeological Society' (L F Salzman), 'The library and museums' (Thomas Sutton), 'The prehistoric collections' (E C Curwen), 'The Roman and Anglo-Saxon collections' (I D Margary), and 'Meetings held, 1846-1945', all appear in vol LXXXV *Centenary 1846-1946*. The *Collections* appeared in a larger format in 1974. General indexes to vols I to XXV (1874) and to vols XXVI-L (1914) were published separately, and brief subject indexes to vols XXVI-XL, vols XLI-L, vols LI-LX, vols LXI-LXX appeared in the XLI (1898), LI (1908), LXI (1920) and LXXI (1930) volumes of the *Collections*. In addition a *General index to vols LI-LXXV of the Collections (1908-1934) and vols I–IV of Notes and queries (1926-1933)* compiled by Brig Gen E G Godfrey-Fausset with a special *Bibliographic index of archaeological matters relating to Sussex appearing elsewhere than in the publications of the Sussex Archaeological Society* compiled by Eliot Curwen was issued in 1936. This bibliographic index was a continuation of a feature 'Sussexiana topographica' which had appeared in the *Collections* vols XV-XVIII 1863-1866 and vols XXXII–XXXIII 1882-1883. A *General index to vols LXXVI-C of the Collections (1935-1962) and vols V-XV of the Notes and queries 1934-1962* compiled by Grace W Holmes, was published in 1966. An extract from G and R Thurston Hopkins' *Literary originals of Sussex* (1936), quoted by the editor in his 'A society anthology 2' (vol 113, 1975: 151) cannot be resisted here: 'valuable material, though presented with much tediousness of details and pomposity, is to be found in the *Collections* of the Archaeological Society, published every year since 1848'.

599 Sussex Archaeological Unit is based on the Institute of Archaeology, University of London and works in close cooperation with Group 11 of the Council for British Archaeology. It has published a survey of archaeological sites in the county and has conducted a number of excavations and surveys.

600 'The Sutton Hoo ship-burial' *a handbook* by Rupert Bruce-Mitford, published in a second edition by British Museum Publications in 1972, descends from a *Provisional guide* which first appeared in 1947 and went through many impressions before being replaced by the present handbook in 1968. Besides an account of the excavations culminating in the ship's discovery in 1939 there is a description of the ship itself, a comparative study of the nature of the burial, a discussion of the significance of the

small hoard of coins uncovered, some informed speculation on the identity of the person for whom the burial was arranged and a full examination
of the splendid silver and jewellery recovered from the site which is now
considered as not least amongst the museum's treasures. Extensive notes
and an annotated bibliography together with a large number of colour
and monochrome photographs, ensure that the handbook fully measures
up to the customary immaculate standard of the museum's publications.
It is also available in a paperback version.

601 'The techniques of archaeological excavation' by Philip Barker (Batsford, 1977) is a comprehensive illustrated guide to excavation covering
every stage from the initial fieldwork to final publication. It is published
in hardback and in limp covers.

602 'Techniques of industrial archaeology' by J P M Pannell is an illustrated guide for the industrial archaeologist 'who wishes to extend his
skills and knowledge with the object of making his studies more complete'. The various types of primary source material are investigated,
elementary surveying is explained and demonstrated, and the art of
measuring and drawing machines, plant, and buildings, also receives practical treatment. The most effective ways of compiling accurate written
records and photographic evidence are closely examined in a commend-
ably straightforward manner, whilst a substantial classified bibliography
itself forms the basis of extensive research into all the topics covered in
the text. The book was first published by David and Charles in their
'Industrial archaeology of the British Isles' series in 1966.

603 'Technology and culture' *the international quarterly of the Society
for the History of Technology* began publication with a winter 1959
issue. It includes general articles dealing with the relationship of technology with society and culture in addition to more specialized papers on
the history of technological processes and appliances. Other regular
features are book reviews and surveys of museum activities. Volumes 1-5
were published by the Wayne State University Press, volumes 6 onwards
have appeared under the imprint of the Chicago University Press.

604 'Terms used in archaeology' *a short dictionary* by Christopher Trent
(Phoenix House, 1959) is designed 'to give as clear a definition as possible of the terms likely to be encountered in reading books about archaeology or listening to lectures' and is intended primarily for the interested
278

layman with no subject knowledge although it might conceivably be of
use to the student as a quick reference guide to the chief periods, industries
and sites of prehistory. The emphasis is clearly on British archaeology but
a few terms relating to other areas are included. A savage, single-paragraphed
review in *Antiquity* XXXIII (130) June 1959: 156 denounced its errors and
omissions.

605 Thames and Hudson have for many years specialized in publishing
lavishly illustrated works on archaeology. Many famous series have appeared under their imprint: 'Ancient peoples and places'; 'New aspects of
antiquity'; 'The world of archaeology'; and 'Library of the early civilizations'.
In addition the firm is responsible for the publications of the British School
of Archaeology at Athens and of the British Institute in Eastern Africa. In
1972 they were appointed to distribute the Research Reports of the Society
of Antiquaries of London. Full notes on all these series may be found elsewhere in this handbook.

606 The Thoroton Society *an antiquarian society for Nottingham and Nottinghamshire* owed its inception to the efforts of two men, Lord Hawkesbury
and W P W Phillimore, who were of the opinion that it was high time that
Nottinghamshire could boast of a county society similar to those found in
most other counties. Proposals issued in January 1897 engendered so much
interest that a formal inaugural meeting was arranged in the Grand Jury
Room, Shire Hall, Nottingham for the 1st June. The objectives of the society were declared in these words: 'to promote, generally, the study of
the history and antiquities of the shire, to print ancient records relative
to the county , and an annual illustrated volume of *Transactions*, containing
accounts of the society's meetings and papers read, relating to the antiquities
of the county, local meetings and excursions to places of interest within
the county'. A report of the inaugural meeting is to be found in the first
volume of the *Transactions* 1897. Papers of more than usual interest are
W P W Phillimore's 'The work we have to do' vol 1 1897: 47-52, 'a few
directions in which we may usefully work', including ethnography and
dialect, an archaeological survey and map of the county's pre-Norman
Conquest antiquities, an analysis of the Nottinghamshire parts of the Domesday Book, and a history of monasticism in the county. R M Butler's 'Archaeology in Nottinghamshire—achievement and prospects', LVIII, 1954:
1-20 is a brief chronological survey with undertones of disappointment.
An intriguing account of the personalities who made the society is set down
in 'The Thoroton Society: some memories of its first thirty years' by T M

Blagg, himself the sole survivor of the inaugural meeting, appears in vol L
1946: 13-24.' 'Fifty years of the *Transactions*' by A C Wood, included
in the same volume, is noticed separately in this handbook because of its
wider implications. A note of anxiety is struck in 'Diamond Jubilee The
Thoroton Society 1897-1957' vol LXI, 1957: 1-7 which compares the
society's achievements and failures with its original aims. There is more
than a hint of conflict (also to be noticed in Wood's article) between the
picnickers and the earnest seekers after archaeological truth demanding
more erudite articles in the *Transactions*. A change to a larger format
in 1967 allowed the 1969 volume to be given over entirely to various
aspects of the Roman settlement at Margidunum excavated 1966-1968.
A consolidated classified list of scheduled ancient monuments in the
county to 31 December 1964 appeared in vol LXX (1966) and this was
augmented by additions listed in volumes LXXI (1967) and LXXVIII
(1974).

607 '**To illustrate the monuments'** *essays on archaeology presented to
Stuart Piggott on the occasion of his sixty-fifth birthday* edited by J V S
Megaw (Thames and Hudson, 1976) possesses a unique intrinsic value in
that it includes an original John Piper painting of Pentre Ifan, Dyfed, as
a frontispiece and also a dedicatory poem by John Betjeman. A truly
remarkable collection of essays is assembled, among them are 'Cultural
heritage, archaeological museums and public opinion' (Lili Kaelas);
'Druids-as-wished-for' (Stewart Sanderson); 'Stone, bronze and iron'
(Glyn Daniel); 'Conserving societies and independent development' (A M
Snodgrass); 'Some thoughts on the megalith tombs of Ireland' (Michael
J O'Kelly); 'Ritual rubbish? The Newstead Pits' (Anne Ross and Richard
Feachem); 'The archaeologist in fiction' (Charles Thomas; and a 'Biblio-
graphy of Stuart Piggott's publications' (Marjorie Robertson).

608 '**Town and country in Roman Britain'** by A L F Rivet published in
the archaeology section of Hutchinson's University Library in 1958 was
intended for 'the growing body of intelligent and energetic amateurs who
attend summer schools and provide the labour force of innumerable excavations'. The first chapter 'The nature of the evidence', considers in turn
the literary, epigraphic, archaeological, and comparative evidence and
the opinions of modern scholars, each being furnished with a very useful
outline of the relevant literature. Other chapters look at the Celtic background, the Roman administration, towns, countryside and political
geography, with constant references to appropriate sites and discoveries,
and each concluding with a detailed bibliography.

609 'The towns of Roman Britain' by John Wacher (Batsford, 1974) is an authoritative account based on the numerous 'rescue' excavations over the past decade of the remains of urban Britain in the Roman period. There are full surveys of London, Colchester, Lincoln, Gloucester, York, Canterbury, Chelmsford, St Albans, Caistor, Chichester, Silchester, Winchester, Cirencester, Dorchester, Exeter, Leicester, Wroxeter, Caerwent, Carmarthen and Aldborough, together with an analysis of the reasons for the choice of sites, the factors which influenced their foundation, and their effect on provincial life. Numerous maps, plans, diagrams and photographs and a very full documentation of sources, ensure its appeal to scholar and general reader alike.

610 Ulster Archaeological Society came into existence in the autumn of 1946 when the general committee of the *Ulster journal of archaeology* decided to regularise its position and give a legal status to the journal by forming the society. The committee transformed itself into the society and co-opted every subscriber on 1st January 1947 as a member. The declared objectives are (a) the publication of the *Journal*; (b) the management of an excavation fund and the carrying out of archaeological excavations and other field work; and (c) the furtherance of all forms of knowledge and research into the archaeology, history, folk-lore, and geography of Ireland and in particular of Ulster. The *Journal* was revived in a third series in 1938 as a direct result of the new prospective afforded Irish archaeology by the considerable increase in archaeological research. Its scope included 'all branches of study comprised in the somewhat elastic term "archaeology" ' and was designed to attract general readers and specialists alike. Two previous series had been published 1853-1864 and 1895-1911. Papers of particular interest include O Davies' 'A summary of the archaeology of Ulster', volumes 11, 1948: 1-41 and 12, 1949: 43-76; E E Evans' 'Archaeology in Northern Ireland 1921-1951', 16, 1953: 3-6 and 'Archaeology in Ulster since 1920' 31, 1968: 3-8; and O Davies' 'Stone circles in Northern Ireland', 2, 1939: 2-14. Cumulative indexes to vols 7-12 (1944-1949) and 13-30 (1950-1967) were published in volumes 16 (1953) and 30 (1967) respectively; these are also available as offprints.

611 University of Pennsylvania: the museum of the university has played a preeminent part in pioneering excavations in the Holy Land and on the American continent. A list of its sections will illustrate the breadth of its activities: African, American, Biblical, Egyptian, Far Eastern, Mediterranean, Near Eastern, Oceania, South Asian, underwater archaeology, and general anthropology. There is also an Applied Science Center for Archaeology. In the 1968-1969 winter it mounted an exhibition describing its current field research programme. 'Where in the world', two special issues of the museum's magazine *Expedition* (*qv*) 11(1) fall 1968 and 11 (2) winter 1969 commemorated the exhibition.

612 'The value of the publications of the archaeological societies to a public library', a paper read at the annual conference of the Library Association in Leeds, 1926 by E W Crossley, discusses the contents of the journals, proceedings, transactions and other publications of general, county and local societies. It is printed in the *Library Association record* March 1927: 12-18 and the validity of its argument and conclusions has not diminished over the years.

613 'Vetusta Monumenta' *quae ad rerum Britannicarum memoriam conservandam Societas Antiquariorum Londini tabulis aeneis incidi curavit*, an irregular series of large sized engravings with short explanatory notes was issued by the Society of Antiquaries in volume form 1747-1893. Indexes were published in 1810 and 1897. Its varied history can be followed in Joan Evans' *A history of the Society of Antiquaries* (1956).

614 'The Victoria history of the counties of England', describes itself as 'an historic portrayal of the English counties founded upon the most careful original research'. It came into existence in 1899 when G L Gomme interested H A Doubleday, then a partner in the publishing firm of Archibald Constable, in a project he had in mind to mark Queen Victoria's diamond jubilee.

It is intended that eventually it will cover the whole of England except for Monmouthshire and Northumberland although coverage at the moment is far from complete. Each set of county volumes consists of 'general' and 'Topographical' volumes: the general volumes include those subjects it was deemed advisable to treat on a county-wide basis—natural history; prehistoric, Roman and Anglo-Saxon remains; architecture; ecclesiastical, political, maritime, social and economic history; industry, art and manufactures—and a translation of the appropriate parts of Domesday Book, with an identification of place names and a detailed study of its features and problems. The topographical volumes, deliberately intended as works of reference, describe each city, town, and village within the county. The standard of archaeological sections varies, the older contributions on prehistory were written long before the study

282

of that discipline made such impressive advances and are thus a little out-dated. On the other hand F J Haverfield's articles on the Roman remains of Cornwall, Derbyshire, Hampshire, Kent, Norfolk, Northamptonshire, Shropshire, Somerset, Surrey, Warwickshire and Worcestershire, have lasted well, his unpublished manuscript notes on several other counties are in the library of the Ashmolean Museum in Oxford and may be con-sulted there on application.

At first it was anticipated that the *History* would be completed in 160 volumes within six years, disillusionment when it came must have been mercifully swift. After a complex and precarious existence for thirty years the *History* was acquired by the University of London in 1933 and housed in the Institute of Historical Research which is now responsible for appoint-ing the general editor and nominating a committee of management. The most significant step in post-war years has been the cooperation of various local authorities who have financed local editorial staff who work under the supervision of the general editor. In this way the central organisation of the *History* has acquired extra staff at no cost to itself whilst the local authorities are guaranteed a high standard of scholarship.

To see the serried ranks of the *VCH* volumes standing in bright red array on library shelves is to imagine an extraordinary conformity of con-tents but in this instance appearances are deceptive. Later volumes differ greatly from their forerunners. For example the Wiltshire volumes, all published since 1953, were planned along different lines: natural history was dropped altogether, prehistoric coverage was contrived in a more mo-dern way, and a gazetteer of archaeological sites was introduced. Never-theless a measure of uniformity remains; the *History* has been built up over seventy years and it would be folly indeed to drastically alter its com-position, for readers and users have become acclimatized, so to speak, to its arrangement, and comparative study between county and county is made very much easier if each volume is arranged on a uniform pattern.

The fullest statement so far on the birth of the *History* and its advance to the reputation it enjoys today is '*The Victoria history*: its origin and progress', an essay by R B Pugh, the present general editor, to be found in the *General introduction* published in 1970 to commemorate the appear-ance of the 150th volume. This includes a complete list of the contents of all the volumes published to that date thus providing a most convenient conspectus of the whole work. There is also a three page 'Bibliographical excursus', a close look at the various title pages, dedications and similar *minutiae*. The *Handbook for editors and authors* (1970) edited by C R Elrington, is a revised and enlarged version of the *Handbook for contributors* (1954) which offers clear instruction in such matters as printing style in the text, the nature and structure of footnotes, and the submission of copy, illustrations, and the correction of proofs. This seems certain to become a recognized guide to historical publication.

Bibliography: L F Salzman's 'The Victoria county histories', *Bulletin of the Institute of Historical Research*, XIII, 1935-36: 65-68 is a brief summary of the *History* up to its acquisition by the University of London; R B Pugh's 'The Victoria history of the counties of England', *Amateur historian*, 1(1) Aug-Sep 1952: 2-5 refers to the *History* as an 'amalgam of hard facts, tersely presented and implying in the reader a certain familiarity with the main trends of English domestic history . . . designed to be consulted in the library rather than read before the fire'. The same writer's 'The structure and aims of the Victoria history of the counties of England', *Bull of Inst Hist Res*, XL, 1967: 65-73 contains some interesting material not included in his essay in the *General introduction*. W B Powell's 'The Victoria history . . .' *Library Association record* August 1957: 260-262 glances at earlier county histories and describes the supplementary bibliographic volume introduced for Essex. Two *TLS* review articles are also of interest: 'Parish by parish' (13 March 1969) considers the place of the *VCH* in the revolution of historical method since 1950 whilst 'From antiquarianism to professionalism' (13 November 1970) concludes that 'it is ceasing to be just a string of county histories and is becoming increasingly a work to which scholars are turning for material to provide them with a fuller picture of national history'.

Volumes published to date:

General introduction (1970)

Bedfordshire: I (1904); II (1908); III (1912); index (1914); (complete)

Berkshire: I (1906); II (1907); III (1923); IV (1924); index (1927); (complete)

Buckinghamshire: I (1905); II (1908); III (1925); IV (1927); index (1928); (complete)

Cambridgeshire and the Isle of Ely: I (1938); II (1948); III (the city and university of Cambridge, 1959); IV (1953); index to vols I-IV (1960); V (1973)

Cornwall: I (1906); II pts 5 and 8 (1924)

Cumberland: I (1901); II (1905)

Derbyshire: I (1905); II (1907)

Devonshire: I (1906)

Dorset: II (1908); III with index vols II-III (1968)

Durham: I (1905); II (1907); III (1928)

Essex: I (1903); II (1907); III Roman Essex with index vols I-III (1963); IV (1956); V (1966); bibliography (1959)
Gloucestershire: II (1907); VI (1965); VIII (1968); X (1972); XI (1976)
Hampshire and the Isle of Wight: I (1900); II (1903); III (1908); IV (1911); V (1912); index (1914)
Herefordshire: I (1908)
Hertfordshire: I (1902); II (1908); III (1912); IV (1914); index (1923)
Huntingdonshire: I (1926); II (1932); III (1936); index (1938)
Kent: I (1908); II (1926); III (1932)
Lancashire: I (1906); II (1908); III (1907); IV (1911); V (1911); VI (1911); VII (1912); VIII (1914)
Leicestershire: I (1907); II (1954); III (1955); IV (1958); V (1964)
Lincolnshire: II (1906)
London: I (1909)
Middlesex: I (1969); II (1911); III (1962); IV (1971); V (1976)
Norfolk: I (1901); II (1906)
Northamptonshire: I (1902); II (1906); III (1930); IV (1937)
Nottinghamshire: I (1906); II (1910)
Oxfordshire: I (1939); II (1907); III (University of Oxford, 1954); V (1957); VI (1959); VII (1962); VIII (1964); IX (1969); X (1972)
Rutland: I (1908); II (1935); index (1936)
Shropshire: I (1908); VIII (1968)
Somerset: I (1906); II (1911); III (1974)
Staffordshire: I (1908); II (1967); III (1970); IV (1958); V (1959); VIII (1963); XVII (1976)
Suffolk: I (1911); II (1907)
Surrey: I (1902); II (1905); III (1911); IV (1912); index (1914)
Sussex: I (1905); II (1907); III (1935); IV (1953); VII (1940); IX (1937)
Warwickshire: I (1904); II (1908); III (1945); IV (1947); V (1949); VI (1951); index to vols 1-6 (1955); VII (1964); VIII (1969)
Wiltshire: I pt I (1957); II (1955); III (1956); IV (1959); V (1957); VI (1962); VII (1953); VIII (1965); IX (1970); X (1975)
Worcestershire: I (1901); II (1906); III (1913); IV (1924); index (1926)
Yorkshire (general): I (1907); II (1912); III (1913); index (1925)
Yorkshire East Riding: I (1970); II (1974); III (1976)
Yorkshire North Riding: I (1914); II (1923); index (1925)
Yorkshire City of York: I (1961); (complete)

Since 1935 the *History* has been published by the Oxford University Press. W R Dawson, Cannon House, Folkestone, Kent are engaged upon a continuing programme of photographic facsimile reprints.

615 Victoria history of the counties of Wales never really progressed
beyond the planning stage. Preliminary moves in 1901 by the proprietors
of the *VCH* led to the formation of a general committee, an executive
committee, and an editorial committee responsible for drawing up a
scheme. Appeals for support were launched and a prospectus was issued
outlining a proposal for two 'general volumes' covering the whole of
Wales and forty-eight 'topographical' volumes arranged county by county.
But by the autumn of 1903 there was no real prospect of the scheme
coming to fruition and regrettably the project had to be abandoned.

616 '**Viking antiquities in Great Britain and Ireland**' edited by Haakon
Shetelig and published in Oslo by Aschehoug in 1940 in five volumes
was the result of a project of the Norwegian Science Research Fund of
1919 which decided to make a comprehensive investigation of Viking
remains in the British Isles one of its principal activities. The actual task
of collecting the material for such a work was undertaken by Norwegian
archaeologists on visits to Britain. Later it was decided to add a survey
of corresponding antiquities on the European mainland and also a complete catalogue of British antiquities of the Viking period found in
Norway. *Volumes*: *An Introduction to the Viking history of Western
Europe* (Haakon Shetelig); *Viking antiquities in Scotland* (Sigurd Grieg);
Norse antiquities in Ireland (J Boe); *Viking antiquities in England with a
supplement of Viking antiquities on the continent of Western Europe*
(Anathon Bjorn and Haakon Shetelig); and *British antiquities of the
Viking period found in Norway* (Jan Petersen). A sixth volume, *Civili-
sation of the Viking settlers in relation to their old and new countries*
(Alexander O Curle, Magnus Olsen and Haakon Shetelig) was published
in 1954.

617 '**Wales: an archaeological guide**' *the prehistoric, Roman and early
medieval field monuments* by Christopher Houlder was published as one
of Faber's series of archaeological guides in 1974. The author divides
the Principality into eight regions which are further sub-divided into a
total of forty-five selected named and numbered areas designed to
facilitate convenient motor tours of one or two days' duration. The
history and geography of each area is sketched before more explicit details are given of the archaeological sites which, it must be remembered,
include only a very small proportion of the total available to anyone
requiring to study a particular area, period, or type of structure in more
depth. Sites are either graded as 'primary' (those which form the basis of
286

the suggested tours) or as 'secondary' which are worth a visit if time allows, priority in both cases being given to the most accessible or the best preserved. Besides a generous quota of maps and photographs, and a bibliography listing readily obtainable books and pamphlets, the guide also provides useful explicatory notes on the national grid and Ordnance Survey maps and general information on the Welsh Tourist Board, national and local museums and societies, and on government publications relating to Wales.

618 'Wales museums and art galleries' was published as a pictorial, pocket-size booklet in 1976 by the Welsh Tourist Board in conjunction with the Council of Museums in Wales. Introductory notes on prehistoric and Roman archaeological finds and on the development of industries in the Principality lead on to a gazetteer of museums in north, mid, and south Wales. Opening hours, admission charges, and a brief indication of outstanding exhibits are included in each entry.

619 'Welsh antiquity' *essays mainly on prehistoric topics presented to H N Savory upon his retirement as Keeper of Archaeology* (of the National Museum of Wales) edited by George C Boon and J M Lewis was published by the museum in 1976. *Contents*: 'How the west was won: prehistoric land-use in the southern marches' (D P Webley); 'A view of the early prehistory of Wales' (Arthur Ap Simon); 'Towards a chronology of megalithic tombs in Wales' (Frances Lynch); 'Burials with metalwork of the later bronze age in Wales and beyond' (Colin Burgess); 'Twyn-y-Gaer hill fort, Gwent: an interim assessment' (L A Probert); 'The Seven Sisters hoard: a centenary study' (Jeffrey L Davies and Mansel G Spratling); 'A Don Terret from Anglesey, with a discussion of the type' (Robin G Livens); 'The shrine of the head, Caerwent' (George C Boon); 'A survey of early Christian monuments of Dyfed, west of the Taf' (J M Lewis); and 'Cambrian antiquity: precursors of the prehistorians' (Donald Moore). Elizabeth H Edwards contributes a bibliography of Dr Savory's writings.

620 Wessex Archaeological Committee, formed in February 1974 with the support of the Department of the Environment, acts as the coordinating body for archaeology in Berkshire, Dorset, Hampshire, Isle of Wight and Wiltshire.

621 'Wessex before the Celts' by J F S Stone (1958) was the ninth volume to be published in Thames and Hudson's 'Ancient peoples and places' series. The aim was 'to present in small compass a summary of its earlier prehistory, of man's gradual control of his environment in this most vital region of Britain'.

622 West Midlands Rescue Archaeology Committee (WEMRAC) was formed at the end of 1973 to coordinate archaeological effort throughout the region. It has published the results of a survey of the immediate threats to archaeological sites in the region. Urban sub-committees to organise excavations and surveys in historic towns like Shrewsbury and Hereford have been set up.

623 'Which degree? 1977', a complete guide to first degree courses in the United Kingdom, edited by Audrey Segal, and published by Haymarket Publishing Limited, is an expanded version of the former *Which University?* In the 'Degree courses' section courses are grouped under main subject headings, archaeology taking its place under arts and humanities. An introductory section stresses that archaeology is not a romantic treasure hunt but a painstaking attempt to reconstruct the material history of man and emphasises that it is no longer the province of virtuoso antiquarians but is now based on teamwork, embracing a large number of biological and physical sciences. Courses are listed alphabetically by university, each entry gives the title of the course, its length, structure and content, whatever options may be offered within it, and details of examinations.

624 'White horses and other hill figures' by Morris Marples, first published by Country Life Ltd in 1949 and now reprinted by S R Publishers Ltd of East Ardsley, Wakefield, Yorkshire, begins with a general survey and then considers in turn the Offington Horse, the Westbury Horse, nine Wiltshire horses, the Red Horse of Tysoe, some other horses, white crosses, the Cerne giant, the Long Man of Wilmington, four other giants, and some miscellaneous figures. Their design and execution, their aesthetic appeal, and their possible raison d'etre, all come under the author's scrutiny. Each chapter except the first concludes with a bibliography and over fifty photographs and nearly as many drawings illustrate the text.

625 The Wiltshire Archaeological and Natural History Society, unquestionably one of the most flourishing of the country archaeological societies, whose territory contains several monuments of national and international importance, was inaugurated at a meeting in the Town Hall, Devizes, 12

288

October 1853, held at the instigation of William Cunnington whose family was intimately associated with the society for close on eighty years. Earlier in the year Cunnington had received a letter from the veteran Wiltshire antiquary, John Britton, who had laboured unsuccessfully to keep the Wiltshire Topographical Society (1839-1850) in being. Britton wished to dispose of his library either to a gentleman of the county or to a public society who would preserve it for future topographers to use. The response to Cunnington's enquiries was so heartening that he determined to form a society for the specific purpose of establishing a museum and a library. Over two hundred people attended the inaugural meeting including the Marquis of Lansdowne who presided, and the society was formally constituted 'to cultivate and collect information on archaeology and natural history , , , and to form a library and museum illustrating the history, natural, civil and ecclesiastic, of the county of Wilts.'

The society's history is fully documented: B H Cunnington's 'The origin and history of the Wiltshire Archaeological and Natural History Society', *Magazine*, XLV(152), June 1930: 1-9; *1853-1953 A centenary history* (1953) compiled from the society's minute books and annual reports, considers earlier efforts to form a county society and to collect archaeological and historical material, the *Magazine* and other publications. the annual meetings and excursions, the museum and library, and its work of maintaining and preserving the county's ancient monuments. *The Wiltshire archaeological and natural history magazine* was first issued in 1854 and appeared twice yearly thereafter. A larger format was assumed with vol LVII (206-208) June 1958-December 1960 when it became an annual publication. A feature 'Excavation and fieldwork in Wiltshire', an archaeological register for the previous year, also made its debut in the same number. 'Wiltshire books, pamphlets and articles' was introduced in 1947, and lists of accessions to the society's museum and library also became a regular feature. A further innovation came in 1970 (vol 65) when as an experiment the *Magazine* was published in two parts, (a) natural history and (b) archaeology and local history.

Papers and articles of especial interest include W J Harrison's 'Bibliography of the great stone monuments of Wiltshire, Stonehenge and Avebury', vol XXXII (XCVI) December 1901: 1-169; E H Goddard's 'A list of prehistoric, Roman and pagan Anglo-Saxon antiquities in the county of Wiltshire arranged under parishes', XXXVIII(CXX) December 1913: 153-378; 'A complete list of the ancient monuments in Wiltshire scheduled under the Ancient Monuments Act 1913' (up to March 1925), XLIII(CXLIII) December 1925: 175-179; Maud E Cunnington's 'Romano-British Wiltshire:

a list of sites occupied during the Roman period', XLV (CLIII) December
1930: 166-216 and her 'Wiltshire in pagan Anglo-Saxon times', XLVI
(CLVIII) June 1933: 147-175; Stuart Piggott's 'Notes on some North
Wiltshire chambered tombs', LII(CLXXXVII) December 1947: 57-64;
R W H Willoughby's 'The Salisbury and South Wiltshire Museum founded
1860', LVII (CCVIII) December 1960: 307-315; and R E Sandall's 'Sir
Richard Colt-Hoare', LVIII (CCIX) September 1961: 1-6. R B Pugh's
'The society: today and tomorrow', LVI (CCIII) December 1955: 87-101,
the text of his presidential address, summarizes the society's efforts to
modernize its structure and administration. Of special importance is
'Conservation and the countryside', 63, 1968: 1-11, the text of three
memoranda edited by P H Fowler: 'Recommendations for improving the
existing legislation for the preservation of Ancient Monuments' submitted
to the Field Monuments Committee, August 1966 (the society was one
of only three invited to submit evidence); 'Leisure in the countryside
with special reference to the preservation of archaeological treasures'
and another on the natural history of Wiltshire, both forwarded to the
County Council following the publication of *Report of the second conference on the countryside in 1970*, published by the Royal Society of
the Arts in 1965. 'An archaeological survey and policy for Wiltshire', 64,
1969: 1-20 consists of two papers 'Palaeolithic' (Derek Roe) and 'Mesolithic' (Jeffrey Radley), the first in a series commissioned by the archaeological sub-committee of the society designed to assess the current state
of knowledge in the county and to provide a guide in planning future
research. Part III neolithic and bronze age (Stuart Piggott) appeared in
vol 66, 1971: 47-58. The sub-committee has in preparation a supplement
to L V Grinsell's 'Wiltshire archaeological gazetteer', published in the first
of the Victoria County History's *Wiltshire* volumes (1957), which will
carry the record from 1951 to 1970.

From 1971 the Wiltshire Archaeological Register, an annual survey of
excavations and chance finds, incorporating 'Excavation and fieldwork
in Wiltshire' and the accessions list of the library and museum, keeps the
record permanently up to date. Entries are grouped into eight periods,
palaeolithic, mesolithic, neolithic, bronze age, pre-Roman iron age, Roman,
early medieval (c AD 400-1000), and medieval (AD 1000-1500), and
listed under civil parishes. A bibliography is included. W J Ford's 'The
role of the County Council's library and museum services in field archaeology', 68, 1973: 39-41 outlines the council's policy with regard to the
protection of ancient monuments and includes a list of archaeological
sites contained within their designated conservation area. Cumulative
290

indexes appear in the *Magazine* from time to time. Separate publications
have included A C Smith's *British and Roman antiquities on the North
Wiltshire Downs*, W Long's *Stonehenge and its barrows* and J E Jackson's
The topographical collection of John Aubrey 1659-1670. More recently
in 1976, the society published Jeremy Haslam's *Wiltshire towns—the archaeological potential* which not only sets down each town's historical development but also in a final chapter urges further historical and archaeological
work while there is still time.

626 Winchester Research Unit was set up under Martin Biddle with the
help of a substantial grant from the Gulbenkian Foundation in 1968 specifically to publish the results of excavations carried out at Winchester since
the summer of 1960. Its true significance for British archaeology is that
for the first time the principle was established that the writing up of excavations is just as much a team effort as the excavations themselves and
need not be the responsibility of one man alone. Some old time archaeologists, of course, might have had their own views on this! A detailed
report is included in *Current archaeology* No 9 July 1968: 247-248 and
may be complemented by an 'Interview with Martin Biddle' in the same
magazine 11(9) No 20 May 1970: 256-258. *Winchester in the early middle
ages*, the first volume in the series 'Winchester studies', was published by
Oxford University Press in 1977. Today the unit is responsible to the City
of Winchester Council for the conduct of rescue archaeology within the
district.

627 Woolley, Sir Charles Leonard (1880-1960) was the director of a joint
British Museum/University Museum of Pennsylvania expedition to excavate
sites at Ur and Eridu in 1922 and was occupied there for the next twelve
seasons. The results were staggering—nothing less than the uncovering of
the Sumerian civilization. Apart from the official expedition reports,
Woolley published four volumes and left two others in manuscript. He was
the author of *Ur of the Chaldees* (1929), a conducted armchair tour of
the excavations, and *Excavations at Ur, a record of twelve years work*
(1954). *Digging up the past* first published in 1930 went through a number of editions including one in paperback by Penguin Books. Woolley
was also co-author with Jacquetta Hawkes of *Prehistory and the beginnings
of civilization* (1963) the first volume in Unesco's *History of mankind*,
generally recognized as the most scholarly and most readable volume in a
disappointing project.

628 Worcestershire Archaeological Society was formed in 1854 as the Worcestershire Diocesan Architectural Society along the lines of several other similar societies. Its purpose, as outlined in its constitution was 'to promote the study of ecclesiastical architecture, antiquities and design by the collection of books, casts, drawings, etc, and the restoration of mutilated architectural remains within the diocese and to furnish suggestions, so far as may be within its province, for improving the character of ecclesiastical edifices hereafter to be erected or restored'. The society faltered a little in the late 1870s but was invigorated by a decision to include the fields of historical and antiquarian studies within its scope and the society duly changed its name to the Worcestershire Diocesan Architectural and Archaeological Society. It remained an official diocesan organisation until 1910 when membership was thrown open to non-churchmen and the society assumed its present title. Its objectives were redefined in 1924 as 'the study and preservation of ecclesiastical and other architectural antiquities, and to form a collection of books, photographs etc concerning matters of antiquarian interest, which shall be placed within its library'. They remain much the same to this day. The society's *Transactions* reflect its unusual history: the old series were published as an annual report and one or two papers among the *Reports and papers of the Associated Architectural Societies*, 1854-1922. This not altogether satisfactory position was remedied in 1923 when E A B Barnard, the president, convinced the committee that the society should issue its own *Transactions*. A subject index to the old series, compiled by Margaret Henderson, was printed in volume XXX new series 1953: 48-53; A third series was initiated with the 1965-1967 volume when a change to a quarto format was effected in order to allow the inclusion of drawings, plans and diagrams on a much larger scale. Recent issues have varied between annual and biennial volumes but other than this publication has been prompt. Contents are very much as to be expected although the 1968-69 volume was given over entirely to 'The origins of Worcester'. Items of special interest are 'Ancient Monuments, Worcestershire' (Scheduled in 1913) volume II ns 1924-25: 176-177 and 'Worcestershire scheduled monuments' vol XII ns 1935: 72-73. Two unusual compilations that might profitably be emulated were H R Hodgkinson's List of papers on Worcestershire subjects in the *Transactions of the Birmingham Archaeological Society vols I-LX*, vol XVII ns 1940: 50-60 and a similar list from *Archaeologia, The antiquaries journal* and *The archaeological journal*, vol XVIII ns 1941: 41-46; An account of the early years of the society, its membership, fieldwork and other activities, together with the
292

history of the society's library and a description of the society's head-quarters, a fine old Tudor house known as Greyfriars, is available in W R Buchanan-Dunlop's 'A hundred years, 1854-1954', vol XXX, ns 1953: 2-15.

629 'World archaeology' is a scholarly journal published by Routledge and Kegan Paul three times a year since 1969. Its aim is to synthesize contemporary thought on matters of common interest to archaeologists the world over, each issue concerns itself with a particular theme. *Recent issues:* Bioarchaeology (February 1977); Island archaeology (June 1977); Architecture and archaeology (October 1977); and Landscape archaeology (February 1978).

630 'The world museum guide' edited by Barbara Cooper and Maureen Matheson and published by Threshold/Sotheby Park Burnet in association with Qantas Airways in 1973 is a popular guide, designed mainly for tourists, to some two hundred of the world's great art galleries and museums. Arrangment is by city A-Z and each entry provides concise information on the history and architecture of the museum or gallery, a description of its collections, a list of outstanding treasures (supplied by the institution concerned), opening times, public transport, admission costs, the guidebooks available, the tours and lectures arranged, children's facilities, the sales desks, the restaurants and coffee shops, photography regulations and fees, education and library facilities, and membership benefits. There is an index of countries and an index of museums and galleries by title.

631 'The world of archaeology' a Hart-Davis series, is designed to outline the growth of archaeological interest and knowledge in areas of major importance which have been thoroughly explored and to describe how archaeological evidence has been deciphered and interpreted. *Titles: Southern Mexico* (Norman Hammond); *Scandinavia* (Stanley Thomas); *Ancient Egypt* (J R Harris); *Prehistoric Greece* (Frank Stubbings). These slim volumes of less than one hundred pages are beautifully illustrated and include a book list arranged by chapters.

632 'The world of archaeology', a Thames and Hudson series, deals with broader themes and larger geographical areas than the 'Ancient peoples and places' series (*qv*). Some volumes are concerned with regions, others with particular periods of prehistory, and still others with the history of archaeology in countries which have substantially contributed to its development and progress. There are also volumes on archaeological techniques. The series is designed to accommodate the needs of the university student and of the general reader with an interest in archaeology. *Titles: Archaeological atlas of the world* (David and Ruth Whitehouse); *Archaeology into history* (D P Dymond); *A history of American archaeology* (Gordon Willey and Jeremy A Sabloff); *A history of Scandinavian archaeology* (Ole Klindt-Jensen); *The neolithic of the Near East* (James Mellaart) and *The story of decipherment: from Egyptian hieroglyphic to Linear B* (Maurice Pope). Other titles are in preparation. The general editor is Glyn Daniel.

633 'The world of the past' edited and with an introduction and notes by Jacquetta Hawkes (Thames and Hudson, 2 vols, 1963) remains the most comprehensive and satisfying of all anthologies of archaeological writings. A long essay on the purposes and pleasures of archaeology, its history, the lost civilizations, scientific prehistory and the evolution of man, modern archaeology, excavations and discoveries, introduces what is in effect a massive history of archaeological progress in the words of some of its most notable practitioners. Volume 1 relates archaeology's great discoveries about the stone ages and in the Fertile Crescent from Babylon to Egypt whilst volume 2 tells of famous episodes in the archaeology of the Classical World, Asia, Northern Europe and America. This attractive work fully conforms to its publisher's high standards of production.

634 'The wreck detectives' by Kendall McDonald (Harrap, 1972) is a popular narrative of the search for sunken ships off the coasts of the British Isles. The story of each ship found—'how, why, when and where she sank'—is also told. Scholarly substance and research value are added in a series of whimsically named appendixes: (1) 'Sources for wreck location, including a full guide to the way to identify a wreck, the places to go for information, and how to use those sources once you get there'; (2) Cannon, anchors, pins and bottles, including the way to identify cannon and the poeple who will do it for you, an investigation into those mysterious 'fins', and good advice on sources for further help'; (3) 'The diver and the law, including the way a diver can protect his wreck, how he stands legally about diving on other people's wrecks, the law's shortcomings and how it could be improved'; (4) 'Bibliography including those books you ought to have read, those you should read, and those that ought to be on your bookshelf'; (5) 'What to do with your wreck when you find her including some advice from Joan Du Plat Taylor of
294

the Committee for Nautical Archaeology'; and (6) 'Wrecks around the coasts of Britain including a sensible wreck list of the ships you can hope to find if you dive for them, but not including any stupid treasure stories of ships which don't exist!' This list gives date of sinking and a brief account of the circumstances.

635 Yale University Publications in Anthropology 'embody the results of researches in the general field of anthropology which are directly conducted or otherwise sponsored by the University Department of Anthropology or by the Division of Anthropology in the Peabody Museum of Natural History'. To date seventy-six of this numbered series have appeared, ranging in size from brief papers to extensive monographs.

636 York Archaeological Trust was founded in 1972 and has been engaged since then on a programme of archaeological research and excavation in advance of development to answer outstanding problems concerning the origins and early growth of the city. Because individual excavations are of necessity completed very rapidly the trust plans to publish the basic data of its work as expeditiously as possible. To this end, and also to retain the coherence and integrity of the continuing programme, a series of eighteen volumes is planned under the general title of *The archaeology of York* to be published for the trust by the Council for British Archaeology. Fascicles of these volumes will be issued as soon as they are printed, they will be bound together with a thematic preface and an index when the volume is complete. In this way scholars will be able to acquire fascicles relevant to their interest without going to the expense of purchasing the complete set of volumes. The scheme of volumes is *Sources for York history to AD 1100*; *Historical sources for York archaeology after AD 1100*: *The legionary fortress*; *The Colonia*; *The Roman cemeteries*; *Roman extra-mural settlement and roads*; *Anglian York (AD 410-876)*; *Anglo-Scandinavian York (AD 876-1066)*; *The medieval walled city south-west of the Ouse* and *north-east of the Ouse* (2 vols); *The medieval suburbs*; *The medieval cemeteries*; *Early modern York*; *The past environment of York*; *The animal bones*; *The pottery*; *The small finds*; and *Coins*. The general editor is P V Addyman who contributed 'Excavations in York 1972-1973, first interim report' to *Antiquaries journal* 54, 1975: 200-231. Subsequent annual interim reports will be published in a similar format to the fascicles of the definitive volumes.

637 'York historian', an annual journal devoted to the archaeology, architecture and history of York, was first published by the Yorkshire Architectural and York Archaeological Society in 1976.

638 Yorkshire Archaeological Society traces its origins to private meetings in the spring of 1863 of a few gentlemen interested in archaeological pursuits in each other's houses in Huddersfield to discuss matters of archaeological interest in the neighbourbood. Gradually these gatherings increased in numbers and soon it was proposed to form an archaeological society for two parishes but such was the interest aroused that it was decided instead to extend the society's area to the whole deanery of Huddersfield. A prospectus was circulated under the heading of the Huddersfield Archaeological and Topographical Association seeking support and giving notice of a public meeting. The duties of the association would be '(1) to preserve and illustrate the ancient monuments, history, and customs of our ancestors; (2) to collate and transcribe ancient charters, deeds and documents, with the ulterior view of employing them as material for a compilation of the history and topography of this locality; (3) that the immediate sphere of their researches and operations shall be primarily connected with . . . the deanery of Huddersfield; but not to exclude any matters of a kindred character which the executive of the association shall deem necessary or interesting.'

The first public meeting took place in the Gymnasium Hall, 8th July 1864 and a second, 11th November 1864, in the rooms of the Huddersfield Literary and Scientific Institute, at which rules were adopted, council members nominated, and officers elected. The association was now in being and two years later its objects were further defined as the 'examining, preserving, and illustrating the ancient remains which exist around us—whether in the form of earthworks, Druidical or Roman remains, ecclesiastical buildings or other ancient edifices; the transcribing of ancient charters, deeds, pedigrees, and other documentary evidence'. The next important step forward was a resolution to publish *The Yorkshire archaeological and topographical journal* which first appeared in 1870 titled thus 'because the area from which articles may, consistently with the rules, be contributed embraces all Yorkshire'. And then at Pontefract in August 1870 the name of the association was changed to that of the Yorkshire Archaeological and Topographical Association. In March 1893 a further change was effected when the association was incorporated under the Companies Act of 1867 as the Yorkshire Archaeological Society.

Besides the activities of the main society there are also seven sections—prehistory research, Roman antiquities, medieval, Georgian, local history study, industrial history, and family history and population studies—which organize their own lectures and summer schools, courses, excavations and fieldwork. Local groups either composed of members of the society, or affiliated to it in a not too precise manner, ensure that the society's interests and activities are widespread. The history of the society is efficiently chronicled: Sir Thomas Brooke's 'Huddersfield Archaeological and Topographical Association, founded in 1864', *Journal*, XVI, 1902: 227-237 narrates the early history down to 1870 and includes extensive quotations of the first report of the Huddersfield Association. This is heavily quarried and expanded upon in S J Chadwick's 'The Yorkshire Archaeological Society: an account of its origin in 1863 and of its progress from that date to 1913', XXIII, 1915: 1-91. Verbatim reports of the speeches and addresses of the July 1864 inaugural meeting are included along with details of everything of concern to the society, its activities, its library, and its meetings and excursions; extravagant descriptions of the jubilee dinner, the menu, the toasts and replies form a second section; and then a final section consists of obituary notices of the society's deceased founders and secretaries. *The history of the Yorkshire Archaeological Society*, an undated booklet by J W Walker (1947?), still available from the society's headquarters, is a useful summary. 'Commemoration of the centenary of the society (1863-1963)', *Journal*, XLI, Pt CLXII, 1963: 134-159 is especially useful for its account of the growth of the groups and sections.

The original purpose of the *Yorkshire archaeological journal* (the title adopted in 1893) was that it should form a medium for the collection of facts and documents, not previously published, relating to the antiquities and history of the county. Two parts were usually issued every year and numbered in biennial volumes but on the occasion of the *Journal*'s centenary in 1970 the opportunity was taken to change to annual volumes, ending this composite system which was apt to cause bibliographical confusion. The *Journal* has undoubtedly taken its bibliographical responsibilities very seriously, the contents of the *Transactions* of Yorkshire societies, the papers of Yorkshire interest appearing in non-Yorkshire journals, and a 'Yorkshire bibliography', were all printed in each issue from the mid-1920s to the 1940s. Additions to scheduled monuments in the county (although not it seems a consolidated list) and 'Roman Yorkshire', an annotated record of excavations and discoveries arranged alphabetically by location, were two other regular features. The 'Yorkshire Archaeological Register', an annual record of casual finds with brief notes on excavations throughout Yorkshire relying on information from archaeologists and local research workers was introduced in Part CLXI, vol XLI, 1963. At first sites were listed under names of parishes or nearest villages A-Z with a period index but since 1971 they have been arranged under chronological headings and then alphabetically by location. 'Bibliography, archival notes, book reviews' first appeared in vol 44 (1972) and was succeeded by 'Book reviews and bibliographical notes' in vol 47 (1975). An *Analytical index of contents of the first thirty volumes of the journal* was published in 1939 and a similar index for volumes XXX to XL (1934-1962) in 1963. It was announced in 1971 that a regular quinquennial index was under consideration.

639 YOUNG RESCUE for all children interested in archaeology, was formed by Kate Pretty in 1972 and was initially regarded as a pilot scheme in the Cambridge area. Its aim 'is to enable young people interested in archaeology to make full use of the archaeological facilities available to them, to understand the principles and purpose of RESCUE and above all to break away from the commonly held idea that archaeology and excavation are synonymous by promoting archaeological activities which are unrelated to excavation' (Corbishley). The next year, helped by articles in the *Times* and *Times educational supplement*, it developed into a national organization. There is a wide range of activities for the 9-16 age group including a bi-monthly newsletter. Perhaps its most amazing achievement has been to persuade some directors of excavations to allow members to assist on their sites! Kate Pretty's 'Young Rescue reports', *RESCUE news*, 6, Spring 1974: 6-7, tells how it branched out on a national basis and includes a distribution map showing density of membership. Gill Corbishley's 'YOUNG RESCUE holidays', *RESCUE news*, 10, Winter 1975: 8-9 is an account of two separate long week-ends enjoyed by over sixty members.

INDEX

References are to entry numbers

Cooper, Barbara and Maureen Matheson *World museum's guide* 630

Copley, Gordon *An archaeology of south-east England* 121

Corbett, John M'River basin salvage in the United States' 9

The Coritani Malcolm Todd 478

Cornish archaeology 234

The Cornovii Graham Webster 478

Cornwall, I W *Soils for the archaeologist* 576

Cossons, Neil and Kenneth Hudson *Industrial archaeologist's guide* 352

Cotswolds and Upper Thames James Dyer 266

Cotton, M Aylwin and P W Gathercole *Excavations at Clausentium, Southampton 1951-54* 254

Cottrell, Leonard *The Concise encyclopaedia of archaeology* 255

Council for British Archaeology 5, 60-61, 74, 81, 91-92, 100, 107, 168, 170, 174, 199, 223, 227, 229, 236-237, 245, 263, 267, 307, 312, 315, 329, 373, 397, 410, 417, 441, 458, 487, 502-503, 516, 525, 529, 550, 552, 556, 595, 599, 636

'A County society: The Cornwall checklists' Peter Sheppard 297

Cradle of England Barry Cunliffe 178

Crawford, O G S *Air photography for archaeologists* 242; *Air survey and archaeology* 242; (ed) *Antiquity* 55; 'Archaeological surveys in Wales' 201; 'Archaeology and the Ordnance Survey' 464; *Archaeology in the field* 105; *Field archaeology* 242; *Said and done* 55, 464; *Wessex from the air* 242

Crook, J Mordaunt *The British Museum* 184

Crossley, E W 'Value of the publications of the archaeological societies to a public library' 612

'The cult of Mithras and its temple at Carrawburgh on Hadrian's Wall' I A Richmond 511

Cultural change and continuity Charles E Cleland 586

Cunliffe, Barry (ed) 'Archaeology of Britain 110; *Cradle of England* 178; *Excavations at Fishbourne 1961-1969* 572; *Fishbourne* 302, 450; *Iron age communities in Britain* 110, 377; *Making of the English* 178; *The Regni* 478; *Roman Bath* 572; 'A university department of archaeology' 297

Curiosities of British archaeology Ronald Jessup 583

Current and forthcoming offprints on archaeology in Great Britain & Ireland 245

Curwen, E Cecil *The archaeology of Sussex* 123, 240

Cussans, John Henry *History of Hertfordshire* 218

Daniel, Glyn (ed) 'Ancient peoples and places' series 37; 'Archaeology and broadcasting' 178; 'Archaeology and television' 178; 'Archaeology of megaliths' 161; (ed) Faber's Archaeological Guides 69; *A Hundred and fifty years of archaeology* 244, 345, 484; *Idea of prehistory* 347; *Man discovers his past* 178; *New Grange and the Bend of the*

318